Butterworth Architecture Design and Development Guides

Hotels and Resorts

Hotels and Resorts
Planning, Design and Refurbishment

Fred R. Lawson, MSc, PhD, CEng, Eur Ing

Butterworth-Architecture
An imprint of Butterworth-Heinemann

Butterworth Architecture
An imprint of Butterworth-Heinemann Ltd
Linacre House, Jordan Hill, Oxford OX2 8DP

 A member of the Reed Elsevier plc group

OXFORD LONDON BOSTON
MUNICH NEW DELHI SINGAPORE SYDNEY
TOKYO TORONTO WELLINGTON

First published 1995

British Library Cataloguing in Publication Data
Lawson, Fred
  Hotels and Resorts: Planning, Design and
  Refurbishment
  I. Title
  728.5

ISBN 0 7506 1861 2

Library of Congress Cataloguing in Publication Data
Lawson, Fred R.
  Hotels and resorts: planning, design and
  refurbishment/F. R. Lawson
  p. cm.
  Includes index.
  ISBN 0 7506 1861 2
  1. Hotels – Planning. 2. Resorts – Planning. 3. Hotels – Design and
  construction. 4. Resorts – Design and construction. I. Title.
  TX911.3.P46L39   94–26993
  647.94'068–dc20   CIP

Composition by Scribe Design, Gillingham, Kent
Printed and bound in Great Britain by Bath Press, Avon

The information and statements herein are believed to be reliable, but are not to be
construed as a warranty or representation for which the author or publishers assume
legal responsibility. Users should undertake sufficient verification and testing to
determine the suitability for their own particular purpose of any information or products
referred to herein.
  No warranty o fitness for any particular purpose is made.
  The appearance of any illustrative material is not a representation that the owners of
patents or copyrights have granted any release to users of this book.

Contents

Contents

Preface

With increasing opportunities for leisure coupled with technological advances in transport and communication, the last thirty years has witnessed a vast growth in travel and tourism. At the same time, there has been widening diversification in accommodation, from exotic resorts and complex city hotels to budget priced units, each planned to serve specific markets. Changing economic circumstances have also brought about their own impacts with cyclical periods of escalating investment often followed by difficulties of recession.

This is the third of my books on hotel planning and design written over those years. The first could cite relatively few cases of new projects while, in this present version, it has been difficult to choose between so many outstanding developments. Throughout the new text, emphasis has been given to condensing information as a convenient source of reference although it must be stressed that each project involves individual consideration and factual details are intended only as a guide in preliminary analysis.

Criticism is often levied that hotels and tourism development can destroy the attractiveness of a sensitive location. This must be balanced against the extensive economic benefits derived from tourism: carefully sited development can provide the means for financing conservation; hotels are often formed out of restored historic buildings and are used as catalysts in attracting reinvestment into depressed urban and rural areas. Mindful of the need to constantly attract discriminating visitors, most designs carefully respond to their environmental settings whether this is to blend into the landscape or to make a dramatic statement in otherwise bland surroundings. Equally important, more than most buildings, hotels and resorts provide for continual maintenance and life-cycle refurbishment.

The compilation of a book of this nature requires the cooperation of many specialists and I am extremely grateful for the generous help provided by numerous Chairmen and Directors of hotel companies, their architects, designers and consultants. The examples illustrate the work of many of the leading international specialists in this field, but credit is also due to those responsible for directing and coordinating development, like Patrick Brown of Accor (UK) Ltd, Diane Dumashie of Scotts Hotels, Ermes Oretti of Swallow Hotels, Mrs Olga Polizzi of Forte, Ken Sailor of Hilton International, Malcolm Turner of Hyatt International, Jeremy Logie and many others omitted only by lack of space. The valuable roles of the World Tourism Organization and International Hotel Association must also be acknowledged.

Not least, I must express my gratitude to my wife for her long forbearance and to Sue Kitching for secretarial help.

Fred Lawson

1

Profile of hotel industry

1.1 Scale of hotel provision

1.1.1 Influences on development

The successful development of hotels and tourist facilities depends on many factors, which can be grouped generally under five headings:

- *Marketing* an increasing and unsatisfied demand for accommodation stemming from the tourism, recreation and business attractions of a locality.
- *Economics* the state of the economy and financial inducements or constraints which may favour or restrict investment.
- *Location* availability of appropriate sites with adequate infrastructural services and opportunities for development.
- *Enterprise* correct interpretation of requirements and entrepreneurial organization of the necessary finance and expertise to successfully implement a project.
- *Planning and design* careful planning and design of facilities to create an attractive hotel which will satisfy the marketing, functional and financial criteria.

These aspects, together with the need for maintenance and refurbishment, are examined in later chapters of this book.

1.1.2 Types of accommodation used

Hotels are not the only types of accommodation used by tourists, travellers and temporary visitors. In Europe some 75 per cent of all *domestic tourists* – people travelling or taking vacations in their own countries – stay with friends and relatives, use camp or caravan sites or rent houses and apartments. In many resort areas a high proportion of visitors own second homes, condominium or time-shared properties.

Business travellers and *foreign tourists* represent a significant part of hotel usage as illustrated by the statistics for the United Kingdom (Figure 1.1).

The distinction between serviced hotels and rented accommodation is increasingly blurred. In many budget hotels and lodges the restaurant is operated independently from the accommodation; *hotels-garnis* and bed and breakfast establishments restrict meal service and most resorts offer the option of self-catering or serviced rooms.

The World Tourism Organization groups accommodation into two main categories:

- *hotels* and similar establishments
- *supplementary accommodation* including rented houses, apartments, camping and caravan sites, hostels and convalescent homes.

1.1.3 Definitions and standards: hotels

In most countries a 'hotel' is defined as a public establishment offering travellers and temporary visitors, against payment, two basic services: accommodation and meals.

The precise definition of what constitutes a hotel and conditions for hotel registration and grading are set out in more than one hundred classification systems worldwide operated by governmental or representative agencies.

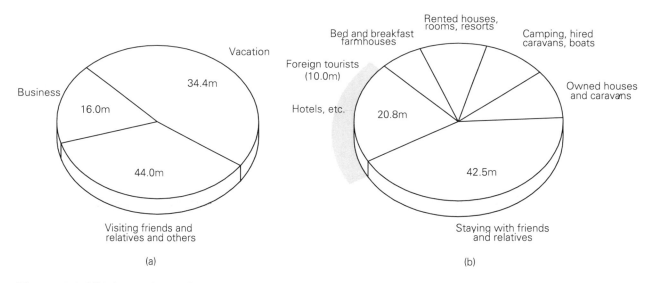

Figure 1.1 UK domestic tourists 1992. (a) Visits by purpose; (b) accommodation used. (Source: BTA, ETB)

National systems of classification vary both in the range of categories and method of designation (letters, figures, stars, crowns and other symbols) and may be compulsory or voluntary (see section 1.1.6).

Circumstances of hotel operation also vary: resort hotels may be operated under exclusive contract to one or more tour operators; they may restrict food service to residents and remain open only during the holiday season. Hotels may also include many different types of accommodation: guestrooms, suites, self-catering units and supplementary apartments using the hotel services.

Motels, motor hotels and motor courts
Motel accommodation is located and arranged to serve the particular needs of the motorist traveller and ranges from the simple court or lodge to more elaborate motor hotels offering extensive conference and banqueting facilities. In most countries, motels are ranked with hotel accommodation and are subject to the same standards. Specific legislation has been introduced for motel requirements in six countries. For example, in France there are three categories classified by location, standards of rooms and fittings and collective amenities.

Motel facilities in Turkey require the provision of a service station.

Boarding houses, guest houses, pension, pension de famille
This type of accommodation generally involves the use of domestic-type property which may be shared with the resident family. Facilities and meals are limited to use by resident guests and standards in a number of countries are subject to regulation. Sophisticated facilities for paying guests may be provided in stately houses and chateaux.

Bed and breakfast accommodation, hotels-garnis
Premises offering bed and breakfast services range from converted hotels to shared domestic properties. Services are generally limited and many premises operate only during the tourist season.

1.1.4 Numbers of rooms: distribution and densities

Worldwide there were some 11 312 000 rooms in hotels and similar establishments in 1991, an increase of 30.4 per cent in the ten years from 1981 (Figure 1.2).

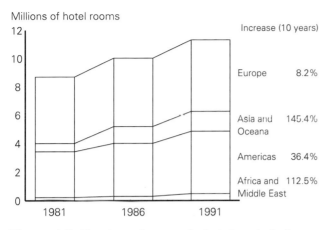

Millions of hotel rooms

Increase (10 years)

Europe 8.2%

Asia and 145.4%
Oceana

Americas 36.4%

Africa and 112.5%
Middle East

Figure 1.2 Number of rooms in hotel and similar establishments worldwide. (Source: World Tourism Organization, *Yearbooks* and *Compendiums of Tourism Statistics* 1981–1993)

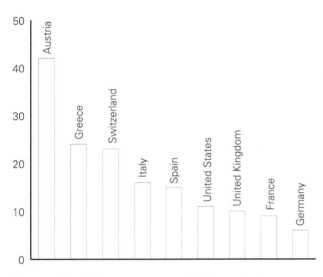

Figure 1.3 Hotel rooms per 1000 population 1991. (Based on World Tourism Organization statistics and other sources)

The ratio of beds:hotel rooms averaged 1:93. In developing tourist areas, the number of bed spaces is a more useful guide for the overall tourist population density, and includes other types of accommodation (rented apartments, villas, camping sites, etc.).

Hotel room densities and ratios

The number of hotel rooms in comparison to the population of a country is an indication of the level of investment in international and domestic tourism (Figure 1.3). Trends in tourism demand and hotel room densities are an indication of potential for investment on the risk of hotel saturation in a country.

1.1.5 Supplementary accommodation

Supplementary accommodation ranges from temporary camping and caravan sites to rented and owned properties.

Holiday villages

Holiday villages are centres of accommodation, usually planned as self-contained resorts, with extensive opportunities for sport and recreation in an attractive natural or created setting. The accommodation is typically in multiple small-scale units clustered around recreational focuses or dispersed in landscaped grounds. Self-catering or serviced options, including a choice of restaurants, are normally offered with a high ratio of family units, each providing a convertible living room, bedroom(s), bath/shower room and kitchen.

Commercial holiday villages (holiday centres, camps and clubs) are usually large (600 to 1200 or more bed capacity) with a density of about 150–200 beds/hectare (60–80 beds/acre). Design emphasis may be given to sport and contact with nature (Club Méditerranée, Club Robinson), to enclosed subtropical leisure pools (Center Parcs) or entertainment attractions (Butlins, Pontins).

Specific regulations may apply, as in Spain where holiday villages are classified into three categories according to the amenities and services provided. In France, regulatory standards apply to commercial holiday villages and to social holiday centres like those of the Association *Villages Vacances Familles* (VVF).

Village style accommodation may also feature in large integrated resorts and marina developments, in pavilion hotels and as part of resort hotel complexes.

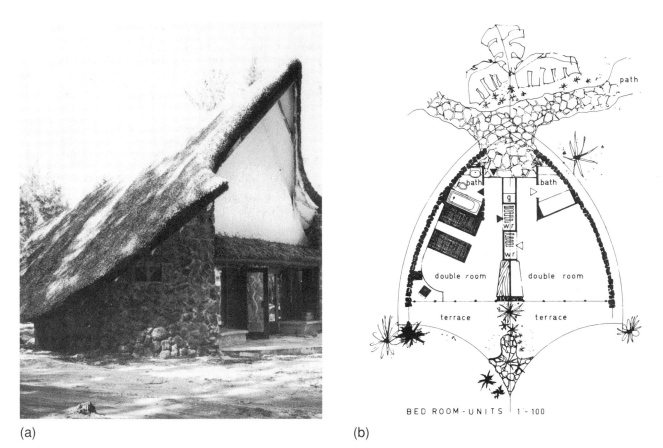

(a)　　　　　　　　　　　　　　　　　　　(b)

Figure 1.4 *La Pirogue Hotel, Mauritius* This holiday village uses dual bedroom units built in stone with thatched roofs arranged in curved rows facing the sun around a large central building. Architects: Melick & Associates

Condominiums

Condominium development involves joint ownership of a complex. The condominium owner purchases and has full benefit of a unit (guestroom, suite, apartment, villa) while also sharing in the costs common to the whole complex. The latter usually include property taxes, maintenance of the premises, upkeep of grounds, roads and recreational facilities and the provision of services such as security, management and letting.

The condominium has many advantages over simply leased property, enabling the owners to enjoy extensive recreational facilities which are exclusive to the complex. Mortgages are gener-ally available, with tax benefits of property ownership, and capital invested can appreciate with rising values, particularly in prime locations.

Condominiums are often used in multiple developments to generate capital and to provide accommodation back-up for other hotel and convention centre projects. Various schemes have been devised to widen opportunities for investment including single, joint or multiple ownership, sale and leaseback for letting, time-sharing and property exchange arrangements.

Terms of purchase and contractual arrange-ments for management and owners' representa-tion are widely variable and may be subject to legislation or Codes of Practice.

Individual villas, apartments, suites, cottages
Much of the recent investment in resorts has been in privately furnished villas and apartments for owner occupation or/and letting. Land allocations, financial loans and credits are often available for appropriate development which will contribute to capital costs of resort infrastructure and public amenities. In many European countries, notably France, there are incentives for conversion of redundant farm buildings and cottages (Gîtes) to provide self-catering tourist accommodation.

Residential accommodation is subject to the general law relating to housing and public health. Specific legislation for rental apartments has been introduced in several countries. Regulations generally cover such aspects as the capacity, furniture, fittings, amenities, services and sanitation and may include classification based on location, size and furnishings.

Individual investment in rooms and suites may also be provided in aparthotel and marina developments.

The demand for second residences for weekends, holidays, letting and retirement has led to extensive conversion of traditional properties (cottages, farm buildings, mills) as well as large scale real estate development in areas of scenic and climatic attraction (as in Florida, the Mediterranean and European Alps).

In most countries, control over development is provided though Town and Country Planning legislation. In addition, positive steps must be taken to reduce the environmental impact and ensure an attractive resort image. (See Tourism and Recreation Facilities)

1.1.6 Grading

Since 1962 the World Tourism Organization (WTO) – previously the International Union of Official Tourism Organizations (IUOTO) – has sought to develop a universally accepted hotel rating system. Similar proposals have been considered by the International Hotel Association (IHA). The Confederation of National Hotel and Restaurant Associations (HOTREC) of the European Union has devised an alternative system using symbols to represent the facilities without classification.

In 1995 there were over 100 classification systems in operation, the majority based on the WTO model but customized to suit local conditions.

Systems fall broadly into two groups:

1 *Official classifications* Standards set by governmental agencies – usually the Ministry of Tourism or Regional Tourist Board – either as a compulsory requirement for registration or licensing or as a voluntary scheme.
2 *Independent ratings* Hotels inspected and assessed by associations (such as hotel or automobile associations) or commercial bodies (Mobil and Michelin Travel Guides).

1.1.7 Benefits and limitations

Grading of accommodation offers a number of advantages: the published ratings provide channels for direct promotion, give guidance on the facilities, and reassurance that standards will meet expectations. Grading also sets standards and incentives for improvement of quality and contributes towards an image of reliability for a destination.

Difficulties can arise in introducing or changing a system where there is a large stock of existing hotels. Some schemes allow modified or compensatory standards for existing premises and others exclude traditional forms of guesthouses (such as the Ryokans in Japan).

Other considerations include:

1 *Local infrastructure* – fundamental requirements such as pure water supply, sanitation, ceramic tiles, which are generally assumed, may need to be specified in developing countries.
2 *Overall quality* – some properties, whilst lacking certain amenities may have outstanding features (history, location, character). Some schemes are based on points awarded.
3 *Factual basis* – all schemes consider tangible factors (space, facilities, amenities, services

(a) Site layout

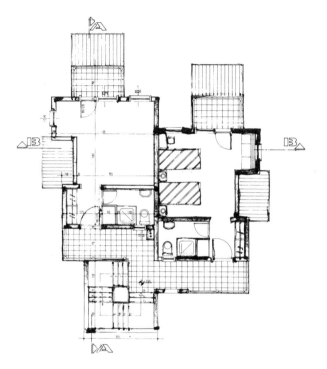

(b(i)) Plan of chalets

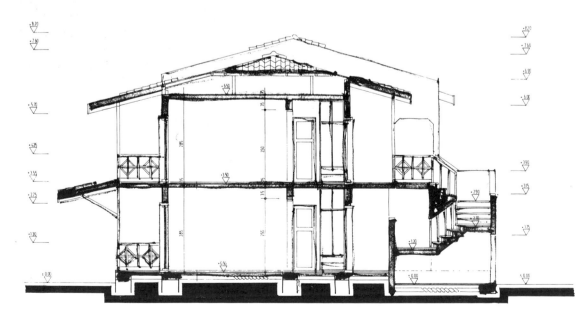

(b(ii)) Section A–A of chalets

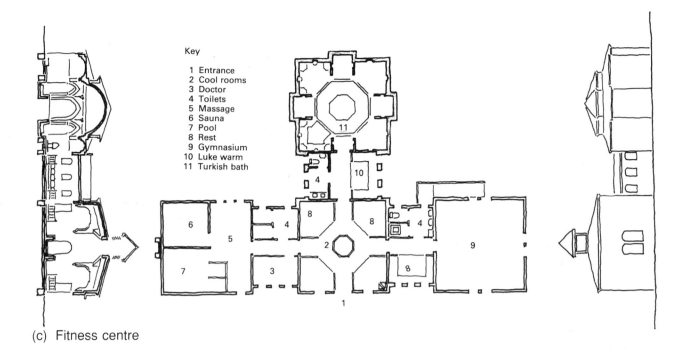

Key

1 Entrance
2 Cool rooms
3 Doctor
4 Toilets
5 Massage
6 Sauna
7 Pool
8 Rest
9 Gymnasium
10 Luke warm
11 Turkish bath

(c) Fitness centre

Figure 1.5 *Turtel Sorgun Resort Village, Turkey*
Located on the edge of the Sorgun Forest, 80 km
from an international airport and 5 minutes from
the ancient city of Side, Turtel Sorgun is designed
as a self-contained resort.

There are 346 standard rooms, 14 duplex and 2
suites, a total of 738 beds and central public
buildings set within a 7.2 hectare (18 acre) wooded
site. Each standard room has a private balcony,
WC, shower, heating and air-conditioning and the
rooms are grouped into small dispersed chalets
and blocks amongst the mature trees. Five
swimming pools provide focuses of interest and
include pool bars and a landscaped 54 m long
waterslide.

The public facilities are mainly grouped into a
large central complex with 2 restaurants, 3 bars,
shopping centre, beauty parlour, conference halls,
TV room and fitness centre. There is an outdoor
theatre and disco, 4 tennis courts and watersports
adjacent to a 300 m long, sandy beach.

Car park, reception and service buildings are
located at the entrance restricting traffic on the site.

Seating capacities: Restaurant, 750; 3 bars,
(total) 650; disco 150.

Developers, owners: Turtel Turizm Isletmeleri AS.

(d) View of chalet

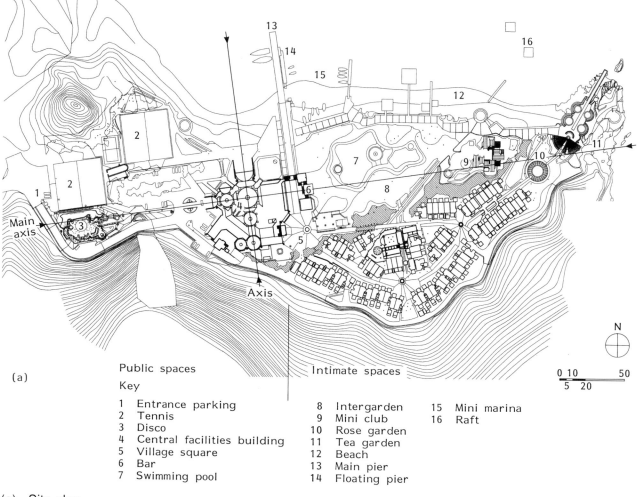

(a)

Public spaces		Intimate spaces	
Key			
1	Entrance parking	8	Intergarden
2	Tennis	9	Mini club
3	Disco	10	Rose garden
4	Central facilities building	11	Tea garden
5	Village square	12	Beach
6	Bar	13	Main pier
7	Swimming pool	14	Floating pier
		15	Mini marina
		16	Raft

(a) Site plan

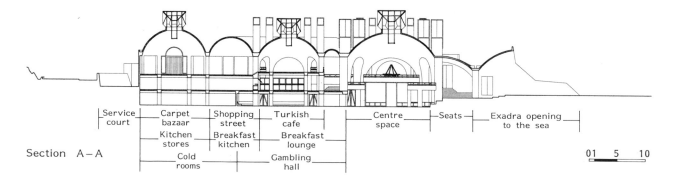

Section A–A

(b) Plans of central facilities building
    (i) Section

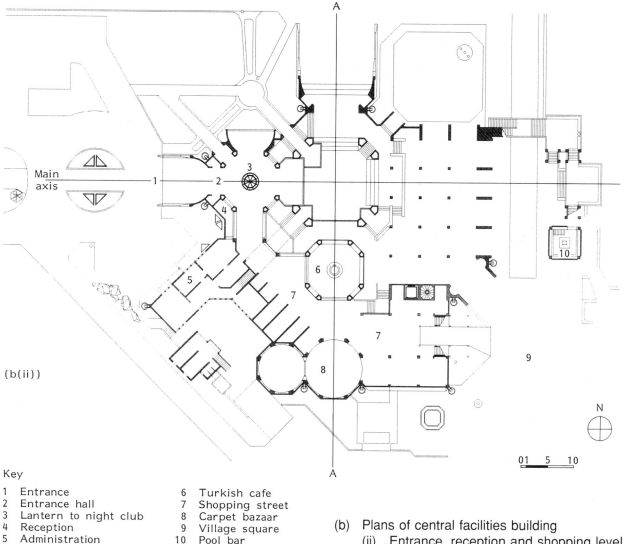

(b(ii))

Key

1 Entrance	6 Turkish cafe
2 Entrance hall	7 Shopping street
3 Lantern to night club	8 Carpet bazaar
4 Reception	9 Village square
5 Administration	10 Pool bar

(b) Plans of central facilities building
(ii) Entrance, reception and shopping level

Figure 1.6 *Eldorador, Phaselis Kemer*
Encircled by tree-covered mountains between two rocky outcrops jutting into the Mediterranean, this new village resort has been planned around three main zones:

- Intimate residential areas of individual and terraced houses which occupy the quiet backland surrounded by trees and gardens.
- Grouped public facilities accessible to the entrance, car park and pier.
- Open recreational areas forming the interzone which extends to the beach.

Architect: Professor Cengiz Eren

Figure 1.6 *continued*

(b) Plans of central facilities building
     (iii) Main restaurant, lounge and
           kitchen level

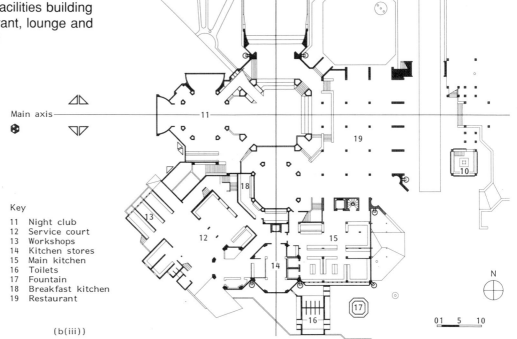

Main axis

Key

11 Night club
12 Service court
13 Workshops
14 Kitchen stores
15 Main kitchen
16 Toilets
17 Fountain
18 Breakfast kitchen
19 Restaurant

N

0 1   5   10

(b(iii))

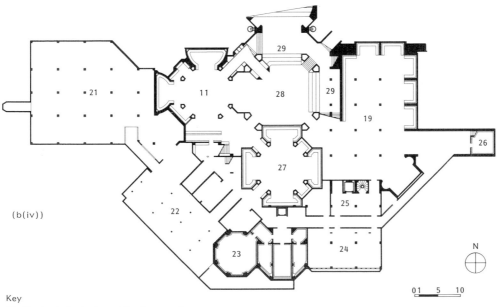

(b(iv))

N

0 1   5   10

Key

21 Mechanical plant   26 Bar service
22 Laundry   27 Gambling hall
23 Cold rooms   28 Central space for entertainment
24 Stores   29 Spectator seats
25 Service kitchen

(b) Plans of central facilities building
     (iv) Basement restaurant, night club,
          gambling hall and performance areas.
          Back of house support facilities

(c) Plan of Turkish
Bath with roof
area for showers
and resting

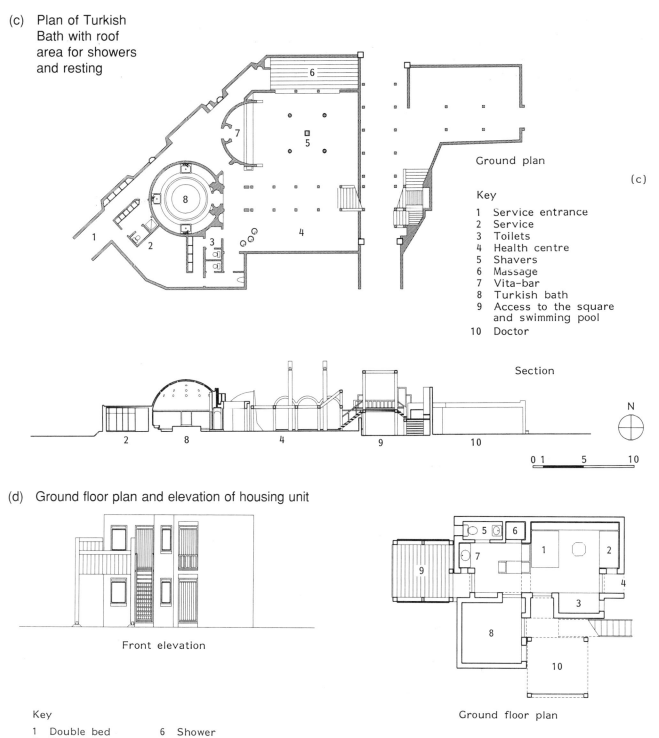

Ground plan

(c)

Key
1 Service entrance
2 Service
3 Toilets
4 Health centre
5 Shavers
6 Massage
7 Vita-bar
8 Turkish bath
9 Access to the square
   and swimming pool
10 Doctor

Section

N

0 1   5   10

(d) Ground floor plan and elevation of housing unit

Front elevation

Ground floor plan

Key
1 Double bed   6 Shower
2 Sofa   7 LB
3 Mashrabiya   8 Suite
4 Entrance   9 Wooden terrace
5 WC and LB   10 Terrace to upper unit

0 1   5

(d)

(e)   Aerial view of site

(f)   View of pool

Figure 1.6 *continued*

provided). Qualitative aspects (performance, personal service) which involve subjective judgements tend to be more variable. Some schemes (Korea) provide for two types of awards, others have a combined points system (China).

4 *Location and market needs* – user requirements for resort hotels differ from those in a city. Separate standards may apply (Austria).

5 *Maintenance* – hotel quality depends on standards of cleanliness, upkeep and maintenance which can impair comfort and safety but may be difficult to monitor.

1.1.8 Model schemes

Table 1.1 indicates minimum standards based on the classification proposed by the World Tourism Organization and is broadly comparable to minimum standards adopted in most countries.

Rating General characteristics

1 Hotels with good basic facilities and furnishings ensuring comfortable accommodation. Meals services may be limited. Includes small private hotels.

2 Hotels having higher standards of accommodation and more facilities providing good levels of comfort and amenity. Includes private hotels and budget orientated accommodation.

3 Well appointed hotels with spacious, very comfortable accommodation, mostly with ensuite bathrooms. Full meal facilities are provided as well as a range of amenities.

4 High quality hotels, well equipped and furnished to a very high standard of comfort, offering a very wide range of services and amenities for guests and visitors.

5 Outstanding hotels with exceptional quality accommodation and furnishings to the highest international standards of luxury, providing impeccable services and extensive amenities.

Table 1.1 WTO minimum hotel standards

	1 star	2 star	3 star	4 star	5 star
Physical requirements					
Size	Minimum of 10 letting bedrooms				
Entrance	The hotel must have its own independent entrance			Hotel restaurants must have their own external as well as internal entrances. Separate service entrance	
Staircases	To comply with legal requirements →			Separate service staircase	
Construction	Architecture, design, furniture and decoration should reflect the local style with the degree of sophistication increasing with category →				
Furniture, fittings and equipment	Moderate cost construction, simple, durable equipment and furniture of standard design		Medium cost construction materials and fittings. Custom made furniture	High cost construction and fittings. Custom made equipment and furniture	Top cost construction, fittings, equipment and furniture. Individualized decor
Emergency power supply		Emergency light sources	Stand by generator to supply basic lighting and power up to 24 hrs	Stand by generator to supply energy for lighting, lifts, water treatment, cooking and refrigeration, and heating	
Heating and cooling	Heating or fan cooling when necessary	+ central heating and comfort cooling seasonally available	+ individual heat control in bedrooms. Temperature maintained between 18 and 25°C	+ individual air conditioning control in all rooms. High quality equipment with very low noise emission	
Lift(s) available to match room capacity	Where more than three upper floors	When more than two upper floors		When more than one upper floor	
Service lift				Separate from main guest lift	
In room communication	Call bell	Internal only telephone. Telephone available on request	Telephone connected through hotel switchboard	Direct dial telephone to other rooms and for national calls	Direct dial telephones for national and international calls. Telephone in bathroom
	One externally connected telephone per floor				

Table 1.1 WTO minimum hotel standards *(continued)*

	1 star	2 star	3 star	4 star	5 star
Public telephones	Telephone available through reception	Telephone booth in the lobby	Telephone available near all public rooms	Soundproof booth in lobby with national and international connections	
Bedrooms					
Size	Adequate for free movement, comfort and safety. Minimum area in square metres (excluding bathroom and lobby):				
Single	8	8	10	12	13
Double	10	10	12	14	16
Triple	12	12	14	16	19
Suites				Some suites available or connecting rooms to make temporary suites	Independent suites of various types and connecting rooms
Single bed minimum size	1900 mm x 800mm			2000 mm x 800mm	
Linen/towels	Bed linen changed with each new occupant.	Bed linen changed twice a week		Towels changed with each new occupant and daily ↑ Bed linen changed daily	
Room cleaning	Daily ↑			Additional room cleaning on request up to 12.00 pm	24 hour additional room cleaning
Storage	Closet or wardrobe with hangers plus shelves or chest of drawers. Increasing in sophistication ↑				
Seating	Minimum of one chair per person			Minimum of one armchair per person	
Tables	One bedside table per guest ↑	Table in room	Writing/dressing table	Writing/dressing table with drawers	
Lighting	Natural light through windows during the day. Artificial light at night adequate for reading. Ceiling light with switches at entrance and bedside. One bedside lamp per person ↑		Reading lamp at armchair/writing table		
Floor covering	Suitably tiled or covered floors with bedside rugs or carpets where appropriate		Wall to wall carpets or high quality flooring and floor coverings		

In-room entertainment		Radio/central music system controlled by the guest	TV available	Colour TV	Colour TV with video channel
Other room facilities	Window coverings to provide privacy and exclude light ↑			High quality furnishings	
	Waste basket. Ashtray (if not non-smoking room). At least one waterglass per person.				
	Written information on hotel services and procedures provided in one other language.		Written information on hotel services and procedures provided in two other languages.		
	Do-not-disturb sign	Fire safety instructions		Local regulations may require display of tariff ↑	
		Luggage rack			
		Mirror other than in bathroom or at washbasin.			Plus full length mirror
			Stationery		
				Mini fridge/mini bar	
Soundproofing		Tolerable for day and night stay	Good to tolerable		High standard soundproofing
Door	Lockable with individual keys or other means. Easily identifiable from outside. Internal security fastening ↑				
Bathrooms					
Availability	Wash-basin with mirror, light, shelf, towels, soap and electric socket marked with voltage	+ at least 25% of rooms with private bathrooms		All rooms have private bathrooms	Spacious bathrooms / Separate toilet
Size	Adequate for free, comfortable and safe movement ↑				
Standard facilities	Natural or induced ventilation providing at least 3 air changes/hr ↑				
	Hot and cold running water. Colour coded. Thermostatically controlled ↑				Chilled drinking water
	Wash-basin with mirror, light, shelf, towels, soap and electric socket marked with voltage ↑				
	Water closet with toilet paper. Waste bin ↑				
	Shower cabinet or bath with showerhead and curtain or screen			Bath with showerhead minimum 1600mm long	Bath with showerhead minimum 1600mm long. Separate shower cubicle
	Minimum of one hand and one bath towel per guest ↑				
		Bath mats			
		Shampoo provided			Shampoo and other toiletries provided
				Cabinet for personal effects	
					Hairdryer, telephone

Table 1.1 WTO minimum hotel standards *(continued)*

	1 star	2 star	3 star	4 star	5 star
Shared bathrooms (minimum)		One bathroom per five bedrooms sharing. Two on each floor (one for each sex). Equipped with shower cubicle or bath tub, washbasin, mirror, wc (unless separate and standard facilities			
Shared water closets (minimum)		One wc per five bedrooms sharing. Two on each floor (one for each sex) with washbasins and standard facilities			
Public areas					
Public toilets		Separate for each sex. Normally each should have a minimum of two water closets with toilet paper, washbasins with hot and cold running water, mirror, soap, towels or hand drier and waste bin. Separate cubicle for the disabled equipped with appropriate fittings. Suitably sited near public areas with interiors screened from view. Ventilation with at least 3 air changes/hr			
Corridors		Well lit 24 hours a day by natural and/or artificial light. Adequately ventilated. Free from obstacles or hazards. Suitably signposted with emergency exits clearly indicated		Carpets, wall to wall carpeting or special floor finishes	
Reception area		Seating and appropriate furniture commensurate to hotel capacity.	Coffee and/or writing tables. Carpets, wall to wall carpeting or special floor finishes. Plants. Music/PA system.	Well lit. Carpets, wall to wall carpeting or special floor finishes.	
Parking		Free access by car. Some reserved parking space	Parking space reserved for average number of car-using guests	Exclusive parking or garage to accommodate all hotel guests and casual visitors. 24 hr security	As four star plus basic care servicing available
Green area				Some garden area or terrace with plants	Green area for guest use such as terrace with plants, roof garden, patio or adjoining gardens

Food and beverage, leisure and recreation facilities

	1	2	3	4	5
Lounge	Area with lounge seating, music and/or television services. May also be used for breakfast and reception of guests	Lounge area or sitting room with music and television services, newspapers and/or magazines	Lounge area or sitting room as before seating at least one-third of hotel bed capacity in combination with reception area	Choice of lounge(s) or sitting room(s) as before, plus service of drinks and refreshments	Choice of lounge(s) or sitting room(s) as before with 24 hour lounge service
Breakfast	Provided in hotel or facilities in immediate proximity	As above or by service to rooms	Resaurant(s) provided within hotel with adequate seating capacity for breakfast and other meals	Breakfast served 7.00 am to 10.00 am	7.00 am to 11.00 am
Room service	The option of self-catering facilities may be provided → Breakfast served in rooms where no breakfast area available	Limited room service may be offered		Breakfast service including newspaper. 24 hour beverage and light meal service	24 hour full meal and beverage services
Restaurant	Restaurant or cafeteria where meals are served at lunchtime and evening or in immediate proximity to appropriate independent facilities	Restaurant or coffee shop where meals are served at lunchtime and evening. Seating not less than half of hotel bed capacity		Main restaurant or choice of restaurants serving a variety of meals. Private dining or function rooms available. Total seating not less than hotel bed capacity. High quality food and beverage services	Highest standards of cuisine and services
Bar			Separate bar	Separate bar(s) and cocktail lounge	
Conference facilities				Meeting and conference rooms with appropriate conference facilities	
Cloakroom			Cloakroom and toilets near public rooms		
Entertainment				Music and public address system. Night club, dancing area or discotheque available in hotel or near proximity	
Recreation				Sauna or swimming pool or health club cr a combination	Sauna, gymnasium/ health club, swimming pool/jetpool

Table 1.1 WTO minimum hotel standards (continued)

	1 star	2 star	3 star	4 star	5 star
Hairdresser					Hairdresser/beauty studio
Services					
Reception services	Reception desk manned throughout the day. Night bell. Guest luggage handling on request.		Permanent reception service. 24 hour check-in	Paging service/public address system	Hall porters, luggage handling and doorman
Medical services	Emergency medical/first aid service ↑			First aid room	
Cashiers services	Safety deposit ↑	Credit cards accepted	Currency exchange service	24 hour currency exchange service	Individual safety deposit boxes
Laundry services	Laundry only	Laundry and dry cleaning		Express laundry including washing, ironing and dry cleaning	
Postal services	Service to include mail delivery and dispatch and sale of postage stamps and stationery ↑		Dispatch of telex or telefax	Dispatch and receipt of, telex and telefax	
Tourist and travel services	Local maps available on request	Tourist information available at reception. Booking tickets for local entertainment and cultural events	Tourist information service at reception	Travel agency/tourism service (tourist information, excursions, guiding, insurance, etc.) Ticketing and booking service for transport, hotels, entertainment and cultural events	
Tourist and travel services	Taxi on call			Taxi service. Hotel minibus available if isolated location	Taxi and rent-a-car service. Free hotel vehicle if isolated location
Retail services				Sale of newspapers, books, postcards, tobacco and photographic supplies	

		Sale of cosmetics and souvenirs	Sale of cosmetics, souvenirs and flowers
Language services	Adequate knowledge by reception staff of one key international language	Working knowledge of two key international languages by customer contact staff	Good knowledge of two key international languages by customer contact staff	Good knowledge of two key international languages by management positions and very good knowledge of three such languages by customer contact staff

Conditions

Buildings, grounds, equipment, fittings and furniture maintained in clean, safe and sound condition, in good working order and free from defects which could impair use ↑

Public and guest areas cleaned at least daily, maintained in good decorative order and provided with clean furnishings in good sound condition. Attention given to defects with minimum of delay

Exceptionally clean and in excellent decorative order and condition. Rapid response to any matter requiring attention

Full compliance with legal and licensing standards in respect of fire, means of escape and other safety precautions, hygiene, conditions for places of work and habitation, hotel insurance and other stipulated requirements ↑

Notes

↑ General requirements which apply to all hotels
Column requirements apply to hotels of the grade indicated and above

1.2 Hotel categories

1.2.1 Identification

Hotels may be described by their locations, standards of quality, operation as a chain or independently and extent of specialization (Table 1.2).

1.2.2 Sizes

The stock of hotel accommodation in most developed countries is characterized by a high proportion of small family-run hotels, inns and guest houses. New hotels are generally in the mid- to large size range to justify commercial investment and group operation. The optimum

Table 1.2 Hotel identification

Identified by	Examples	Characteristics: emphasis
Location	City centre, provincial town	Business travel, urban visitors
	Resort, country house	Vacation and conference users
	Airport, motel	Transient and staging needs
Quality	Official or voluntary grading systems denoted by 1 to 5 stars, crowns, diamonds, etc.	Standards of space, facilities and services appropriate for hotels of that grade
	Company tiering or sub-branding of products to serve differentiated markets.	Budget, mid-markets and luxury hotels distinguished by brand names, specific design features and range of services offered
Operation	Large hotel companies operating as a chain or group of company-owned, managed or franchised properties	Similar standards of quality, facilities and services. Branding is usually adopted to provide a recognizable and consistent product at a common national tariff
	Individual hotels which may be fully independent or associated with a marketing consortium	Emphasis is often placed on the distinctive character of the hotel and personal service
Specialization	Hotels offering particular facilities and services, e.g.:	
	Resort hotels	Orientated around resort and leisure attractions
	Convention hotels	Including extensive facilities for meetings and conventions
	Spa hotels	Providing medical, paramedical, fitness and convalescence services
	Casino hotels	With gaming rooms, spectacular entertainment and public facilities

Figure 1.7 *Guildford YMCA*

(a) Front elevation

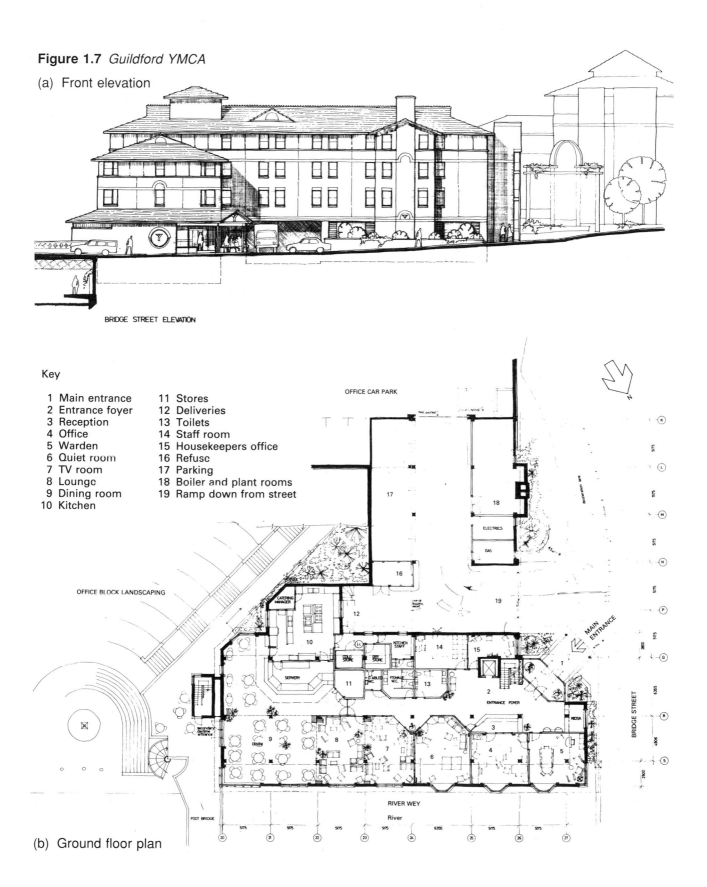

Key

1 Main entrance	11 Stores
2 Entrance foyer	12 Deliveries
3 Reception	13 Toilets
4 Office	14 Staff room
5 Warden	15 Housekeepers office
6 Quiet room	16 Refuse
7 TV room	17 Parking
8 Lounge	18 Boiler and plant rooms
9 Dining room	19 Ramp down from street
10 Kitchen	

(b) Ground floor plan

Figure 1.7 *Guildford YMCA*
The 'Y' hotel in Guildford is part of a new development in the centre of the town next to the river. Although 5 storeys high it has been designed so that that only 4 storeys are evident giving a human scale to the building. The ground floor has a generous foyer with glazed walls to the activity rooms and restaurant with scenic views of the river beyond. There is a divisible community hall on the lower ground floor and residential accommodation:

114 bedsits with shower/WC shared between 2 bedsits
3 bedsits suitable for wheelchairs with private shower/WC
3 ambulant bedsits with adjacent bathroom
1 0ne-bedroom staff flat.
The building is constructed of reinforced concrete framework on the ground and lower ground floors – for future flexibility – with loadbearing brickwork to the residential floors above.

Building cost (1989) £760/m² ($105/sqft). Total floor area 3237m² (34 840 sqft). Clients: YMCA. Architects: Hurley Porte and Duell. Structural Engineer: Peter Olley & Associates. M & E Consultants: Engineering Design Consultants

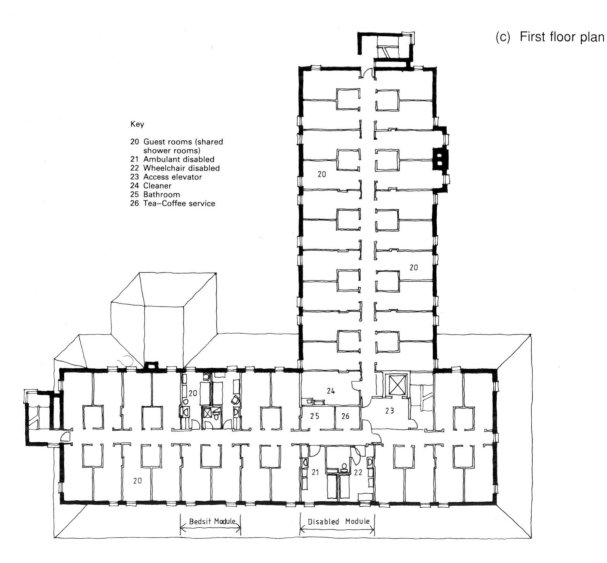

(c) First floor plan

Key

20 Guest rooms (shared
   shower rooms)
21 Ambulant disabled
22 Wheelchair disabled
23 Access elevator
24 Cleaner
25 Bathroom
26 Tea–Coffee service

for efficient staffing is usually around 200 rooms (120 rooms for budget/mid-tariff hotels) while larger units can provide savings in property operation and advantages in marketing. In prime locations (city centres, resort prominence) the high cost of site acquisition will usually dictate the minimum size and grade to achieve a viable cost/room ratio (Table 1.3).

Table 1.3 Characteristics of various sizes of hotel

Size range	Characteristics
Fewer than 25 rooms	Typical guesthouses, farmhouse and cottage conversions, small private hotels and traditional inns and lodges. Usually family run and individually owned. This form of small-scale dispersed tourism development is actively encouraged in many rural tourist areas
50–80 rooms	Includes the smaller independent hotels and country houses and luxury conversions of stately houses, Paradors (Spain). Hotels of this size are large enough to employ a separate manager and may be operated independently or as part of a company or marketing consortium
80–120 rooms	Most new budget hotels, inns, lodges and motels are in this size range providing standard rooms with an independent restaurant. Depending on location the development may include a small outdoor swimming pool and children's play area
120–200 rooms	New provincial hotels in Europe tend to be in this size range. The number of rooms allows for better utilization of space and facilities – which usually include some business meeting/private function rooms, a separate coffee shop and restaurant and health-fitness centre
200–300 rooms	Typical size for resort hotels supporting more extensive dining areas, lounges and recreational facilities. This size is also representative of mid-scale city centre hotels and many airport hotels
150–250 rooms	Luxury hotels in resorts and spas. Hotels of this size can retain a personal service while offering a wide range of exclusive facilities (private beach, golf-course, speciality restaurants, remedial treatments)
300–500 rooms	High grade hotels in city centre, downtown and prime resort locations. Invariably these provide more than one restaurant, a health–fitness club including an indoor pool and extensive business facilities. This size is also necessary to support more extensive convention facilities
300–800 rooms	Most integrated resorts, holiday centres and club complexes have a large capacity to support extensive recreational and entertainment facilities and marketing costs
800–1000+ rooms	Mega city centre hotels where economies of scale can allow spectacular designs and cost savings in construction and operation. This includes the larger convention hotels and casino hotels

(Continued on page 30)

23

Figure 1.9 *Holiday Inn Crowne Plaza, Istanbul*
Completed in 1993, this 27 storey, high rise of 5 star quality is on the edge of the Bosphorus near the centre of Istanbul and only 5 km from the international airport. It is part of an extensive tourism complex covering 50 hectares which includes a 1050 boat marina, a yacht hotel and club and 55 500 m² shopping galleria with its own skating rink.

The hotel has a total of 298 guestrooms with 593 beds and 60 sofa beds comprising 264 standard rooms (4 types), 2 rooms for the disabled, 28 junior suites and larger suites. Seating capacities of public areas are:

Restaurant	126
Roof bar	62
Meeting rooms (5)	224
Lobby lounge	50
Patisserie	114
Piano bar	62
Outdoor terrace bar	200
Restaurant	176
Function room suite (3 sections)	400: banquet or 780: conference

The basement health club includes a 10 m × 5 m indoor pool, whirlpool, sauna and massage rooms and bar. There is also an outdoor swimming pool, 25 m × 13.5 m and paddling pool within a surround extending to 3140 m². Covered garaging is provided for 136 cars and open parking for 167 cars.

Floors:

2 basements	Total construction area 34 510 m²
1 ground floor	
1 meeting room	Construction period, Sept 1987–June 1993
3 installations	
19 guestrooms	Total costs excluding land (leased) but including finance $95 million of which: furniture & furnishings – 10.00%; operating equipment – 10.5%; landscaping 0.50%; and cost/m² – $2753
1 roof restaurant, bar	
27	

(a) Front entrance

Architect and coordinator: Dr Hayati Tabanlioğlu.
Structural engineer: Ali Terzibasoğulu.
Mechanical engineer: Ersin Güdol.
Electrical engineer: Bulent Cedetas.
Project managers: Nurer Ozcan.
Main contractor: Atakoy Otecilik AS

(b) Exterior

(c) Lobby

(d) Standard bedroom

Figure 1.9 *Holiday Inn Crowne Plaza, Istanbul (continued)*

Key
1 Shopping mall galleria
2 Multi-storey parking area
2a Multi-storey parking + movie theatres
3 Hotel Holiday Inn Crowne Plaza – Istanbul
4 Restaurant
5 Convention centre (planned for future)
6 Beach club (planned for future)
7 Yachters' hotel (Holiday Inn – core brand)
8 Leisure and sports facilities (planned for future)
9 Health club
10 Yachters' club
11 Marina
12 Marina admin. building with tower
13 Boat maintenance area
14 Sea bus port
15 Marina shopping arcade (regatta)
16 Landscaped area for public use

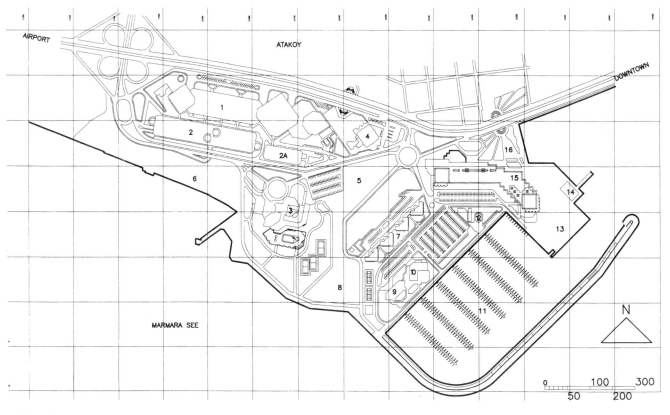

(e) Atakay tourism complex general layout plan

(f)   Section

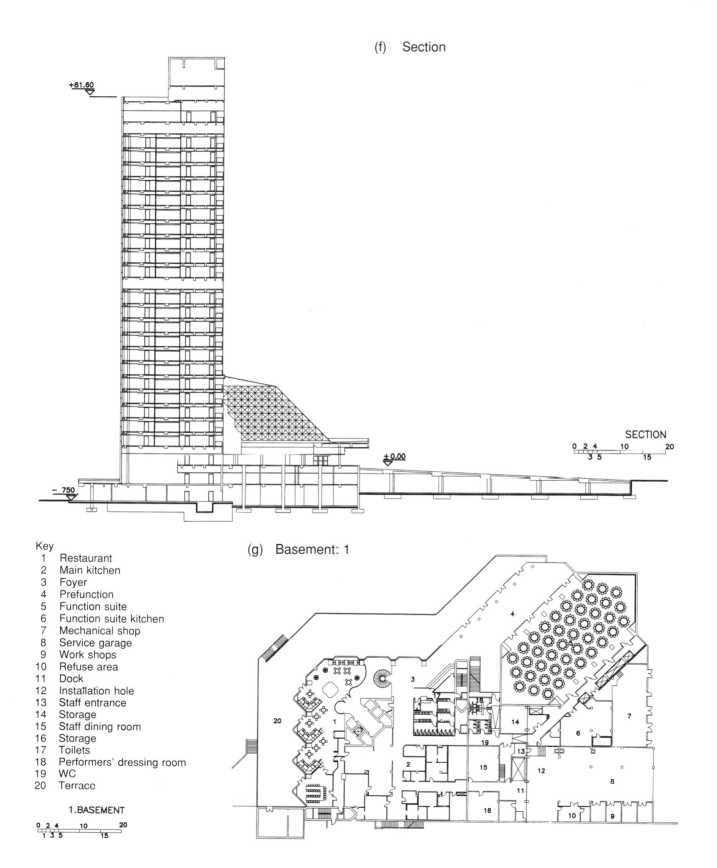

Key
1   Restaurant
2   Main kitchen
3   Foyer
4   Prefunction
5   Function suite
6   Function suite kitchen
7   Mechanical shop
8   Service garage
9   Work shops
10 Refuse area
11 Dock
12 Installation hole
13 Staff entrance
14 Storage
15 Staff dining room
16 Storage
17 Toilets
18 Performers' dressing room
19 WC
20 Terrace

(g)   Basement: 1

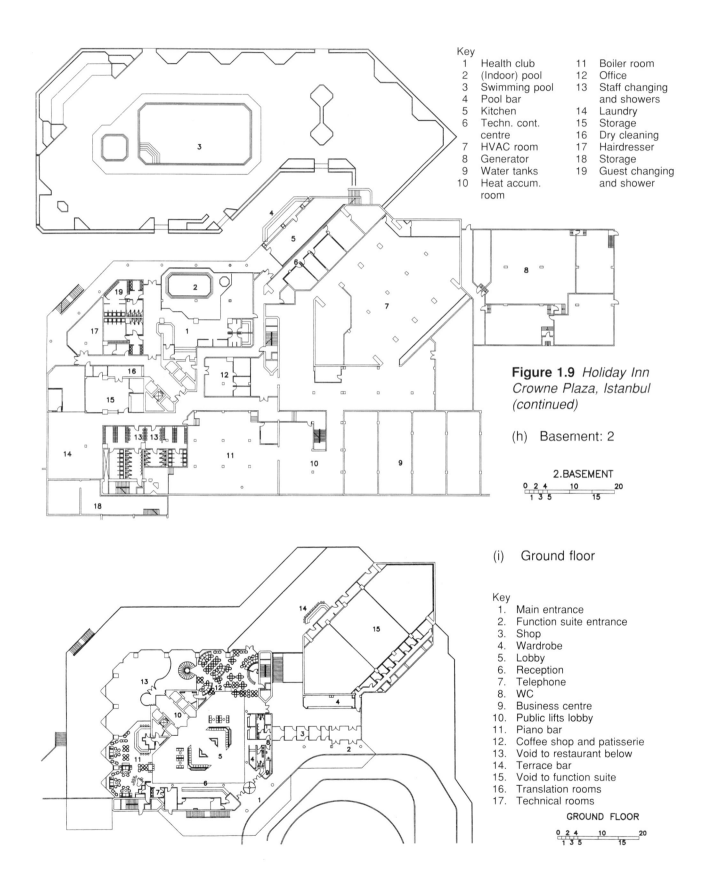

Key
1 Health club
2 (Indoor) pool
3 Swimming pool
4 Pool bar
5 Kitchen
6 Techn. cont. centre
7 HVAC room
8 Generator
9 Water tanks
10 Heat accum. room
11 Boiler room
12 Office
13 Staff changing and showers
14 Laundry
15 Storage
16 Dry cleaning
17 Hairdresser
18 Storage
19 Guest changing and shower

Figure 1.9 *Holiday Inn Crowne Plaza, Istanbul (continued)*

(h) Basement: 2

2.BASEMENT

0 2 4   10   20
  1 3 5   15

(i) Ground floor

Key
1. Main entrance
2. Function suite entrance
3. Shop
4. Wardrobe
5. Lobby
6. Reception
7. Telephone
8. WC
9. Business centre
10. Public lifts lobby
11. Piano bar
12. Coffee shop and patisserie
13. Void to restaurant below
14. Terrace bar
15. Void to function suite
16. Translation rooms
17. Technical rooms

GROUND FLOOR

0 2 4   10   20
  1 3 5   15

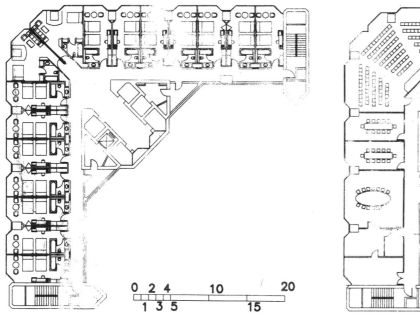

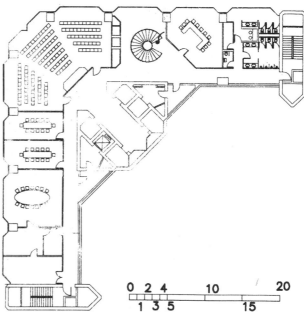

(j) Guestroom floor

(k) Meeting room floor

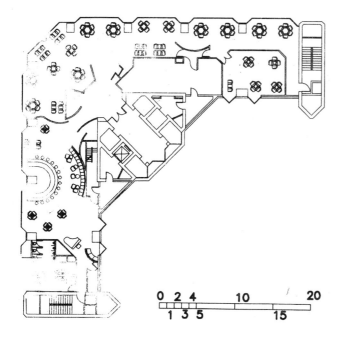

(l) Roof floor

Figure 1.9 *Holiday Inn Crowne Plaza, Istanbul (continued)*

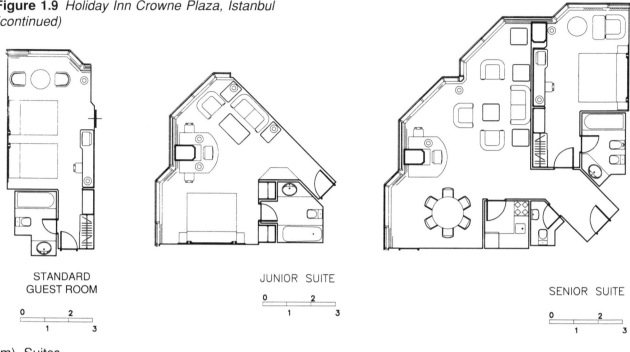

STANDARD
GUEST ROOM

0   2
1   3

JUNIOR SUITE

0   2
1   3

SENIOR SUITE

0   2
1   3

(m) Suites

(Continued from page 23)

1.3 Ownership and operation

1.3.1 Ownership structures

Whilst most family-run hotels are owned and operated on an individual basis many company hotels have an increasingly complex ownership structure (Table 1.4).

Separating hotel property ownership from the trading business enables a hotel company to expand at a faster rate and run more hotels than it could finance from its own resources. The

Table 1.4 Types of hotel ownership

Hotel ownership/operating structures	Examples
Land owner – ground lessor	Development of leasehold sites Sale and leaseback of freehold Joint venture schemes with landowner
Hotel developer – sub-lessor	Development of property and sale to an institution, investment group or unit owner
Hotel lessee	Leasing of property by hotel company or hotel investment group
Franchisee	Investment in franchised hotel property by an individual or company. Master franchise rights may be obtained for a country or region
Hotel management – operator	Operation by hotel management company under contract agreement

acquisition of existing hotels may be funded in part by the purchase and simultaneous sale and lease-back of the property or site. The method of releasing capital assets (property, land) is also used to reduce company borrowings and is particularly important in times of low growth in property values, (see section 1.4.7).

1.3.2 Independent hotels

Although family-owned and individual hotels run on an independent basis comprise the majority of units there is a continuing move towards company-affiliated hotels or conversion to self-catering. Small independent hotels are often under-capitalised, limited in scope for expansion and have difficulty in financing marketing and facility improvements.

However, the benefit from tourism incomes is often a valuable direct contribution to the local economy and governmental authorities are increasingly seeking ways of assisting this type of provision. Current approaches include:

- resort and regional promotion, collective advertising and syndication of purchasing
- development of national and regional reservation networks for tourist information and reservation systems
- direct aid in grants and subsidized or guaranteed loans for improvements in standards.

1.3.3 Company hotels

Company-affiliated hotels include those:

- owned or leased and operated by a hotel company
- managed by a hotel company on a management contract with remuneration to the operator linked to revenue or profit
- operated by the owner but forming part of a marketing and reservation consortium
- operated by the owner or investor under a franchise agreement with a major hotel chain.

Company hotels, in general, have less difficulty in financing refurbishment and expansion and

the professional standards of management enable performance to be monitored and operated with higher efficiency. Large international chains can develop central reservation systems either alone or linked with other international networks.

To identify with specific market segments and optimize the range of facilities and investment, hotel groups increasingly differentiate their properties into a number of tiered brands with specific characteristics and pricing levels (Table 1.5).

Table 1.5 Hotel descriptions by market tier

Market tiers	Examples of descriptions
Luxury	Grand, Regency
Mid-tariff	Garden Court, Courtyard
Budget	Inn, Lodge
Resorts	Resort, Club, Village

1.3.4 Standardization

The degree of standardization depends on company policy and the extent of brand conformity required. Some groups lay down precise specifications to achieve a uniform quality for their products; others adopt very broad guidelines to allow individual architectural and interior design diversity.

Most hotel chains have to detail requirements for their technical systems and operating equipment (front office and back-of-house) in order to achieve quality control, operating efficiency and compatibility throughout the chain.

As a broad division the degree of control over design depends largely on the need for cost control over construction and subsequent operation (Table 1.6).

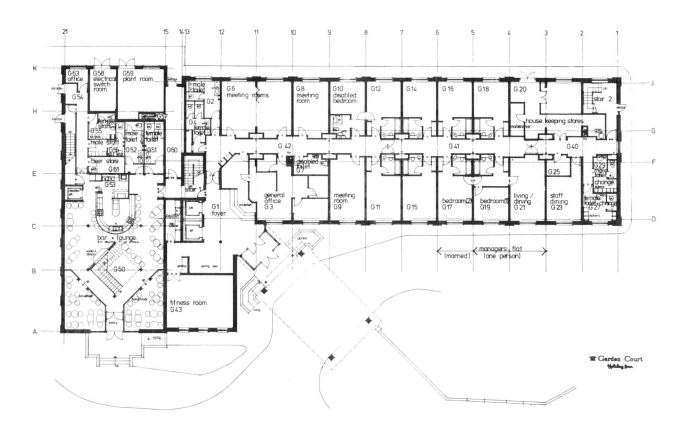

(a)   Ground floor plan

(b)   View from marina

Table 1.6 Degree of standardization

Types of hotels	Standardization
Luxury and high class hotels with emphasis on quality and sophistication	Individual designs within requirements laid down for space, range of facilities and quality. Company represented in the graphics, operating procedures and quality control
Mid-scale hotels with branded identity for reliability of products	Detailed design brief with standard requirements for guest rooms and precise guidelines for planning of public and back of house areas. Operating equipment usually specified
Budget hotels with cost-efficient accommodation	Highly standardized design and repetitive construction techniques, often using prefabrication and systems building. Rationalized requirements for public facilities with detailed specifications including equipment suppliers

Figure 1.10 *Courtyard Marriott, Lincoln*
Scotts Hotels, which are part of a large Canadian development group, owned and operated hotels in the United Kingdom under Holiday Inn franchises. In 1992 the company secured the Master franchise for Marriott hotels and effected the changeover of brands. The Courtyard Marriott is a mid-standard hotel (equivalent to 3 star) which targets the market gap between the more sophisticated Marriott hotels and budget accommodation. Like the Holiday Inn Garden Court, the primary markets are business and transient visitors with weekend promotions.

The Courtyard Lincoln (1992) illustrates the functional layout. There are 95 rooms on five floors, a bar and lounge on the ground floor – with a restaurant, seating 75 on the floor above – a small fitness room and two meeting rooms.

Although the construction is systems built the height and facades relate to each site. In Lincoln the Courtyard fronts a marina and resembles a traditional warehouse. All the hotels have a characteristic tower. Architects: Cobban & Lironi. Developer: Scotts Hotel

1.3.5 Hotel portfolios: changes in ownership

Following the escalation in hotel prices and values in the 1980s, the recession period 1987–93 witnessed major changes in hotel grouping. Large-scale portfolio sales alone resulted in some 2150 hotels (more than 450 000 rooms) changing hands at this time as well as numerous individual properties.

These included the sale of 104 Inter-Continental Hotels by Grand Metropolitan to the Seibu Saison Group (Japan), 110 Ramada Inns to the New World Development Corporation (Hong Kong) and sixty-two Westin Hotels and Resorts to the Aoki Corporation (Japan). Some 1589 Holiday Inns were acquired by Bass plc (UK) and 140 Hilton International Hotels were sold to the Ladbroke Group (UK).

Other changes in ownership in the United Kingdom resulted from the takeover of fifteen Norfolk Capital Hotels by the Queens Moat Group and the purchase of thirty-five Thistle Hotels by Mount Charlotte Hotels. The Allied Lyons group withdrew from hotel operation with the sale of forty-three Embassy Hotels to Jarvis Hotels Ltd.

In subsequent disposals of acquired hotels, Bass plc sold its forty-seven Crest Hotels to Forte plc, Queens Moat sold two hotels to Balmoral and Ladbroke put six of its hotels on the market.

1.3.6 Company strategies

In pursuing strategies leading to the sale or acquisition of other hotels, companies are influenced by several factors (Table 1.7).

In most disposals, sales have excluded particular areas of the company's operation such as profitable casinos and specialised hotel subgroups. Sales included company owned, franchised and managed hotels in the group.

While hotel sales – including companies going into receivership – featured prominently in the 1989–93 economic recession, the leading 150 international chains reported over 980 new hotels scheduled for opening between 1990 and 1993 in addition to extensive refurbishments. In part, these projects reflect market positioning and expansion plans but also the development time delay in response to changing conditions.

The increasing value of prime city centre locations has also led to higher investment in upgrading and refurbishment.

1.4. Investment

1.4.1 Commercial feasibility

Hotel development involves a high investment intensity with a long-term commitment of the bulk of the capital in fixed assets. Revenues are invariably dictated by external conditions and profit margins affected by operating expenses (Table 1.8).

1.4.2 Influences on investment

Investment in hotels tends to follow cyclical changes in economic growth. Conditions influencing the direction and timing of capital expenditure include those listed in Table 1.9.

The conditions usually apply generally over the region or country rather than to individual projects. Thus hotel development tends to occur in cycles when investment is favoured and this may lead to overbuilding with the resultant competition lowering occupancies and profitability.

Table 1.7 Factors influencing sale and acquisition of hotels

Strategy	Company objectives
Purchase	
Operation	Synergy of identity and advantages of enlarged group. Acquisition of balanced portfolio in one transaction with immediate prospects of increased cash flows, market representation, extension of reservation and referral systems and flexibility of staff movement
Overseas expansion	Entrée into overseas markets following near saturation of home demand
Competitive costs	Costs per room advantage compared with new development
Sale	
Reduction of gearing	Lowering of borrowings at time of high interest on debt
Realization of high property values	Sale in anticipation of falling rates of return on property investment
Sectorization	Market repositioning and concentration on particular sectors of hotel and resort operation

1.4.3 Development Incentives

The overall climate for investment in a country, region or locality may be improved by government encouragement and assistance:

- *Government cooperation* includes measures such as enacting legislation which is conducive to investment and direct information for prospective investors, guarantees and fiscal concessions.

- *Planning and infrastructure provisions* through Development Plans and government-financed infrastructure services (utility services, roads, airports, etc.).

Table 1.8 Considerations involved in hotel investment

Hotel investment	Consideration
Costs	
High capital costs	Usually 2 to 4 times annual revenues[a]. Sensitive to opportunity costs of capital. High fixed costs limit operational flexibility
Fixed use	Trading orientated rather than property investment. Location and efficient design critical. Cannot be easily converted to other uses
High operating costs	Expends some 65–75% of revenues[a]. Difficult to reduce without affecting standards and prices
Revenues	
Price sensitivity	Prices set by competition and comparison. Tourism and budget markets tend to be discretionary and cost sensitive
Demand variation	Usage is affected by short term and cyclical fluctuations[b], economic and political influences[c] and changes in locality
Perishability of products	Revenues are highly dependent on maintaining occupancy levels. Involves costs in marketing and reservation systems as well as rack rate discounting

Notes: [a] Depending on sales mix.
[b] Particularly seasonal and weekday/weekend variations.
[c] Particularly risks to personal security.

Table 1.9 Conditions influencing capital expenditure

Changes	Conditions
Economic	Low rates of interest charges on loans and the availability of capital for investment
Business	Progressive increase in hotel prices and property values compared with other sectors (price and cost indices)
Demand	Expansion of demand arising from growth in tourism or/and investment in the attractions of the area
Incentives	Government-regulated incentives for new investments and conversion/refurbishment schemes (see section 1.4.3)

- *Reducing investment requirements* by provision of land at less than market value (often in return for equity participation), by awarding grants to offset specific project costs, through loans on favourable terms and duty concessions.
- *Fiscal and operational requirements* to improve the profitability of specific projects such as profit tax concessions, subsidies and the provision or financing of vocational training.

Development incentives are generally targeted at deprived areas such as neglected inner city districts, or redundant industrial wasteland.

In order to stimulate tourism, grants and other incentives are also provided on a selective regional basis, assisting those areas with relatively high unemployment and limited resources for alternative development.

Specific incentives may be available more generally in certain countries to encourage the provision and improvement of tourist accommodation, mainly to increase foreign tourism and currency exchange earnings but also to extend opportunities for domestic and social tourism (see section 1.4.9).

1.4.4 Risk limitation

A hotel investment may be separated into the land, building shell, interior assets and operating systems. The land and building shell may be:

- separately owned as part of a mixed development of shops, offices etc., and leased to a hotel company
- sold to a property company or financial institution under a leaseback arrangement
- assessed on a rental basis as part of company policy to provide financial control over its property assets
- operated through a management contract arrangement by a separate hotel company.

Various other financing arrangements may also be adopted to reduce initial investment outlays, defer capital repayments or raise additional cash:

- Rental or hire purchase of equipment and furnishings
- Loan negotiation and restructuring, including repayment of interim and short-term finance (see sections 1.4.6 and 1.4.7).
- Increase in company equity through stock market flotation or cash calls on investors.

1.4.5 Benefits of development

- *The market value* of a hotel building which is well located and managed tends to appreciate compared with the book value represented by the original cost less depreciation. Revaluation of assets may be used to increase the level of borrowings and depreciation allowances.
- *Hotel tariffs* can respond rapidly to inflationary trends compared with properties which have long intervals between rent reviews.
- *Preference to hotel developments* (by earmarking sites or offering planning concessions) is often used as a means of stimulating and supporting other commercial investment in urban redevelopment schemes. Hotel use is also compatible with the restoration or conservation of many redundant buildings.
- *Taxation benefits* in the form of capital and depreciation allowances also have a significant impact. These vary both in place (district region country) and time (government policies, specific concessions). Fixed assets may be depreciated over agreed periods using the straight line or diminishing balance methods. In exceptional circumstances (to encourage investment) accelerated depreciation may allow all or a large part of the plant to be written off for tax purposes in the initial years.

1.4.6 Sources of finance

Methods of financing projects and sources of funding depend on the location and scale of development. For a large project capital finance is often in two or more phases:

- *Interim finance*: high risk or venture capital to cover the costs of investigation, site development and building works, hotel fitting out and pre-opening costs through company equity together with short-term loans. Interim costs may also be met by bank overdraft facilities and mezzanine financing of projects in anticipation of sale.
- *Long-term development finance*: repaid over a period of amortization secured by the collateral of land and/or property.

Sources of capital funding can be considered under three main categories: equity, loans and public funding.

1.4.7 Equity

Equity usually covers the initial funding and a significant part of the capital requirements. This may be provided out of retained profits, issue of share capital or sale and roll-over of finance from other assets. Typically, the equity amounts to 30–40% but this will depend on the level of other borrowings (gearing or leverage) and economic conditions.

Equity finance may be provided by:

- *Hotel companies* either directly or as part of a larger conglomerate.
- *Development or investment companies* in association with hotel groups or independently (prior to management contract).
- *Franchisees* (entrepreneurs or companies) investing in development as part of a licence or contract agreement with a hotel group. Financing of development of specific projects may also be assisted by simultaneous
- *Sale and leaseback* of land or property to release capital asset values.
- *Forward sale* of property by development to investment groups (which may include hotel companies).

1.4.8 Loans

Loans from commercial banks, etc., are charged at a percentage above the base lending rate

depending on the borrower and security provided. It is often necessary to organize a package of loans to cover the capital requirements and the terms and conditions may allow for initial suspension of interest or a moratorium on repayments:

- *Merchant Banks*: venture capital and funding packages. Higher interest rates charged for unsecured loans and the bank may seek a share of the equity.
- *Clearing Banks*: similar short-term loans (up to 3 years). Usually require additional security.
- *Institutions*: (Insurance companies, Pension Fund Management, etc.): long-term loans secured by appreciating asset value of property or land.
- *Mortgages*: long-term loans (10–25 years) with repayments of debt at intervals and agreed scheduling of interest. The first mortgage is usually limited to a percentage (e.g., 70%) of the agreed value of the project.

High gearing (leverage) of loan to equity is most advantageous at times of an upturn in property values. However, the higher fixed costs also make profitability highly sensitive to changes both in performance and interest rates.

1.4.9 Public funding

Public funding is generally limited to specified projects or areas and in time and amount. The contribution may be in loans or direct grants (generally, no more than 20–30%) and must be agreed prior to commencement. The range of public funding agencies is wide and changes with economic and political circumstances as represented by the following examples:

International agencies
- International Bank for Reconstruction and Development (IBRD) and its affiliates
- United Nations Development Fund (UNDP) – often working in association with the World Tourism Organization (WTO)

- Organization for Economic Cooperation and Development (OECD) mutual aid programmes
- European Union (EU) and other regional and national organizations as well as bilateral aid agreements between countries.

Regional agencies
- European Regional Development Fund (ERDF) and other EU coordinated programmes
- European Development Bank

National funding
- Specific funding for infrastructure (roads, airports, technical services)
- Urban Development Grants, Derelict Land Grants
- Selective grants for small businesses, rural industries
- Buildings of Historic or Architectural Interest
- Development Grants for Assisted Regions

- Grants and loans for specific projects approved by the Tourist Boards.

1.4.10 Valuations

Valuation of hotel properties is normally on a value per room basis broadly assessed from:

- earnings achievable: commercial return on capital invested
- comparative per room values for similar properties (sales indices)
- estimates of new building costs less depreciation (cost indices).

A standard approach is to use discounted cashflow methods to calculate expected receipts, payments and operating performance of a hotel together with expected capital expenditure over a period of time and any residual value.

Property surveys take into account the individual details listed in Table 1.10.

Table 1.10 Property survey considerations

Details	Considerations
Location	Benefits (prestige, convenience, prominence), surroundings, progressive changes in area (positive or detrimental)
Facilities	Numbers of rooms and extent of other facilities, recent expenditure incurred and assessment of improvements/ refurbishments required.
Markets	Analyses of trading patterns, operating revenues and costs, market trends and potential for changes
Investment	Capital requirements balanced against current borrowing costs. Trends in property asset values (effects of adverse conditions)
Tenure	*Freehold* – asset value for gearing purposes *Leasehold* – more problematic: length of unexpired lease, current rental value, frequency of rent reviews, rental charges relative to the open value of property *Managed* – value highly dependent on operator's expertise and reputation

2

Hotel characteristics

2.1 Influences on design

2.1.1 Parameters

Hotel design is normally dictated by three parameters:

- *Location and site considerations*: space, surroundings, development constraints
- *Market and operator requirements*: facilities, mode of use, extent of standardization
- *Cost and time*: level of sophistication, cost limits, programme requirements

To a large degree these are interdependent since market requirements are generally related to the need to stay in a particular location and standards affect costs.

2.1.2 Types of hotels

Although there are many variations, current hotel development tends to be identified with five main types of property:

- *Mid-range*: commercial hotels in suburban areas, near airports, ferryports and towns
- *High-grade*: city centre hotels, including adaptive re-use and mixed development
- *Budget hotels*: for transient users
- *Resort hotels*: including mixed development resorts, vacation villages and adaptive re-use of country houses
- *Suite hotels*: condominiums and serviced apartments.

Good quality city centre and resort hotels, in particular, may provide specialized facilities for conventions and spa treatment.

2.1.3 Other tourist accommodation

In addition to development of hotels, there is extensive investment in rented accommodation, self-catering units and property ownership schemes (single, multiple and time-shared arrangements). The provision of tourist accommodation and associated facilities may be encouraged and assisted by incentives and cooperative marketing and regional reservation systems. Examples include:

- conversion of redundant farm buildings, dock warehousing, institutional buildings and uneconomic hotels
- provision of temporary holiday accommodation in schools, student residences, caravan and camping sites (sensitively sited)
- adaptation of chateaux, stately houses and other residential properties.

Details are given in the companion book *Tourism and Recreation Facilities*.

2.2 Mid-range: suburban hotels

2.2.1 Influences on development

The development of hotels in suburban areas has been accelerated by:

- high land costs and taxes affecting inner city and town development
- development restrictions in sensitive city areas
- traffic congestion in towns and trends towards pedestrianization

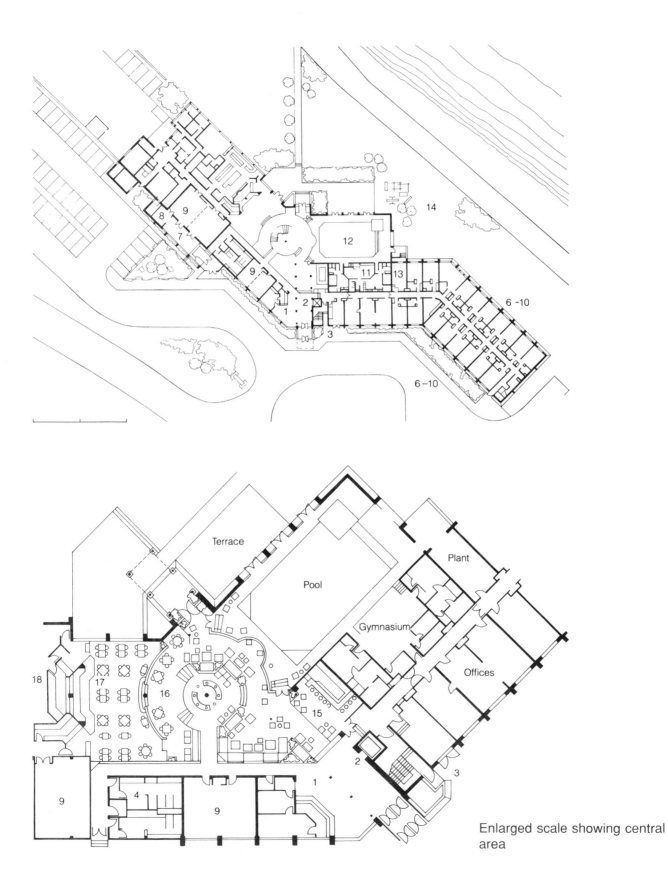

Enlarged scale showing central area

Key

Hotel facilities
1 Reception
   desk & front office
2 Lift & invalid hoist
3 Fire exit
4 Toilets &
   powder room
5 Housekeeping
6 Family, twin &
   disabled
   bedrooms

**Meeting &
Function Rooms**
7 Entrance foyer &
   anteroom
8 Chair store
9 Meeting &
   boardrooms
10 Syndicate rooms

**Fitness &
leisure facilities**
11 Gymnasium &
   changing rooms
12 Pool
13 Filtration plant
14 Children's
   play area

**Food preparation &
Service**
15 Cocktail bar
16 Restaurant
17 Display servery
18 Main kitchen

Food storage
19 Wine & beer
   stores
20 Cold stores
   deep freeze
   & dry stores

Staff areas
21 Staff changing
   rooms
22 Personnel
   & control
23 Staff dining

**Hotel servicing
areas**
24 Loading bay
25 Electricity
   sub-station
26 Plant room
   maintenance
27 Switchroom
   & PABX
28 Laundry
29 Service lift

Figure 2.1 *Forte Posthouse, Lancaster*
One of the world's largest hotel groups, Forte plc has also been responsible for many of the advances in hotel design. In the UK the group operate seven distinct hotel brands, ranging from Travelodges and Welcome Lodges to Posthouses (3 star), Crest (4 star), Grand (4–5 star), Exclusive (5 star) and historical Heritage hotels.

There are 200 Forte Posthouses strategically located along major routes near towns. These are progressively undergoing refurbishment to provide new, western style, trailer restaurants. The Lancaster Posthouse on route to the Lake District provides an indoor leisure pool and 115 adaptable rooms

---

- decentralization of offices and perimeter siting of new industries.

Suburban developments generally permit more convenient access and parking, more space for amenity and leisure and larger room sizes without cost penalty. The hotel location may be advantageously associated with other new commercial properties, including business and research parks and institutions such as hospitals and universities, trade centres and airports. In other situations hotel development is usually subject to planning and zoning restrictions and specific controls over access and signing, including directional signing on the highway.

2.2.2 Airport hotels

Special situations arise near airports and ferryports where transfers are likely to require overnight or day accommodation. Other markets include aircrew and airport staff accommodation in addition to the needs of other tourism developments around the airport. Airport hotels also provide a convenient meeting place for international representatives and most offer extensive conference facilities.

Disadvantages may arise from the lack of character in the surroundings, height restrictions, noise disturbance and isolation from other amenities. To counter this new airport hotels are increasingly designed with distinctive styling to serve as landmarks and may be in atrium form (Hyatt Regency, Roissy, Hilton Hotel Heathrow) using impressions of light and transparency to contrast the restrictions of travel. In developing airports, hotels may be directly linked by walkways to the terminal buildings. For other locations, transport to and from the terminals must be provided but the hotel may offer extended parking.

(a) Plan: Ground floor

(c) Entrance

Figure 2.2 *Elstree Moat Hotel*
Redevelopment of an existing hotel which had
become uneconomic involved replacement of most
of the older premises with a new three-storey
building. Eighty new guestrooms were added to a
retained wing of sixty refurbished rooms.

Public and support areas occupy the ground
floor and include a banquet conference suite for
up to 400, business centre and leisure centre with
6.8 m pool. Construction was carried out during
1990–1991 at a cost of £9.0 million ($13.4 million)
excluding furnishings and loose equipment.
Completion was arranged in stages to allow
progressive takeover and furnishing. Developer:
Queens Moat Houses plc. Architects: Nellist
Blundell Flint, Partnership. Structural Engineer: A
B Dailey, Son & Clarke. Interior Design: Trevillion
Interior.

(d) Lobby

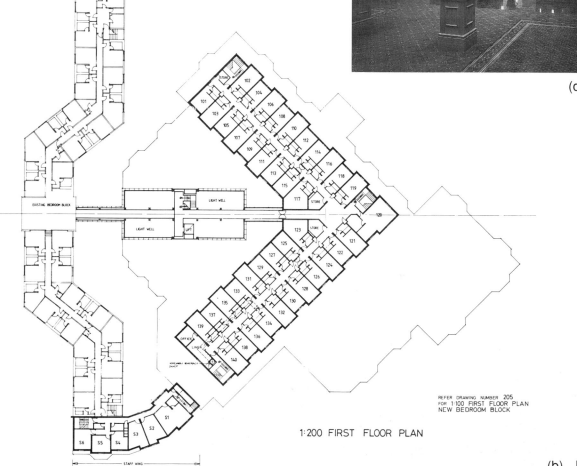

REFER DRAWING NUMBER 205
FOR 1:100 FIRST FLOOR PLAN
NEW BEDROOM BLOCK

1:200 FIRST FLOOR PLAN

(b) First floor

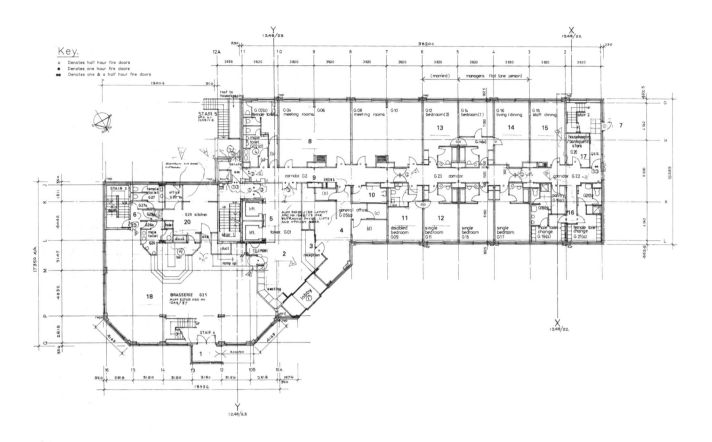

Figure 2.3 *Courtyard by Marriott, Slough–Windsor*
Located off a main junction to the motorway this
Courtyard style of hotel is owned by Scotts Hotels
and operated under the Marriott Franchise. The
hotel caters for the mid-tariff range of markets and
offers a café-bar and main restaurant, a small
gymnasium and small suite of meeting rooms.
Developers: Scotts Hotels. Architects: Cobban &
Lironi

Key

1 Entrance
2 Lobby
3 Reception
4 General office
5 Elevators
6 Public toilets
7 Fire escape
8 Meeting rooms
9 Vending

10 Disabled toilet
11 Disabled bedroom
12 Single bedrooms
13 Twin bedrooms
14 Managers flat
15 Staff dining
16 Staff changing
17 Housekeeping store
18 Brasserie
19 Bar
20 Kitchen

2.2.3 Categories

New suburban hotels mostly fall into two tiers
of standards:

- *Main company hotels* with superior accommodation, conference facilities, business and
  leisure centres – including enclosed
  swimming pool and choice of restaurants.
- *Motor and courtyard-style hotels* offering
  less sophistication with a simpler style of

building. The facilities generally include one
or more small meeting rooms, a fitness
room and a café-restaurant open to non-
residents.

Suburban developments also include:

- *Individual older hotels or converted houses*,
  usually set in their own grounds, which
  require refurbishment and/or appropriate
  extension.

(a)

(b)

Figure 2.4 *Hyatt Regency, Paris-Roissy*
An ultra-modern hotel (a) incorporating a 21 m (69 ft) high glass atrium (b) linking parallel buildings, the Hyatt Regency, which opened October 1992, is just 5 minutes from both the Charles de Gaulle airport and the Villepinte trade show and exhibition centre.

The hotel provides 388 rooms: 9 handicapped, 55 doubles, 236 Kings and 13 suites; all fully air-conditioned and sound-proofed. There is a modern-style brasserie, open all day, an entertainment centre and bar lounge in the atrium. Extensive facilities are provided for business visitors including a 450 seat divisible ballroom and a function room suite. Set in its own landscaped grounds, which include two tennis courts, the hotel also has an indoor fitness centre with a swimming pool, spa, sauna and massage and beauty service. Architects: Helmut Jahn, Arte Jean-Marie Charpentier. Interior design: Hirsh Bedner International

2.2.4 Planning issues

Suburban hotels cater for diverse markets (transient, business, conference and local visitors). Visibility, convenience of access and first impressions are important considerations. Normally, the lobbies and public areas need not be extensive unless there is a local catchment demand for quality restaurant and function rooms. Leisure facilities can provide a marketing advantage (particularly for weekend promotions) and may attract local club memberships.

Car parking

For motor hotels and suburban locations car parking is usually provided in the ratio 1.25 spaces per room (see section 5.2.4).

(Continued on page 48)

(a)

Figure 2.5 *Hotel complex, Haludovo, Croatia*
Large development of villas and apartments grouped around the 5-star Palace Hotel (d) which contains shops, restaurants, a night club and casino, swimming pools and other recreational facilities. One-storey villas are linked together in small groups each with a distinctive elevated roof (b). At one end of the site buildings of conventional design are clustered together in the manner of a fishing village (a), (e). Brodokemerc Hotel Group. Architect: Boris Magaš

(b)

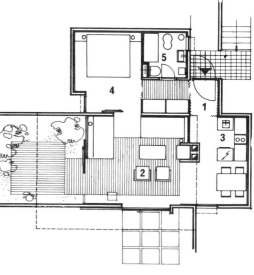

Key
1 Entrance
2 Living
3 Kitchen
4 Bedroom
5 Bathroom
6 Service-bedroom
(c) 7 Independent bedroom

(d)

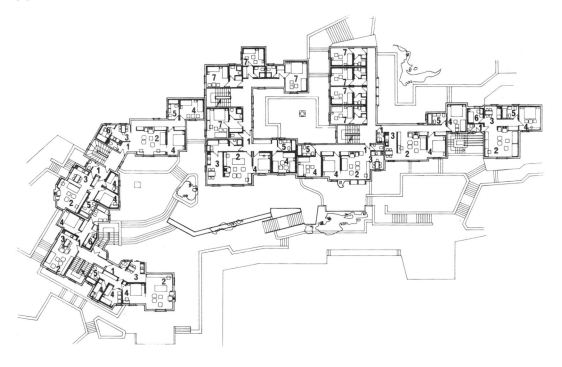

(e)

(Continued from page 45)

Guestroom

Standard twin rooms are generally required with a proportion of alternative double bed studio rooms. Corridors may be off-centre to provide rooms in two sizes and specific blocks of ground floor rooms may be designed for easy conversion into syndicate rooms for business use.

Special needs

High sound insulation standards are essential – 40 dBA near motorways and airports and 35 dBA generally – requiring double glazing and insulation of roof areas. This will usually necessitate full or partial air-conditioning unless rooms are well screened.

2.2.5 Trends

- Sensitivity in location and design to meet environmental concerns.
- Greater distinction from budget hotels with better facilities for business, meetings and functions.
- Accelerated checking in and out systems, including in-room registration and account presentation.

2.3 City centre and downtown hotels

2.3.1 Restrictions on development

Sites in the most prestigious city locations in Europe are usually limited and subject to stringent town planning controls. In these situations most hotel development arises from the conversion of other buildings (e.g. the Lanesborough, Hyde Park) and the refurbishment and complementary enlargement of existing hotels to maximize the advantages of their siting and character (Langham Hilton).

Conversion and refurbishment generally applies to medium size hotels (150–350 guestrooms) offering a distinctive individual character and personal service. Plot ratio and height restrictions generally limit the massing of

hotels to five to ten storeys but there are many notable exceptions such as the Hôtel Concorde la Fayette, Paris with 1000 rooms towering 130 m high.

In other urban areas affected by obsolescence and declining employment, redevelopment may be positively encouraged by planning proposals, local tax concessions and other incentives (see section 1.4.3). Hotels may be included in large-scale mixed developments or provided by conversion of redundant industrial and docklands buildings.

2.3.2 Commercial zones

Elsewhere, new city hotels tend to be large and impressive, featuring amongst the most prominent buildings in downtown districts. To gain advantages in marketing as well as economies of scale in high-rise construction, hotels commonly have 300–600 rooms and sometimes more.

With some reservations as, for example, in the City of Washington and for reasons of safety, there are virtually no limitations on height. Many of the new urban hotels are over twenty-five storeys high. The Westin Stamford in Raffles City, Singapore, at seventy-one storeys is the world's tallest hotel and the tallest structure in Asia; the Peachtree Plaza in Atlanta (1200 rooms) is seventy storeys high, at fifty-six storeys the Island Shangri-La (565 rooms) is the tallest hotel on Hong Kong Island.

Current trends in building design are to emphasize sophistication by the use of distinctive architectural silhouettes, the elegant styling of components like windows and the discreet use of graphics.

2.3.3 Mixed developments

Urban redevelopment programmes are usually on a large scale to attract the levels of investment and appreciation of land and property values required for regeneration. Hotels often feature as part of comprehensive schemes, combined with office buildings, shopping malls, convention centres, exhibition and trade centres and serviced apartments.

(a) Sketch

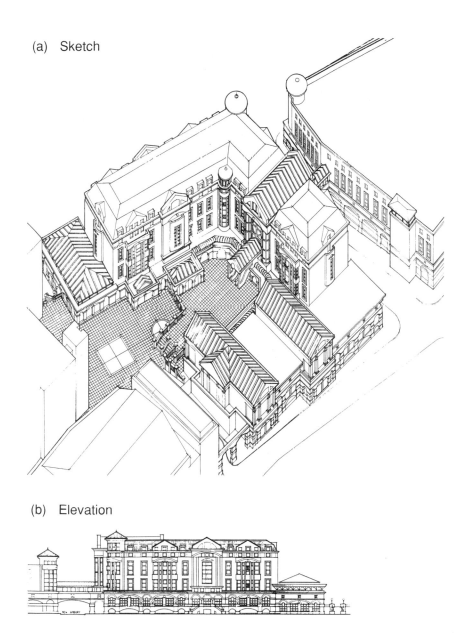

(b) Elevation

Figure 2.6 *Redevelopment of sensitive city site in Bath* This design was the winning entry selected by the city authorities. The proposals will provide 150 hotel bedrooms, function rooms, catering and leisure amenities. Closely linked to the hotel is a large auditorium designed to accommodate business events and a full range of performing arts. Additional multistorey car parking will be built below and above ground level. Architects: Nellist, Blundell Flint Partnership

The hotel accommodation may occupy only upper floors as part of a vertical complex but must be served by exclusive elevators or escalators from a distinctive lobby or reception hall at street level. The main lobby providing front desk and lounge services may be located at the hotel floor levels. Separate goods and service access is required together with appropriate control, temporary storage and transportation to the 'back-of-house' areas. In drawing up leasing arrangements for the building, the areas, equipment and engineering services provided for hotel use need to be clearly defined.

The hotel's marketing and facility requirements may be strongly influenced by the associated use – for example, in convention and exhibition centres. As a rule, extensive public facilities (restaurants, cafés, bars, shops, meeting rooms, recreation club) are required for the local shopping and business markets generated by the development.

(Continued on page 61)

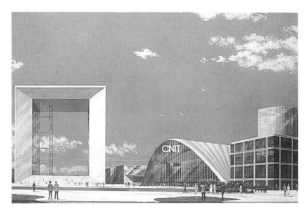

(a) Environment

(b) External view

(c) Ground floor lobby

(d) Reception

(e) Restaurant

Figure 2.7 *Hotel Sofitel, CNIT, Paris*
Located next to the sensational La Grande Arche and forming part of the CNIT complex in Elysées Le Defense, this new Hotel Sofitel is planned around a circular lobby located within a partially glass fronted atrium. The design is highly innovative yet achieving high standards of sophistication. Guestrooms and bathrooms are preformed and planned to maximize the internal use of space. Developers: The Accor group. Architects: Andrault & Parat, Ennio Torrier, Bernard Lamy. Project Management: Sari Engineers, Socotec, Qualiconsult. Interior Design, Jean Quesneville

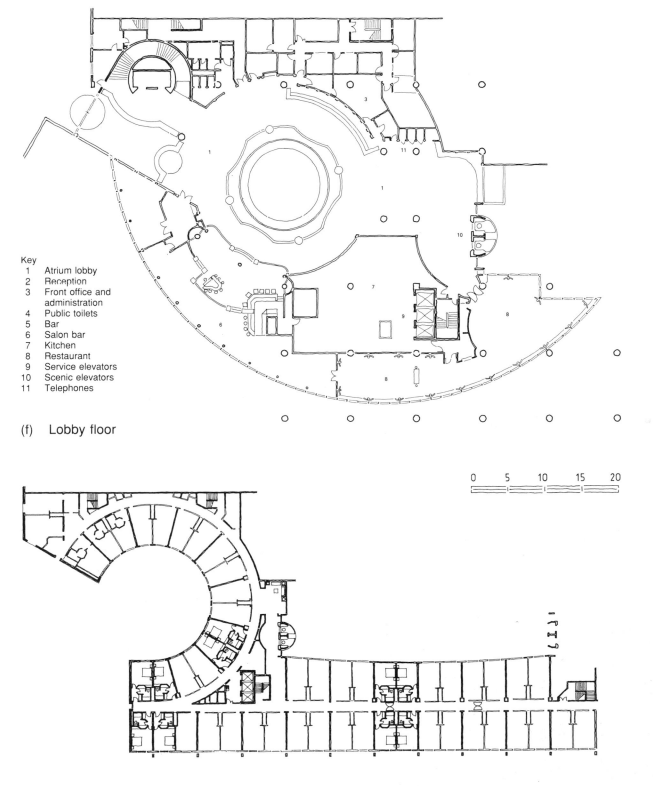

Key
1   Atrium lobby
2   Reception
3   Front office and
    administration
4   Public toilets
5   Bar
6   Salon bar
7   Kitchen
8   Restaurant
9   Service elevators
10 Scenic elevators
11 Telephones

(f)   Lobby floor

0   5   10   15   20

(g)   Typical guestroom floor

0   5   10   15   20

Figure 2.8 *The Oriental, Singapore*
Designed by John Portman, the 21 storey Oriental Hotel forms part of the spectacular Marina Square development in Singapore. Together with two other hotels, it rises above a 59 000 m² two-storey mini-city of shops, department stores, cine centres and 2300 vehicle car park and is also linked to an exhibition–trade fair complex.

Fan shaped in plan, the 518 rooms and suites form the perimeter of an 18 storey atrium and gives panoramic views of the harbour and city. The soaring Atrium lobby is ringed by two restaurants, a bar, a sensational pagoda-shaped lounge suspended between the fourth and fifth floors, a business centre, art gallery, lobby shop and reception area. Tapering inwards on one side the atrium is lit by a spectacular skylight and features six chandeliered bubble elevators.

Deluxe quality is emphasized by marble linings, brass balustrades, bronze reliefs, sculptures and artwork.

There are a total of seven restaurants and bars, a large ballroom and six banquet rooms. Out of the 518 rooms, 417 are standard deluxe, 39 executive deluxe, 50 one-bedroom suites, 10 two bedroom suites and 2 presidential suites. Total area 54 600 m² (587 700 sqft).

Specifications for Mandarin Group Hotels require rooms to have an area of 37.2 m² (400 sqft) with 4.6–5.6 m² (50–60 sqft) bathrooms. Design Architectural Consultants: John Portman. Architects: DP Architects Pte Ltd. Structural

(a)   View of the Oriental

(b)   Lobby

Engineers: Ove Arup & Partners. Mechanical, Electrical Engineers: Ewbank Preece Partnership. Interior Design: Don Ashton.

Hotel Group: Mandarin Oriental Hotels, Members of the Leading Hotels of the World

(d) Eleventh floor plan

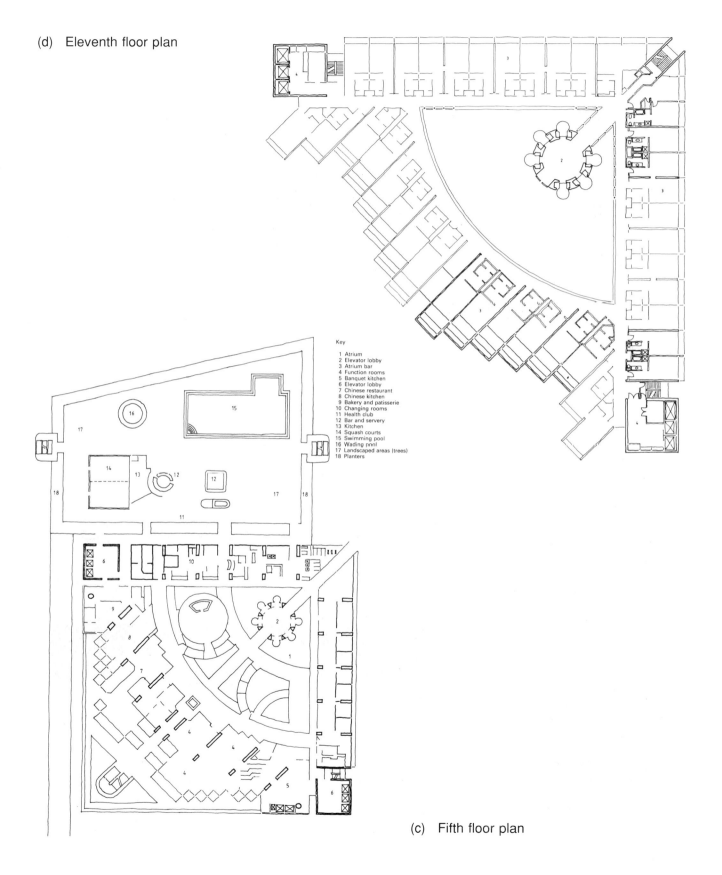

Key

1 Atrium
2 Elevator lobby
3 Atrium bar
4 Function rooms
5 Banquet kitchen
6 Elevator lobby
7 Chinese restaurant
8 Chinese kitchen
9 Bakery and patisserie
10 Changing rooms
11 Health club
12 Bar and servery
13 Kitchen
14 Squash courts
15 Swimming pool
16 Wading pool
17 Landscaped areas (trees)
18 Planters

(c) Fifth floor plan

(a) View

Figure 2.9 *Hotel Concorde La Fayette, Paris*
Integrally linked with the International Congress
Centre of Paris, this hotel extends to form a
gracefully curved tower 130 m (450 ft) high. There
are 1000 guestrooms, three restaurants seating
750, three bars and a banquet hall for 2000.
Developers: Chaire des Hotels Concorde.
Architects: G. Gillet, H. Guibout and S.
Maloletenkov

(b) Plans

Key					
1	Reception	7	Coffee shop	14	Receptionist	21	Tourist restaurant
2	Lobby	8	Telephones	15	Porter	22	Escalator
3	Seating area	9	Convention hall	16	Bathroom	23	Service room
4	Luggage	10	Entrance	17	Service lift	24	Kitchens
5	Lifts	11	Lounge	18	Guestroom	25	To hotel
6,	Left luggage	12	Bar	19	Fire escape	26	Function rooms
		13	Cashier	20	Speciality grill		

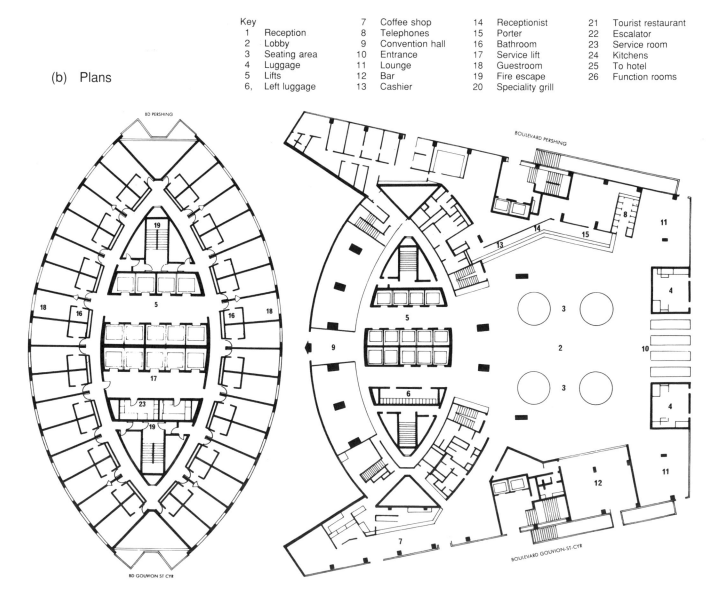

(a) View

(b) Restaurant

Figure 2.10 *Shanghai Hilton International Hotel*
Situated in a low rise residential district in the heart of Shanghai the 800 room Hilton International Hotel provides one of the most elegant landmarks of the city. The hotel tower shimmering in satin aluminium and glass rises 42 storeys to a height over 140 m (426 ft). Triangular in plan, accommodating 25 rooms per floor, the tower is orientated towards the sun. Glass wall-climbing elevators, providing panoramic views of the city, transport visitors to a speciality Chinese restaurant and Western entertainment lounge on the 39th floor.

Surrounding the tower is a 20 m high podium clad in reddish granite blending with the scale and yellow ochre roofs of the surroundings. From the entrance, space extends to a full height atrium over the lobby naturally illuminated with a rooflight view of the adjacent tower. An atrium coffee shop and surrounding Chinese and Japanese/International restaurants, ballroom and function rooms are clearly discernible and the flow of space, natural landscaping and simple decoration express comfort and harmony.

The swimming pool is located below the roof of the podium, designed to allow entry of sunshine.

Back-of-house areas are on four floors of the podium with a basement for the boiler room, water tanks and car parks. There are service floors at the 5th, 22nd and 41st–42nd level:

Total size area:	11 500 m² (123 800 sqft)
Gross floor area:	69 240 m² (745 300 sqft)
Storeys:	42 plus 1 basement
Car park:	100 cars (underground)
Tour bus bays:	7
Site possession:	Dec 1984
Commencement:	Feb 1985, Operational: Dec 1987
Grand opening:	Jun 1988

Owner and developer: Cindic Hotel Investment Co. Ltd. Architects: A P Architects Ltd. Structural Engineers: Ove Arup Partners HK Ltd. Mechanical and Electrical Engineers: Parsons Brinckerhoff (Asia) Ltd. Hotel Consultants and Operators: Hilton International

Figure 2.10 *Shanghai Hilton International Hotel (continued)*

(c)　Swimming pool

(d)　Plan of site

(e)　Section

(f)　East elevation

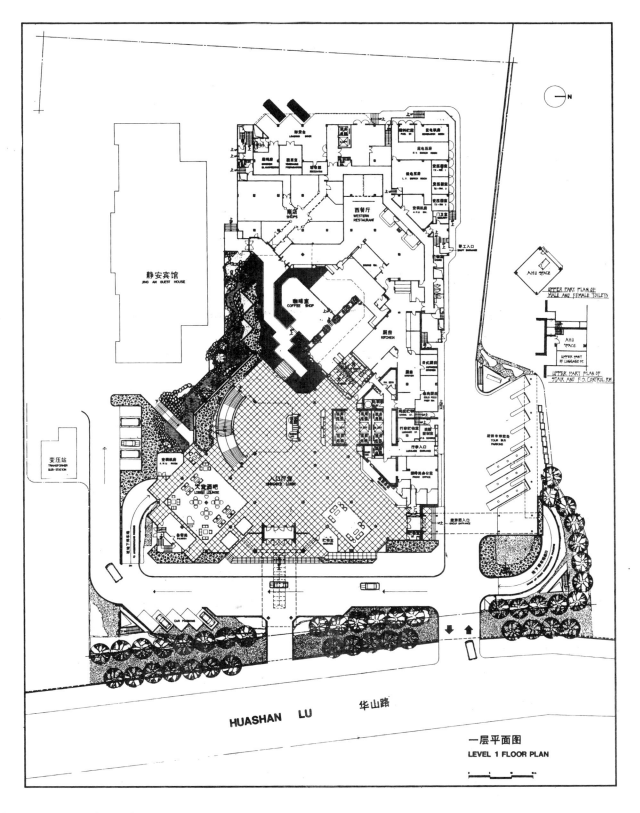

一层平面图
LEVEL 1 FLOOR PLAN

(g)   Level one floor plan

Figure 2.10 *Shanghai Hilton International Hotel (continued)*

(h)   Level thirty-nine floor plan

(i)   Typical floor plan

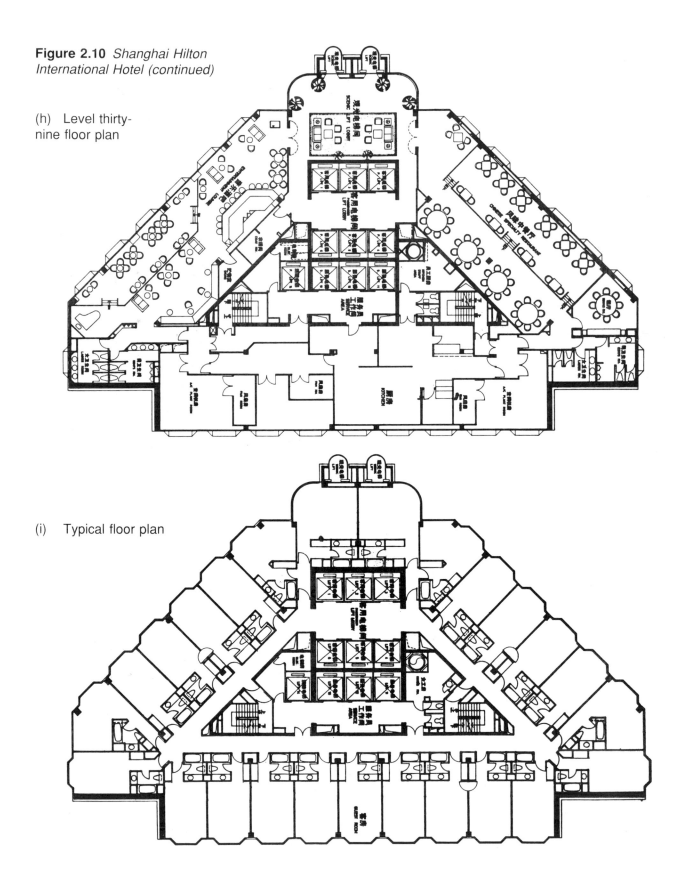

(a)

(b)

Figure 2.11 *Four Seasons Hotel, New York*
With 367 rooms in 52 storeys on a tight midblock site between Park and Madison Avenues, the Four Seasons Hotel, which opened June, 1993, is New York's tallest hotel at 208 m (682 ft). Clad in limestone, with four-storey base rising in a series of setbacks, the tower reflects the style of the 1920s and 1930s. The grand foyer provides a huge symmetrical entry space, 10 m (33 ft) high, with limestone columns, back-lighted onyx ceilings, glowing wall sconces and restrained plating giving an air of lofty grandeur (a). All public spaces are furnished with modern pieces recalling the Art Moderne period (b), while the guestrooms and suites have a softer urbane style (c).

(c)

Standard guestrooms average 55.7 m^2 (600 sqft) and a 278 m^2 (3000 sqft) Presidential suite occupies the entire top floor. The facilities include a 465 m^2 (5000 sqft) fitness centre and spa, a full-service business centre and 12 meeting rooms for 10 to 150 persons but no large convention/function areas. Architects: Pei Cobb Freed & Partners, Frank Williams Associates. Interior design: Chhada, Siembieda & Partners. Owners: Hotel Investment Corporation. Operators: Four Seasons Hotels and Resorts

(a) View of hotel (building on the right)

(b) The Embassy

(c) Typical guestroom floor plans:
East tower

Key

1 Guestrooms
2 Bathrooms with
  separate wc and
  shower cubicles
3 Service area
4 Stairs
5 Glass enclosed
  bridge to West
  Tower

Figure 2.12 *The Mandarin Oriental, San Francisco*
Located in one of the most prestigious business addresses in the city, the Mandarin Oriental, San Francisco, has its 160 guestrooms in twin towers linked by a spectacular glass sky bridge between the 38th and 48th floors of the First Interstate Center. Each tower has seven rooms per floor – few of which are square – with a large area of 49.2 m² (530 sqft) per guestroom.

The Mandarin Group specify bathrooms to be 4.6–5.6 m² (50–60 sqft) in area with 1.6 m (5' 6") bath, a separate shower, spacious vanity basin, bidet, magnifying mirror, hairdryer and make-up lighting. The room decor and furnishings are carefully selected for appearance, durability and maintenance of standards.

The hotel has its own entrance and the lobby, reception area and business centre are on the ground floor. Marble walls and inlaid marble floors provide a luxurious backdrop to the circular lobby.

Deluxe mandarin Oriental hotels are located in key business areas and the clientele are 80% business, 20% leisure travellers. The San Francisco Hotel was recently voted among the top 10 US hotels.
Architects: Structural Engineers: Skidmore, Owings & Merrill. Mechanical, Electrical Engineers: Cammisa Wipf. Design consultants: Babey Moutlon, Pfister, Don Ashton

Figure 2.13 *Westin Hotels, Raffles City, Singapore*
Completed in 1986 the Westin Hotels complex in Raffles City occupies 3.2 hectares (8 acres) in the heart of Singapore around a multitiered atrium designed as an enclosed town square. Above the public concourse of shops and restaurants is a complete floor of convention and exhibition areas accommodating over 5000 people.

Three of the four corner towers comprise two hotels offering 2052 guestrooms and 127 suites. The Westin Stamford occupying the highest tower rises 71 storeys, making this the world's tallest hotel. The second and third twin core towers of 28 storeys form the Westin Plaza.

All operations in the hotels are fully computerized with interlinked reservations, group reservations, food and beverage outlets, energy control, fire life safety systems and security providing instant service and safety to guests.

The meeting rooms are accessible from both towers by banks of 12 escalators and 31 elevators. There are 20 restaurants and lounges with service for over 3000 people, a fully equipped health club, 4 squash and 6 tennis courts and 2 swimming pools. Architect for the complex: I M Pei & Partners. Hotel operators: Westin Hotels

(Continued from page 49)

2.3.4 Building design

Adaptive re-use
Where hotels are provided by extension or conversion of existing buildings, the shape and character is largely predefined. Often the sizes of rooms and proportions of space cannot be easily changed and a disproportionately high ratio of public areas and circulation space usually results. Wide window spacing, high ceilings and single loaded corridors may limit the number of rooms which can be achieved without major structural and cost implications.

Some of the main considerations in planning are the provisions for service access, circulation and the installation of technical equipment (including elevators, air conditioning and individual bathrooms). In particular buildings, fire protection and means of escape may dictate specific treatment.

On the credit side, the converted properties often have unique character, historical associations and a personal atmosphere which attracts discerning guests and visitors.

Purpose-designed buildings
While new hotels are planned around the functions and spaces specified there is often wide scope for architectural interpretation.

2.3.5 Planning issues

Lobbies
In bustling urban surroundings, hotel interiors generally create an environment which is inviting

and reassuring as well as interesting. The lobby is invariably spacious and provides the focus for reception and public facilities. Alternative design approaches include the use of huge spectacular atriums, more traditional halls expressing grandeur and interlinked spaces providing more intimate areas for personal attention.

Public facilities

High-standard city hotels generally provide extensive facilities for visitors as well as guests. The larger scale and accessible location usually justifies a choice of restaurants, an arcade of shops, a ballroom and function room suite, business centre and health and leisure club. Unless the hotel attracts regular convention business the percentage residential take-up of such facilities after breakfast is likely to be low and feasibility will depend on external marketing. The peak demands for breakfast meals can be moderated by offering continental menu room service with planned circulation from pantry facilities.

Conference and function facilities

Being accessible to populous catchment areas, city centre hotels are well placed to offer facilities for business meetings, conventions and social events. This advantage is reflected in the high annual occupancy rates generally achieved, marketing being mainly targeted to create off-season and weekend attractions.

A high percentage of conference usage increases the extent of food and beverage facilities. The size and location of large column-free ballroom and function areas also has a major influence on the design of the building (in structural, servicing and access requirements).

Guestrooms

Guestrooms in high-grade city hotels are generally to standard 3.65 × 8.5 m dimensions with some 5–10 per cent being suites, but the high percentage of single occupancy in business hotels may justify rooms of 3.6 ×8.0 m in studio-style layouts. Full room service is invariably required.

Parking

A major consideration in development cost is the extent of parking in basement construction. This will depend on local authority requirements and the availability of alternative public car parks – including contract arrangements. A fairly common standard is 0.3 car spaces per room but in some areas 1.0 spaces per room may be stipulated. In luxury hotels valet car parking may be offered.

2.3.6 Trends

The trend is towards increasing technical sophistication in the business facilities available in individual rooms and personalized information/reservation services. Operational developments have been mainly towards card accessing of rooms and facilities, accelerated reservation and checking out arrangements and the extended use of management systems for accounting, personnel and property operations.

2.4 Budget hotels

2.4.1 Characteristics

Budget hotels and motels cater for mainly transient markets requiring reliable accommodation at economy room rates. They may be described as Inns, Lodges, Motels or by more specific product names (e.g. Arcade). To control quality and costs the designs are highly standardized with extensive prefabrication in building and fitting out. Rooms are normally planned for family use with *en suite* bath or shower rooms but some units (e.g. Formula 1, targeted mainly at drivers) offer shared toilet facilities (which are automatically sanitized after use).

2.4.2 Planning issues

Public facilities and back-of-house areas are rationalized and accommodation units may be conveniently associated with other public restaurants, cafés and garage service stations to share investment and infrastructure costs.

(Continued on page 67)

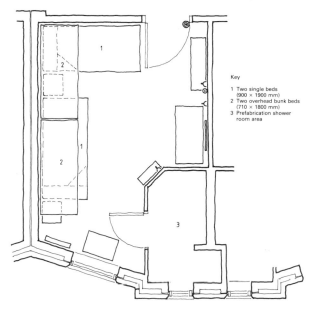

Key

1 Two single beds
  (900 × 1900 mm)
2 Two overhead bunk beds
  (710 × 1800 mm)
3 Prefabrication shower
  room area

(a) Typical room plan

Figure 2.14 *Arcade Hotel, Ladywell Walk, Birmingham*
The Arcade Group are International leaders in developing the budget hotel concept. Arcade brand hotels are constructed to detailed designs using extensive prefabrication to reduce costs and time. The standard bedrooms provide two 900 mm (3 ft) beds with overhead bunk beds for family use within an area 3.205 m wide × 4.413 m (10'6" × 14'6"). Prefabricated 2.23 m² (24 sqft) shower-rooms are interset on external walls and the division walls provide for interspacing of furniture and shower fittings.

Different facades and roof treatment can be incorporated. Public facilities can range from minimal to full restaurant/lounge/meeting room provision – as illustrated by the Birmingham Arcade. Developer: Accor (UK) Properties Ltd. Design: Fowlers Design and Build

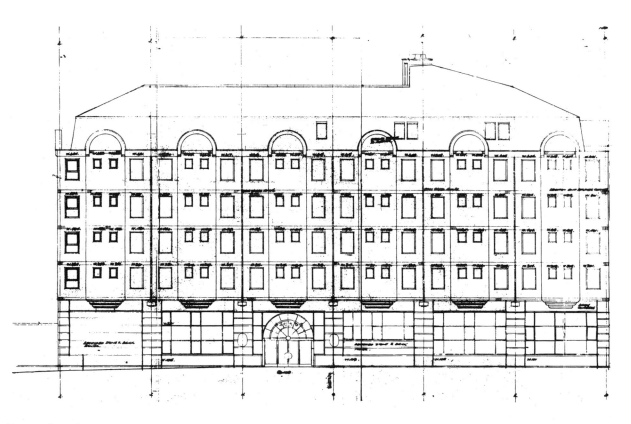

(b) Front elevation

(a) Layout plan

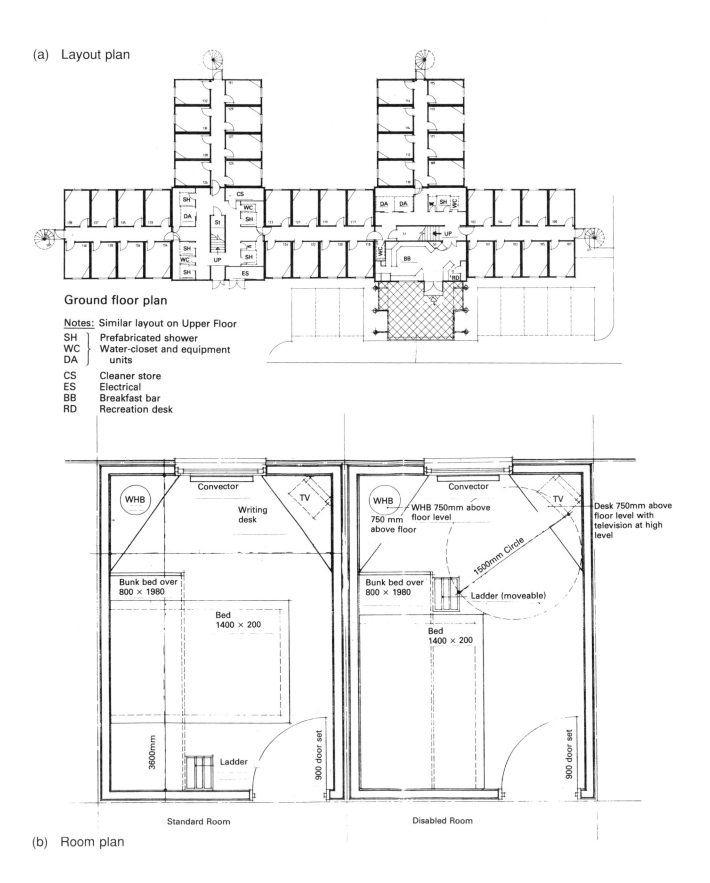

Ground floor plan

Notes: Similar layout on Upper Floor

SH ⎤ Prefabricated shower
WC ⎬ Water-closet and equipment
DA ⎦   units

CS   Cleaner store
ES   Electrical
BB   Breakfast bar
RD   Recreation desk

(b) Room plan

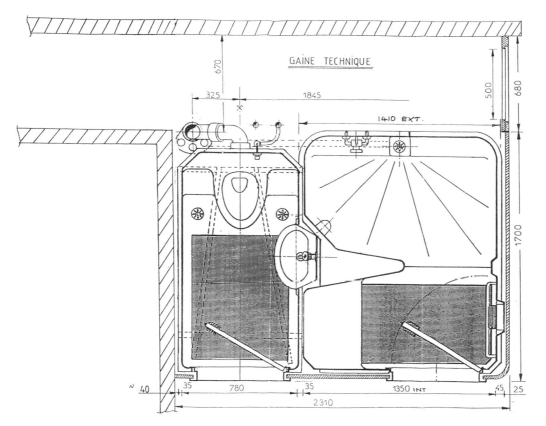

GAINE TECHNIQUE
1410 EXT.
1350 INT
2310

(c) WC and shower rooms

Figure 2.15 *Accor: Formula 1*

With 2098 hotels encompassing 238 900 rooms in 66 countries the Accor Group was the fourth largest international corporate chain in 1993. The company offers a wide range of brands each targeting identified markets from luxury to budget requirements, including Sofitel, Novotel, Mercure, Motel 6, Pullman, Ibis and Formula 1 hotels.

Accor has been the pioneer of many budget concepts, adopting innovative design, rationalized facilities and prefabricated construction to achieve both cost reduction and efficient operation.

The Formula 1 is an example of a low-budget hotel. Popular in Europe, the plans show the first development in Great Britain in 1992. 78 standard rooms plus 2 rooms for the disabled are provided in a two-storey prefabricated building. Rooms are 9 m², attractive, comfortable and easy to clean. Designed for 1 to 3 persons each has a vanity washbasin, double and bunk beds, a writing desk and TV and closet hanging space. There are 14

shower rooms, 14 WCs and 4 WC/shower rooms combined (disabled use) which are installed as complete units and provide automatic sanitizing after use. A studio flat is included for the resident manager.

The compact reception area is adjacent to a breakfast bar and has a small service pantry for trayed continental breakfast with self-service of coffee.

Space analysis (based on 64 room model):

Gross space per room	15.09 m²
Bedrooms (net)	59.7%
Room corridors	12.6
Other circulation, stairs	10.4
Entrance hall	3.0
Sanitary services	6.3
Studio apartment	3.2
Plantrooms, ducts	4.8
Storage, etc	100.0

Designers: Accor Group

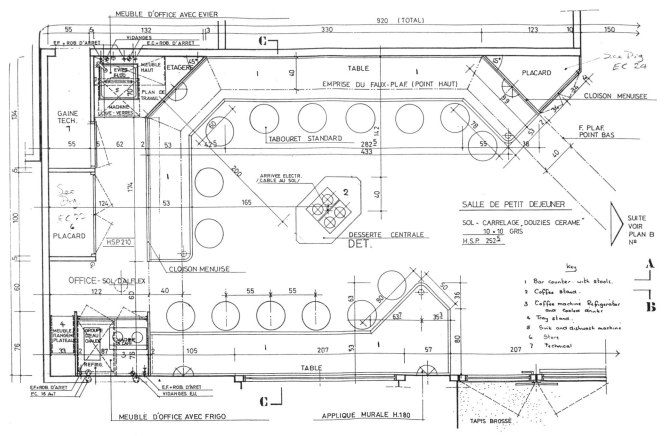

MEUBLE D'OFFICE AVEC EVIER
920 (TOTAL)

55 5 132 13 330 123 10 150

E.F.+ROB. D'ARRET VIDANGES E.C.+ROB. D'ARRET C

EVIER MEUBLE HAUT ETAGERE 45° TABLE PLACARD

MEUBLE HAUT EMPRISE DU FAUX-PLAF (POINT HAUT) See Drg EC 24

PLAN DE TRAVAIL CLOISON MENUISEE

MACHINE LAVE-VERRES

GAINE TECH. F. PLAF. POINT BAS

55 5 62 2 53 425 TABOURET STANDARD 282 78 53 2

433 55 38 40

See Dv ARRIVEE ELECTR. /CABLE AU SOL/ SALLE DE PETIT DEJEUNER SUITE VOIR PLAN B N°

EC 22 124 53 165 2 SOL - CARRELAGE DOUZIES CERAME A

PLACARD DESSERTE CENTRALE 10 × 10 GRIS B

HSP 210 DET. H.S.P. 252

key

OFFICE - SOL D'ALFLEX 1 Bar counter with stools.

CLOISON MENUISE 2 Coffee stand.

122 40 55 55 50 3 Coffee machine Refrigerator and cooled drinks

4 Tray stand.

MEUBLE RANGEMENT PLATEAUX GROUPE D'EAU CHAUDE MACHINE A CAFE 637 353 5 Sink and dishwash machine

33 87 76 2 105 207 53 57 207 6 Store

REFRIG. 7 Technical

E.F.+ROB. D'ARRET P.C. 16 A+T E.F.+ROB. D'ARRET VIDANGES EU. TABLE C

MEUBLE D'OFFICE AVEC FRIGO APPLIQUE MURALE H.180 TAPIS BROSSÉ

(d)   Reception/breakfast area

(a)

Figure 2.16 *Bahari Beach Hotel, Tanzania*
Complex of 25 two-storey round cottages built of
coral rock with thatched roofs in village grouping
around a central public building. Each cottage
contains four adaptable family bedrooms, all air-
conditioned with private shower, WC and balcony
(a). The central restaurant, bar and lounge are
covered by a large tent-like thatched roof having
open sides. Architects: Van Melick, Globeconsult
BV

Developments are mainly one or two storeys and may be in motel style, courtyard grouping, pavilion arrangement with separate blocks or in individual purpose-designed buildings. Most budget hotels and motels are small, separating broadly into 20–50 room units for family operation and 50–100 room units for company or franchise management.

2.4.3 Trends

Trends in budget hotels are towards more innovative design to achieve attractive, compact layouts with minimal cleaning and service attention. Budget hotels are also increasingly branded to serve a wider range of market needs with different pricing levels, styles and catering services.

2.5 Resort development

Hotels in resort destinations show wide diversity, responding to the tourist attractions of the locality as well as marketing requirements. The large-scale dominant resort developments catering for the mass travel and packaged holiday markets of the 1970s have been overtaken by more sensitive designs reflecting concerns over the environment and the need to cater for more diverse tourism interests. In particular many new resort developments offer residential ownership (condominiums, time-sharing and residential properties) and self-catering options in addition to hotel services (Table 2.1).

Integrated developments, including the improvement and revitalization of existing resorts, are covered in the companion volume *Tourism and Recreation Facilities*.

2.6 Beach resort hotels

2.6.1 Location

Most resort hotels are based on the leisure attractions of water both as a visual setting and recreational amenity. The hotel sites may front beaches, lagoons or lakes directly or provide elevated views with convenient access to the waterfront activities.

Planning and regulatory controls generally require beach areas and sensitive coastlines to be kept free from obscuring development and hotel building is usually subject to zoning requirements. Controls include wide setbacks from the beach front (often sixty to eighty

Table 2.1 Development of resort locations

Location	Emphasis in development
Existing traditional resorts	Improvements in resort facilities and environment to increase convention and recreational use: pedestrianization, urban and beach-front landscaping, investments in sophisticated sports/entertainment facilities
Concentrated resorts in new destinations	Integrated development with control over zoning and planning. Include themed resorts, marinas, mountain resorts and beach resorts near airports (within one hour transfer) in expanding tourist regions
Individual resort hotels in secluded areas	Mainly high-grade hotels based on exclusive golf, parkland, beach or lakeside attractions. Include converted mansions and chateaux
Vacation villages and mixed developments mainly in isolated areas	Resorts catering for family vacations and/or specific interests in sport. Generally low-rise vernacular buildings carefully integrated with the landscape, and recreational facilities

(a) Hotel courtyard

(b) Lobby

(c) Standard room

(d) View from villa

Figure 2.17 *Iberotel Art-Kemmer, Turkey*
This new deluxe holiday resort forms part of a planned tourism development area in Antalyia which will eventually accommodate 24 000 tourist beds. The site is 38 km from Antalya City and international airport and 10 km from the developed resort at Kemmer.

The site is approximately 10 hectares (25 acres), covered with pine trees and fronting a 150 m long fine sand beach with a dramatic mountain background.

The Iberotel resort occupies 5 hectares (12.5 acres) and has been designed to harmonize with the environment and architecture of the region. A hotel building of 286 rooms arranged as a courtyard has been placed at the back and kept to four-storeys to merge with the mature trees. There are 50 two-storey villas and extensive facilities arranged as an interlinked chain of action areas leading to the beach.

Facilities:
  Main restaurant with terrace, speciality and snack restaurant
  Lobby, bar, pool and sports bars, nightclub
  Amphitheatre, two conference centres, shopping arcades
  Health club (with Turkish hamam, sauna, jacuzzi, indoor pool)
  Swimming pool (650m^2 water area), childrens, club and pool
  Full sports facilities

Site area: 50 000m^2 (12.5 acres).Construction area: 22 000 m^2 (236 800 sqft). Developer and Contractor: Artlek Co. Architectural Design: Eren Boran MA

---

metres) and, in many cases, restrictions on building height and density. In new resorts, plot ratio limits of 2:1 are common.

To protect the environment and other views, hotels may be integrated into the backland with appropriate landscaping; built into cliffs and amongst rocky outcrops to reduce the outline; stepped down slopes screened by planted terraces or kept below the height of the indigenous trees.

While the views and setting of the sea or lake are critical, much of the recreational activity is

(Continued on page 74)

First floor level

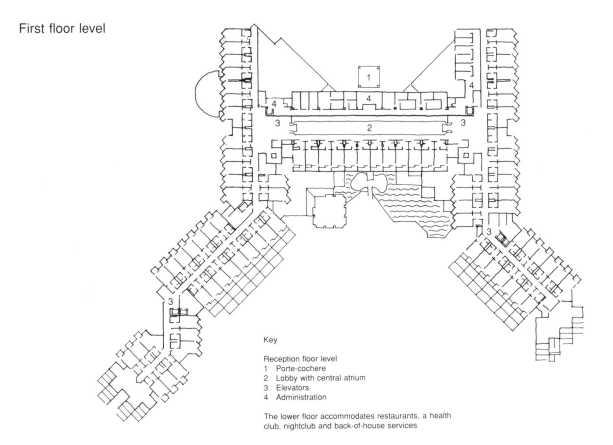

Key

Reception floor level
1   Porte-cochere
2   Lobby with central atrium
3   Elevators
4   Administration

The lower floor accommodates restaurants, a health club, nightclub and back-of-house services

Figure 2.18 *Albeach Golf Hotel, Belek – Antalya, Turkey*

The deluxe Albeach Hotel is an example of the tourism development taking place in Antalya and is a 25 minute bus ride from the international airport. Set in 10 hectares (25 acres) of landscaped grounds it has a 200 m beach of white sand and a mature pine forest at the back.

There are 269 rooms, 33 suites and 6 bungalows all fully equipped with ensuite bathrooms, air-conditioning, direct dial telephones, satellite TV, audio visual equipment and minibars.

Two main prerequisites influenced the plans:

• all rooms had to be provided with sea views, and balconies or patios
• the building had to be low rise (four storeys) to integrate with the natural landscape and link focuses of interest.

Public areas and guestrooms are arranged around a spacious lobby which lies under a four-storey atrium served by panoramic elevators at both ends. The bedrooms extend into wings at

each corner around the pool, fountains and other features.

Facilities:
Main restaurant with terrace, à la carte and snack restaurants
Lobby bar, pool, health club and sports bars
Indoor nightclub, shopping arcade and bazaar
Multifunction conference hall, banquet and meeting rooms
Peninsula-shaped swimming pool (900 m²), cascade and jacuzzi
Golf school (10-lane driving range, putting green, sand bank)
Pony riding stables, tennis club (10 courts)
Watersports, boat house, children's club
A car park is provided at the entrance to the site and the tourist areas are fully pedestrianized.
Accommodation for some staff is provided on site.

Site area: 10 000 m² (2.5 acres). Construction area: 24 000 m² (258 300 sqft). Developer & contractor: Alarko Group of Companies. Architectural Design: Eren Boran, MA

(a) Ground floor plan showing the entrance lobby, shops, day restaurant and service area. The back of house is concentrated in 3 floors above the service area, under guestrooms extending from floors 5 to 11

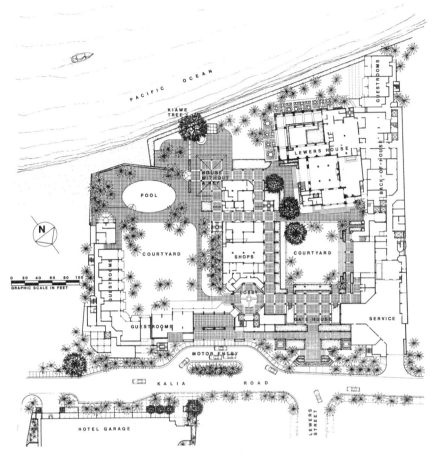

Figure 2.19 *The Halekulani, Honolulu, Hawaii*
Located near the crowded centre of the famous 1.4 mile crescent of Waikiki Beach, the Halekulani, 'House befitting Heaven', provides an oasis of quiet elegance. The 2 hectare (5 acre) compound consists of five inter-connected buildings arranged around courtyards, gardens, swimming pool and terraces giving a sense of isolation from the urban surroundings. Nearly all 456 guestrooms and 44 suites have ocean views and the buildings are stepped down from 16 storeys at the rear to one and two storeys at the ocean front. Completely rebuilt in 1984, the hotel retains the cottage style of the original 1920 grand estate including the restored and refurbished Lewers House. Each room has a spacious private lanai.

The pool is a classical oval shape lined with millions of tiny blue tiles which form the petal shape of an enormous underwater orchid. Fountains and pools provide a soothing white noise to mask outside traffic sounds.

There are all-day and night-time restaurants in Lewers House, informal snacks, evening cocktails and entertainment in the 'House without a Key', four function rooms and a ballroom.

Space analysis
Residential area 71.3%; Public space 11.5%; Administration 2.3%; Back of House 17.2%;
Covered floor area 36 900 m² (397 200 sqft); Area per room 73.8 m² (794 sqft) excluding lanai

The Halekulani has been selected as the World's Best Tropical Resort by the US readership of *Conde-Nast Traveler Magazine* for the last three consecutive years (1990–1992). Architect: Killingsworth Brady & Associations (now Killingsworth, Stricker, Lindgren, Wilson and Associates). Structural Engineer: Richard M Libbey Inc. Mechanical Engineer: Ferris & Hamig Inc. Electrical Engineer: Albert Chang Associates Inc. Contractor: Hawaiian Dredging & Construction Co. Photographs: Julius Shulman

Figure 2.19 *The Halekulani, Honolulu, Hawaii (continued)*

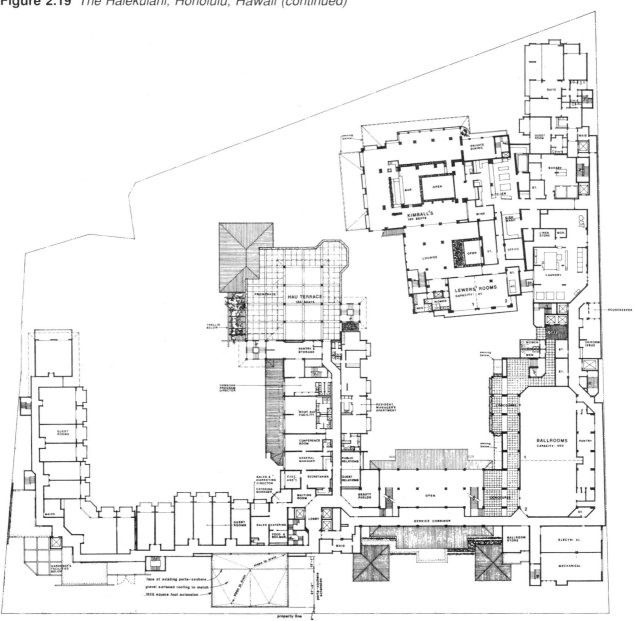

(b)   Second floor

(c)   Ocean elevations

(d)   Guestroom floor

(e)   Swimming pool

Figure 2.20 *Hyatt Aruba*
In 1994 there were 166 Hyatt hotels and resorts worldwide. Hyatt International through its subsidiaries operated 46 hotels and 16 resorts in 30 countries with a further 11 under construction. Hyatt Hotels Corporation, a separate company, operated 89 hotels and 17 resorts in the USA, Canada and Caribbean. The Hyatt Aruba is one of the largest designs blending stylish buildings in landscaped grounds.
Photograph: Hyatt Hotels, R. Mack

(Continued from page 69)

normally focused in the grounds of the hotel itself. The location and landscaping of swimming pools may be used to create an interest for rooms and restaurants separated from the beach. In larger hotels compensatory views may be provided through the development of associated golf courses and other outdoor sporting interests.

Generally, beach resorts offer a range of attraction for family vacations but high-grade hotels may specifically target markets seeking more sophisticated requirements.

2.6.2 Planning

Individual hotels often need to be large for effective marketing and to finance extensive recreational provision. 300–400 rooms are common for major developments and 200–300 rooms for more exclusive luxury hotels. Hotels associated with existing resorts generally cover a wider range. In addition to the main hotel building the development may include supplementary accommodation in the form of executive lanai suites, individual villas or village-style developments to provide alternative choice for long-stay or family visitors. Smaller-scale units can be integrated into the grounds, associated with particular recreational interests (golf, riding, fishing) and constructed to traditional design. Site areas are usually extensive to allow for recreational needs and landscaping. Future phases of extension and infrastructure

requirements need to be incorporated at the initial planning stage.

Orientation of the guestroom wings perpendicular to the sea or lake is most efficient allowing rooms on each side of a double loaded corridor to enjoy 90° views. External walls and balconies may be serrated to increase the viewing angle. Single loaded corridors add 12–15 per cent to the cost but may be required for linkage areas or high-value rooms and suites. Tower, atrium and step-terraced buildings may also be warranted by increased value.

2.6.3 Facilities

Rooms
The guestrooms in a resort hotel need to be large allowing for vacation (1–2 weeks or more) and convention (4–7 days) user requirements. Extensive wardrobe and luggage storage must be provided with adequate day space as well as sleeping areas. Balconies are an advantage and must be at least 1.5 m (5ft) wide for two sets of loungers and chairs plus a table. Rooms are normally planned for twin beds with a proportion of double bedrooms and family room combinations.

Public areas
In resort hotels the lobby serves as a focus for information, assembly and relaxation. Shops may form part of the lobby or an arcade outside the main building to allow easier access.

(a)

Figure 2.21 *Bali Hilton International*
Planning infrastructure development and primary landscaping of the Nusa Dua Beach in Bali was initially funded by the World Bank and this is now the setting for many world-famous hotels.

On its opening the Bali Hilton International was proclaimed to be the most beautiful hotel in Indonesia. 544 guestrooms (b)(d) including 23 suites, are grouped into wings around a created landscape with a lagoon island pool (c) and open Balinese theatre. Footpaths extend to the beach beyond. Throughout the hotel carvings and artifacts express the mythological characters of the legend of the Ramayana (a).

The main entrance encircles a vast cascading pool 30 m wide with monumental carvings of the Monkey King and his army. A sheltering *porte-cochère* leads directly to the 30 m high lobby with its three-tier tiled roof and intricately detailed interior like a great Balinese temple (f).

Back-of-house areas at first floor level are supplied via a separate service road and are linked to all units through a large underground service tunnel. Amenities include all-day seafood and Japanese restaurants; cocktail lounge, fun pub and pool bar; multispace ballroom; health spa; covered and open tennis courts; and an associated 18 hole golf course and country club.

(b)

The design carefully characterizes Balinese architecture, incorporating authentic styles and the work of the finest artists and sculptors. Open roofs provide shelter while utilizing cooling air streams and the low rise buildings blend naturally with the landscaped environment. Owner: P T Banigati Betegak. Hotel Management: Hilton International. Architects: Killingsworth, Stricker, Lindgren, Wilson and Associates, Long Beach California. Consulting Engineers: Teddy Boen & Associates (structural design). Mechanical and Electrical Engineers: Lehr Associates. Interior Designers: Chhada Siembieda & Associates Ltd. Lighting: Tino Kwan

Figure 2.21 *Bali Hilton International (continued)*

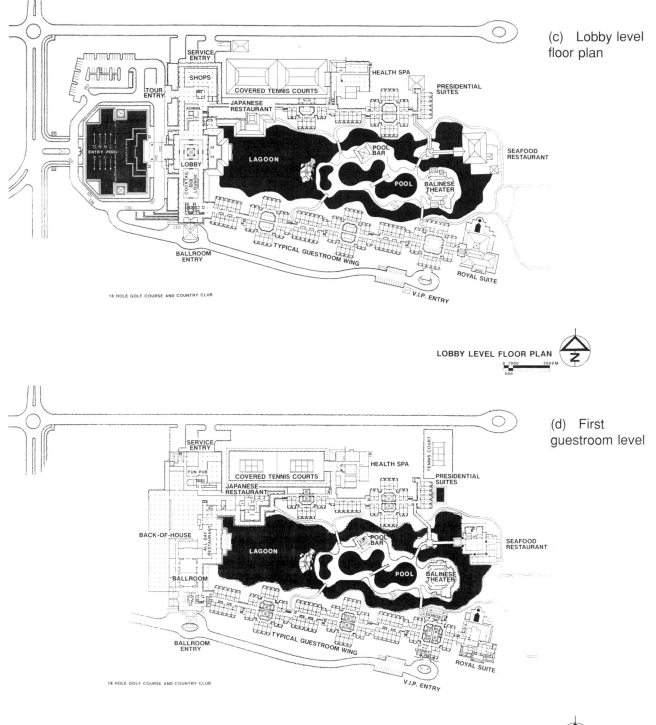

(c) Lobby level floor plan

(d) First guestroom level

(e)   Plan of guestrooms

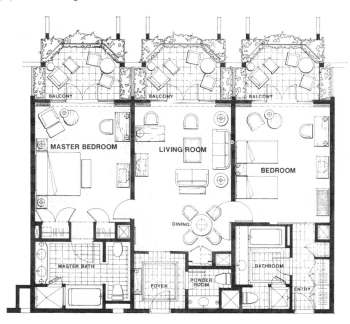

SUITE

TYPICAL GUESTROOM

(f)   Section through lobby

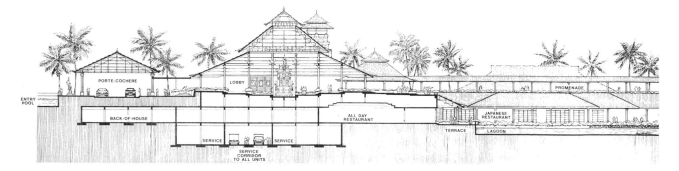

(g)   South elevation

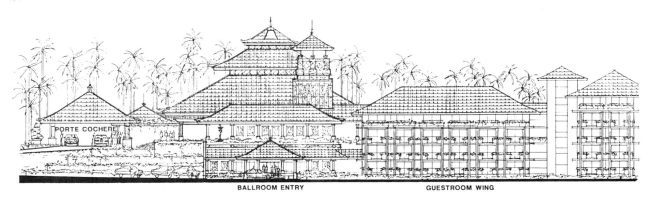

(Continued from page 74)

Restaurants and lounges are more extensive to provide for the high coincidence of demand at breakfast and evening meals. The lounge, piano bar and traditional areas may be adjacent to allow extension for entertainment events. The main restaurant is often subdivided to create more personal space and variety of choice is offered, typically with a themed speciality or gourmet restaurant, café-bar, pool bar and barbecue area.

Back-of-house

The extent of individual provision for kitchen, laundry, maintenance and plant areas is usually large because of the lack or remoteness of outside services. In developing countries, in particular, local utility supplies may be inadequate or unreliable requiring extensive installation of storage, treatment and generating plant.

Recreation

Facilities are mainly sited externally in landscaped grounds but an indoor swimming pool, activity area and gymnasium may be required for extended season marketing. Clubhouse facilities are usually provided where there are high-standard tennis courts and golf courses. Hotels may also be associated with other recreational developments (marinas, harbours, theme parks).

2.6.4 Trends

- Provision of spa and therapeutic treatment for non-seasonal marketing.
- Mixed development of hotel and serviced residential accommodation.
- Innovative extension of recreation and learning experiences.
- Environmental sensitivity in the siting and integration of hotel buildings.

2.7 Marinas

2.7.1 Marina development

The planning of marinas and harbours involves wider considerations than hotel requirements alone. In addition to market studies of the demands for moorings and harbour facilities, extensive surveys must be undertaken to assess the suitability of the locality for this purpose and the extent of protection works required.

Range of provision

- *Minimal development:* light sailing craft drawn up on beach with one or more jetties for motor boats (for water skiing, sea-fishing, etc.).
- *Yacht and dinghy centre:* for craft stored on shore with boat standings, car and trailer parking and launching slip or ramp to sheltered water areas.
- *Small boat harbour:* providing piers and moorings for yachts and motor boats, protected by breakwater, with shore services to boats and separate parking areas.
- *Marinas:* extensive development of harbour and shore-based services (including clubhouse and shops), generally feasible for upwards of 150–250 boats.
- *Locked basin marinas:* for tidal rise–fall of more than 3 m and to maintain water levels for individual jetties and moorings. Usually required for more than 500 boats.

Harbour and basin areas are usually estimated on 75–100 boats per hectare (30–40 boats per acre) plus an equivalent space for car park and light boat storage. The minimum basin depth is typically 4.6 m (15ft) with berths 2.5–3.7 m (8–12ft) deep. Sea protection (by breakwater, groins or levées) is usually required, together with channels for flushing the basins. Metered services to moorings are installed for potable water, electricity and fuel together with drainage connections and garbage collection points. The extent of parking for cars and trailers depends on the location and local club membership: resort-based, 0.4 car spaces:boat; club-based, 0.8–1.0 car spaces:boat. A hardstanding should separate the waterfront and areas for parking, storage, etc.

2.7.2 Resort planning

Water-based activities form a focus of interest and the development of hotels, public areas, shops and residential properties must be closely integrated around the marina. Alternative approaches may be to:

- set back buildings leaving the harbour frontage clear as public space (for promenades, terraces, squares)
- extend properties on piers over the water edge providing individual boat moorings and walkways (1.0 moorings:residential unit).

In both cases, provision must be made for servicing and vehicle access which should be separated, as far as practical, from pedestrianised areas.

Marinas invariably include retail shops (provisions, fishing, sports, boutiques) cafés, marine stores and calendering, an administrative office and yacht clubhouse. Boat overhaul and repair workshops (including derrick or lifting crane) should be available either as part of the facilities or nearby.

Hotel facilities are generally of high-grade catering for yacht owners as well as sailing and watersport enthusiasts. The ratio of boat moorings allocated per guestroom depends on market emphases but is usually in the range of 0.3–0.5 per room. A high proportion of suites is usually required with balconies overlooking the waterfront. Restaurant, café and bar areas may spill out onto the harbour surround. A swimming pool is essential and a second pool may be provided as part of the yacht owners' club facilities.

Other outdoor sporting facilities (tennis courts, gardens, childrens' play areas) are usually provided as an interest for rooms facing away from the marina.

2.7.3 Trends

The expansion of flotilla and crew cruising favours simpler accommodation in traditional style being provided at ports of call.

Sailing, snorkelling and most aqua sports call for training and instruction schools as part of resort development with scope for marketing organized courses and services.

2.8 Health resorts and spas

2.8.1 Development of health resorts

Development of health resort hotels derives from the therapeutic benefits of local mineral springs and other related forms of treatment. Traditional spa resorts are well established, particularly in Europe and Japan, and have experienced a resurgence in demand arising from a combination of several factors: increasing concerns over stress, diet, health and fitness; ageing populations; and, in some countries, health insurance reimbursement of treatment costs.

Modern spa hotels cater for a variety of needs and include wide-ranging provisions for individual and family recreation. In existing resorts many hotels have undergone extensive refurbishment, installing the latest sophisticated equipment. New hotels may also be located in or near traditional spa towns or be individually developed to provide self-contained health and fitness centres.

Depending on location, spa hotels may give emphasis to: intensive sport and fitness programmes, health and beauty rejuvenation; treatment of rheumatoid and other conditions; stress relief and body toning (relaxation and revitalization); or dietary and weight loss regimes.

Set programmes may extend over days, 1–2 weeks or longer. The quality and range of restaurant and lounge facilities is important. Although spa usage is mainly non-seasonal, provision should be made for special events, entertainments, competitions, exhibitions and festivals.

2.8.2 Planning

Spa hotels have broadly similar planning requirements to those for high-grade resort hotels but need also to provide for specific needs:

- Car parking and spa reception area for day visitors as well as resident guests
- Spa complex with changing, wet and dry zones as a focus for interest and activities

(a) View

(b) Pools

Figure 2.22 *Thermal Hotel, Aquincum, Budapest*
The Danubius Hotel Aquincum is a modern 4 star spa hotel located on the Buda side of Budapest overlooking the Danube and green Margit Island. This was the camp site of the first Roman legions at the end of the 1st century and of subsequent castles and palaces. Thermal water is piped from Margit Island at a temperature of 70°C (158°F) which is cooled down to 40°C (104°F) and 36°C (91°F) for spa use.
The facilities cater for business, tourist and spa treatment markets and include:

312 rooms: 176 double, 80 twin, 44 single, 8 suites, 32 connecting rooms, 4 double rooms for the handicapped
Parking: up to 91 cars and 5 buses with garage (57 cars)
Business centre, travel agency, drugstore, antiques-craft shop, beauty salon, laundry and valet services
Two restaurants: Hungarian/International cuisine, light meals, salads, snacks
Café
Themed bar, poolside bar
One large meeting room for 300 divisible into 80 + 220
Swimming pool 8×15 m with sauna, fitness room, solarium
Medical services include two large spa pools and specialist departments for balneotherapy (water-based), physiotherapy (gymnastics, massage) and electrotherapy

Quadrangle rooms are mainly single corridor. A central glazed atrium allows natural light into the basement spa area. Developers: Joint venture between Danubius Hotels Shares Company, Müszertechnika Share Company and Swiss Hafina Bau AG

- Planned circulation to provide for disabled access and shelter in all weathers
- Generally more spacious guestrooms with large bathrooms and dressing areas
- Some or all of the bathrooms equipped with showers and jacuzzis in addition to dual washbasins, water closets and bidets

- Facilities for disabled guests and visitors. Depending on marketing, 5–10 per cent of guestrooms should be equipped for ambulant disabled with a higher ratio in hotels specializing in treatment. Adaptable rooms (removable fittings) may be provided.

2.8.3 Spa design

Spa facilities can be grouped into separate 'wet' and 'dry' areas with access via a reception area and changing rooms. The locker and changing facilities for men and women are also usually separated and some spa areas may be designed for exclusive use by women or men. Pools may be arranged on different levels, or separated into leisure–exercise and spa treatment areas. The pools for spa treatment (plunge pools, surge and jet pools) are often surrounded by alcoves or rooms for individual treatments (sauna, steam, massage, therapy). Similarly, the 'dry' areas for exercise, body toning and fitness may be associated with the clubhouse facilities for sports (golf, tennis, squash, etc.).

2.8.4 Facilities

The range of services and facilities varies widely and may include:

- *Reception hall* or gallery with pro-shops, supervision and stores. Consulting rooms, beautician, hairdressing manicure–pedicure, boutique services.
- *Lockers and changing rooms* with washing, shaving, shower and drying facilities.
- *Spa areas* with hot and cold plunge pools, surge pools, jet pools, swiss showers, sauna, steam and environmental rooms or cabinets. Wet and dry massage, including hydrotherapy (underwater jets); fango (volcanic mud), thalassotherapy (seaweed) and aromatherapy (massage with aromatic oils) treatments. Inhalation and specialist treatments. Reflexology.
- *Exercise and leisure pools* with solarium areas.
- *Dry areas* with workout rooms for weight training, body building, cardio-muscular exercise.
- *Gymnasium equipment* including nautilus and free-weight machines, rowing, treadmill, cycling and stretching machines, trampolines.
- *Mirrored classrooms* for aerobics, dance and movement, stretching and toning, yoga and bar exercises.

- *Sports hall* for basketball, volleyball, racquet ball, badminton, indoor tennis courts, squash courts.
- *Clubhouse facilities* for golf, tennis, croquet, volleyball, horseriding.
- *Outdoor leisure pool*.

2.9 Rural resorts and country hotels

2.9.1 Development

Inland resort hotels are more difficult to market than those offering beach, lake or mountain attractions. Hotels in rural surroundings, isolated from business and local users, need to create their own individual amenities. In many cases the property is surrounded by extensive grounds for golf courses (championship standard), tennis, equestrian, fishing and/or shooting interests. More exotic sports may be offered (hot air ballooning, wargames, archery, river rafting, rock climbing) and professional instruction programmes included.

Country hotels are usually combined with club facilities for wider marketing and, invariably, provide banquet halls and meeting rooms for executive conferences and functions. Indoor swimming pools, health and fitness facilities (including spa equipment) squash courts and tennis/badminton halls are usually included.

The quality standards of high-grade country hotels are similar to those for beach resorts. Many of the hotels are converted from historic buildings to provide unique character. Others may be integrated with the larger scale development of property for lease or sale under management agreements.

2.10 Mountain resorts

2.10.1 Development of ski resorts

Ski hotels and mountain lodges are planned to serve the markets for winter sports. They are located in areas of high altitude having access to mountain slopes suitable for skiing. Most of the traditional resorts in Europe are founded on

(a) View

Key
1 Riding school
2 Visual-instruction
3 Bar
4 Patio
5 Swimming pool

(b) Section

(c) Plan

Key
1 Entrance
2 Car park
3 Olympic riding school and
   stables
4 Jumping course
5 Tennis
6 Administration
7 Guestrooms
8 Riding school
9 Visual-instruction
10 Bar

11 Swimming pool
12 Restaurant, stables
13 Kitchen
14 Exercise paddock
15 Children's riding school and
   pony stables
17 Trekking horses
18 Horses' sick bay
19 Forge
20 Maintenance shops
21 Riding school 20 × 60 m

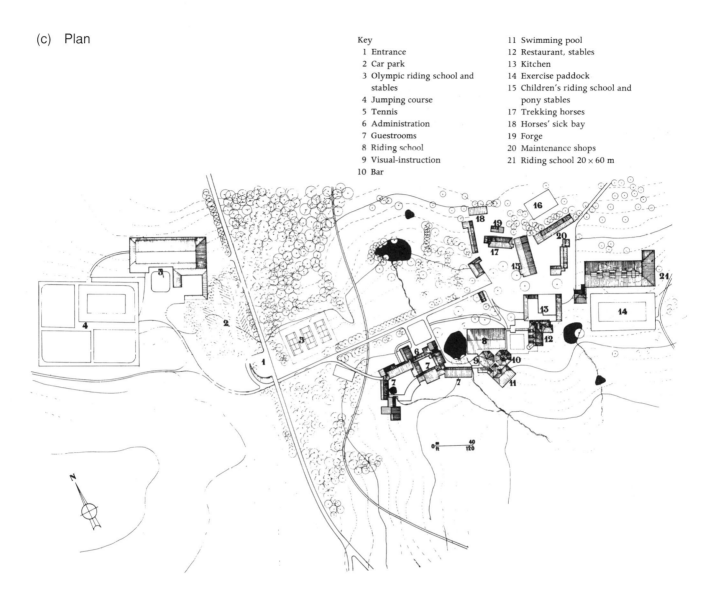

Figure 2.23 *Village Equestre de Pompadour,
Corrèze, France*
Reflecting the architectural style of the area, the
equestrian holiday village for 400 persons is
housed in farm-like buildings. Architects: Noëlle
Janet and Christian Demonchy. Operators: Club
Méditerranée

original mountain villages at altitudes of 1200–1500 m although some of the new resorts are at 1500–2000 m. This higher altitude allows longer skiing seasons but, being above the treeline, is less attractive for dual summer use. As a rule a minimum of four months' snow cover is necessary for national marketing. The potential of an area for skiing depends also on the gradients of the mountain slopes (average 25–35% with short sections up to 60%), the vertical drop for downhill ski pistes (1000–1500 m for national standards), tree cover and terrain and orientation avoiding long exposure to sun (melting) and wind.

2.10.2 Planning

The high cost of new development and infra-structure generally calls for multiple hotel complexes, usually combined with other properties for sale or lease (condominiums, time share and individual ownership). Strict environmental controls invariably apply defining the zoning and extent of development permitted. Most resort 'master plans' favour high concentration of buildings in the style of traditional mountain villages to minimize encroachment on the surrounding landscape. Development may be partially hidden at the head of a valley, on a natural terrace or built into a gradual slope utilizing the stepped underground areas for parking and other services. The resort areas must be clear of any risk of avalanches, avoiding steep slopes of 60% or more.

Preferably hotels should be sited around the assembly and activity area (*la Grenouillère*) at the base of the ski lifts as a focus of interest. Skiers should be able to ski directly from hotels to the departure station. Steep gradient paths and continuous slopes must be avoided and ski trails should not cross road traffic routes (except in tunnels or over bridges).

2.10.3 Hotel and lodge design

Hotel rooms and balconies should be orientated towards the sun and be sheltered from wind. Roof design is important to create character

and also minimize danger from dislodged snow, including damage to balconies.

The design of the hotel must allow for protective lobbies, ski rooms and equipment storage, located adjacent to the entrance. Public areas are designed to create a social atmosphere of comfort and warmth as part of the *après-ski* attractions. Log fires are often used and durable materials (wood panelling, ceramic tiles) should be softened with rugs, tapestries and curtaining. Guestrooms tend to be smaller than in other resorts and may provide bunk beds for family use.

Mountain resorts provide extensive facilities for sports (enclosed swimming pools, hockey/ice-skating rinks, curling rinks) and for entertainment; hotels may also provide individual pools and gymnasia but usually on a smaller scale and, in some cases, with shared facilities. The summer season is important for commercial viability and provision must be made for dual use of central areas, such as for tennis courts and gardens in the summer months.

Parking requirements depend on the modes of transport provided to the resort. In some isolated locations cars may be restricted or banned to ensure freedom from noise and pollution. A secure alternative parking base should be available conveniently near the transport terminal.

2.10.4 Trends

- Concern over the environmental damage of high altitudes and bleak summer appearance tends to favour lower, traditional village-style developments.
- Technical advances in artificial snow, helicopter and cable transport and the wider range of winter sports activities (cross-country skiing, skating) allows a wider diversity of resort locations.
- Much of the large-scale sophisticated development stems from events such as the Winter Olympics financed in part by government and commercial sponsorship – including televised coverage.

2.11 Themed resorts

2.11.1 Development

Themed resort hotels cover a wide range of developments:

- associated with themed leisure parks, entertainment complexes (Eurodisney)
- offering specific attractions (Safari Lodges, Dude Ranches)
- providing `atmosphere' and experiences (historical/archaeological restorations).

In each case the hotel complex is designed to complement and extend the experience of the situation and emphasis is given to sensitive interpretation of the environmental setting. Where appropriate, historic and otherwise unique buildings and features may be incorporated into the development as a means of securing their conservation.

The range of facilities and standards of accommodation depend on the particular attraction and its market appeal. Hotels associated with leisure parks cater for families; safari lodges and ranches are designed for reasonably comfortable escapism; historic buildings – converted by the owners or government – are invariably to the highest standards of craftsmanship and quality (Paradors – Spain; Pousadas – Portugal; Palaces – India; Châteaux – France).

Further details of resort planning are given in *Tourism and Recreation Facilities*.

2.11.2 Specialized needs: casino hotels

Casinos and gaming rooms are restricted to areas in which casino gambling is legalized and are subject to licensing conditions. They may be operated independently of hotels – the traditional European casino is more typically a resort-based complex – in separate premises linked to the hotel or part of the hotel design itself.

Specialist casino hotels tend to be concentrated into specific resorts (Reno, Las Vegas, Atlantic City, Sun City) or located in tourist destinations having access to large affluent markets such as the Caribbean. In addition to hotel residents (average stay four days) many resort hotels attract large numbers of day visitors.

Casino hotels in resorts are generally large (500 rooms plus) with glitzy signage and ornate interiors to create an air of excitement and fantasy. Most provide extensive amenities including multiple-choice restaurants and bars, health clubs, convention facilities and entertainment ranging from cabaret/piano bars to sophisticated nightclubs (Table 2.2).

Table 2.2 Planning considerations for casino hotels

Games rooms	Planning considerations
Access, circulation	For public and staff (including staff dining, rest and dressing rooms)
Games tables	Usually in the ratio of 1 roulette, 1 dice table (craps) to 3–5 card tables (Baccarat, Blackjack) plus more specific needs, Poker, Keno, Big Wheel, etc.
Space	Roulette – 30 m². Dice – 20 m², Card tables – 15 m² average. Tables with supervisor stations may be grouped to attract players or in regular rows. High ceilings
Coin slot machines	In adjacent area in rows and clusters with bright lights, low ceilings, high noise. 1–2 m² per machine
Cash, chips handling	Conspicuous cash desk (cage) with secure access and transfer of money to counting rooms, safes and loading dock
Security	Direct observation (mirrored), camera surveillance, video recording room, detention area
Other facilities	Spectator viewing of gaming tournaments. Electronic games

Guestrooms tend to be large – 30–35 m² (330–380 sqft) with a high proportion of suites. A high degree of security is maintained with individual safes in rooms as well as safe deposit facilities near the cashier desk.

Floors must be designed for heavy loading: 14 kN/m² (300 lb/sqft) from machines and cash accumulation; and be vibration free, unobtrusive and noise absorbent. High-quality air conditioning and lighting is necessary.

2.11.3 Convention and conference hotels

Large conventions are mainly held in autumn and spring, extending the peak vacation season by some four months. Average delegate expenditure is typically 2.5 times the rackrate and most large hotels provide ballrooms, with meeting and banquet areas for conventions. In resorts, multipurpose congress/arts centres may be developed through public investment to increase the resort amenities and accommodate larger groups.

Room accommodation is often extended through the letting of condominiums and rented properties. In city centres, valuable supplementary markets may arise from weekend visitors and functions, banquets, parties, weekday business lunches combined with meetings and exhibitions. Many resort hotels also attract incentive travel groups and corporate meetings.

A more specialized facility is provided by conference centres which are planned – often in university and college campuses – to meet the needs of executives and others requiring sophisticated meeting, tutorial, lecture and professional training programmes. This is usually combined with high-standard sports facilities.

Details are given in section 8.4 and in the companion book *Conference Convention and Exhibition Facilities*.

2.12 All-suite hotels

2.12.1 Benefits

A suite offers several advantages over the large conventional guestroom:

(a) View

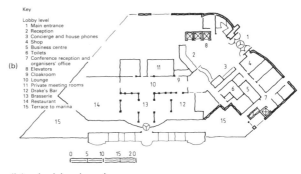

(b) Lobby level

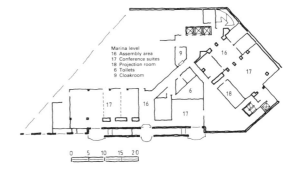

(c) Marina level

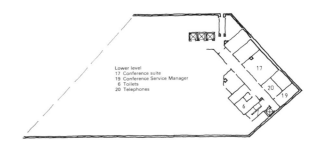

(d) Lower level

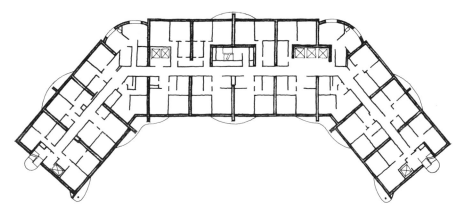

(e) Guestroom floor

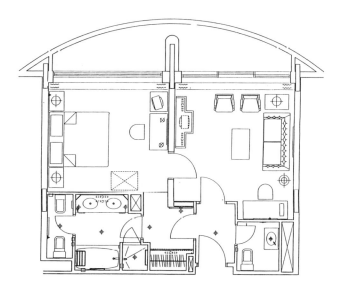

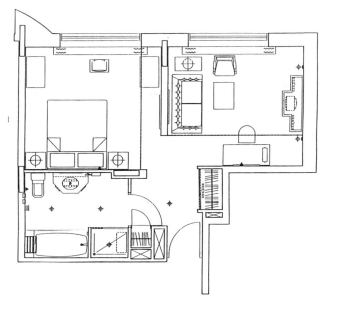

(f) Suite plan

(g) Disabled suite plan

Figure 2.24 *Conrad Hotel, London*
Located in the new Chelsea Harbour development on the River Thames, the Conrad Hotel is the first all-suite hotel in London.

The 160 suites cover several designs and each provides a bedroom, bathroom and separate living room. As a state-of-the-art business hotel every suite has an executive desk, colour satellite TV and VCR, three telephones with two lines for in-room facsimile, and personal computer, individually controlled air-conditioning and electronic safety locks.

Hotel facilities include:

- Business centre with full support services
- 15 conference/banquet rooms for 10 to 210 delegates
- Fitness health centre with gymnasium, indoor heated swimming pool, massage and beauty treatment
- A brasserie with views over the harbour, Long Gallery for snacks and drinks, bars and terrace plus 24 hour room service
- Pre-registration and rapid checkout.

Operator: Conrad Hotels (subsidiary of Hilton Hotels, USA).

- Meetings and other work, entertainment and dining are separated from the privacy of the bedroom.
- Suites allow wider flexibility for sale as condominiums or residential apartments.
- In some cases the building plan can be more efficiently used (in single corridor and atrium arrangements).
- Suites can often be more easily provided in building conversions, particularly where the installation of bathrooms is restricted or the existing rooms are small.
- Although a suite takes up some 50 per cent more net space than an equivalent quality guestroom and can increase the gross factor in double loaded corridors by 80 per cent, there may be savings in space required for public facilities.

There is an increasing market demand for business suites – in which the living room serves as an office – as well as hotel suites for executives (especially females), families and long-stay visitors. With self-contained suites, hotels may be relatively small, provide minimal public facilities and be operated with few staff – many of the services being contracted out. At the other extreme, all-suite hotels can be designed with an extensive range of amenities to deluxe standard. Purpose-designed suites may also be provided as an alternative type of accommodation in conventional hotels, either on one or more floors of the main building or as units within the grounds.

2.12.2 Planning

By separating the living room, the bedroom area can be reduced – for a standard twin-bedded to 14.5 m² (156 sqft). With a smaller lobby to the bedroom, the bathroom can be enlarged or an entrance dressing room provided.

The living room is usually to a similar size and can include a fully equipped kitchenette or a bar with limited cooking facilities. The latter avoids ventilation problems and is more suitable when a public restaurant is available or a room catering service provided.

The living room and bedroom may be back to back at right angles to the corridor or side by side in parallel. Bathroom and kitchenette areas are adjacent, sharing common ducts and shafts for the engineering services. The back-to-back arrangement requires borrowed natural light to the living room (with sound insulation and curtaining) from either a glazed single loaded corridor or atrium layout with roof lighting. With bedroom and living rooms side by side both rooms can have outside windows and the living area may extend into a balcony.

Alternatively, the living room and bedroom may be on a different floors linked by internal stairs in the form of duplex units. This also

Table 2.3 Size specifications for suites

Minimum for suites[a]	Dimensions		Areas	
	(m)	(ft-in)	m²	(ft²)
Width	3.8	12'6"		
Lengths				
Bedroom and Bathroom	6.2	20'3"	23.6	254
Living Room and Kitchenette[b]	5.0	16'4"	19.0	204
Total areas			42.6	458

Notes: [a] Measured to centrelines, including partitions. Allows reasonable standards comparable to 4 star grade. High-grade suites are some 30% larger.
[b] May have a balcony extension 1.5 m (5ft) wide.

allows mezzanine arrangements, which can be useful in designing or converting rooms with high ceilings and tall windows (Table 2.3).

2.13 Condominium, time-share and residential developments

2.13.1 Association

Residential properties are often included in the overall development of resorts to contribute to the financing and marketing of the sophisticated amenities which are invariably required. The condominiums and other units for sale and/or letting provide a wider variety of choice and are usually designed to a smaller domestic scale and more closely integrated with the recreational facilities of the resort.

In city centre hotels, the residential apartments may be on one or more floors (usually upper floors) of the main building or in a separate, linked block. Access may be shared but an exclusive entrance, lobby and elevators must also be provided for residents' use. Service circulation to the residential units must be planned as part of the hotel's operation and may require a service tunnel to separated buildings.

The benefits of incorporating properties for sale are particularly important in reducing capital debt at times of high interest charges and the hotel is able to let and service rooms and suites on behalf of the owners for a fee income. In addition to managing condominiums in individual ownership, the hotel may provide similar services under contract for other resort properties.

2.13.2 Planning

Condominiums and other residential units may be self-contained houses and apartments, convertible studios or suites of one or more bedrooms. Since letting rates are usually based on the number of persons accommodated, living rooms are often adaptable with convertible sofas and fold-away beds.

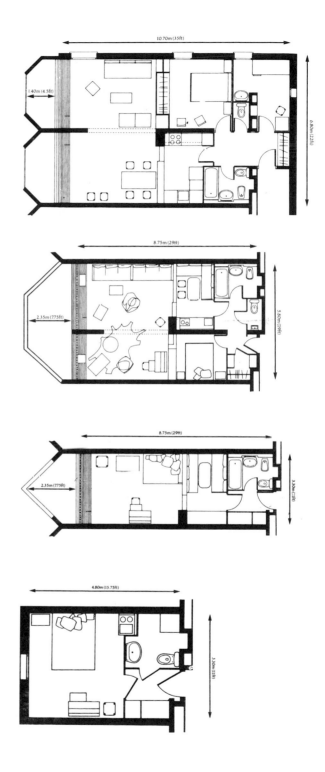

Figure 2.25 *Isola 200*
Floor plans of typical apartments in a ski resort in the Maritime Alps. Developer: Bernard Sunley Group

In resort developments the trend is away from uniform rows to variety with a choice of sizes and shapes of property in compatible designs clustered around particular attractions (piazzas, marinas, swimming pools, gardens, golf courses, etc.). Duplex units may be preferred in marinas and other activity-related properties. The landscaping is closed integrated with buildings providing contact with the environment and screening where required. Zoning requirements for resorts must provide for the separation of cars and other traffic from pedestrianized areas.

Urban development of condominiums is often closely integrated with that of hotels enabling the rooms to be operated as part of the hotel complex. As a rule this necessitates multi-storey buildings with planned guest and service circulations together with hotel support facilities. Secure storage for the owner's personal items is usually required in each condominium.

3

Organization and marketing

3.1 Developers' agencies: organization

3.1.1 Developers

The developer is the person or organization who initiates a project, bringing together the various resources needed to carry it out (site, finance, professional inputs). This may be an individual (hotelier, entrepreneur), a company (development company, hotel group) or a public organization (local government or government agency).

The extent of direction by the developer varies considerably depending on experience and the resources of expertise available.

Public agencies and *established hotel companies* usually initiate projects themselves and may directly organize surveys, select sites, instruct consultants, gather and coordinate information, prepare detailed briefs and documents and monitor the programme. Prestigious schemes may be open to competitive designs but, more commonly, tenders are invited from selected architects and consultants.

Private developers often leave some or all of these functions to appointed professional advisers. The developer may have a specific interest in the project (ownership of the site, expansion strategy) or be involved in a range of development schemes.

3.1.2 Development strategies

Company development programmes require both internal and external organization and, in particular, will be affected by:

- company objectives, resources and stage of expansion
- availability of finance and the opportunity cost of capital
- availability of suitable sites.

Internal company organization generally involves the stages shown in Figure 3.1.

3.1.3 Hotel company development

The major factors influencing hotel company plans for development and refurbishment are shown in Table 3.1.

3.1.4 Public sector

The role of the public sector is normally to promote and assist private sector investment and development of hotels. In some countries or specific locations where the land is in public ownership the authority concerned may fund the development or participate in a joint venture scheme.

Public sector assistance for hotel-related projects can be justified on several grounds (Table 3.2).

3.2 Consultancy requirements

3.2.1 Appointments

The development of a large-scale hotel or resort project generally calls for a wide range of professional skills and experience. This may be provided by specialists employed by the

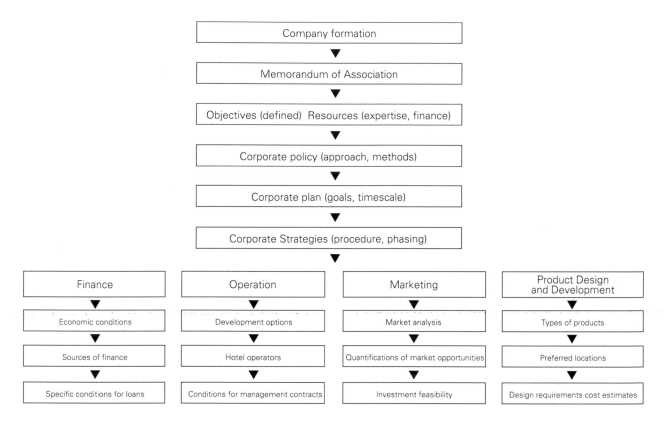

Figure 3.1 Stages of internal company organization

Table 3.1 Factors affecting hotel company development plans

Development plans	Objectives
Increasing company portfolio of properties	Economies of scale in marketing and operation Improved geographic spread of sales and security for profits Increased scope for referral marketing
Securing company representation in specific locations	Sectorization and `niche' development of particular hotels Prestigious prime site development and marketing advantages `Gateway' entry to developing countries and regions
Development of new products	Differentiation or tiering of company hotels into specific types each with a distinctive brand image and operating policy Introduction of innovative designs and new facilities for competitive expansion Diversifying into related investments (health care, catering, leisure projects) or shared developments (partnership and linked schemes, franchising, project and operational management, joint investments)

Table 3.2 Public sector assistance for hotel-related projects

Benefits	Method
As a stimulus to inner city and downtown development	Tax concessions, inner city grants, planning and zoning allocations
Economic gain through employment, direct and induced expenditure in the region, increased opportunities for training and acquisition of skills	Assisted regional development grants and loans
Generation of foreign earnings	Specific development of tourist hotels and tourism services
Expansion of conference, convention and exhibition business, prestige and publicity from hosting international sports and expositions	Direct public investment in convention halls, multipurpose arts/congress centres, sports complexes

Table 3.3 Consultancy or employee appointments

Aspect	Consideration
Selection	Background, experience, resources, local knowledge, reputation, personality, market conditions
Arrangement	Appointment, roles, duties and responsibilities, finance/budget, fee structure, payments
Briefing/programming	Method, meetings, records of decisions, circulation of documents, liaison with developers' representatives
Organization	Coverage of tasks, resources needed, specific responsibilities, subcontraction
Timescales	Work phases, key decision stages, critical timescales, work programme

development/hotel group or independent professional consultants. Consultancy or employee appointments require a number of matters to be clarified at the time of engagement (Table 3.3).

3.2.2 Coverage

Many of the professional services overlap and are interdependent. A structured arrangement of main and secondary responsibilities is necessary to ensure:

- coverage of all requirements without duplication
- contractual assignment of responsibilities
- establishment of channels for communication
- management and coordination to control quality, costs and time.

The assignment of key responsibilities will normally be dictated by the main consultancy work involved, for instance:

- *Architect*: individual hotel design and conversion
- *Project manager*: standardized hotel projects
- *Interior designer*: refurbishment, brand development
- *Engineer*: installation of equipment and systems.

Table 3.4 Consultancy inputs

Building function			Programme	Hotel function	
Specialist	Main inputs	Coordination		Coordination	Specialist
Environmental impacts; Development plans	Land agencies	Preferred locations	Concept; Site selection	Development opportunities; Market positioning	Market identification; Financing conditions
Conditions for approval; Preliminary requirements; Conditions for supply	Planning conditions; Ownership and legal constraints; Infrastructure and utility services	Site survey	Development option	Investment requirements	Regional/local incentives; Tourism etc. Authority support; Purchase and development costs; Sources of finance loan conditions
Proposed changes; Access conditions	Traffic flow analysis		Planning approval	Feasibility analysis	Market surveys; Competition analysis; Estimates of revenues costs and sensitivity
		Legal services	Purchase/lease	Financing agreement	
Ground surveys; Infrastructure works; Special systems: lifts/elevators; Food service and laundry equipment; Telephone and computer systems; Fire safety	Civil and structural engineering; Mechanical and electrical engineering	Architectural design	Instruction; Briefing/ Programming	Hotel requirements	Space standards; Room requirements; Leisure, conference and business facilities; Food and beverage services; Operating systems
Building control; Environmental health and sanitation; Car parking	Statutory requirements	Architectural design; Project manager	Schematic design; Cost estimates	Development liaison; Development approval	Administration and back-of-house requirements; Hotel negotiation
Recreation; Lighting, signage, drainage	Landscaping	Architectural design	Detailed design and specification. Local planning etc. agreements	Hotel operator	Brand requirements; Special systems

Left items	Left party	Stage	Right party	Right items
Equipment and fittings / Furniture; Furnishings / Graphics	Interior design	Interior design and specifications	Hotel operator	Specified requirements; Graphics; Uniforms
	Quantity surveyor/ cost consultant; Project manager	Cost appraisal	Investment agreements	Banks and mortgage agencies; Associated companies
	Project manager	Contract documentation	Developer	Hotel operator
		Tender/bid agreement		
Subcontractors; Suppliers	Main contractor; Project manager	Construction programme	Developer	Nominated suppliers; financing programme
Architect specialist details	Contractors; Project manager	Phased development	Staged payments	Key appointments
Interior design details	Contractors; Project manager	Fitting out commissioning	Hotel operator	Staff recruitment; Special installations
	Contractors; Project manager	Completion fault listing	Hotel operator	Graphics and printing; Suply arrangements; Cleaning, checking
	Project manager	Pre-opening	Hotel operator	Furnishing and housekeeping supplies
		Opening	Hotel operator	Food & beverage supplies; Staff training; Operating systems; Promotion
	Contractors; Project manager	Defects, liability period	Hotel operator	Hotel maintenance department; Departmental checklists

While the structure for consultancy organization will depend on the role and resources of the developer, this is a representative arrangement.

3.2.3 Consultancy inputs

See Table 3.4 on pp. 94–95

3.3 Market classification and characteristics

3.3.1 Market studies

As a preliminary to planning it is necessary to quantify the level of demand for hotel accommodation, the characteristics of the markets involved and the extent to which their requirements are being met by the existing supply of facilities. Market studies may have different emphasis.

General surveys, undertaken by tourism organizations and planning authorities, are normally concerned with the changing needs of tourism and the adequacy or otherwise of existing provisions. Their objectives are to ensure appropriate economic development through improved information services (promotion), planning (and allocation) and incentives (financial, technical). Surveys may be repeated at intervals to show patterns and trends or ad hoc to examine particular aspects in depth.

Specific surveys, carried out by hotel companies and development agencies, are usually more directly concerned with quantifying market demands for hotel facilities in particular locations, the nature and extent of competition and the feasibility of investment. The objectives may be to identify opportunities for future development (short, medium and long-term) or to assess the suitability of a particular site.

Coverage. Market research for specific projects may be local, regional or national in coverage depending on the main origins of tourists and business visitors to the area and on the scale of development involved. Reference is usually made to tourism statistics, economic indicators and social and demographic censuses in comparing prospects and projecting future trends.

3.3.2 Commercial feasibility

Market studies give an analysis of the nature and scale of products required (hotel accommodation, leisure facilities, convention services, resort development). This also provides the basis for determining the commercial feasibility:

- Development requirements and estimates of investment costs
- Estimates of revenues and operating expenses
- Sensitivity to changes in occupancy levels and prices.

Even though a large unsatisfied demand may be known to exist, commercial development may not be viable in particular situations, for example:

- budget accommodation in prime sites
- areas lacking essential infrastructure
- hotels in areas having a short tourist season.

In determining economic feasibility it is also essential to have advance knowledge of local planning requirements and tourism development incentives. The latter may apply generally or locally, to particular types of hotels and accommodation and under specified conditions.

Building grants and loans towards the costs of development, sites at low rent, subsidies and other fiscal benefits will often create development opportunities which might otherwise be uneconomic (see section 1.4.3).

3.3.3 Segmentation of market demands by activity

The demand for hotel services and accommodation is largely generated by the *resource attractions of a locality* whether inherent (seaside, mountain, lake, ancient monument, historic town) or created (themed park, resort, marina) and by *the activities* which draw visitors, tourists, business and investment to the area (Table 3.5).

(Continued on page 102)

(a) Aerial view

(c) Bedroom showing separate dressing room

(b) Lobby

Figure 3.2 *Hotel Nikko Guam*
On a promontory overlooking the emerald green coral reef of Tumon bay, the luxury Hotel Nikko Guam has been designed to enable all 500 guestrooms to enjoy an ocean view. Like an ocean wave the two curved wings step down into a series of terraces. The wide open lobby serves as the focus for the resort activities providing views of the swimming pool set in landscaped gardens as well as the ocean beyond. From the rooftop restaurant there is a panoramic view of the entire bay. Client: TNN Guam Inc. Architect-Engineer: Nikken Sekkei.

Site area	85 000 m^2
Building area	14 040 m^2
Total floor area	57 050 m^2
Area/room	114 m^2
Guestrooms	500
Building height	55 m
Construction period	Oct 1988–Jan 1992

Figure 3.2 *Hotel Nikko Guam (continued)*

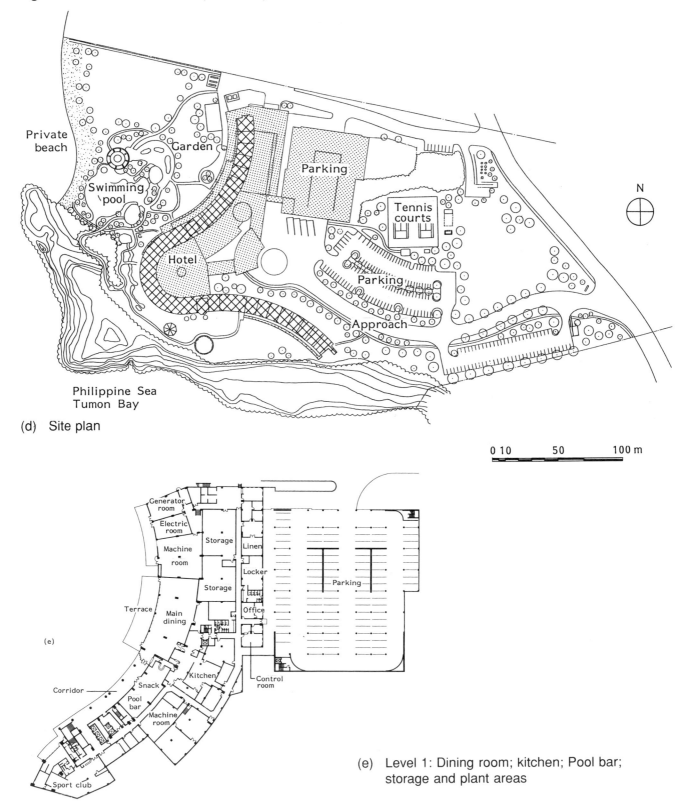

(d) Site plan

0 10   50   100 m

(e) Level 1: Dining room; kitchen; Pool bar;
storage and plant areas

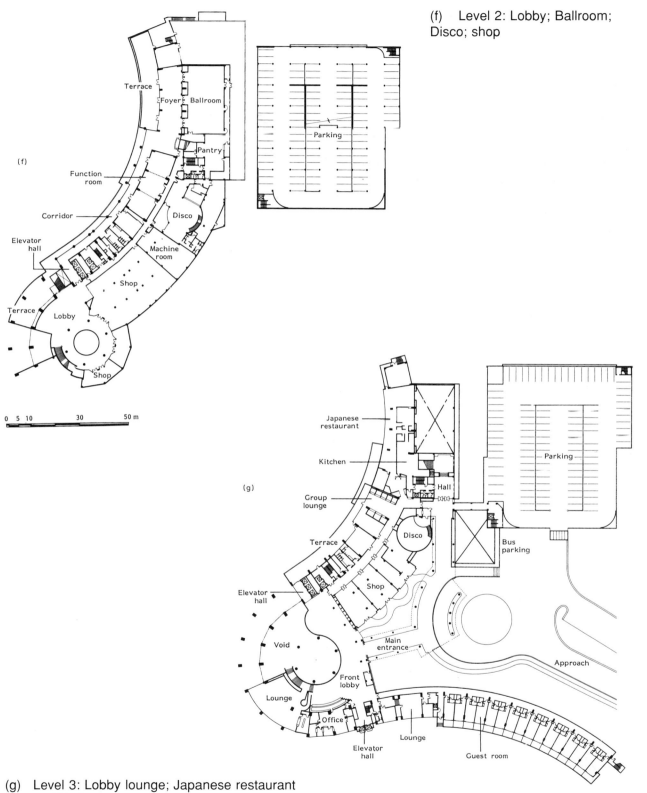

(f)   Level 2: Lobby; Ballroom;
Disco; shop

(g)   Level 3: Lobby lounge; Japanese restaurant
and kitchen.

Figure 3.2 *Hotel Nikko Guam (continued)*   (h) Typical guestroom floor.

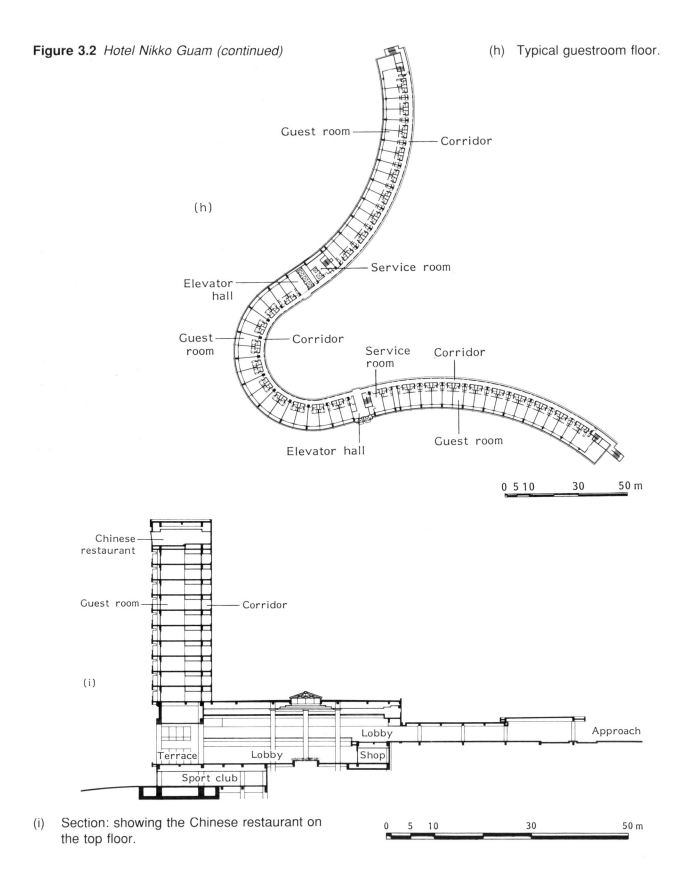

(i) Section: showing the Chinese restaurant on the top floor.

(a)

(b)

(c)

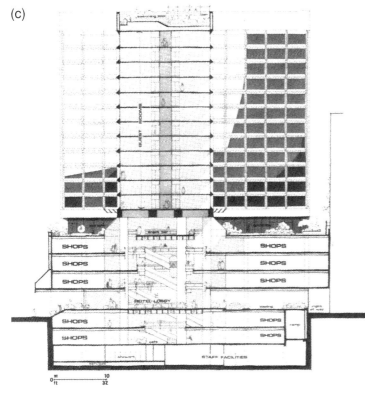

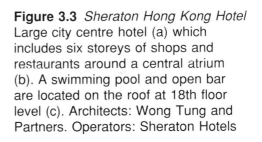

Figure 3.3 *Sheraton Hong Kong Hotel*
Large city centre hotel (a) which
includes six storeys of shops and
restaurants around a central atrium
(b). A swimming pool and open bar
are located on the roof at 18th floor
level (c). Architects: Wong Tung and
Partners. Operators: Sheraton Hotels

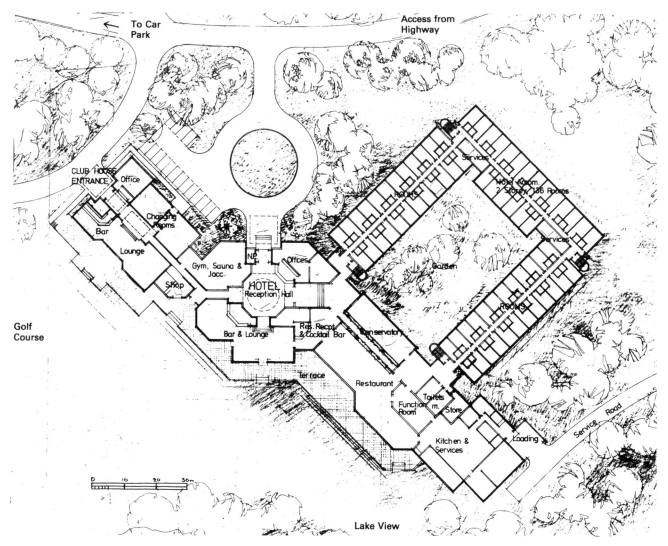

Figure 3.4 *Ellington Hotel*
Plan of proposed hotel serving transient, business and leisure (golf) markets. Architects: Biscoe and Stanton

(Continued from page 96)

There may also be a substantial demand for permanent or seasonal accommodation for retirement or clinical care, for investment in serviced apartments, holiday villas and condominiums and for families or employees in course of relocation.

In some instances the hotel or resort accommodation may be built for a specific market (packaged tour operation, holiday club) with precise requirements. More commonly the market demand will be made up from a segmented mix of activities, with similar accommodation requirements.

Segmentation is useful in:

- identifying guest profiles and particular requirements
- comparing relative growth rates and trends in demand
- assessing market shares and strengths of competition

102

Table 3.5 Types of activity

Activity	Examples
Leisure	Sun seeking, sightseeing, seaside and lakeside vacations
Recreation	Sailing, golf, skiing, climbing, riding, walking
Cultural	Interests in local art, history, archaeology, pageantry
Religious	Ceremonies, pilgrimages, festivals
Entertainment	Theatres, concerts, popular events, casinos, nightclubs
Meeting	Conferences, conventions, training sessions, incentive travel
Institutional	Visitors to institutions, hospitals, universities
Business	Business and commercial travel, executive meetings
Representation	Promotional shows, exhibitions, representative offices
Medical	Health, dietary, spa and convalescence requirements
Social	Visits by friends, relatives, societies, clubs
Travel	Transient and staging requirements along route, at terminals
Government	Officials, representatives, formal visits, associated agencies

- developing innovative attractions to create new demands.

In practice, markets are generally grouped into four main segments:

- vacations
- business travel
- transient and local visitors
- conference and convention groups.

3.3.4 Fluctuations in demand

In most situations it is desirable to achieve a balanced mix of market segments to avoid:

- over-dependence on particular sources (tour operators, company business) which require heavy discounting and may become volatile (external economic and political changes)
- pronounced seasonality (vacations) and weekday use (business visits) which create difficulties in staffing, operation and distribution of fixed costs.

Figure 3.5–3.7 illustrate these issues.

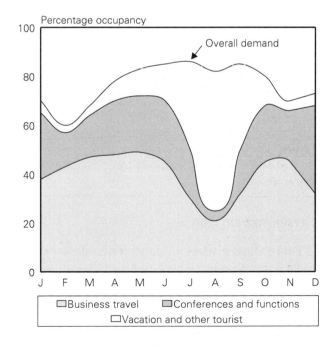

Figure 3.5 Typical seasonality of demand (smoothed): city centre hotel, northern hemisphere

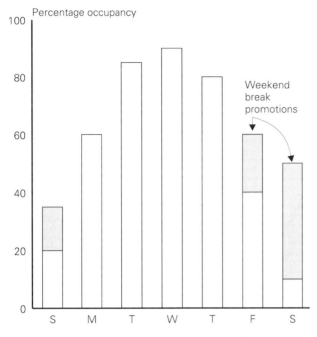

Figure 3.6 Typical weekday/weekend fluctuations: city centre hotel

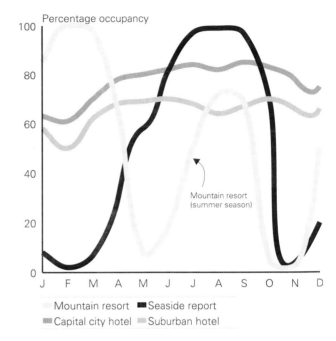

Figure 3.7 Comparative occupancy levels

3.3.5 Tiering by price

Markets can also be grouped by social and economic characteristics which indicate the standards of sophistication likely to be expected (in facilities and services) and price ranges acceptable (Table 3.6).

With changes in society and modes of living, class distinctions are tending to become blurred and variable depending much on the situation and circumstances, such as the stage in life-cycle, level of disposable income and role-playing required of the occasion. In tourism, destination expenditure is often linked to the travel distance origins of the tourists.

Security and confidence in standards are also necessary in establishing an effective connec-

Table 3.6 Accommodation preferences by socio-economic class

Socio-economic class		Accommodation preference
UK	*USA*	
A	UU/LU	Exclusive 5 star individual hotels, country houses
B	UM	High class 3–4 star group hotels, motor hotels
C1	LM	Mid-tariff 2–3 star hotels, motels, inns
C2	UL	Chain, budget hotels, lodges, guesthouses
D		Self-catering, guesthouse, B&B
E	LL	Self-catering, B&B, out of season hotels

tion with branded products while the level of responsiveness to innovative concepts or price competition is important in penetrating established markets.

3.3.6 Guest profiles

User requirements can be more precisely identified by examining typical characteristics of the market segments, namely:

- purpose of visit and main categories involved (business, pleasure, transient, long term)
- average lengths of stay, percentage of double occupancy, ratio of female:male guests
- main periods of use, frequency of visits, price sensitivity and average spend
- facilities required.

Further analyses can be used to show the main marketing channels (tour operators, corporate businesses, tourist agencies) and rack-rate discounts. Such data is readily available from computerized reservation systems. See Table 3.7.

3.3.7 Market distinction

A hotel aims to satisfy a particular tier of the market (whether luxury, economy or intermediary level) and the standards of sophistication, service and pricing must reflect this aim. It is not feasible within a single hotel unit to introduce wide variations in standards:

- There may be changes in room style (e.g. suite) and prices provided these are warranted by obvious benefits in position, aspect, space and facilities.
- Alternative styles of catering may be offered to meet differing needs (coffee shop, speciality restaurant, banquet rooms) but must complement rather than contradict the overall image.

Where the markets are widely mixed in character, separate accommodation and price structures may be offered in:

- *separate hotels* designed to different levels of price/grades (see section 3.1.3)

- *resorts* providing a range of facilities from high-grade hotels to self-catering family units.

3.3.8 Complementary business

Complementary markets are important in achieving the overall levels of annual occupancy required for investment feasibility (Table 3.8).

3.3.9 Locational factors

The location of a hotel must be appropriate to serve the needs of the intended market and satisfy a number of requirements (Table 3.9).

The time–distance is usually critical in determining the catchment area for restaurants, functions and other local users as well as the limits for convenience of travel (Figure 3.8).

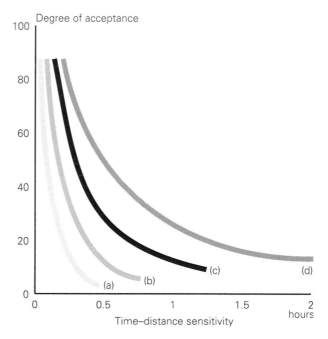

Figure 3.8 Time–distance sensitivity. (a) City centre catchment for hotel restaurants; (b) convenient proximity to commercial areas and tourist sights; (c) transfers to main resorts from airport; (d) catchment for regular functions and meetings; transfer to individual hotels from airport

Table 3.7 Characteristics of the market segments

Purpose and main categories involved[a]	Typical guest profiles[b]	Hotel requirements[c]
Business		
Individuals Sales representatives. Company executives. Consultants. Government officials. (independent or via travel agency)	1–2 nights 100% single occupancy. 80% men 20% women. Weekdays. Non-seasonal. Frequent travel. Price insensitive. High average spend. 1.3:1	High-grade hotels with good business services and meeting rooms. City centre or convenient suburban locations. Well-equipped guestrooms with large lounge, work area. 10% suites, room service
Groups Professional seminars. Association conventions. Sales force meetings. Management conferences. (Independent or via conference organizer)	2–4 nights. 90% single occupancy. 75% men 25% women. Weekdays. Low to mid-season. Regular or periodic events. Price insensitive. Av. spend 2.3:1 Conferences. Product launches	High-grade hotels with extensive conference and function rooms and support facilities. Well-furnished guestrooms with lounge, work area. 5–10% suites
Management training sessions Company orientation programmes (Usually independent)	3–6 nights. Usually 100% single occupancy. 65% men 35% women. Weekdays. Low season. Often part of on-going programme. Price sensitive	Mid-grade hotels with good conference facilities and seminar rooms. Standard guestrooms with lounge, work area
Incentive travel programmes. Corporate conventions (Incentive travel agency)	5–8 nights. 80% double occupancy. Mainly mid-season. Periodic. Price insensitive. Av. spend: 2.5:1	High-grade hotels in exotic locations with convention facilities. Well-furnished guest rooms with lounge/balcony. 5% suites
Contract business Airline crews. Tour groups. Regular visitors	1–2 nights. 60% double occupancy. Specific requirements. Repeat business. Discounted rates	Good standard hotels near airports, tourist areas, hospitals, institutions, universities, research parks
Pleasure		
Mature couples and individuals Tours, sightseeing, cultural interests. Special promotions. Weekend breaks. (Independent or via travel agency)	1–3 nights. 25% single occupancy (high ratio of females). Weekdays. Mid-season. 2–3 times per year. Price sensitive to discounting. Moderate to high spend	Mid–high grade hotels and guesthouses in mainly historic city and country areas. Well-furnished guestrooms
Vacations (tour organized or independent)	7–10 nights. 20% single occupancy. Mid and high seasons. Annual. Price: relatively insensitive. Moderate to high spend	Mid–high grade hotels in attractive resorts and country areas. Well-furnished spacious guestrooms with balconies
Retired couples and individuals (tour organized)	7–14 nights. Sometimes longer. 30% or more single occupancy. Low season packages, Annual. Highly price sensitive. Low–moderate spend	Mid-grade hotels in quiet resorts with range of amenities. Well furnished spacious guestrooms with balconies

Category	Reasons for visits	Pattern and spend	Accommodation
Families	Vacations. (Tour organized vacations. Independent short visits)	7–14 nights in resorts. High season: peaked during school holidays once or twice per year. Price sensitive. Low–moderate spend	Mid-grade hotels in resorts. Holiday clubs. Village resorts. Guesthouses. Self-catering houses or flats and camping with range of recreation and entertainment facilities. Well-furnished, large family rooms or combinations with balconies or terraces
Young professionals	Singles and couples. Vacations. Clubs. Associations. Winter sports. (Tour organized)	6–12 nights. 70% single occupancy. Mid–high season: summer and winter. Often twice a year. Price sensitivity depends on resort attractions. Moderate to high spend.	Mid-grade hotels or shared self-catering in recreation-based mountain or seaside resorts, safari parks, etc. Standard rooms in hotels with sociable public facilities
Young singles	Vacations. Tours sightseeing. Exploration. (Independent or tour organized)	1–3 nights touring. 6–12 nights in resorts. High–mid season. Annual. Highly price sensitive. Low spend	Budget hotels, hostels or shared self-catering. Basic rooms. Showers or shared facilities

Transient[d]

Category	Reasons for visits	Pattern and spend	Accommodation
Couples and individuals	Visits in area. Events. Stopovers. (Independent)	1–2 nights. Mid–low season. Weekends. Often periodic. Moderately price sensitive. Limited spend	Mid-grade chain hotels, motels or guesthouses in convenient locations with restaurants
Families	Visits in area. Stopovers. (Independent)	1–2 nights. High season. Weekends. Occasional. Price sensitive. Limited spend	Budget hotels, motels or guesthouses with large or linked family rooms and play area for children. Mainly bed and breakfast

Long-term residence

Category	Reasons for visits	Pattern and spend	Accommodation
Business	Employees in course of relocation. Professionals working in area	Several weeks. All year. Moderately price sensitive. Moderate spend	Suites in hotels and associated self-catering villas and apartments with separate lounge/office area.
Pleasure	Retired couples and individuals	Several weeks – semi-permanent. Moderately price sensitive. Low–moderate spend	Mainly self-catering apartments or villas, in condominiums or aparthotels

Notes: (a) Main categories and reasons for visits. Couples include persons sharing rooms with twin beds. Mature couples: independent of children. Individuals include wide range of ages.

(b) General descriptions only with main periods of use. Price sensitivity – influencing choice of hotels but subject to corporate and group discounts. Average spend – total expenditure in hotel. Typical ratio compared with median for hotel guest. Exceptions not included.

(c) Hotel preferences and main facilities required. Excluding rented houses.

(d) Transient includes day visits to friends, relatives, institutions and events. Stopovers in long journeys and at terminals.

Table 3.8 Major and complementary markets

Location	Major markets[a]	Complementary markets[b]
Resorts	Vacation tourists Recreationists	Incentive travel. Conventions. Special events. Out of season training
Towns/cities	Business travellers Conferences and meetings	Long and short vacations. Weekend packages. Exhibitions
Suburban	Business travellers Transient visitors	Visitors to locality. Social functions. Recreation clubs
Terminals	Passenger transfers Airline crews, etc.	Business meetings. Training sessions. Recreation clubs
Country houses	Business visitors Recreationists	Recreation clubs. Social events. Health and fitness treatments

Notes: [a] Typical characteristics.
[b] Programmed to balance demand. May require higher investment in space and facilities and should be checked for feasibility.

Table 3.9 Requirements of the location of a hotel

Key factors	Considerations
Trading advantage	Proximity to key attractions (beach frontage, recreational interests, fashionable shopping areas, etc.)
Aspects	Vantage position (views of river, historic buildings, parks, recreational activities)
Convenience	Time–distances, access, relationship to major highways and junctions, visibility, signing
Surroundings	Suitability of environment (attractive surroundings, quality of other buildings, valuation of area)
Space	Land area for cost-efficient planning, design, car parking and recreational requirements
Restrictions	Planning and zoning limitations, legal restrictions, conservation requirements
Costs	Costs of land and development (site works, infrastructure, construction)

3.4 Market feasibility studies: procedure

3.4.1 Organization

Table 3.10 Organization of market feasibility studies

Marketing and operation	Location and development	Economic and financial analysis	Stage

Market definition
  Target markets and characteristics. Viability, potential for growth
	Location identification
	  National and regional patterns of development. Optimum locations for investigations
		Investment sourcing
		  Economic climate, trends, price:earnings ratios. Sources and conditions for finance
			Policies

Local data analysis
  Catchment areas. Socio-economic trends. Business activities. Tourism demands
	Survey of potential sites
	  Locational advantages. Planning conditions. Traffic transportation. Future developments
		Funding considerations
		  Development incentives. Local incentives and benefits. Sources and conditions for finance
			Areas

Competition assessment
  Locations. Main markets. Advantages. Weaknesses
	Site requirements
	  Area. Access. Car parking. Infrastructure
		Labour and services available
		  Employment in area. Wage rates. Services available
			Sites

Demand analysis
  Segmented categories. Projections over period. Sensitivity to change
	Building needs analysis
	  Number. Type of rooms. Range of facilities. Net and gross areas
		Operating forecasts
		  Business mix. Average room rate. Occupancy levels
			Plans

Operational needs
  Organization. Contract arrangements. Staff requirements. Procedures
	Initial planning
	  Brief style of hotel. Facility programming. Schematic plans. Options for development
		Investment feasibility
		  Construction cost model. Budgets: revenues. Costs. Profit and loss forecasts. Sensitivity analysis
			Feasibility

3.4.2 Market survey data

Table 3.11 Market survey data

Subject	Data required
Demand and support	
Tourism demand	Statistics, cyclical and long term variations, projections, visitor profiles
Tourism attractions	Quality, visitor numbers, investment, proposed changes
Planning policies	Structure and development plans, proposals for tourism and hotels
Incentives	Regional and local incentives, terms and conditions for support
Local community	Catchment population, demographic and socio-economic structures and trends
Local economy	Economic activities and trends, main employers, planned developments
Institutional visitors	Universities, colleges, hospitals and major companies: visitor and meeting requirements
Competition and operation	
Existing hotels	Locations, standards, facilities, prices, occupancy levels and variations
Other services	Competing restaurants, banquet and meeting facilities
Planned provision	Proposed new hotels and refurbishments. Stage of development
Market gaps	Deficiencies in facilities. Scope for improvements in standards/services
Investment climate	Economic conditions, sources of finance and requirements
Hotel operation	Staff shortages, availability of supplies and support services
Location and site development	
Traffic flows	Through primary and secondary routes. Traffic characteristics, main origins and destinations
Access	Major junctions, access and signing restrictions. Visibility
Planned changes	Highway improvement programmes, traffic restrictions and diversions
Local transport	Public transport, time–distances to terminals and town centres
Available sites	Locations, areas, accessibility and development potential
Existing use	Existing buildings, trees. Conservation restrictions. Utilization and conversion potential
Advantages	Views, proximity to attractions. Prominence. Environmental benefits
Restrictions	Planning conditions, plot ratios, easement and lease restrictions
Development	Space, requirements, possible layout and massing of buildings
Site works	Contours, soil conditions, excavation to levels, basement works, drainage
Utility services	Availability, conditions and costs of supplies, emergency provisions
Vehicles	Entrance drives, car parking, provisions for service vehicles, loading docks
Landscaping	Space and locations for recreation, landscaping and screening
Weather	Seasonal and diurnal ranges in temperature, humidity, rainfall, prevailing winds
Noise	Proximity of road, rail and flight ways, noise climates, insulation needs

3.4.3 Quantification of demand

The level of customer demand for a new hotel can be estimated from forecasts of future growth in tourism and the percentage share of the market likely to be attracted. This data is more usefully separated into different market segments to compare relative performances.

- *Future growth* based on extrapolation of time series, tourism statistics and socio-economic data for the area. Opportunities for creative marketing (short breaks, incentive travel, referral business) may be included.
- *Market shares* includes new customers and those displaced from competitive hotels (better location, facilities, standards, prices) and other latent markets whose needs can be serviced (club membership, convention facilities, banqueting).

3.4.4 Example

Location	Attractive riverside site in city with increasing commercial and high technology developments.
Proposal	High-grade hotel of 200 rooms with good conference and indoor leisure facilities.
Primary Markets	Business-related travel, conferences, complemented with vacation tourists.
Competition	3 existing hotels of similar grade but less well equipped. Total: 460 rooms. Average occupancy 71.5%.

Tourism data

Current Year: 1994 — Market demand analysis[a]

	Total hotel visits	Business related	Conferences and events	Vacation tourists	Others
Visitor numbers[b]	53 000	12 000	6 000	20 000	15 000
Average stay (nights)		1.5	3.0	6.0	1.2
Bednights	174 000	18 000	18 000	120 000	18 000
Double occupancy[c]		1.0	1.2	1.6	1.5
Room nights	120 000	18 000	15 000	75 000	12 000
Annual growth		5%	10%	2%	4%
Projections 1997[d]	134 300	20 800	20 000	80 000	13 500
Room nights 2000	150 400	24 100	26 600	84 500	15 200

Hotel supply analysis

Year	Hotels	Rooms provided	Room nights available	Average occupancy (%)	Room nights used	Business related	Conferences and events	Vacation tourists	Others
1994	3[e]	460	167 900	71.5	120 000	18 000	15 000	75 000	12 000
1997	3	460	167 900	80.0	134 300	20 800	20 000	80 000	13 500

New hotel completed: market share distribution

Year	Hotels	Rooms provided	Room nights available	Average occupancy (%)	Room nights used	Business related	Conferences and events	Vacation tourists	Others
1997[f]	New	200	73 000	54.8	40 000	6 000	11 000	20 000	3 000
	Others	460	167 900	56.2	94 300	148 000	9 000	60 000	10 500
	4	660	240 900	55.7	134 300	20 800	20 000	80 000	13 500
2000[g]	New	200	73 000	65.0	47 500	8 000	14 000	22 000	3 500
	Others	460	167 900	61.3	102 900	16 100	12 600	62 500	11 700
	4	660	240 900	62.4	150 400	24 100	26 600	84 500	15 200

Seasonal analysis[h] year 2000: third year of new hotel operation

New hotel only	*Spring*	*Summer*	*Autumn*	*Winter*	*Year*
Available room nights	18 250	18 250	18 250	18 250	73 000
Demand					
Business related	3 500	500	4 000	1 000	8 000
Conferences, events	6 000	1 000	6 000	1 000	14 000
Vacation tourists	4 000	12 000	6 000	–	22 000
Others	1 000	1 000	1 000	500	3 500
Total room nights used	14 500	14 500	17 000	2 500	47 500
Occupancy factor	0.795	0.795	0.932	0.137	0.65
% room occupancy	79.5%	79.5%	93.2%	13.7%	65.0%

Notes: Figures rounded for illustration.

[a] Based on tourism and visitor bureau statistics.

[b] Visitors staying in hotels, segmented by types of visitors.

[c] Double occupancy factor: average number of guests per room.

[d] Extrapolated from time series data.

[e] Occupancy breakdown of individual hotels may be shown.

[f] +3 years programme of planning, construction and finishing hotel.

[g] +6 years to allow for initial build-up of business

Targets	Market share (total market)
33%	Business related (central location)
50 to 55%	Conferences and events (better facilities)
26%	Vacation tourists
20 to 25%	Others (transient, local visitors)
31 to 32%	Overall

Room occupancy

$$\left.\begin{array}{l} 65\% \text{ by year 3} \\ 54\text{–}55\% \text{ year 1} \\ 60\% \quad \text{ year 2} \end{array}\right\} \text{Build up period}$$

[h] *Formulae*

$$Bn = \frac{Gn + St}{Pt + Of}$$

$$Rn = \frac{Bn}{Df}$$

Bn = Number of beds
Gn = Number of guests
St = Average stay (nights)
Pt = Period (nights)
Of = Occupancy factor
Rn = Number of rooms
Df = Double occupancy factor

Alternative approach

The numbers of beds and rooms to achieve a desired occupancy may also be calculated.

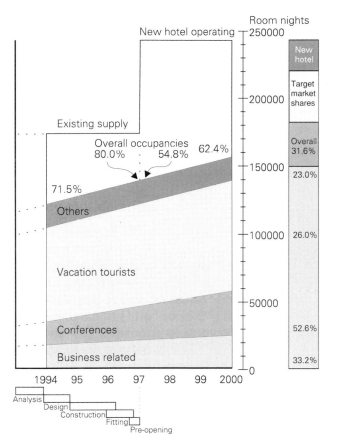

Figure 3.9 Example of opening a new hotel

4

Facility programming and cost analysis

4.1 Factors affecting space

4.1.1 Hotel functions

Table 4.1 Hotel functions

Functions	Operational areas	Considerations
Revenue earning	Guestrooms, suites	Major source of revenue. Main contributors to gross profits
	Food and beverage services	Usually major source of revenue, but incur high operating costs
	Minor related services	Telephones, business services, hire of meeting rooms, exhibit areas
	Rental charges	Shops, kiosks, representative offices and suites
	Casino, discothèque and entertainment facilities	Management/operating charges and commissions
	Ancillary, buildings/ serviced apartments	Service charges, food and beverage sales
	Club operations, spa facilities	Membership fees, admission charges, charges for individual treatments
Cost contribution	Staff accommodation, staff feeding	Deducted or allowed in setting employee wages/salaries
Non-revenue earning	Car parking	Enclosed parking – high-cost area, may utilize associated public car park
	Public areas – lobbies, lounges, libraries	Usually associated with revenue earning services (food, beverages, promotions)
	General recreation areas	May include charges for equipment, etc., hire and instruction
Administrative	Front desk and administration offices	Including interviews and training areas, security and telephone, etc., services usually linked to business centres
Operational support	Food and beverage production and service	Rationalized by centralization of production
	Housekeeping and laundry	Laundry may be contracted out or off-site
	Loading dock and storage	Location critical (access, noise, disturbance, garbage storage)
	Staff facilities – changing, dining and rest areas	Linked to staff entrance, supervision, personnel and training areas
	Mechanical and engineering, plant, workshops and stores	Plant may be located in basement, roof penthouse or/and intermediary service floors.

(a) View of the hotel from the sea

(b) The hotel terrace

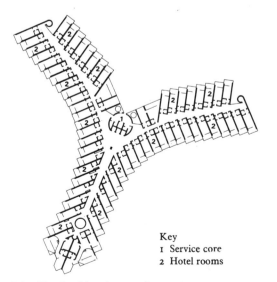

Key
1 Service core
2 Hotel rooms

(c) Typical bedroom floor plan

Figure 4.1 *Royal Cliff Beach Hotel, Pattaya Beach Resort, Thailand*

A self-contained luxury resort hotel overlooking the Gulf of Siam, four floors of which are terraced into the cliff face. The main building has a Y-shaped plan with seven floors of hotel bedrooms and suites above mezzanine level.

At ground level there are extensive recreational facilities, an arcade of shops, a cinema/theatre, coffee shop, grill room, night club, lounge and bar-restaurant. The mezzanine floor provides a single-storey convention hall for over 1000 persons and five other conference rooms, offices and another shopping arcade. In total there are 623 twin guest rooms or suites.

Typical bedroom floor plan

	m²	%
Guest rooms	49 774	62
Facilities	13 648	17
Common area	4 175	5.2
Offices	1 846	2.3
Services and storage	10 838	13.5
Total	80 281	100.0

The cost breakdown gives:

	%
Land and site development	5
Building	56
Equipment	26
Decoration and finishes	13
	100

Architects: Wirachai Wongpanit. Contractors: United Construction Co. Clients: The Royal Cliff Beach Hotel Co. Ltd

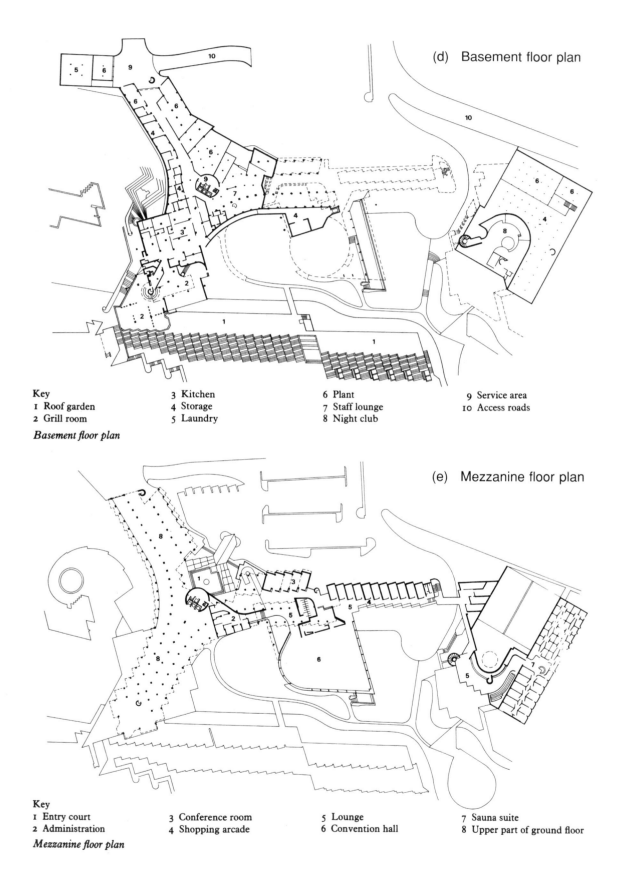

(d) Basement floor plan

Key

1 Roof garden	3 Kitchen	6 Plant	9 Service area
2 Grill room	4 Storage	7 Staff lounge	10 Access roads
	5 Laundry	8 Night club	

Basement floor plan

(e) Mezzanine floor plan

Key

1 Entry court	3 Conference room	5 Lounge	7 Sauna suite
2 Administration	4 Shopping arcade	6 Convention hall	8 Upper part of ground floor

Mezzanine floor plan

4.1.2 Variations in requirements

The areas of built space required for hotel functions vary with:

- hotel company standards
- grade of hotel
- specific facilities offered
- location.

Hotel groups generally lay down space standards as company policy to ensure consistent quality (for merchandising) and to characterize their products. Standardization is also an essential feature of cost saving (bulk purchasing, preplanning, prefabrication) in multiple accommodation units (see section 1.3.4).

The total area per room will depend on the extent of public facilities offered. These are dictated by location and marketing requirements (see section 3.3). The number of rooms compared with the total area is usually critical in ensuring feasibility of investment (Table 4.2).

Table 4.2 Space considerations

Variations	Effects on space
Grade or standard	Overall space/room increases from some 26 m^2 (budget) to 76 m^2 and over (deluxe hotels)
Proportion allocated to rooms	Residential areas represent 80% or more in budget hotels, reducing to 75% in mid-grade and 71% or less in deluxe hotels
Product differentiation	US chains tend to offer more generous bed sizes and larger rooms. Resort hotels generally require larger areas per room
Relative cost of land	Affects the ratio of land:building area, massing and unit building costs. Public facilities on multiple floors duplicate lobby and circulation space and require satellite food and beverage services
Specialist facilities	A higher percentage of public space is required for convention hotels, indoor leisure facilities, casinos, etc. The location of ballroom and convention halls (column-free) affects the positioning of guestroom floors
Building design	The proportion of space taken up by circulation and services to rooms varies with the shape and format of guestroom floor plans:

Typical plans	Gross factors
Slab building: central corridor (double loaded)	0.25–0.35
Slab building: side corridor (single loaded)	0.35–0.40
Atrium building, tower building	0.40–0.45
Motels and holiday village resorts (without corridor access)	0.15

Back-of-house	Laundry and other services may be contracted out reducing total areas by 2–3%; zoned air conditioning and other plant may be housed in the associated roof spaces
Basement car parking and loading dock	Basement car parking addition to the built area of a high-grade hotel: 1 car space/room + 33% 0.3 car space/room + 11% A basement loading dock can add a further 3% together with problems of increased headroom and ramping

4.1.3 Preliminary estimates of space

Initial allowances for planning may be based on typical areas for hotels of similar grade (Table 4.3).

4.1.4 American and large international hotel chains

The concept of the compact economy-style hotels has not been widely developed in America. Most US and international chain

Table 4.3 Size range of European hotels, 150–350 rooms[a]

Grade	Economy[b]	Moderate	Average	High	Deluxe
Rating	*	**	***	****	*****
Room area (net)	17.5[c]	21.7	25.2	30.0 (+5%)	36.0 (+5%)
Gross factor[d]	0.25	0.25	0.30	0.40	0.40
Gross residential area	22	27	33	44	53
Public support areas[e]	5.5	8	12	18	22
Total area/room	27.5	35	45	62	75
Residential % of total	80%	77%	72%	71%	71%

Notes: Provisional figures rounded. In square metres. Room areas (plus 5% suites).
[a]Typical of European hotels: US comparisons below.
[b]Double bedrooms. Restaurant may be separate provision.
[c]Shower room may be used.
[d]Depends on building format. Allows for room service and greater variety of design for high-grade hotels including part single loaded corridors. Refers to gross internal areas. 0.10–0.15 for external access.
[e]Gross areas for non-specialist hotels. For specialist requirements, see section 4.1.5.

Table 4.4 Size range of US hotels, 250–500 rooms

Grade		Budget	Mid-price	First class	Luxury
Rating		**	***	**** (a)	***** (a)
Room area (net)	m²	21.9	29.0	32.5 (+5%)	37.2 (+5%)[b]
	(ft²)	(240)	(312)	(350)	(400)
Gross factor[d]		0.25	0.35	0.40	0.45
Gross residential area	m²	27.9	39.0	47.8	56.6
	(ft²)	(300)	(420)	(515)	(609)
Public/support areas	m²	7.0	13.0	18.6[c]	22.3
	(ft²)	(75)	(140)	(200)	(240)
Total area/room	m² [d]	34.8	52.0	66.4	78.9
	(ft²)	(375)	(560)	(715)	(846)
Residential % of total		80%	75%	72%	72%

Notes: Provisional figures rounded.
[a]Typical range: First class 330–380 sqft; Luxury 400–450 sqft.
[b]Plus nominal 5% suites.
[c]Depends on extent of convention facilities (see section 4.1.5).
[d]Gross areas measured to outside faces of walls.

hotels adopt larger room sizes to accommodate double or oversized twin beds with a mix of king and queen sized individual beds. The standard 3.65 m (12') room width is widely used although 4.1 m (13'6") or wider rooms may be used in first class and luxury hotels to allow design flexibility.

New hotels tend to be larger than those in Europe, permitting some economies in public areas giving a higher overall percentage of residential space per room (Table 4.4).

4.1.5 Specialized requirements

Hotels meeting more specialized market requirements involve further analysis. For example, convention hotels will have more extensive provision for ballrooms, banquet and meeting rooms together with additional foyer space and banquet kitchen and furniture storage (Table 4.5).

In view of the higher investment area and operating costs involved most specialized hotels tend to fall into the high class (****) standard.

4.2 Space analysis

4.2.1 Briefing and programming

Each hotel will have specific requirements dictated by the particular location and marketing opportunities. At an early stage of the briefing or programming procedure the hotel operator will need to define the scale and content of the project to meet the commercial objectives. This will include a general statement of the company's intentions, programmes or details of the facilities to be provided, operational requirements and cost targets within the overall budget for the project. As the conceptual design develops, the information will become more detailed and possibly modified to respond to spatial constraints or opportunities (for improved efficiency or marketing advantage).

Statement of intent
- Type of hotel required, location, intended markets
- Number of rooms, principal facilities, nature of use
- Broad concept of architectural design.

Site utilization
- Area of site, features, planning constraints
- Site conditions, surveys to be undertaken
- Access requirements for guests, special groups, services
- Parking to be provided, basement construction implications
- Provisions for phased expansion, future changes
- Landscaping and recreational areas.

Facility requirements
- Number of rooms of each category, special needs (Royal suites, etc.)
- Space standards with significant minimum dimensions

Table 4.5 Specialized market requirements

Type of hotel	Gross areas/room		Total
	Residential	Public and Support	
Convention/conference	44	22	66
Casino	45	25	70
Spa	45	25	70
All-suite	62	14	76

(a)   View of hotel

(b)   Plan of site at lobby entrance level

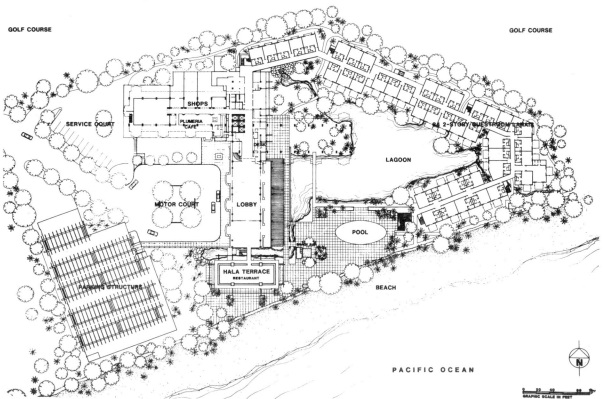

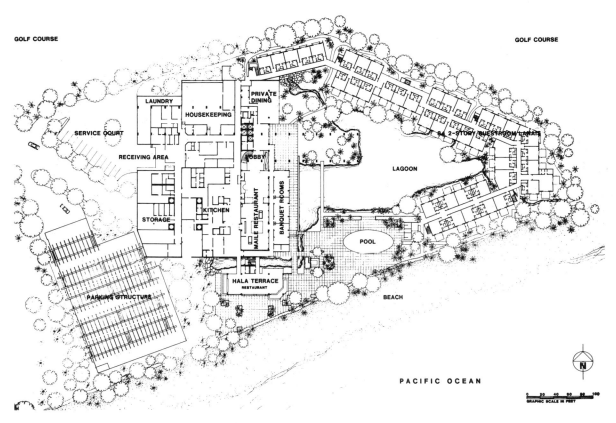

(c)   Ground floor, back-of-house and restaurant areas

Figure 4.2 *The Kahala Hilton, Honolulu, Hawaii*
Blending architecture with landscape the 370 room Kahala Hilton rises 10 storeys above its own lagoon in lush landscaped grounds. Designed with a prestressed concrete and beam structure the buildings form a giant trellis for trailing bougainvillaea.
Space analysis:

Total floor area   31 600 m² (340 000 sqft) excluding lanai

Residential space	74.1%
Public space	13.5
Administration	1.0
Back-of-house	11.4
Services	100.0

   Architects: Killingsworth, Brady & Smith (now KSLW). Structural Engineer: Alfred Yee. Landscape Architect: Wilbert Choi. Photographs: Julius Shulman

- Main furniture and fittings (including bathrooms)
- Room services to be provided (technical, operational).

Lobby
- Architectural character, space and functions to be accommodated
- Entrances, elevators, main circulations within the lobby
- Provisions for the front desk and guest services
- Retail shops, lounges and other public facilities.

Food and beverage areas
- Numbers and characteristics of restaurants, bars, lounges, etc.
- Seating capacities and nominal space allocations
- Optimum locations; requirements for food service operations
- Room service provisions, staff feeding arrangements.

Function and conference areas
- Ballroom or/and banquet hall seating and space provisions
- Meeting and function rooms: numbers, sizes and specific needs
- Foyer/prefunction spaces, food service and ancillary areas
- Business services and special needs (exhibits, promotions).

Recreational areas
- Recreational emphasis, range of built and external facilities
- Swimming pool, location, size, character, ancillary requirements
- Gymnasium, sports and leisure areas, childrens' facilities
- Specialized requirements, spas, beautician, hairdressing.

Administration
- Space and dimensions for front desk and front office

- Areas for accounting, executive, sales and catering offices
- Circulation and interfacing needs, ancillary areas
- Provisions for personnel, engineering and training.

Back-of-house: service areas
- Loading dock, receiving area, general storage, garbage disposal
- Main and subsidiary kitchen areas, food storage requirements
- Housekeeping, laundry and valet areas, circulation arrangements
- Employee changing and toilet areas, dining rooms, supervision
- Engineering offices, plantrooms, maintenance workshops.

Each of these requirements is considered in detail in later chapters.

4.2.2 Basis for estimates

Space requirements for each functional part of a hotel can be estimated in two ways:

- *Estimated occupancy*: based on the numbers to be accommodated multiplied by an appropriate space allowance per person. This can be applied to the numbers of seats or covers in restaurants, function rooms, conference rooms and lounges. It can take account of local demands, in addition to residential use, which may be more significant in food and beverage provisions.

The same approach can be used for kitchens (meals supplied).

- *Allowance per room* based on typical provisions for hotels of the grade and type planned. Allowance should be made for particular requirements such as convention hotels. In larger premises (over 500 rooms) economies of scale can allow savings in administration and back-of-house areas.

4.2.3 Unit areas

Table 4.6 Residential areas

Residential areas	Net areas	
	European hotels (m²)	American hotels (sqft)
Moderate/budget	6.2×3.5 = 21.7	20'×11'6" = 230
Standard	7.0×3.65 = 25.2	26'×12' = 312
High grade (range)	7.5×3.65 = 27.4	27'×12'6" = 340
	8.0×3.75 = 30.0	27'×13'6" = 365
Luxury (range)	8.5×4.1 = 34.0	28'×13'6" = 380
	8.0×4.5 = 36.0	26'×15' = 390

Table 4.7 Food and Beverage, function and support areas

	Net area/seat		Notes
	Average (m²)	Average (ft²)	
Food and beverage services			
Main restaurant	1.8	(19)	Mainly tables for two people
Speciality restaurant	2.0	(22)	Also themed restaurant
Café	1.5	(16)	
Coffee shop, grill bar	1.6	(17)	Including counter
Nightclub	2.1	(23)	Including dance square
Staff dining room	1.4	(15)	Cafeteria services
Public bar, lobby bar	1.5	(16)	Themed or pub style
Cocktail lounge	1.6	(17)	
Lobby lounge seating	2.0	(22)	Settee style seats
Entertainment lounge	1.6	(17)	Close seating, includes stage
Function areas			
Ballroom:			
banquet seating	1.2	(13)	1.0–1.4 depending on layout
buffet	0.8	(8.5)	0.7–1.0 depending on display
reception	0.6	(6.5)	Standing
Foyer	0.3	(3.3)	Prefunction or breakout space
Functions:			
party seating	1.6	(17)	Round tables
Conferences:			
theatre style	0.9	(10)	Close seating in rows
classroom style	1.6	(17)	Individual desks/writing pallets
boardroom style	2.0	(22)	10–20 seated round table
Support areas			
Toilets:			
men's	0.04	(0.4)	
women's	0.06	(0.6)	
Cloakroom	0.04	(0.4)	
Circulation	0.2		20% – depending on layout
Furniture and equipment stores	0.14	(1.5)	
Main kitchen	0.8	(8.5)	0.5 min preparation – 1.0 full service
Satellite kitchen	0.3	(3.3)	Supplied from main kitchen
Banquet kitchen or pantry	0.2	(2.0)	Additional to main kitchen
Room service pantry	0.2	(2.0)	Per room served 1:30 rooms
Food and beverage stores	0.2	(2.0)	Based on total seating

4.2.4 Public areas

The extent of public areas is largely dictated by the grade, location and market emphasis of the hotel (Tables 4.8 and 4.9):

Budget hotels: Space allocation to public and support areas kept to less than 20%. Food service may be omitted or shared with other premises.

Mid-range hotels: Rationalization of space is necessary. Function areas are generally kept to small meeting/party rooms.

Higher grade hotels: Space requirements depend on location and market emphasis.

Table 4.8 Space requirements by location and market emphasis

Type of Hotel	Lobby	Cafés, restaurants bars/lounges	Conference and function rooms	Recreation facilities
City centre hotel	Large: impressive, usually includes shops	Moderate: designed to attract non-residents	Usually extensive in large hotel: high standard, business services	Moderate: health club may include internal pool
Provincial or surburban hotel	Moderate: may extend into lounge	Moderate: depends on competition in area	Moderate or limited but high near airport	Usually limited to fitness room, outside pool
Beach resort hotel. Spa hotel	Large: hub of activities, includes shops	Large: cafés, restaurants, bars and lounges	Depends on markets, convention hotel requires large ballroom	Depends on climate: mainly external but large areas required for spas
Resort village. Condominium	Small: front office and luggage handling	Extensive: multiple choice of restaurants. Large entertainment lounge	Small: but may accommodate other conference visitors	Planned around recreation areas. Built facilities include health club
Mountain resort	Moderate with areas for equipment	Extensive: cafés, restaurants, bars, multiple choice	Usually small	Internal health club and pool
Convention hotel. Conference Centre	Large: extensive services. Registration area	Large areas. Choice of restaurants and lounges	Large ballroom Multiple meeting and function rooms	Usually large health club and indoor pool
Casino	Large: ornate	Extensive choice. Several bars and lounges	Usually large ballroom and function areas	Casino and entertainment areas. Health club

Table 4.9 Facilities by provision per guestroom

Facility	Total provision per guestroom		
	Extensive, large	Moderate, rationalized	Limited
Lobby	1.0–1.2 m²	0.8–1.0 m²	0.4–0.8 m²
Restaurants, cafés	1.4–1.8 seats	0.8–1.2 seats	0.6 seats or fewer
Lounges, bars	0.8–1.0 seats	0.6–0.8 seats	0.4 seats or fewer
Function rooms, meeting rooms	3.0–4.0 seats	1.0–2.0 seats	Fewer than 1.0 seats

Table 4.10 Administration and back-of-house areas

	Low[a] (m²)	(sqft)	Average[b] (m²)	(sqft)	High[c] (m²)	(sqft)	Notes
Administration							
front office	0.2	(2)	0.4	(4)	0.4	(4)	[c] High-grade and luxury hotels
other offices	0.3	(3)	0.6	(6)	0.9	(10)	
Kitchen and stores	1.0	(10)	1.5	(16)	2.0	(22)	[c] Including banquet kitchens
Laundry	0.6	(6)	0.8	(9)	0.9	(10)	May be contracted out
Housekeeping	0.4	(4)	0.5	(5)	0.6	(6)	
Receiving – Storage	0.5	(5)	0.7	(7)	0.8	(9)	Depends on enclosure
Employee areas	0.6	(6)	1.0	(11)	1.2	(13)	[c] Luxury hotels
Engineering areas	1.0	(11)	1.8	(19)	2.3	(25)	[c] Resort hotels
Gross factor	x15%		x20%		x25%		

Notes: [a]May be further reduced in budget hotels.
[b]Reduced in hotels of more than 500 rooms.
[c]Increased by range of facilities offered (functions, conventions) and standards of sophistication.

4.2.5 Administration and back-of-house areas

Support areas can also be provisionally estimated as ratios of space per room depending on the standard and range of facilities included, the size of hotel and its location (Table 4.10). In a developed area many of the back-of-house operations (laundry, maintenance workshops, basic food preparation) can be contracted out, reducing space and equipment costs.

4.2.6 Representative hotel examples

Table 4.11 shows indicative facilities and sizes provided in new hotel developments. Variations will be required to meet particular marketing requirements and site conditions.

Table 4.11 Indicative space standards

	Deluxe hotel capital city, prime District *****	High-class business hotel, main city, urban ****	Commercial/motor hotel, provincial city, suburban ***	Budget inn, economy, roadside **	High-class resort hotel, high standard, scenic area ****	Resort village, family and leisure orientated, new resort ***	Notes
No. of rooms	150	500	200	100	300	600	(1)
No. of storeys	8	15+2 basements		2	4	1+2	
Main markets	Business visitors. High-spend tourists	Business visitors, tourists, conventions, functions	Business & local visitors, functions	Transient, local visitors	High spend tourists, conferences, incentive travel, golf tournam'ts	Tourists, out of season courses and conventions	
Residential areas							
Bedroom/bathroom	Bays 150@ 8.0 × 4.5m 5400	500@ 8.0 × 3.75m 15 000	200@ 7.0 × 3.6m 5040	Bays 100@ 6.2 × 3.5 m² 2170	300@ 8.3 × 3.6 8960	600@27 m² 16 200	(2)
Suites: added areas	7@36 250	25@30 750			12@30 360		
Circulation and service: % addition to net areas	+43%	+40%	+30%	+25%	+42%	+15%	(3)
% of total/gross area	71.8% 8080	71.0% 22 050	74.0% 6552	81.8% 2700	69.2% 13 230	70.5% 18 630	
Public areas							
Lobby and front hall				Reception	Lobby and front hall	Reception hall	
Reception, cloakrooms				Cloakrooms	Reception Cloakrooms	Reception and Info.	
Stairs, elevators				Public telephones	Stairs elevators	Cloakrooms	
Bellman, concierge	1.2 m²/room 180	1.0 m² 500	0.9 m²/room 180	Vending area 0.8 m²/room 80	Bellman, concierge 1.0 m²	Luggage transfer 0.4 m²/room 240	
Lounge area	25@2.0 50		10@2.0 20		Lounge seating 1.0 m² 300		
Shops and stands	4 shops	4 shops	General shop 25		Shops and salons 90	Shops and salons 150	(4)
% of total/gross area	2.0% 230	1.9% 600	2.5% 225	2.4% 80	2.0% 390	1.5% 390	
Food and beverage services							(5)
Restaurants — Café or coffee shop		250@1.6 400	100@1.6 160	(a)60@1.6 100	50@1.6 80	400@1.6 640	(6)
Restaurant: High class	75@2.0 150	150@2.0 300			150@2.0 300		
Main	100@1.8 180		80@1.8 140		300@1.8(b) 540	300@1.8(b) 540	
Speciality		75@2.0 150				100@2.0 200	
Bars and lounges — Hotel bars (total)	50@2.0 100	150@1.5 225	80@1.5 120	(a)40@1.5 60	100@1.5 150	200@1.5 300	(7) (8)
Cocktail (restaurant)	75@1.6 120	75@1.6 120					
Entertainment		100@1.6 160			200@1.6 320	500@1.6 800	
Other public rooms	(a)50@2.4 120						(9)
Circulation	+25%	+25%	+25%	+25%	+25%	+25%	
% of total/gross area	7.5% 840	5.4% 1690	6.0% 530	5.8% 190	9.1% 1740	11.3% 2980	
Meeting and function rooms							
Ballroom and banquet hall	150@1.2 180	750@1.0 750	–		200@1.2 240	200@1.0 200	(10)
Foyer	60	250			80		(11)
Conference and function rooms	75@1.6 120	450@1.6 720	100@1.6 160		100@1.6 160	100@1.6 160	(12)
Business centre		500					
Furniture store		100					
Equipment and AVA							
Cloakrooms: toilets							
Circulation	+25%	+25%	+25%		+25%	+25%	(13)

Notes:
(a) Roadside cafe
(b) In 2 adjacent areas with central buffet
(c) Bar-lounge
(d) Library

Hotel area schedule — typical areas for six hotel concepts (leisure, administration, back‑of‑house, food preparation, and employee areas). Percentages are % of total/gross area; areas in m². Per‑unit standards shown as m²/room or m²/seat.

Category / item	Health club, etc. (≈150 rm)	Health club; pool and deck; circulation (≈500 rm)	Fitness room; circulation (≈200 rm)	External pool and play area; games room (≈100 rm)	Golf and health club; external pool; tennis courts; golf courses (≈300 rm)	Health club; external pool and play area (≈600 rm)
Leisure facilities (indoor) — % of total/gross area	4.0%	6.9%	2.3%	0.6%	3.1%	1.7%
Area (external areas separate)	450	2150	560	70 (games room); ext. pool/play 20	600; ext. pool 400 (tennis courts, golf courses external)	450; ext. pool and play area 300
Administration areas — % of total/gross area	1.8%	2.5%	2.1%	0.6%	2.1%	1.1%
Front office	0.5 m²/room → 75	0.5 m²/room → 250	0.4 m²/room → 100	0.4 m²/room (inclusive)	0.4 m²/room → 120	0.35 m²/room → 210
Executive	0.4 m² → 60	0.4 m² → 200	0.3 m² → 60	—	0.2 m² → 60	0.15 m² → 90
Sales and catering	0.4 m² → 60	0.4 m² → 250	—	—	0.35 m² → 100	0.25 m² → 150
Accounting	0.3 m² → 45	0.3 m² → 150	—	—	0.25 m² → 80	0.2 m² → 120
Administration total	190	800	220	70	360	570
Back‑of‑house areas, food preparation — % of total/gross area	2.0%	2.5%	2.7%	1.2%	1.9%	2.2%
Main and satellite kitchens	1.0 m² → 180	0.8 m²/seat → 425	0.8 m²/seat → 140	0.8 m²/seat (inclusive)	0.8 m²/seat → 360	0.7 m²/seat → 560
Banquet kitchen	0.2 m² → 30	0.2 m²/seat → 150	0.2 m²/seat → 20	—	0.2 m²/seat → 60	0.2 m²/seat → 60
F&B stores (total)	0.2 m² → 100	0.2 m²/seat → 235	0.2 m²/seat → 40	—	0.2 m²/seat → 100	0.2 m²/seat → 160
Circulation etc.	+20%	+20%	+20%	+20%	−20%	+20%
Food prep. total	220	800	240	60	360	570
Back‑of‑house (service) — % of total/gross area	3.1%	3.3%	2.7%	1.8%	3.2%	3.6%
Rec. area and garbage store	0.3 m²/room → 60	0.4 m²/room → 150	0.2 m²/room → 80	0.2 m²/room → 20	0.3 m²/room → 90	0.2 m²/room → 120
General stores	0.2 m² → 60	0.3 m²/room → 200	0.3 m²/room → 60	0.3 m²/room → 30	0.5 m²/room → 150	0.4 m²/room → 150
Housekeeping	0.5 m² → 90	0.6 m²/room → 250	0.5 m²/room → 120	0.5 m²/room → 50	0.5 m²/room → 150	0.4 m²/room → 240
Laundry	0.7 m² → 120	0.8 m²/room → 350	0.8 m²/room → 160	—	0.8 m²/room → 240	0.7 m²/room → 420
Eng. offices, workshops	0.4 m² → 60	0.3 m²/room → 200	0.3 m²/room → 60	—	1.0 m²/room → 300	0.4 m²/room → 240
Plant equipment	1.4 m²/room → 210	0.8 m²/room → 700	0.8 m²/room → 160	0.6 m²/room → 60	1.5 m²/room → 450	1.0 m²/room → 600
Service total	370	1850	640	160	1380	1620
Employee areas — % of total/gross area	6.0%	7.2%	7.2%	4.8%	7.2%	6.1%
Staff: guest room (ratio)	1.4:1	0.8:1	0.5:1	0.2:1 [a]	0.7:1	0.4:1
Control, personnel rooms	0.4 m²/room → 60	0.2 m²/room → 100	0.1 m²/room → 20	0.3 m²/room → 20	0.3 m²/room → 90	0.2 m²/room → 90
Changing rooms, lockers	0.8 m²/room → 120	0.6 m²/room → 300	0.5 m²/room → 100	0.7 m² → 100	0.5 m²/room → 210	0.5 m²/room → 300
Staff dining‑kitchen	0.6 m²/room → 90	0.3 m²/room → 150	0.3 m²/room → 60	0.3 m² → 60	0.7 m² → 90	0.2 m²/room → 90
Employee total	270	550	180	180	390	540
% of total/gross area	2.4%	1.8%	2.0%	1.5%	2.0%	2.0%
Hotel Total	100% — 11 250 — 75.0 m²/room	100% — 31 070 — 62.1 m²/room	100% — 8860 — 44.3 m²/room	100% — 3300 — 33.0 m²/room	100% — 19 110 — 63.7 m²/room	100% — 26 420 — 44.0 m²/room

[a] Including contract and part time staff

Notes: [1]Typical but depends on site area, cost, density of building, and particular market requirements.
[2]Net: internal areas of rooms. Gross: including circulation and support/service areas. Typical gross factors indicated for internal areas.
[3]Service areas (linen rooms, pantries, trolley stores) usually 1 per floor wing of 25–35 rooms with separate pantry area for room service.
[4]Rented space is usually viable in larger city centre, convention and resort hotels. Preferably this should also have outside access.
[5]Restaurant facilities – minimum for residents. May be increased for local demand. Restaurant may have specialized theme to create interest.
[6]Coffee shop also used for breakfast. Minimum requirements indicated. Increased for tourist groups. Large areas may be in two adjacent parts.
[7]Lobby bar and lounge adjacent. Cocktail lounge used in high-class hotels – associated with restaurant.
[8]Lounge area of lobby with settee-type seating.
[9]Entertainment lounge may have piano bar, small dance square and stage area. Increased in resort and convention hotel with adjacent open air terrace.
[10]Ballroom/banquet increased to 1.5 seats/room for convention hotels or where there is an extensive banquet demand. In resorts this is a multipurpose area used for entertainment.
[11]Foyer at least one-third of the size of halls served. Usually separate from public lobby but may be combined in small hotels.
[12]Conference/meeting rooms allow 1.2 m²/seat theatre style, 1.6 m²/seat classroom style and up to 2.0 m²/seat boardroom style. Usually divisible for smaller groups.
[13]Toilets 0.15 m²/seat. Furniture, etc., stores 0.1–0.2 m² seat.
[14]Front office includes telephone rooms, safe storage, audit areas, control panels, and accounting functions.
[15]Kitchen areas include the main and satellite kitchens and banquet pantries. Food storage depends on frequency of deliveries.
[16]Receiving area depends on extent of enclosure and may involve basement construction with ramped access.
[17]Laundry may be mainly off-site, reducing the hotel space required.
[18]Plant rooms may be partly sited externally (including roof mounted equipment) but require careful screening.

4.3 Capital costs

4.3.1 Building cost comparisons

Cost comparisons of hotel building projects are complicated by the wide variations in facility requirements and standards of sophistication as well as differences in the siting and design of the buildings. Local prices are also affected by the extent of competition, rates of inflation in the region and exchange rates. To allow international comparisons, figures are often quoted both in local currency and US dollars or European ecus (Figure 4.3).

4.3.2 Cost per room

This indicates the median cost per room for a hotel of the type described and is derived from the total costs/number of rooms. The gross area per room is assumed but the conditions such as location, size, height, type and grade of hotel need to be qualified. Cost per room indices are useful in making comparisons between several types of projects and over a range of timescales. Since accounts for revenues and costs of hotel operations are also summarized on a per room basis, this enables the capital costs to be directly compared.

4.3.3 Cost per square metre (sqft) floor area

Costs based on built areas are more accurate and can take account of the actual facilities specified, the building design and the gross areas required. Unit costs can be projected to forecast future prices, using building cost and tender price indices, and can more accurately represent regional variations (Table 4.12 and Figure 4.3).

4.3.4 Overall costs of investment

Capital investment covers the costs of constructing and fitting out the hotel together with the associated fees and expenses. The outlay also includes provision for initial working capital and the payment of interest during the construction period. In most cases land may be leased – or purchased and leased back. The general building construction cost usually represents between 50 and 60% of the total.

Table 4.13 shows approximate percentages of costs in which (a) represents a prime area with land costs of 15% and interest rates of around 12% with a two-year building and fitting out period; (b) is more typical of underdeveloped land with higher infrastructure costs. Land purchase varies from 5–20%, the higher value applying to city centre and motel developments.

Table 4.12 Typical building costs (see section 4.2.6 for hotel analysis)

A De luxe hotel, capital city, prime site *****	B High-class business hotel, city/urban site ****	C Motor hotel, provincial city, suburban site ***	D Budget inn, roadside site **
Gross area/room			
75.0 m²	62.1 m²	44.3 m²	33.0 m²
(810 sqft)	(670 sqft)	(480 sqft)	(360 sqft)
Building cost/room 1993[a]			
£75 000–100 000	£55 000–80 000	£30 000–50 000	£18 000–30 000
$105 000–140 000	$70 000–110 000	$42 000–65 000	$22 000–42 000

Notes: [a]US Building costs based on Hospitality Valuation Services Inc., 1991, surveys. UK costs based on Spons Architects & Builders Price Book 1993 and analysis of hotel projects.

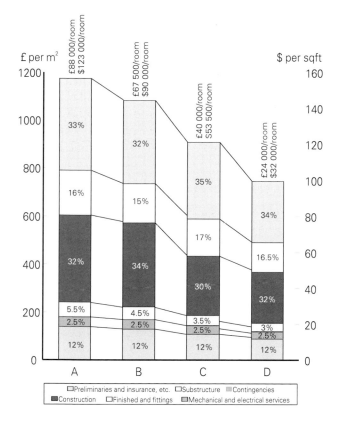

Figure 4.3 Breakdown of building costs. A, deluxe hotel, capital city; B, high-grade business hotel, provincial town; C, mid-grade motor hotel, suburban site; D, budget inn, roadside site

Table 4.13 Overall development costs

Item	Range (a)–(b)%	Coverage
Land purchase	15–5	Leasing or sale and leaseback alternatives
Site works, infrastructure	1½–4	Utilities, roads, surface parking, landscaping
Building construction	50–55	See breakdown of costs
Special systems	1–1½	Telephone, fire safety, audio-visual systems
Furniture, furnishings, equipment	14–16	See below, includes purchasing costs
Professional/legal fees	4–6	Architecture, engineering, interior design, specialist
Pre-opening expenses	1½–2½	Cleaning, recruitment, training
Working capital	1–1	Initial supplies
Financing costs + interest	11–8	Fees, interest during construction, taxes, insurance
Miscellaneous contingencies	1–1	
	100–100	

Furniture fixtures and equipment may be estimated as a percentage (25–30%) added to building cost or based on model schemes. This covers items which may be client supplied – such as loose furniture, furnishings, back-of-house equipment (food service, laundry), front office equipment, inventories (linen, uniforms, china, glassware, silverware, utensils, stationery supplies, printing, etc.). The more specialized equipment is usually leased.

Financing costs and interests depend on the time taken for construction, phased payments for the work and interest rate charged on loans. Agreements may provide for interest to be deferred during the initial year.

4.3.5 Project appraisal

Assessment of financial viability is carried out at an early stage to determine the likely return on the investment. As a rough preliminary indicator the ratio of investment cost per room:room rate = 1000:1 is sometimes used, but this does not allow for changes in interest rates, occupancies, food and beverage income and other variables.

Hotel project appraisal involves the preparation of financial projections covering three main aspects: profit and loss statement, capital invest- ment requirements and cashflow statement (Table 4.14).

Hotel accounts
Operating accounts are useful to compare performance ratios and other data, particularly in setting revenue target figures and budgets for the various cost elements. Analyses of hotel accounts are published on a regular basis by a number of accountancy groups, notably Pannell Kerr Forster Associates and Horwath Consulting. The surveys show comparative figures for hotels by region and generally cover hotels of good international standard.

Methods of investment appraisal
Profit and loss statements are usually expressed in the values which apply at the date of opening. In appraising performance over longer periods, financial modelling is required to handle the large number of calculations involved. This may range from simple estimates of the 'pay-back' periods to complex discount- ing methods such as the internal rate of return which enable the effects of future payments (depreciation allowances, taxation, loan repay- ments) to be more accurately assessed. Cashflow statements typically include adjust- ments for inflation.

Table 4.14 Hotel project appraisal

Analysis	Coverage
Hotel operation: profit and loss statement	Estimates of occupancy rates, revenues and expenses over the initial 3–5 year build-up period. This is usually supported by an analysis of the market and competition
Capital investment requirements	Cost of buildings, infrastructure and land including fees Fittings, furniture and equipment costs (with design fees) and life-cycles Initial costs of finance and working capital Interest and loan repayments. Internal rates of return required Capital and depreciation allowances
Cashflow statement	Gross profits and allowances credited against payments for the loans, depreciation and tax, extending over the loan period (10–20 years) with allowances for inflation

Sensitivity analysis

Revenue projections are calculated for the occupancy indicated by market analysis (typically 60–65%). However, the effects of changes in occupancy levels or prices on revenues and variable costs is also a useful indicator of the sensitivity of profit margins to changes in demand.

This is shown by breakeven analysis to determine the level at which revenues exactly balance all outgoings without profit or loss (Figure 4.4).

4.3.6 Hotel profit and loss statements

These are usually set out in a standard format showing expected revenues from the sale of rooms, food and beverages, minor operations such as telephones and equipment hire and rentals from shops and other concessions.

Operating costs and expenses generally fall into three groups: departmental costs, undistributed costs relating to the hotel as a whole and fixed charges. The first two vary to some extent with the volume of sales achieved while fixed charges have to be met regardless of performance.

Hotel performance is usually compared on a per room basis but even similar grade hotels vary widely depending on location, size and market emphasis. As a very broad division, city centre hotels generally have higher occupancies and a greater proportion of revenue from the sale of rooms than country and resort-based properties. The ratio of food and beverage sales is relatively high in European countries (often 38–43%), which have a tradition of eating out, compared with a median of 32% in the United States and Canada (Figure 4.5).

The revenue for rooms in high-standard hotels usually represents 50–60 per cent of the total but is much higher in budget hotels with limited food and beverage sales. Departmental expenses in operating rooms are relatively low compared with those of food and beverage departments.

Departmental costs as a percentage of departmental income are:

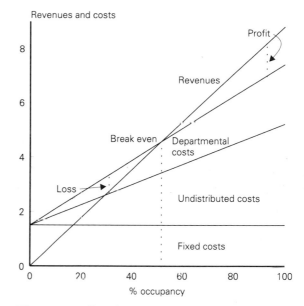

Figure 4.4 Breakeven analysis. Departmental costs are directly variable, undistributed costs are semi-variable

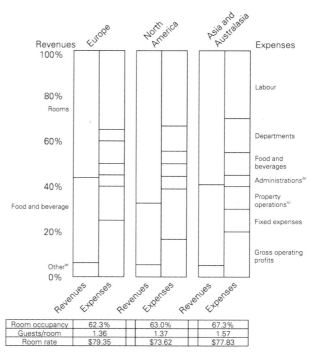

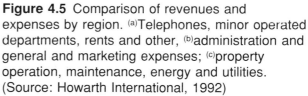

Figure 4.5 Comparison of revenues and expenses by region. (a)Telephones, minor operated departments, rents and other, (b)administration and general and marketing expenses; (c)property operation, maintenance, energy and utilities. (Source: Howarth International, 1992)

Rooms	25–30%
Food and beverage	75–85%
Minor operated	60–80%

Hence, the letting of rooms represents the main contributor to gross profits and the number of rooms and capital cost per room are critical factors in determining the feasibility.

While food and beverage revenues contribute a much smaller percentage, after deducting the cost of sales and labour, these services are important in determining the grade of hotel, room rates and reputation. In many hotels, conventions and banquet sales are also an important source of business.

4.3.7 Fixed charges

Fixed charges are mainly determined by the capital costs:

- *Real estate or property taxes*: related to property values
- *Insurance*: buildings, contents and hotel business insurance
- *Rent*: land and building leasehold costs – if required
- *Management, incentive or franchise fees*: turnover or GOP
- *Depreciation*: allowances for furniture, fittings and equipment replacements
- *Loan interest*: depends on the costs and structure of financing, including
- *Amortization*: phased repayments of loans and mortgages.

4.3.8 Example

The following example outlines a method of appraisal applied to a proposed hotel project. The data is simplified: in practice, various options would be analysed by accountancy software in some detail (see section 4.3.6).

The figures also illustrate the high capital intensity of hotel development and risks involved. It is common for the first two or three years of operation to incur losses.

200 guestroom hotel: 3 star motor hotel in provincial town. Car parking ratio 1 per room. Surface parking.

(a) Overall costs of development

		$000	%
Land	1.6 ha (4 acres) purchase, inclusive of fees, registration and duty	1210	10.0
Siteworks	Parking: 200 bays @ 22 m²	160	1.3
	Utilities, drainage, landscaping	120	1.0
Building	200 rooms @ 44 m²	7000	58.3
Furniture, fittings, equipment 25% of building		1750	14.6
Rooms, public areas: 14%; back-of-house: 7%; Inventories: 4%			
Operating equipment Special systems		160	1.3
Fees Architects, engineers, consultants: 6%		550	4.6
Pre-opening expenses Allowance per room		300	2.5
Working capital and miscellaneous expenses		140	1.2
Finance during construction 50% loan		620	5.2
Development period: 2 years; interest: 10% Interest on cashflow balance plus fees			
Total costs (rounded)		12 000	100.0

Cost per room $60 000 (£42 900)

(b) Financing structure (assumptions)

Capital
Equity 60% $7.2
(own million
finance)
Mortgage 40% $4.8 Amortization 20
or loan million years
(may allow 1 to 2 year moratorium on repayments).

Depreciation allowances (replacements and reserves)
FFE 4% per annum straight line method: reduced to 2% in years 1 and 2 (depends on taxation advantages).

Operating accounts
Based on third year of operation plus 4% of inflation.
Initial years build-up of occupancy: year 1–50%, year 2–60%, year 3–65%.

Revenues Composition

	Percentages
Rooms income	55
Food and beverage sales	40
Minor departments	5
Telephones and rents	———
	100%

Total sales

Expenses	Ratio to total sales
Departmental costs	
Rooms	14
Food and beverage	30
Other departments	3
Total departmental costs	47%
Undistributed costs	
Administration, general, marketing	12
Property operation, maintenance, energy	8
	20%
Gross operating profit before fixed costs	33%

(c) Hotel operations statement

	Year					
	1	2	3	4	5	6
Room occupancy (%)	50	60	65	65	65	65
Double occupancy	1.3	1.3	1.3	1.3	1.3	1.3
Average room rate[a]	$60	$62.4	$64.9	$67.5	$70.2	$73.0
Revenues ($ millions)[e]						
Rooms	2.19	2.73	3.08	3.20	3.33	3.46
Food & beverage	1.59	1.99	2.24	2.33	2.42	2.52
Other	0.20	0.25	0.28	0.29	0.31	0.31
Total Sales	3.98	4.97	5.60	5.82	6.06	6.30
Departmental costs	1.87	2.34	2.63	2.74	2.85	2.96
Undistributed costs	0.80	0.99	1.12	1.16	1.21	1.26
Income before fixed costs	1.31	1.64	1.85	1.92	2.00	2.08
Cashflow statement						
Fixed costs ($ millions)[e]						
Property taxes, insurance[b]	0.40	0.42	0.43	0.45	0.47	0.49
Rents, leases, fees[c]	0.10	0.10	0.11	0.11	0.12	0.12
Depreciation, replacements	0.35	0.36	0.70	0.73	0.76	0.79
Surplus available for debt and tax	0.46	0.76	0.61	0.63	0.65	0.68
Loan interest	0.48	0.47	0.46	0.45	0.44	0.43
Mortgage repayments	0.08	0.09	0.10	0.11	0.12	0.13
Surplus before taxation (loss)[d]	(0.1)	0.02	0.05	0.07	0.09	0.12

Notes: (a) *Hotel operating figures:* may be at constant prices or actual prices (including inflation). Room rates are those achieved after discounts.

(b) *Taxation:* will depend on the location of the project, and trading circumstances of the company. Value Added Tax: net prices are usually taken in preliminary estimates. Property Tax: included in fixed costs. Income tax credits, incentives and allowances added to cash flow statement.

(c) *Fees:* Allowance for management incentive fees.

(d) *Appraisal:* will usually include:
Accumulated interest and GOP surplus over period of loan.
IRR based on income stream only/or including residual value of property.
Return on equity or capital employed.
Annual revaluation of property assets and gearing. (See section 1.4.10)

(e) *Currency conversions:* Direct comparisons may not be precise because of variations in the sales mix, economic conditions, relative costs and exchange rates. The examples are based on 1993 representative currency ratios $1.40 = £1.00.

5

Building plans

5.1 Site developments

5.1.1 Site benefits

Potential sites need to be considered in relation to the main tourist and service attractions (see section 3.3.3). In a *resort area*, views, distance and frontage to the beach or waterfront and surroundings are key factors. In *towns*, proximity to parks, rivers, prime shopping streets, historic areas and entertainment are important. The status of the district and surroundings is particularly critical for luxury hotels.

The *views* influence the plan form, compensatory attractions (garden views, recreational focuses) should be provided for disadvantaged rooms. The *orientation* to sun, shade and prevailing winds will affect building design as well as the location and screening of swimming pools, recreational areas and terraces.

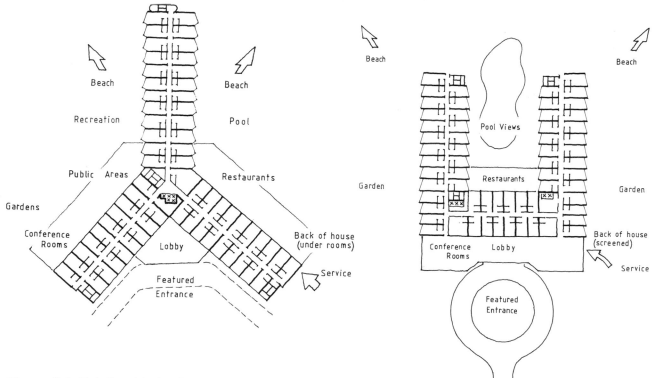

Figure 5.1 Relationship to view

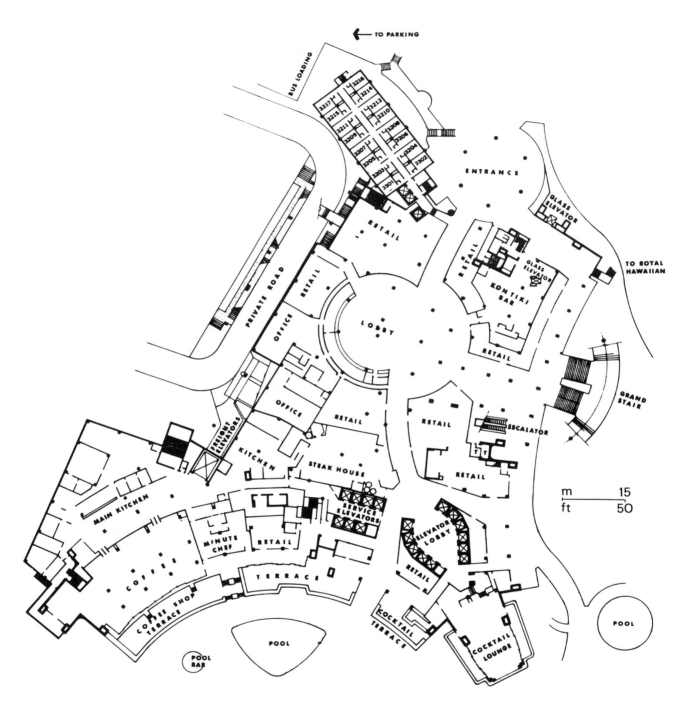

Lobby floor plan

Figure 5.2 *Sheraton Waikiki*
Guestrooms in the Sheraton Waikiki occupy 25
floors in two curving wings overlooking the beach.
The lobby floor extends into the podium between
the guestroom wings with the second floor
accommodating extensive ballroom and
convention areas. Architects: Wimberly,
Whisenand, Allison, Tong and Goo

Figure 5.3 Sensitivity in design
This four-star Forte Crest Hotel with 116 bedrooms and extensive public facilities commands a unique location alongside Exeter Cathedral. The elevations respond to the Georgian conservation zone and incorporate a listed property into the form of the new building. Architects: Scott, Brownrigg and Turner

5.1.2 Environmental and planning constraints

Development may be restricted by town and country planning and zoning conditions. More specific protection is given to existing listed buildings and surroundings through preservation orders and conservation area controls. In sensitive areas, environmental impact assessment and amenity conservation studies may be required to demonstrate that appropriate safeguards have been incorporated in the development.

5.1.3 Traffic analysis

An analysis of traffic flows (including main origins and destinations) is necessary to identify the nature and volume of transient users. Planned changes in road systems and junctions must also be examined.

For transient use, the optimum location is adjacent to a major junction or terminus. Budget accommodation can be sited near garage service stations and roadside cafés for higher visibility and convenience.

Specific consideration must be given to:

- *Counterflows of traffic* and difficulties of crossing opposing traffic lanes.

- *Restrictions on new entries* to the highway and requirements (road widening, separate entry–exit routes, cleared sightlines).
- *Conditions relating to signage* on highway, on and outside the site and on buildings (including illumination). This is likely to be highly restricted in sensitive areas of special control.

The siting of buildings and landscaping requirements will be influenced by the need to reduce exposure to glare, noise and pollution.

5.1.4 Servicing

Separate access routes must be provided for guests and operation services. The service road and goods entry point determine the location for back-of-house and internal servicing circulations.

Basement loading dock and car parking areas require extensive ramping and manoeuvring areas (see section 9.1.1).

5.1.5 Land costs

Costs of land and development affect the area of site and concentration of building. High land costs

137

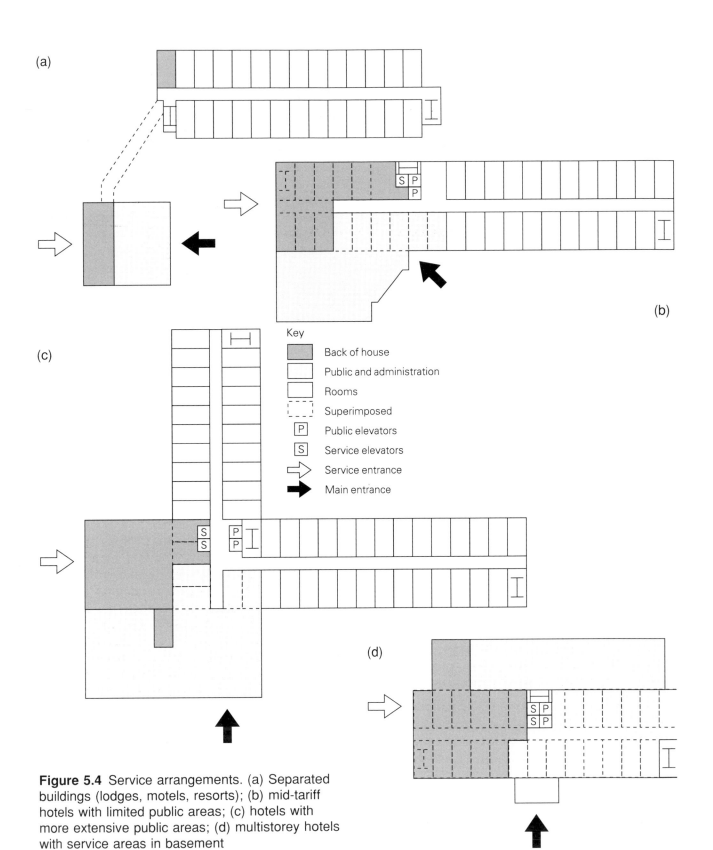

Figure 5.4 Service arrangements. (a) Separated buildings (lodges, motels, resorts); (b) mid-tariff hotels with limited public areas; (c) hotels with more extensive public areas; (d) multistorey hotels with service areas in basement

Key

▨	Back of house
☐	Public and administration
☐	Rooms
⌐ ¬	Superimposed
P	Public elevators
S	Service elevators
⇨	Service entrance
➡	Main entrance

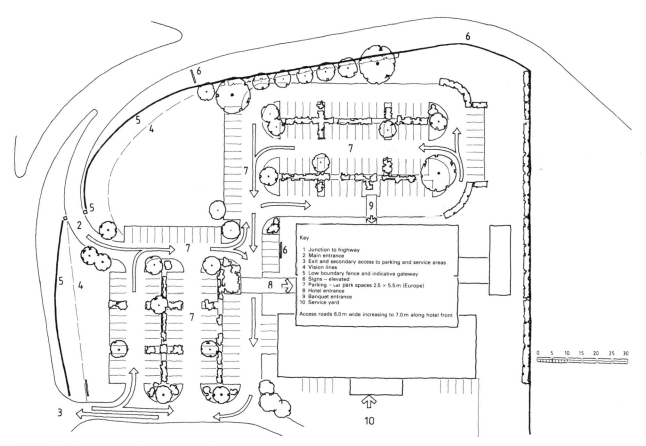

Figure 5.5 Example of access and parking for suburban hotel

generally call for high-density multistorey buildings with basement construction even though the unit building costs may be 10–20% higher.

As a proportion of overall development costs for hotels, land purchase generally represents about:

5% for undeveloped rural areas
10% for suburban and provincial towns
15% to 20% for prime city locations.

Land costs for motels are often 10 to 20% of the total.

Depending on policy, the land may be leased to reduce capital outlay.

5.1.6 Density and height

The development density and massing of buildings is dictated largely by location, land costs and planning conditions. Plot ratios (expressing aggregate of gross floor area/net area of site) used in many European cities and towns broadly range over: 1:1 in sensitive residential districts, 2:1 in mixed urban areas, 2.5:1 in shopping streets rising to 3.5:1 and 5:1 in more concentrated commercial districts like central London and Paris. Plot ratios of 4:1 have been adopted in some of the resorts in Spain with a balance of public open space in promenades and gardens. Height and set-back conditions may also apply to protect the character of the surroundings and restrict intrusion, including existing covenants and rights protected by easements.

5.1.7 Land areas

Typical minimum land areas for 3–4 star hotel development are shown in Table 5.1.

Table 5.1 Typical minimum land areas

Type of hotel	Site	Hectares	Acres
100 room, 2–3 storey	Motor hotel	1.0	2.5
200 room 3–4 storey	Urban, suburban	1.6	4.0
200 room 4–6 storey	City centre	0.8	2.0

Table 5.2 Land areas for recreational and landscaping needs

	m²	sqft
Open air swimming pool (+ children's pool and bar)	750	8 000
Tennis courts (4)	2 700	29 000
Indoor riding stables	450	4 800
Club house	400	4 300
	ha	acres
Golf course 9 holes	14	35
18 holes	28	70

Land areas need to be more extensive to accommodate recreational and landscaping needs, as shown in Table 5.2.

Table 5.3 shows the initial analysis of a 100 room motor hotel.

5.1.8 Future extensions

The initial stage in establishing a hotel is difficult and expensive. Uncertainties arise from possible changes in the economy and markets and the costs of financing large projects and setting up operations are relatively high.

One approach is to provide for a phased expansion of the hotel as future demand increases by ensuring that there is space on site and infrastructure capacity to allow for extensions. As a rule, extensions are comparatively profitable and can be designed to serve known requirements. Guestroom wings may be added, utilizing existing public space capacity, and additional facilities provided (residential suites, conference centre, leisure club, etc.). Future extensions may be provided within the site, by options on further land purchase or by

Table 5.3 Initial analysis of a 100 room motor hotel

	Site coverage (m²)
2 storey bedroom wings	1 650
1 storey public areas	1 350
100 car parking	2 600
Recreation, landscaping	4 400
Overall area	10 000

acquisition of other properties (temporarily used for other purposes). The timing of such extensions is critical and must be planned with other renovation works.

5.1.9 Geographical surveys

Preliminary assessment is usually based on site measurements and available local data. Detailed geotechnical reports will be required for large developments or where there are geological and climate hazards (seismic movements, landslips,

Table 5.4 Utility service requirements for a 100 room 3–4 star hotel

Installed capacity	Conditions
Electricity	3 phase, 415 volt supply (or equivalent) to large equipment. Transformer and emergency generator requirements.
Water	35 000 litre/day (7700 gal/day) domestic supply[a] plus firefighting and irrigation requirements.
Drainage	Foul water discharge 35 000 litre/day. Public sewer location. Peak flow 1.0 to 1.5 litre/s (13–20 gal/min)
Gas	Mains supply availability. Pressure.

Note: [a] Higher in resorts and spas.

faults, adverse soil conditions, potential flooding or erosion). The topography will affect grading and the siting of buildings and car parks. To minimize excavation or fill, existing features may be incorporated into the landscaping. Water-filled ponds may also serve for cooling circulation and land drainage. In a large resort, ground modelling is often used to create features of interest (lakes, canals).

5.1.10 Utility services

The related positions and capacities of public utility services (water, electricity, telephones, gas supplies and sewerage) affect costs and may delay development if additional capacity or wayleaves for services are required.

The provision of generating plants, water bore holes and storage and sewage treatment on site involves careful siting. Emergency requirements must also be planned.

General requirements for 100 room hotel, 3–4 star grades are given in Table 5.4.

5.2 Operational considerations

5.2.1 Circulations

The movements of guests, non-resident visitors, staff and supplies in a hotel tend to follow distinct circulatory patterns. These establish functional relationships between the areas which are associated in providing particular services. In planning layouts it is essential to identify the sequence of steps normally involved in the various hotel operations – both in the 'front-of-house' and 'back-of-house' – and the points at which staff services will interface with guest areas (operational flow diagrams).

Where practical, guest, supply and staff circulations are kept separate

- to avoid disturbances, delay and possible annoyance of guests
- to enable the service areas to be purposely planned for efficiency
- to facilitate control, supervision and security.

It is particularly important to avoid service circulations crossing busy or conspicuous public areas.

In larger hotels some separation of guest and non-resident visitors is also desirable for control and security reasons. This will influence the siting of the front desk and elevators to the guest floors of the hotel.

5.2.2 Public access

Depending on the scale and location of the building, several alternative arrangements may be used:

Table 5.5 Separate public and service access routes

Conditions	Options
Single access from highway (Basement)	Hotel road elevated to prominent entrance Service road ramped down to basement Hotel road direct to conspicuous entrance and car park
(Ground level)	Service road branched off and screened
Separate access from highway	Hotel road from main street or highway Service road from side street

- *Secondary entrances* for restaurants attracting outside custom, to the foyer of the ballroom and function room suite and for the recreational club users, apart from the main hotel reception. Secondary car and taxi access may also be required.
- *Communal lobby or atrium area* giving access to multiple facilities. The lobby may provide a spectacular design. Clear signposting at the entrance and successive points of separation within the lobby is essential.

Convenient routes will also need to be provided direct to the lobby from car parking areas.

5.2.3 External circulation

As a rule separate public and service access roads are provided. Where a common entrance from the highway is necessary because of traffic or site restrictions, the two routes need to be distinctly identified (Table 5.5).

In every case clear street and on-site signposting is essential particularly when shared access or basement car parking is involved.

5.2.4 Traffic generation and parking

Large hotels are major traffic generators and this is often cited as an argument against the development of hotels in residential districts or congested town centres.

Traffic flow predictions are required for cars and taxis used by guests, non-resident visitors and employees. They are also needed for coach and bus parking – for tour and conference groups as well as employees – and for the goods and service vehicles.

The assessment of traffic flows and parking requirements involves a series of calculations using standard formulae for trip generation or computer simulation of the patterns of arrivals and departures (Tables 5.6 and 5.7).

This pattern of movement is fairly typical of business users. In the example, 104 car spaces would be required for hotel guests (1:3 rooms). Evening functions require 24 additional spaces. This could involve increasing the size of the car park or making arrangements to use an alternative park nearby. Local functions and banquets tend to occur at weekends when the hotel demand is lower. Conventions are mainly residential.

Registration, checkout and baggage handling
The same patterns of arrival and departure apply to registration and checkout requirements. Simulation can also be used to estimate the probability of delays and resultant queues.

Registration and checkout at peak times may be speeded by:

- design of front desk with multiple stations linked to both prebooking and accounting systems
- preregistration and direct debit accounting
- additional temporary checkout stations.

For budget hotels, room payment on registration with separate payments for meals and other services is common.

Table 5.6 Example of traffic flow for residents and visitors: four-star city centre hotel

Users	Capacities	Peak occupancy	Multiple factor	Total persons	Cars[a]	Taxis	Others[b] (persons)
Residents	300 rooms	0.8 – night	1.3 multiple room occupancy	312	104	83	31
Restaurants, etc.	100 seats	0.4 – midday	0.6 non-residents	24	8	6	3
		0.6 – evening	0.6 non-residents	34	11	9	4
Conferences functions	150 seats	0.8 – day	0.8 non-residents	96	32	26	9
		0.5 – evening	0.6 non-residents	45	15	12	4
Leisure club	500 members	0.05 – evening	0.95 non-residents	24	8	6	3

Notes: [a]Ratios depend on location and class of hotel, for example:

	Modal split Cars	Taxis	Persons/vehicle Average
City centre hotel	0.5	0.4	1.5
Suburban hotel	0.9	0.1	1.5

[b]Coaches, buses and public transport: may be high near airport terminals or in tourist hotels. Urban planning standards are often based on 1 coach parking bay:200 rooms

Table 5.7 Example of car[a] movement patterns: four-star city centre hotel

Users	07–09 Arr	07–09 Dep	09–11 Arr	09–11 Dep	11–13 Arr	11–13 Dep	13–15 Arr	13–15 Dep	15–17 Arr	15–17 Dep	17–19 Arr	17–19 Dep	19–21 Arr	19–21 Dep	21–24 Arr	21–24 Dep	24–02 Arr	24–02 Dep	Over-night
Hotel guests[b]		−73		−21		−10	+10		+10		+52		+30		+2				
Restaurants, etc.[c]					+8	−4		−4					+10	−5	+1	−5		−1	
Conferences/ functions[a]	+2		+30							−32	+15					−15			
Leisure club[e]											+8			−6		−2			
Net movements	−71		+9		−6		+6		−22		+75		+29		−19		−1		
Spaces occupied	33		42		36		42		20		95		124		105		104		104

Notes: [a]Similar models can be used to show taxi movements.

[b]Departures peaked 70%: 07–09hrs; 20%: 09–11hrs; 10%: 11–13hrs.

[c]Concentrated around meal times.

[d]Highly peaked arrival and departure.

[e]Higher usage at weekends.

Table 5.8 Typical car park ratios[a]

	Motor hotel [b] Suburban hotel	City centre hotel [c]
Guestrooms	1:1	1:3
Restaurant seats	1:5 to 1:2[d]	1:10[e]
Conference seats	1:5	1:10
Resident staff	1:1	1:1
Non-resident staff	1:3	–

Notes: [a] 1 car space:number of rooms, seats, staff.
[b] Overall ratio usually 1:2 spaces per guestroom.
[c] Depends on planning conditions and alternative car parks.
[d] 1:2 for independent restaurant.
[e] For regular non-residential use of restaurant and conference rooms.

5.2.5 Parking

Parking requirements depend on the location of the hotel, market emphasis and local planning requirements for the area (Table 5.8).

In city centres, planning policies may deliberately restrict parking to control urban traffic in any area. For high class hotels off-site valet parking may be provided.

Surface parking

Table 5.9 Spaces and areas per car

	European (m)	American (ft)
Individual parking bay	2.5×5.0	9'2"x19'0"
10% larger bays[a]	2.8×6.0	10'0×22'6"
2% for disabled[b]	3.3×6.0	10'9"×19'6"
Car park areas	m²	sqft
Parking at 90°	18.8	285
Parking at 45°[c]	22.1	345
Overall area with access and landscaping	21–23	320–360

Notes: [a] In higher grade hotels.
[b] Suitably located and marked.
[c] May be reduced by interspacing.

Basement car parking

Basement car parking is expensive and the structural module for column spacing may be dictated by the guestroom dimensions. The width of three parking bays, 7.5 m (27'6") equates to two 3.65 m (13'6") rooms and wall thickness. An overall area of 25–30 m² per car (380–460 sqft) is generally required with a minimum headroom of 2.05 m (7'0"). 10 per cent or more larger bays are provided for limousines and disabled users.

The cost ratio of completely underground parking, under buildings, with mechanical ventilation, sprinklers and two passenger lifts, is 13.0×surface parking on tarmacadam and up to 1.5×an equivalent multistorey carpark with feature cladding and pitched roof.

Taxi ranks

High-grade hotels in city centres and urban surroundings require waiting bays for taxis, additional to the vehicle circulation lanes (Table 5.10).

Coaches

Most large hotels need some provision for coach waiting and parking (for conference and tour groups, airport transfers, staff transport). A minimum requirement is normally 1 parking bay per 200 rooms. Coaches require larger manoeuvring space, wider access roads and high clearances. It is often preferable to allow coach waiting and setting down at a side entrance with luggage storage and transfer facilities adjacent.

Table 5.10 Dimensions required for taxi waiting bays

	European (m)	American (ft)
Waiting bays in line	4.8×1.8	19'0"×6'6" against kerb
Setting down in line	6.1×2.4	23'×9'2" allowing door opening

Typical dimensions of a coach or bus are 12.0×2.5m (European) or 45'×9' (US).

A turning circle of 26 m (compared with 10 m for cars) is usually required together with a wide-swept area for overhang clearances.

5.2.6 External circulation: public

Circulation routes to the entrance must be carefully planned, clearly signposted and well illuminated.

Key considerations are:

- *prominence* of hotel entrance (the approach may be elevated)
- *convenient access* for pedestrians and for setting down passengers
- *wide pedestrian forecourt* clear of traffic – 3.5 to 4.5 m (11'6" to 15'0") for a large hotel
- *one-way approach* to entrance with round-about circulation
- *width in front of entrance* increased to at least 2 lanes for setting down passengers and bypassing
- *taxi and cab* bays, routes for coaches and emergency access

- *porte-cochère or canopy* to shelter and identify entrance
- *signage* and illumination.

Minimum road dimensions (subject to local requirements) are shown in Table 5.11.

5.2.7 External circulation: supplies and services

Vehicle access
Space requirements for the delivery of supplies and removal of refuse and trash depend on the size of the hotel, frequency of vehicle movements and location.

In city centres vehicle access, manoeuvring and loading areas may need to be enclosed within the building envelope. Basement construction is particularly difficult because of the limits on ramping (10%) and high headroom clearances required for trucks and service vehicles (minimum 4.5 m increasing to 4.75 m on slopes).

In other situations, enclosure may be limited to the loading dock itself – if necessary with a canopy extension over vehicle bays.

Typical dimensions for truck movements need to be checked against vehicle characteristics.

Table 5.11 Minimum road dimensions

	Widths		
	European (m)	American (ft)	Considerations
Within hotel site			
In front of entrance	5.5	22'0"	Setting down passengers
Two-lane approach road	4.8	18'0"	Inner radius 6.0 m (20'0")
Single lane (one-way)	3.0	115"	Widened on sharper bends
Footway for pedestrians	2.0	6'6"	Two people with luggage
Street footway	4.0	13'0"	To shops, cafés, bars
Service vehicles and coaches			
Two-lane approach	5.5	22'0"	Inner radius 10.0 m (33'0") widened on sharper bends
Single lane (one-way)	4.1	13'0"	

Maximum incline: 10% on straight; 7% on inner kerb

Table 5.12 Space requirements for loading dock areas

Hotel		Loading dock receiving/refuse storage areas (m²)	Vehicle docking bays[a]
Gross floor area (m²)	Rooms		
5 000	80–100	60	1
10 000	150–200	100	2
25 000	400–500	250	3

Note: [a]A minimum of two vehicle spaces is usually specified. Alternative waiting space may be permitted.

Access will be required for large furniture pantechnicons, refrigerated trucks, refuse vehicles and fire-tenders – in addition to local delivery trucks.

Loading docks

Size increases are in steps with the addition of each docking bay. As a broad guide, space requirements are as shown in Table 5.12. These allow for the frequent deliveries of food and refuse collection by skips.

In addition to the height clearances, access road design must take account of minimum vehicle turning circles and overhangs increasing the swept radius at sharp corners.

5.3 Internal planning

5.3.1 Planning framework

Hotel planning is affected by four main considerations:

- *Location*: site areas, aspects, surroundings, access requirements
- *Scale*: numbers of rooms, range of facilities, space allocations
- *Massing*: concentration of building, structural design, circulations
- *Operation*: guest requirements, standards, service arrangements.

The first three are dependent on the information provided by marketing and site surveys.

Operational requirements take into account service needs and layout efficiency.

Functional relationships

Areas which are associated in use must be identified and linked or grouped together. One approach is to prepare *flow charts or diagrams* in which facilities are arranged in sequence of use.

Other techniques include the use of *method study* to identify which facilities need to be close together for operational efficiency and *computer simulation* to represent the effects of fluctuations in demand and delays in service.

A simplified relationship is illustrated in Figure 5.7. More detailed arrangements are shown in each section.

5.3.2 Spatial requirements

Public rooms   Large spaces: open planned to allow change of function or arrangement.
May need to be column-free (ballrooms, convention halls).
Usually at or near ground level (public access and control).
Individually designed.
External views may be important (vistas, recreational focus).
Close to support areas (foyers, kitchens, equipment stores).

Guest rooms　Compact units with standard-ized fittings and modular dimensions (room layout options within design module).
Repetitive arrangement from floor to floor.
External views important and influence arrangement of floor plans.
Circulation and fire escape requirements may determine number of rooms per floor.
Servicing arrangement incorpo-rated (engineering ducts, housekeeping and room service provisions).

Service and support areas　Areas usually specified for large plant, kitchens, laundries.
Most can be adapted to spaces available.
May need to be near rooms requiring service (kitchens, housekeeping) or near delivery area (stores, plant).
Require separate access and circulation.
Risk of noise or disturbance affecting other areas.

These spatial requirements have a strong influ-ence on the types of structure used in hotel building.

5.3.3 Locations

For reasons of convenience, merchandising and control, the main public areas invariably need to be located at or near street level. Those service areas which are closely associated (front office, kitchens, bar stores) need to be adjacent.

To provide segregation from public activities, quietness, elevated views and greater security, guestrooms are usually on floors at higher levels. Exceptions include:

- Multilevel public facilities where the lobby extends over several storeys as in some atrium designs.

- Restaurant or bars at roof level (sometimes with a revolving floor platform) to take advantage of the views.
- Hotels occupying the upper floors over stores, office, etc. with exclusive elevators direct to the main lobby.
- On steeply sloping sites, the public areas may be more conveniently located at the point of entry above lower guestrooms.
- Resort, villages and pavilion arrangements where the public buildings are separate from accommodation.

High-level public facilities require additional elevators or escalators and provisions for evacu-ation by stairs. Vertical separation of public facilities also increases the space required for satellite kitchens and stores and service circula-tion.

5.3.4 Structural implications

The plan area occupied by the public areas and their support services is generally larger than that of a multistorey guestroom block. To reduce structural and servicing complications of superimposed arrangements particularly over areas which need to be column-free (ballrooms, banquet halls), four main options are possible:

- *Podium extensions* of lower floors to accom-modate the larger public rooms.
- *Atrium or courtyard arrangements* fully or partly enclosing open-plan spaces.
- *Vertical separation* with separate structural blocks as in pavilion hotels, village group-ings and guestroom extension wings.
- *Horizontal separation* using bridging struc-tures to form an intermediary services flow.

In multistorey hotels, layout planning in both public and support areas is affected by the methods of support and drainage given to the guestroom floors above. The numbers of columns in the guestroom structure may be reduced by central positioning on the use of structural crosswalls and/or spine walls with load transference to columns in the lower floors.

(Continued on page 162)

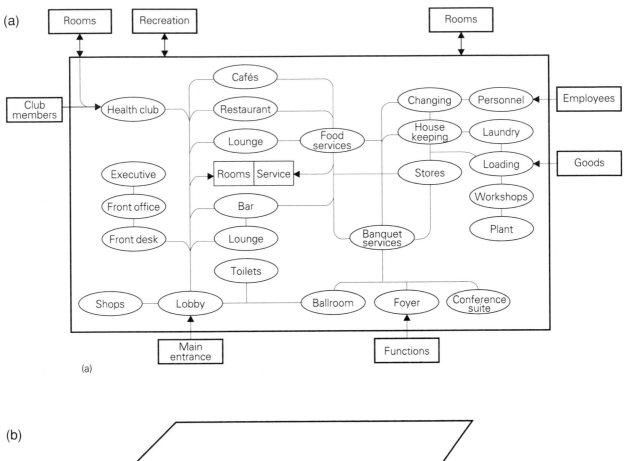

(a)

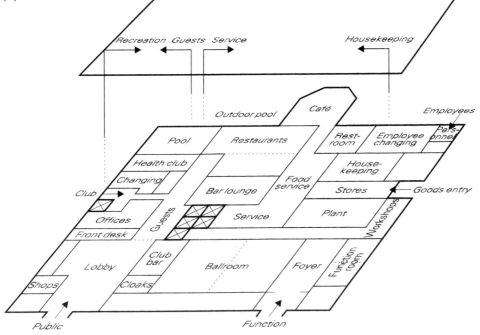

Figure 5.6 (a) Functional relationships and (b) space allocations

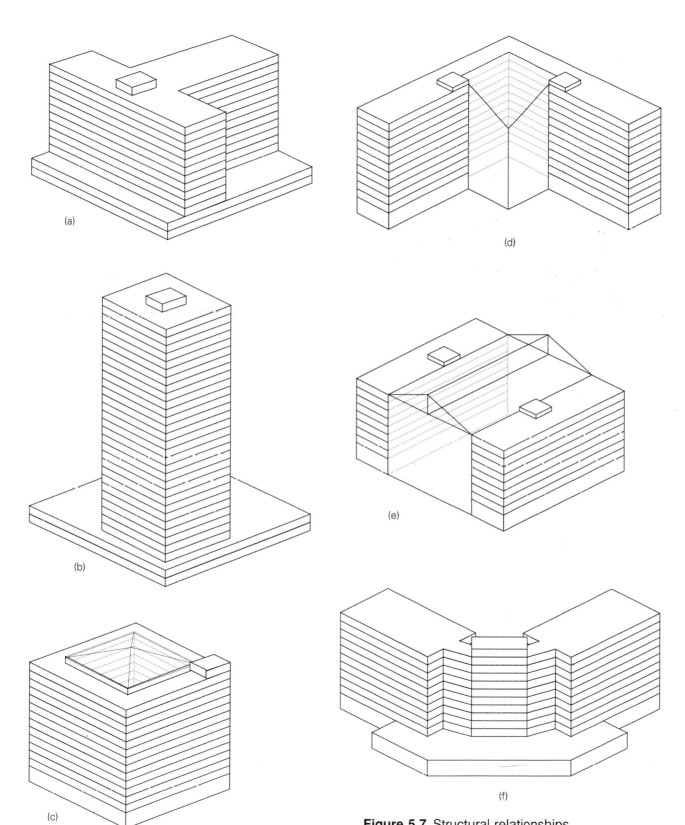

Figure 5.7 Structural relationships

Figure 5.8 *Westown Motor Hotel, New Plymouth, New Zealand*
Entrance to amenities block showing Mount Egmont in background. The four guestroom blocks each contain eight rooms with a central corridor. New Zealand Breweries Ltd. Architect: D.C. Gunter. Photo: Charters and Guthrie.

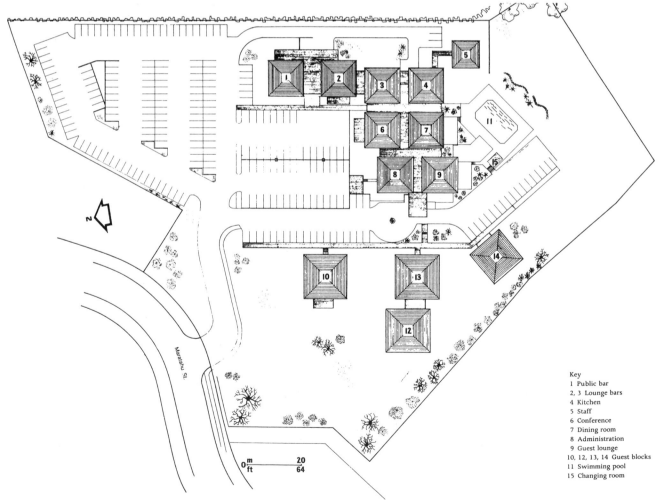

Key
1 Public bar
2, 3 Lounge bars
4 Kitchen
5 Staff
6 Conference
7 Dining room
8 Administration
9 Guest lounge
10, 12, 13, 14 Guest blocks
11 Swimming pool
15 Changing room

(a)   Mayapada Meridien Hotel

Figure 5.9 *Mayapada Meridien Hotel, Jakarta, Indonesia*
William B. Tabler is widely recognized as one of the leaders in hotel architecture and his recent (1987) work is represented by the Mayapada Meridien Hotel, Jakarta.

Occupying a corner site – with provision for linkage to a future commercial centre – this urban hotel is a model of planning for both guest convenience and operational efficiency. In addition to the main entrance there are separate front entries for tour groups and the ballroom and circulations to an underground car park. A rear service drive leads to the loading dock.

The two-storey high lobby forms the hub of circulation, surrounded by a side reception area, speciality restaurant, brasserie and lobby bar which have a view of the landscaped pool. A bazaar-type shopping arcade is located to the side. On the floor above are a business centre and function rooms together with administration offices.

Rooms are grouped into linked blocks containing 11, 8 and 5 guestroom floors respectively, stepping down in a graceful circle from monumental to residential scale proportions, enveloping the pool and landscaped gardens from the exterior traffic. While the design is contemporary it incorporates traditional Indonesian architectural features and motifs.

The back-of-house facilities are at two levels: food storage and kitchens being at ground level adjacent to the food outlets; laundry, housekeeping and employee areas in the basement near the service lifts and plant rooms. A health club is also located in the basement. Architect: William B. Tabler. Consulting Architect: Ateller 6. Structural Engineer: Wayman C. Wing. Mechanical & Electrical Engineers: Howard Osmera & Associates Inc. Interior Design: Inter Art

Building plans

Figure 5.9 *Mayapada Meridien Hotel, Jakarta, Indonesia (continued)*

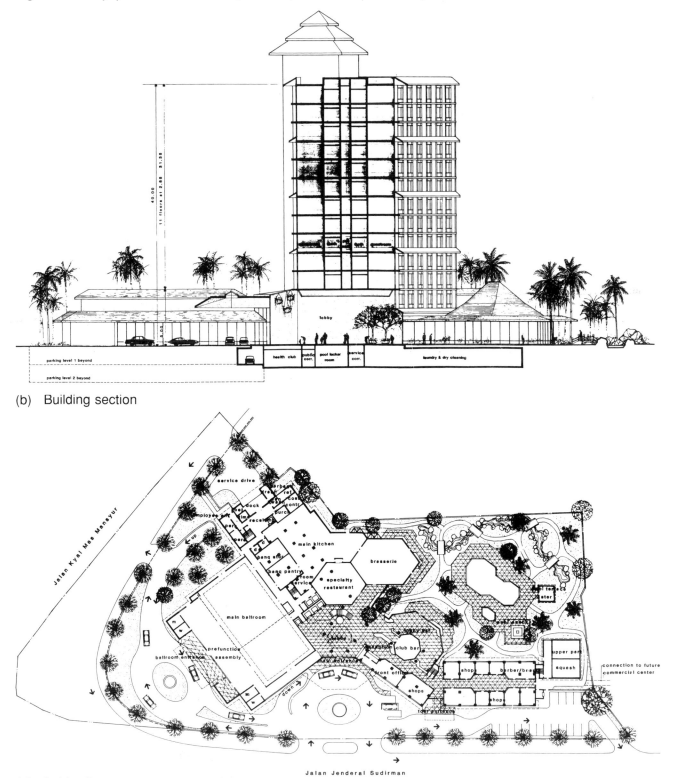

(b)   Building section

(c)   Lobby floor

152

(d) Typical floor

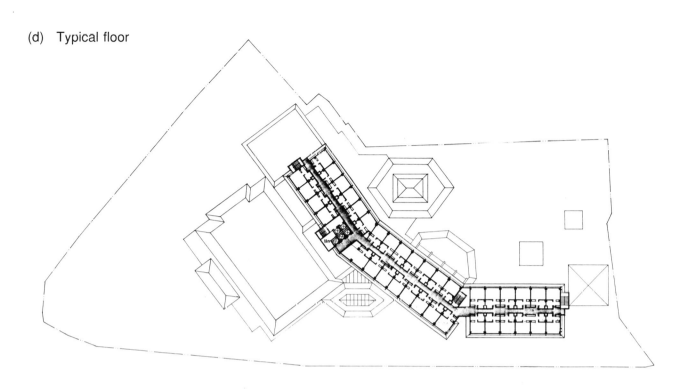

(e) Basement

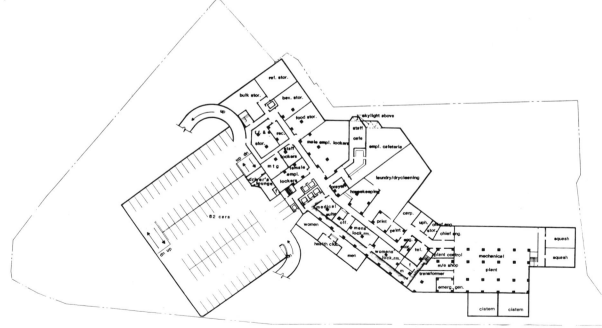

Figure 5.10 *Yokohama Grand Inter-Continental Hotel*
Forming part of the vast Pacifico Yokohama water front development – which includes a Conference centre, Exhibition Hall, National Convention Hall, plaza and parking facilities – the Yokohama Grand Inter-Continental Hotel looks out over the sea resembling a yacht in full sail.

Completed October 1991, the hotel is thirty-one storeys high, with two basements and a penthouse, and offers 600 luxury rooms, including forty-one suites of which seven are in a Japanese style.

Extending into a fourteen storey glass atrium the main lobby features a three storey waterfall and reflecting pool. On the ground floor are group registration facilities and a variety of rooms for wedding ceremonies and conference groups. A

grand staircase and escalators lead to the second floor main registration area together with the lounge and Italian and French restaurants. On the third floor is a 722 m² Grand Ballroom and five private function rooms totalling 426 m², each with an ocean view.

The brief called for international design elements blended with Japanese artwork and styling. Interiors are in cool pastel colours reflective of the seascape. Clients: Pacifico Yokohama; Hotel New Grand Saison Yokohama. Architect-Engineer: Nikken Sekkei (Japan). Interior Design: Media Five (USA); Cheryl Rowley (USA); Consultants: W. Lee Interior Design (Canada) Pierre-Yves Rochon (France).

Site area	100 259 m²
Total floor area	72 672 m² (hotel)
	212 392 m² (including Conference centre, Exhibition Hall, National Convention Hall, Parking facilities and Plaza)
Facilities include	French, Italian, Chinese and Japanese restaurants, all-day cafe, tea lounge, 9 banquet halls, 6 private dining rooms.

Space analysis		
	guestrooms	33.9%
	food and beverage outlets	6.7%
	wedding facilities, retail shops, health club and spa	3.0%
	public areas	20.8%
	administration	4.0%
	kitchens	3.6%
	others	28.0%

(a)   View from Yokohama Bay

(b)   Entrance lobby

(c) Looking up from the foyer

(d) A private dining room of the Chinese restaurant 'Karyu'.

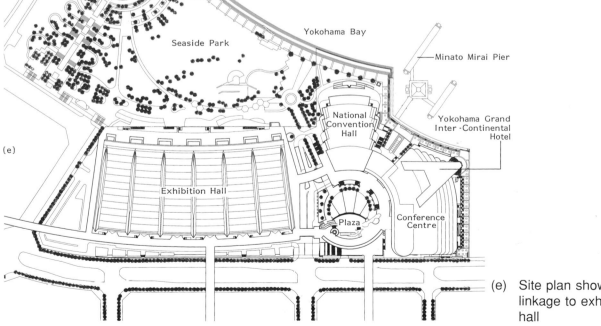

(e) Site plan showing linkage to exhibition hall

Figure 5.10 *Yokohama Grand Inter-Continental Hotel (continued)*   (f)   First floor

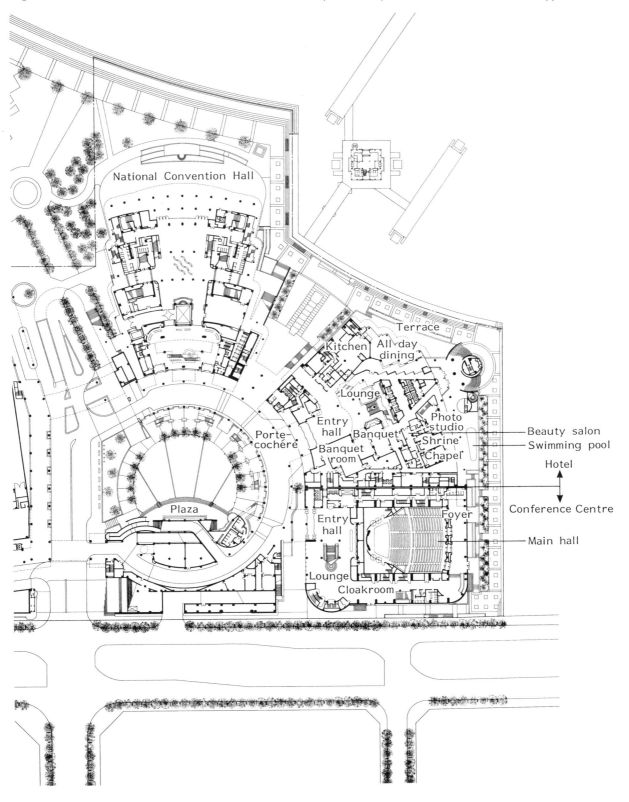

(g) Second floor

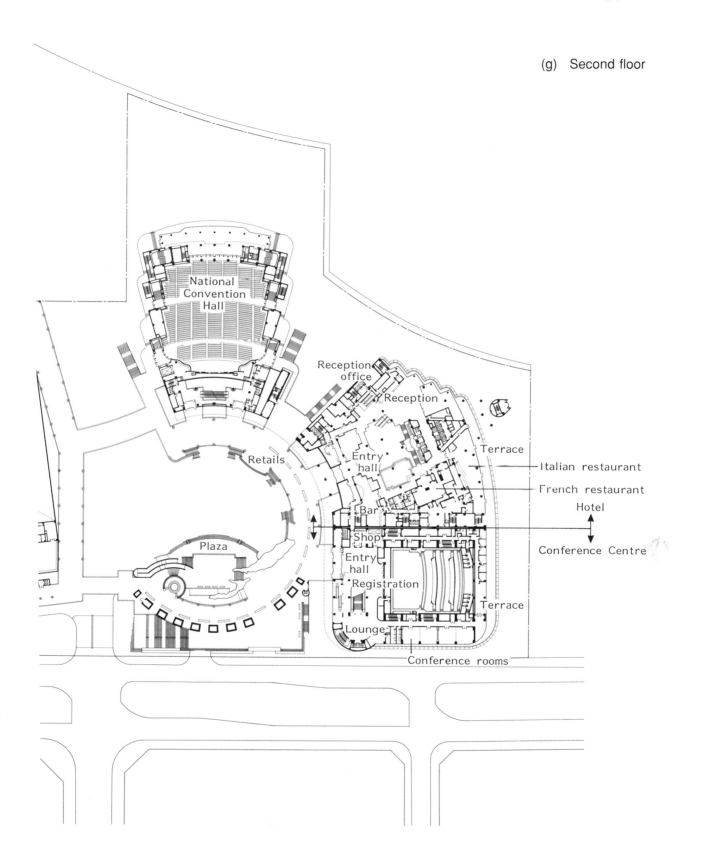

National Convention Hall

Reception office

Reception

Retails

Entry hall

Terrace

Italian restaurant

French restaurant

Hotel

Bar

Shop

Conference Centre

Plaza

Entry hall

Registration

Terrace

Lounge

Conference rooms

Figure 5.10 *Yokohama Grand Inter-Continental Hotel (continued)*

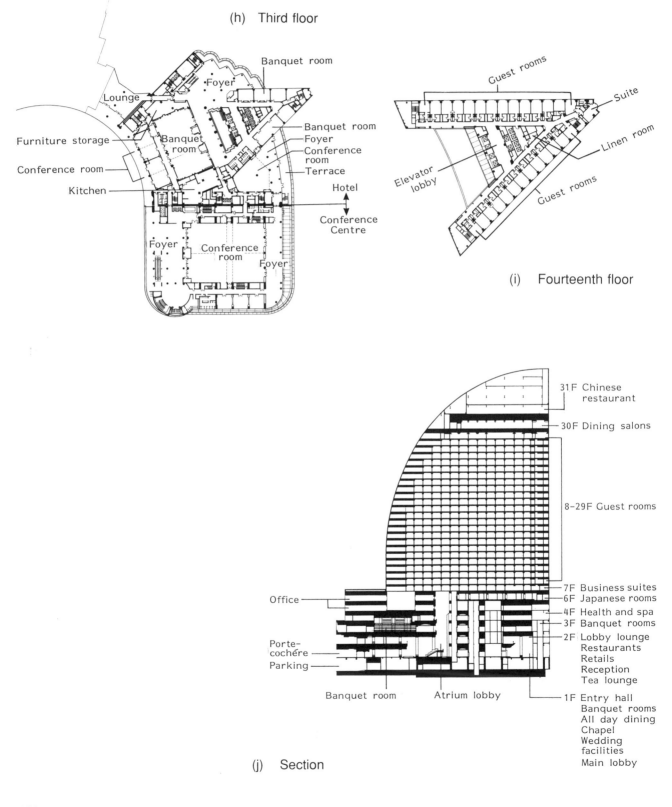

(h) Third floor

Banquet room
Foyer
Lounge
Furniture storage
Banquet room
Conference room
Kitchen
Banquet room
Foyer
Conference room
Terrace
Hotel
Conference Centre
Foyer
Conference room
Foyer

(i) Fourteenth floor

Guest rooms
Suite
Elevator lobby
Linen room
Guest rooms

(j) Section

31F Chinese restaurant
30F Dining salons
8–29F Guest rooms
Office
7F Business suites
6F Japanese rooms
4F Health and spa
3F Banquet rooms
2F Lobby lounge
Restaurants
Retails
Reception
Tea lounge
Porte-cochére
Parking
Banquet room
Atrium lobby
1F Entry hall
Banquet rooms
All day dining
Chapel
Wedding facilities
Main lobby

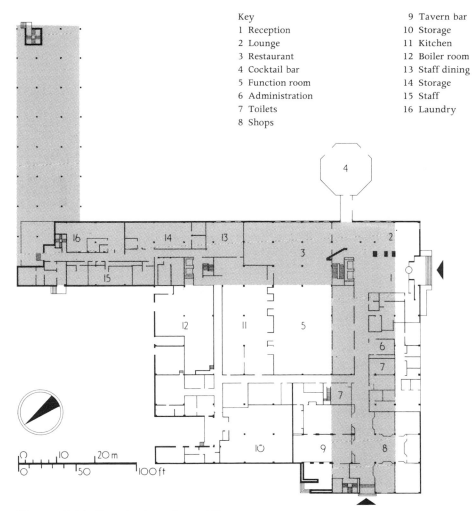

Key
1 Reception
2 Lounge
3 Restaurant
4 Cocktail bar
5 Function room
6 Administration
7 Toilets
8 Shops
9 Tavern bar
10 Storage
11 Kitchen
12 Boiler room
13 Staff dining
14 Storage
15 Staff
16 Laundry

Figure 5.11 *Stratford-on-Avon Hilton*
Layout of public and service areas at ground floor level. The guestrooms, arranged in zigzag wings are partly superimposed. Planning restrictions limited the building height. Architects: Sidney Kaye, Firmin & Partners

Figure 5.12 *Hyatt Regency Hotel, Kansas City, USA*
Sketch of the $50 million Hyatt Regency Hotel with 1000 rooms spiralling upwards to a revolving rooftop restaurant. Architects: Welton Beckett Associates

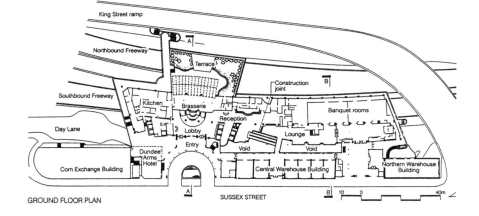

(a) Ground floor plan

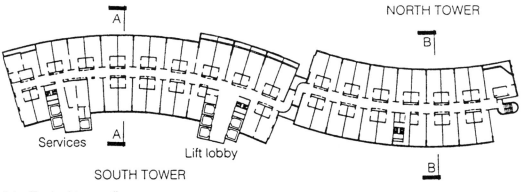

(b) Typical tower floor

Figure 5.13 *Hotel Nikko, Darling Harbour, Australia*

The Hotel Nikko, Darling Harbour is a 645 room hotel comprising a podium at ground and mezzanine levels for retail, hotel reception and services facilities with medium rise towers for hotel accommodation extending 10 and 14 storeys above the adjacent Sussex Street Conservation Area.

A number of existing heritage buildings were refurbished and integrated into the development creating a dynamic and interesting precinct around a historical theme. The shape and structural design were dictated by the long narrow site, within an area of 11600 m² and 210 m frontage bounded by Sussex Street and an elevated freeway along the rear. It was necessary for the building to extend over two lower freeway lanes which are partially enclosed in tunnels.

The hotel is designed to cater mainly for tour coach operations with coach and service access to the basement served by guest and service elevators for baggage distribution to rooms.

The main entrance from Sussex Street leads directly to the lobby and reception with a *porte cochère* between two restored heritage buildings. Function areas for 400 have a separate entrance. Guestrooms are accommodated in two reverse curved towers, the shape, division and textured treatment of the facades giving better visual balance with the historical frontage.

Structural design involved three tiers of requirements:

* structures bridging the in-ground services and freeways

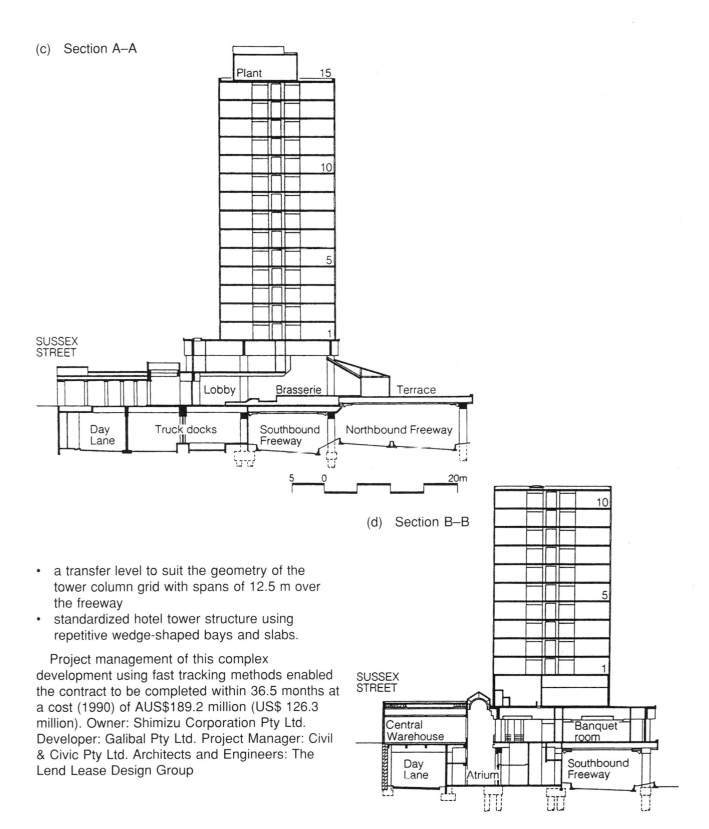

(c) Section A–A

Plant 15

10

5

1

SUSSEX STREET

Lobby   Brasserie   Terrace

Day Lane   Truck docks   Southbound Freeway   Northbound Freeway

5 0   20m

(d) Section B–B

10

5

1

SUSSEX STREET

Central Warehouse   Banquet room

Day Lane   Atrium   Southbound Freeway

- a transfer level to suit the geometry of the tower column grid with spans of 12.5 m over the freeway
- standardized hotel tower structure using repetitive wedge-shaped bays and slabs.

Project management of this complex development using fast tracking methods enabled the contract to be completed within 36.5 months at a cost (1990) of AUS$189.2 million (US$ 126.3 million). Owner: Shimizu Corporation Pty Ltd. Developer: Galibal Pty Ltd. Project Manager: Civil & Civic Pty Ltd. Architects and Engineers: The Lend Lease Design Group

(Continued from page 147)

Larger span clearances may be provided by deep beams acting as bridging structures. The beams may also serve to support structural units suspended below in addition to those built above, to house engineering plant for the public areas as well as terminal and transfer facilities for the ducted services from the rooms, and may be cantilevered out to permit unobstructed sheet facades or overhang other areas.

Outside the plan area covered by guestrooms, public spaces can be relatively unobstructed and lightweight roof structures are generally used.

5.3.5 Guestroom plans: multistorey buildings

Guestrooms may be arranged in rows or one on both sides of a corridor forming a slab plan or stacked around the circulation core of a tower structure.

Slab plans

A linear layout is used for most guestroom plans with staircase cores at or near each end of the corridor. The main vertical circulation is usually central and determined by the positions of the elevators. Double loaded corridors with rooms on both sides are most efficient:

- high net usage of floor space (gross factor: 0.25)
- reduced corridor lengths (for guests and housekeeping)
- structural design and compact engineering services.

As a rule the corridor is central but may be offset in some wings to provide different room formats.

Single loaded internal corridors are used when there are site limitations, (space, aspect, legal restrictions), in terracing down steep slopes and for short linkages. External sheltered corridors are sometimes adopted in pavilion style hotels and budget designs for one- or two-storey buildings.

Atrium designs

These use internal corridors overlooking the central space which may be open or subdivided by mezzanine extensions to increase utilization. Elevators extending through the atrium are invariably transparent for spectacular effect and may be adjacent to the corridor or linked by bridging where there are dimensional changes.

Typically guestrooms are arranged around all sides to facilitate room access, servicing and evacuation. In some cases large areas of glazed wall may be included to improve light penetration and open views to the interior.

The floor space utilization of single loaded corridors is low but can be increased by the use of suites of rooms at right angles to the corridor. Special provisions are required for smoke evacuation and fire protection of the exposed corridors and separate exits to staircases must be provided.

Atriums may be used in urban areas and hostile climates to create an attractive internal environment which can be dynamic and spectacular. The interest created in circulation counters the use of long isolating corridors. To increase space utilization atriums may be extended by guestroom wings of slab construction.

Tower structures

Structural use of the central circulation service core in tower buildings enables the guestrooms to be cantilevered, propped or suspended around the sides. The proportion of space taken up in circulation, including corridors on each floor, is high, and tower structures are primarily used for high-rise buildings where the advantages of views and prominence justify the higher costs involved (unit rates increased by 20% or more). Intensive use of elevators is involved in circulation and servicing (including rooftop restaurant-bar provisions) and special elevators are required for emergency and firefighting access in addition to protected stairs.

Rooms arranged around the perimeter may be in various configurations with optimum ratios of twelve to twenty-four rooms per floor.

5.3.6 Vertical circulation and service cores

Floor plans of multistorey hotel and apartment buildings are affected by the arrangements for

Figure 5.14 Floor plans of slab, atrium and tower structures

Floor plans	Dimensions		Notes

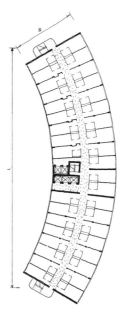

(a) Slab: single loaded corridor (with recessed doorways)

L_1 W_1 — Up to 60 m (195')[a]
Budget 7.9 m (26')
Midgrade 9.1 m (30')
Highgrade 10.8 m (36')[b]
15–18 rooms/floor[b]

Where aspect limited to one side or for short linking sections and in-line suites (corridor lighting)
Low space utilization
Internal gross factor 33–36%.

(b) Slab: double loaded corridor

L_2 W_2 — 65–120 m (195–300')[a]
Budget 13.7 m (45')
Midgrade 16.3 m (53')
Highgrade 19.7 m (65')
44–56 rooms/floor[b]

Efficient use of floor space
Corridors may extend 7.5 m (35') beyond end staircase[a]
Internal gross factor 22–25%.

(c) Offset slab

L_3 W_3 — Up to 120 m (300')[a]
Budget 21.2 m (70')
Midgrade 24.8 m (81')
Highgrade 27.2 m (89')
44–56 rooms/floor[a]

Similar with overlap housing the elevator core and service areas.
Dictates the location of main and service elevators.
Internal gross factor 23–26%.

(d) Curved or segmented slab (with indented closets)

Mid-dimensions similar to (b)

Rooms on inner radius difficult to plan with restricted bathroom widths.
Minimum practical radius 30 m (100').

Figure 5.14 Continued

Floor plans	Dimensions	Notes
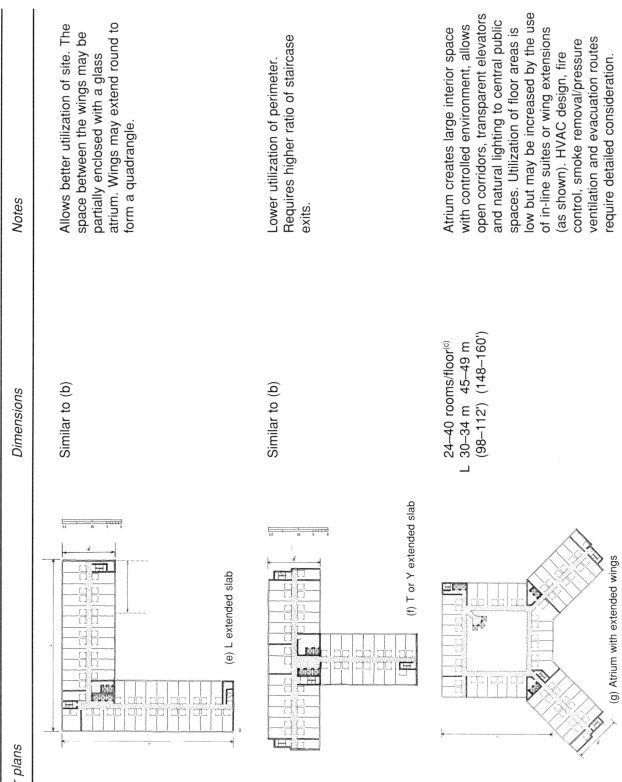(e) L extended slab	Similar to (b)	Allows better utilization of site. The space between the wings may be partially enclosed with a glass atrium. Wings may extend round to form a quadrangle.
(f) T or Y extended slab	Similar to (b)	Lower utilization of perimeter. Requires higher ratio of staircase exits.
(g) Atrium with extended wings	24–40 rooms/floor[c] L 30–34 m 45–49 m (98–112') (148–160')	Atrium creates large interior space with controlled environment, allows open corridors, transparent elevators and natural lighting to central public spaces. Utilization of floor areas is low but may be increased by the use of in-line suites or wing extensions (as shown). HVAC design, fire control, smoke removal/pressure ventilation and evacuation routes require detailed consideration.

Towers require large core structures with single loaded corridors. Space utilization is higher with 16–24 rooms/floor. Internal gross factor 34–36%. With rectangular plans corridor extensions are usually required to corner rooms.

16–24 rooms/floor[c]
L 26–28 m 34–36 m
(85–92') (112–118')

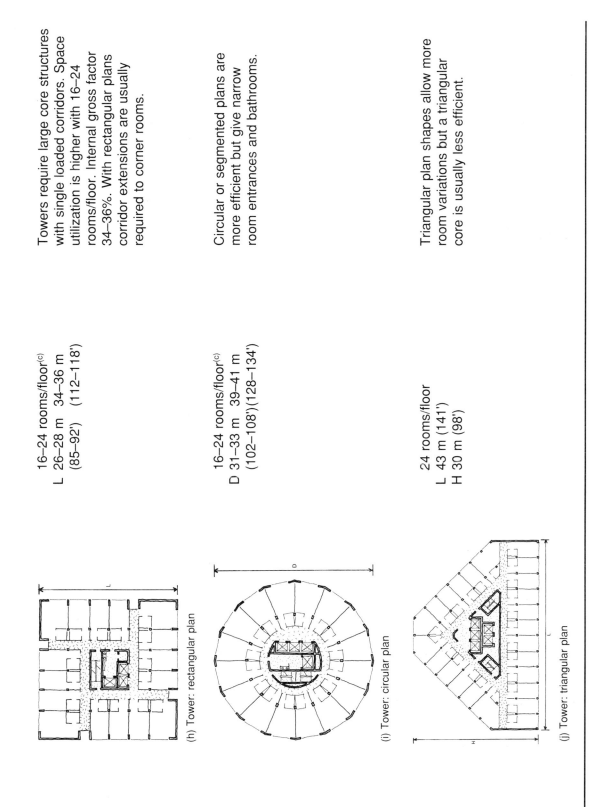

(h) Tower: rectangular plan

Circular or segmented plans are more efficient but give narrow room entrances and bathrooms.

16–24 rooms/floor[c]
D 31–33 m 39–41 m
(102–108')(128–134')

(i) Tower: circular plan

Triangular plan shapes allow more room variations but a triangular core is usually less efficient.

24 rooms/floor
L 43 m (141')
H 30 m (98')

(j) Tower: triangular plan

Notes: (a) Length depends on the permitted travel distance and locations of end and central stairs. The figures are based on London (m) and US (ft) maxima
(b) Based on typical room widths
(c) Optimum number of rooms

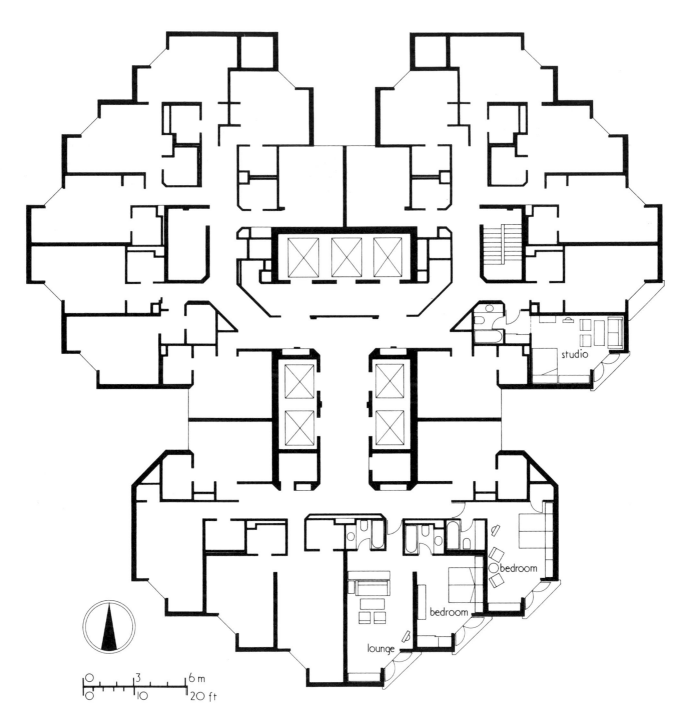

Figure 5.15 *Jerusalem Hilton*
Vertical emphasis provided by three towers
clustered around a central services core, each of
the towers terminating at a different height.
Guestrooms grouped around central circulation
cores. Architects: Y Rechter, M Zarhy. Engineers:
M Peri. Interior Design: Gad-Noy

Figure 5.15 *(continued)*

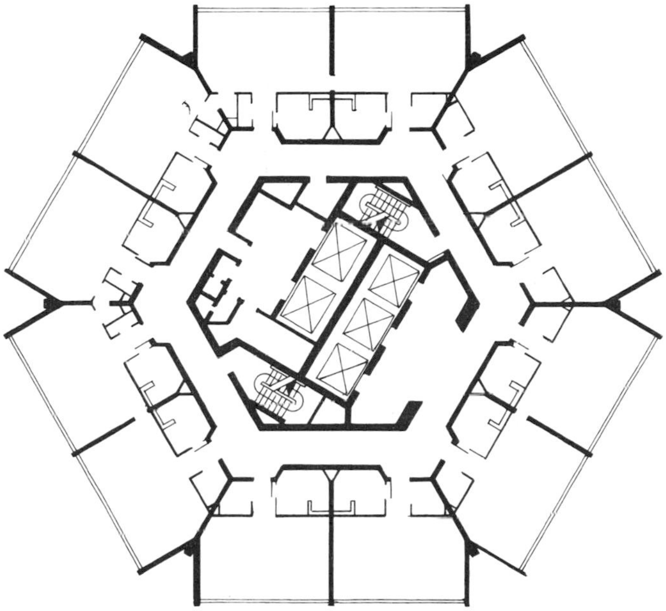

Figure 5.16 *Inn on the Park, Toronto*
Hexagonal tower structure

vertical circulation (stairs, elevators, engineering services, chutes). To avoid risk of fire spreading from floor to floor the shafts and stairwells must be enclosed and protected and there are advantages in grouping vertical circulations together within structural cores.

The positions of stairs are also fixed by fire evacuation requirements which limit the travel distance from any room to a protected exit. Maximum travel distances depend on many factors: the height of the building, fire resistance of construction, availability of alternative routes of escape and installation of automatic water sprinklers. Examples of safety code requirements are given in section 5.6.9.

Apart from relatively short end corridors it is necessary to provide at least two alternative staircases accessible from any room. The secondary stairs can often be utilized for housekeeping and room service access provided fire safety standards are observed.

5.3.7 Location of elevators

As a rule elevators are necessary for hotels over three storeys in height. Some companies require an elevator service for more than one floor level (above the parking level). The needs of the elderly and disabled also influence circulation planning.

Requirements for service elevators for staff, equipment and goods depend on the extent of room service and the relative locations of kitchens, restaurants and function rooms.

There are many practical advantages in grouping the main staircase and banks of elevators together:

- The staircase allows an alternative for emergencies or delays.
- Structural design and equipment installation are rationalized.
- More efficient elevator service, interchange and control.
- Maintenance servicing is concentrated.
- The circulation/service core can be used for structural support or stiffening of the building.

For the same reason, service elevators are often grouped so as to back on to or adjoin the main installation (see section 6.6).

(Continued on page 173)

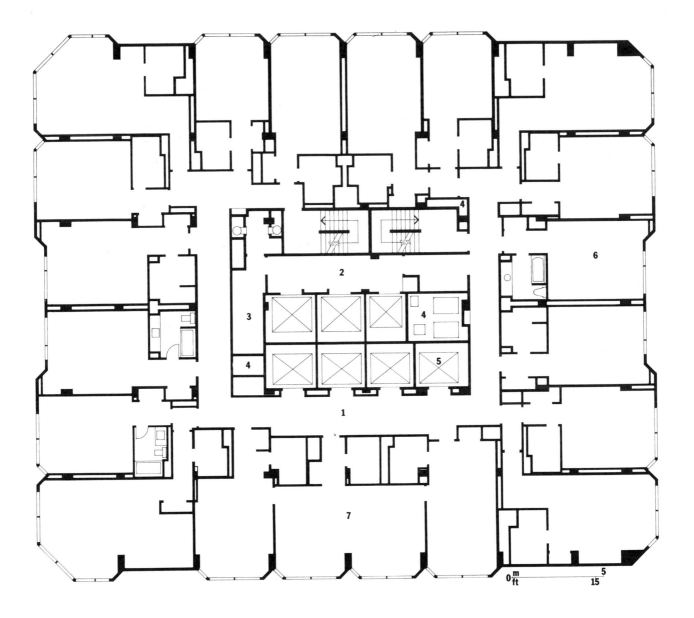

Figure 5.17 *Four Seasons Hotel, Vancouver*
Typical floor plan of tower block accommodating
410 guestrooms on floors 5–27. The hotel is an
integral part of the vast Pacific Center complex.
Architects: McCarter, Nairne & Partners with
Webb, Zerafa, Menkes and Housden

Key
1 Main corridor
2 Service corridor
3 Housekeeping
4 Ducts
5 Firefighters' elevator
6 Guestroom
7 Suite

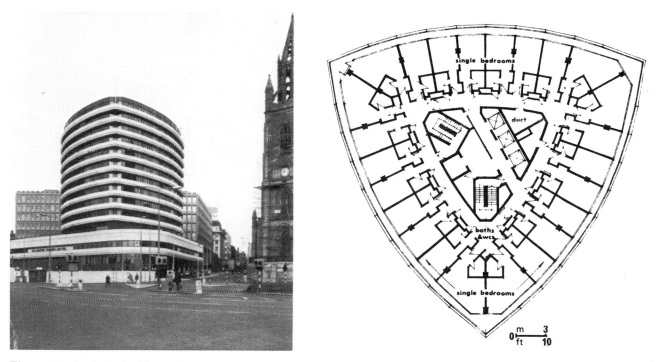

Figure 5.18 *Atlantic Hotel, LIverpool*
(a) Lift slab system of construction, applied to an 11 storey hotel tower block, on a two storey podium. Each floor slab weighed 350 tonnes. (b) Plan of third floor (typical). Thistle Hotels Ltd. Architects: Williams Holford & Associates

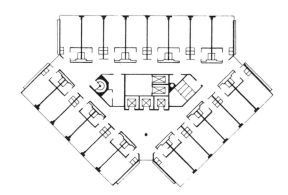

Typical Floor

Figure 5.19 *Sara Hotel Gothia, Gothenburg, Sweden*
Example of triangular tower structure. Architects: Olle Anderson, White Arkitekter Ltd

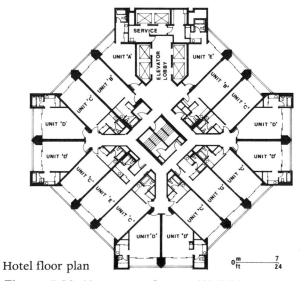

Hotel floor plan

Figure 5.20 *Hemmeter Center, Waikiki*

(b)   Restaurant

(a)   View of lobby

Figure 5.21 *Oberoi Hotel, Bombay*
Completed in 1986 the deluxe Hotel Oberoi, Bombay was interconnected with the earlier and taller Hotel Oberoi Towers to combine the public and service facilities.

The new hotel, on a tight plot, bounded on three sides by avenues, is designed as an atrium building partially open on the west side to allow a scenic view of the nearby bay. Daylight enters the spacious interior through polycarbonate domes, 50 m above the lobby. There are 14 storeys above the lobby level and 3 storeys below including the entrance foyer. A total of 375 guestrooms – 22 of which are 2 or 3 bay suites – occupy the top 11 storeys with the corridors cantilevered out into the atrium in a series of projections housing ventilation grilles and lighting. Architect: P. G. Patki & Associates. Owner: East India Hotels Company Ltd. Operators: Oberoi Hotels

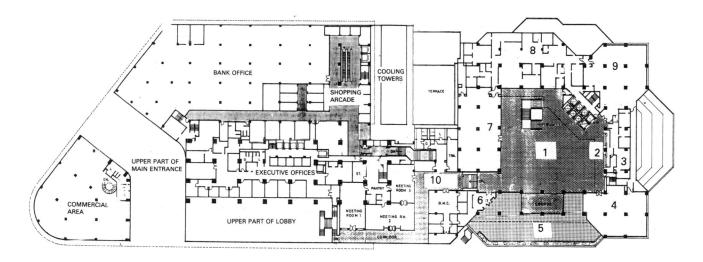

(c) Lobby level

Key

Lobby level (25.5 ft) with shopping arcade below
1 Main lobby in atrium
2 Reception desk
3 Front office
4 Bar
5 Terrace garden
6 Florist
7 Brasseries
8 Main kitchen
9 Rotisserie
10 Corridor to original tower

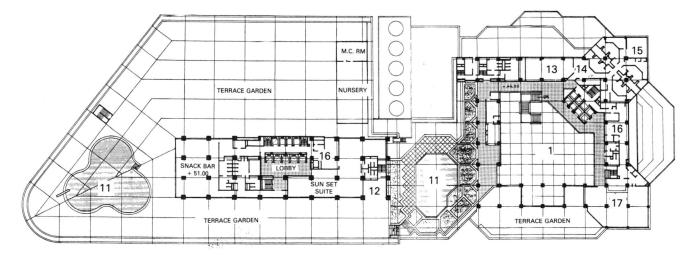

(d) Pool level

Pool level (44.0 ft)
11 Pool
12 Steps to garden of tower
13 Beauty parlour
14 Health club
15 Gymnasium
16 Kitchen
17 Tandoor restaurant

Figure 5.21 *Oberoi Hotel, Bombay (continued)*

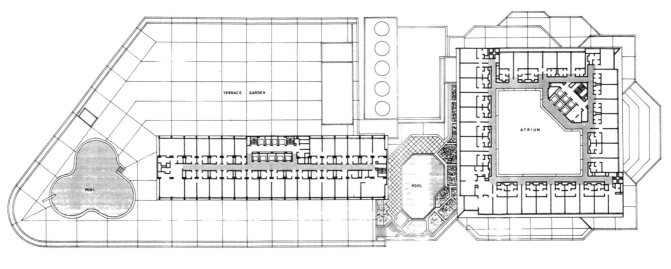

(e) Typical guestroom floor

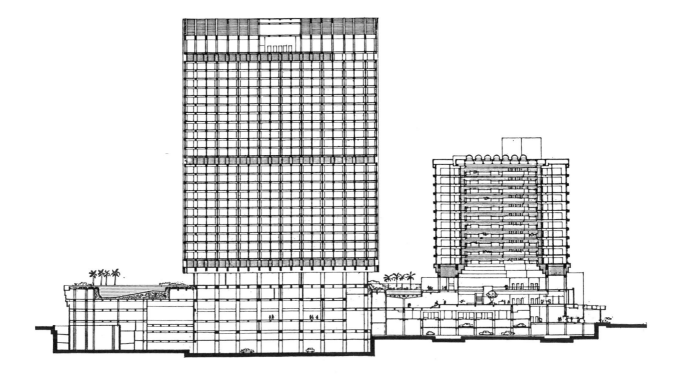

(f) Longitudinal section floor

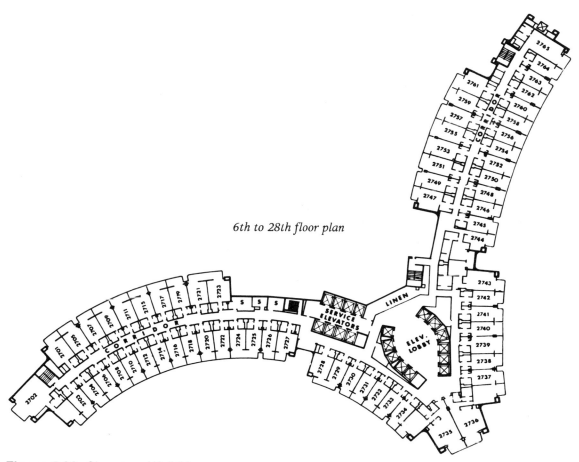

6th to 28th floor plan

Figure 5.22 *Sheraton, Waikiki*

(Continued from page 167)

5.3.8 Room configurations

Linear floor plans may be a single rectangle or combination of rectangles to suit the area and shape of the site. Individual blocks may be straight, curved or circular on plan, uniformly wide or with varying widths to permit different room sizes.

Elevations may show a continuous vertical facade or have projections or indentations to provide balconies and screening or vertical recessing to emphasize height and dominance. Alternatively the superimposed floors may be set back to form terracing or upper levels, or partly projected outward to form overhangs.

Usually the rooms are arranged perpendicular to walls and corridors but acute angled crosswalls may be used with serrated facades.

Curved and circular plan forms, while adding to dimensional changes and constructional costs may be warranted by the extended length and orientation of the frontage.

Towers allow a variety of plan shapes, with the rooms arranged around the perimeter. Square and triangular forms involve extension of corridor access to corner rooms while circular and faceted plans reduce the entry width of rooms.

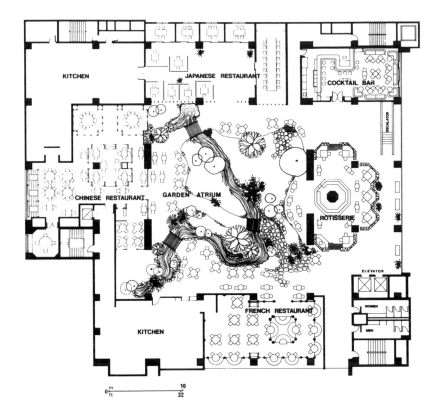

Figure 5.23 *Hayashida Kagoshima Hotel, Japan*
Located in an industrial city the hotel is based on an atrium design with the inner guestrooms viewing into the landscaped courtyard through one-way mirrored glass.

The mirror effect of the courtyard is that of an `infinity box'. Exterior panels are of bronze solar glass and exposed aggregate panels of volcanic ash from the nearby active volcano. Architects: Wimberley Whisenand, Allison, Tong and Goo

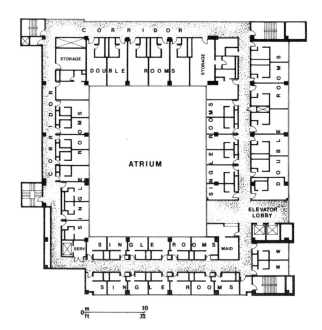

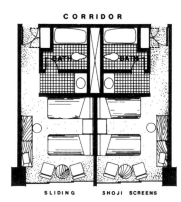

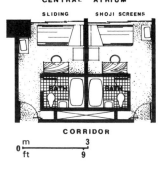

5.4 Building structures

5.4.1 Structural systems

Structural design is affected by many factors: the height and dimensions of the building, stability and loadbearing capacity of the ground and the need for large unobstructed spaces and/or basements underneath are clearly important. The various possibilities in architectural expression are also extensive: emphasis may be placed on individuality of design or on standardization to achieve conformity (Table 5.13) (see section 1.3.4).

The choice of structural systems falls into two main groups:

- Loadbearing walls of masonry or panel construction

- Skeletal structures with floors of beams or slabs supported by a framework of columns and structural cores.

Figure 5.24 Floor slab construction in steel framed building

Table 5.13 Typical design-imposed loads

Area	Intensity of distributed load (kN/m)	(lb/sqft)	Concentrated loads on 300 mm (12") square (Kn)	(lb)
Bedrooms, bathrooms	2.0	40	1.8	400
Restaurants, lounges	2.0	40	2.7	600
Offices – general	2.5	50	2.7	600
Hallways, stairs, corridors[a]	3.0	60		
Kitchens and laundries[b]	3.0	60	4.5	1000
Computer and control rooms	3.5	70	[b]	
Pedestrian plazas, terraces	4.0	80	4.5	1000
Ballrooms, dance halls[c]	5.0	100	3.6	800
Bars, foyers	5.0	100	3.6	800
Gymnasia, exercise rooms[d]	5.0	100	3.6	800
Concentrated storage areas	5.0	100	[b]	
Plant rooms[b]	7.5	150	[b]	
Car parks	2.5	50	9.0	2000
Loading docks, service vehicles[b]	5.0	100	[e]	

Notes: Subject to local codes and regulations.
[a] Not less than the floors to which they give access.
[b] To be determined: minimum loadings indicated.
[c] Higher loadings may be specified for exhibits.
[d] Specific requirements for swimming pools.
[e] Worst combination of wheel loads.

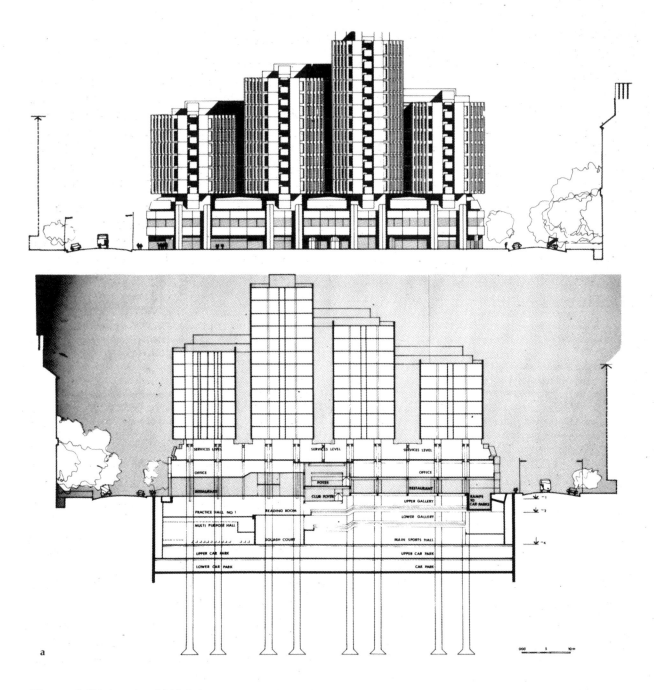

Figure 5.25 *London Y Hotel*
This development of the YMCA provides residential and transient accommodation in four linked blocks above a podium (a), (b). The podium roof is formed by a bridging structure which supports both the towers and the foyer area suspended below. This space also provides a services floor.

Above the podium construction was based on precast load-bearing crosswalls, floor slabs and facing panels (c). Prefabricated services were also used. Room sizes allow for single, double and twin bedded accommodation each having a shower, WC and washbasin(d). Small lounges have been provided in the links between the towers. The tower floors provide extensive recreational areas with two basement car parks. Architects: Elseworth Sykes Partnership. Structural Engineers: Kenchington Little and Partners

176

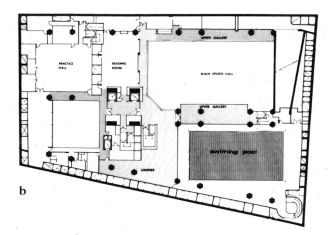

b

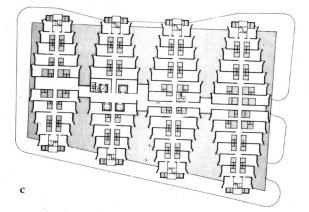

c

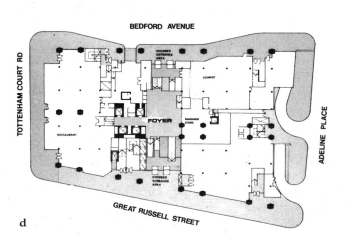

d

5.4.2 Loadbearing walls

Masonry construction

Walls of brickwork or blockwork combine the advantages of traditional construction with durability, good noise insulation and fire resistance. The adaptability and variety possible both in building design and choice of materials and facings allows greater individuality and vernacular styling. Masonry walls are mainly used:

- in low-rise buildings adapted to site conditions particularly in sensitive surroundings
- for crosswall construction separating guestrooms (with the loading transferred to a structural platform having beam and column support over larger span public areas)
- for internal separation of rooms, ducts, corridors, in framed buildings (using non-loadbearing lightweight blocks).

Structural slabs and panels

Widely used in proprietary building systems and prefabrication work, monolithic panels and slabs offer a number of advantages:

- Floor screens and plastering can be avoided by the repeat use of smooth-surfaced forms, power floating and other techniques to leave concrete exposed as the finished surface – saving costs and time.
- Ceiling voids can be omitted – reducing overall building height.
- Precast panels may be used – reducing time and site work in difficult conditions.

Panel constructions in the form of lightweight skin structures on cores of treated wood or metal framing are widely used in prefabricated motel and budget hotel construction.

Buildings may be faced with more traditional masonry or renderings, and can be assembled from panel sections on site or supplied in complete units – such as bathroom shells.

5.4.3 Skeletal structures

Beams or slabs supported by a framework of columns are generally used for large buildings.

Figure 5.26 *The Forum Hotel, London*
Showing the use of slabs and panels in guestroom
wings extending from the elevator core.
Contractor: John Laing & Son Ltd

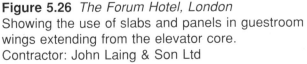

Tall slab and tower structures are of this form and may be designed with the columns extending to the perimeter, or with the floors cantilevered out or suspended from a central framework. Perimeter columns may be incorporated within the wall thickness or arranged outside the wall face as structural mullions.

Structural grids for beams must coincide with the modular dimensions of guestrooms – typically the width of two adjacent rooms – although allowing flexibility in the space and method of division of public areas.

The inherent lightness and structural continuity of framed buildings and lightweight panels tends to create problems from noise transmission, heat transfer and the need for fire resistance.

Noise
- Relatively heavy separating walls will be required between guestrooms.
- Some form of structural isolation may be required for linings (suspended ceilings, floating floors), particularly where adjacent rooms have different functional use.
- Noise penetration through flanking paths (voids) must be sealed.

Thermal insulation and thermal control
- Careful design and selection of external envelope (insulating panels double glazed, shading of windows) is required.
- The internal heating/cooling requirements must be balanced to respond to changing solar radiation, exposure to wind, etc., and the low heat retention of the structure.

Fire resistance
- Protective measures for both structural members and compartments are required.

5.4.4 External envelope: wall construction

Choice of external facing or cladding materials depends very much on the size and scale of the building, structural design, location and characteristics of the area. Company policy may require standardization for merchandising and cost control reasons while, in sensitive areas, the scale of building and external appearances are usually subject to planning conditions.

Greater emphasis is being placed on insulation to reduce both heating and cooling loads and noise entry. Access requirements, life-cycle replacements and maintenance (window cleaning, painting, breakages, decay) are also critical factors.

5.4.5 Roof design

The roof form of a hotel building is often its most prominent feature – either because of its dominating position or due to the topography of the surrounding ground. Coastlines and many other areas of tourist attraction are frequently silhouetted by the outline of hotel buildings and this characterizes the image of resorts. Roof design may also be used to increase awareness – such as in low-rise hotels and motels.

A pitched roof enclosure can house engineering equipment and may be used to add to the accommodation – with dormer windows or mansard roofs. In flat roofs detailed consideration must be given to the location and screening of roof-mounted HVAC plant and prominent features such as chimneys, water tanks and elevator housing as well as the design of any rooftop restaurants or penthouses (Table 5.14).

Structural requirements depend on the spans and loadings involved. The large-span enclosures of public areas may take several forms:

- portal frames – to give maximum ceiling heights over halls
- lattice, truss and other assemblies – to support roof-mounted and suspended equipment in convention and exhibition halls
- space frames – for lightweight enclosures of atriums, swimming pools, etc.
- shell construction for architectural features.

Table 5.14 Roof design considerations

Functional requirements	Details
Exposure, weather conditions, snow loading, thermal movement	Design of roof and coverings for wind and water exclusion, durability, drainage
Reduction of heat loss or gain	Insulation and surface treatment
Noise intrusion (equipment, aircraft, traffic)	Insulation, antivibration mountings, isolation and attenuation
Protection from storm damage, lightning, fire hazard	Specific provisions: lightning conductors, fire resistance
Safety	Barrier rails, access platforms, etc.
Engineering plant, elevator machinery	Loadings, access, maintenance and replacement
Rooftop restaurants	Elevator services, rotating machinery and tracks. Service requirements
Helicopter pads	Areas, loading, access, safety
Natural lighting to internal work areas, etc.	Location and design of roof lights, pavement lights, access, cleaning
Recreational use: swimming pools, landscaped gardens	Specific requirements including loadings, access, drainage, screening

Building plans

(a) Exterior

(b) Lobby

(c) Bar

Figure 5.27 *The Labadi Beach Hotel, Accra, Ghana*
This five-star hotel on a beachside site was constructed and opened within nine months to meet the deadline for a major international conference in 1991–92. Using a Swedish steel frame system, the design satisfied requirements for control, low cost and consistency of materials.

The development includes a conference hotel with two separate two-storey bedroom blocks framing a pool and landscaped lagoon. Interiors utilize extensive locally supplied materials and designs including five hundred pictures commissioned from Ghanaian artists. Architects: Ratcliffe Stott Associates

---

5.4.6 Standardization

To reduce construction, maintenance and restaurant costs it is necessary to adopt standard dimensions for components, fittings and equipment wherever possible. This applies in particular to the repetitive units used in total bedrooms and bathrooms and to most engineering components. Modular dimensions are also essential in structural design and the assembly of building components and must be considered in determining room sizes and relative positions.

Prefabrication is widely used in hotel building to ensure uniform standards and reduce time of construction.

Examples
- Guestrooms may be supplied in parts (or complete shells) for site assembly.
- Bathrooms may be designed as self-contained structures or as fitted out units for insertion within structural voids.
- Pipework services may be assembled in complete sections ready for connecting fittings.
- Much of the engineering plant is in packaged form.

Considerations in prefabrication design
- Risks of damage (e.g. to plastic mouldings or hollow panels) and the facility of repair or replacement without major disturbance or cost
- Life expectancy and resistance to damage, corrosion, decay, leakage, etc.
- Financial limitations in mortgage or loan facilities.

5.4.7 Environmental conservation

While uniformity in design and construction may offer advantages in merchandising and cost control there are many tourism situations which require individual architectural treatment:

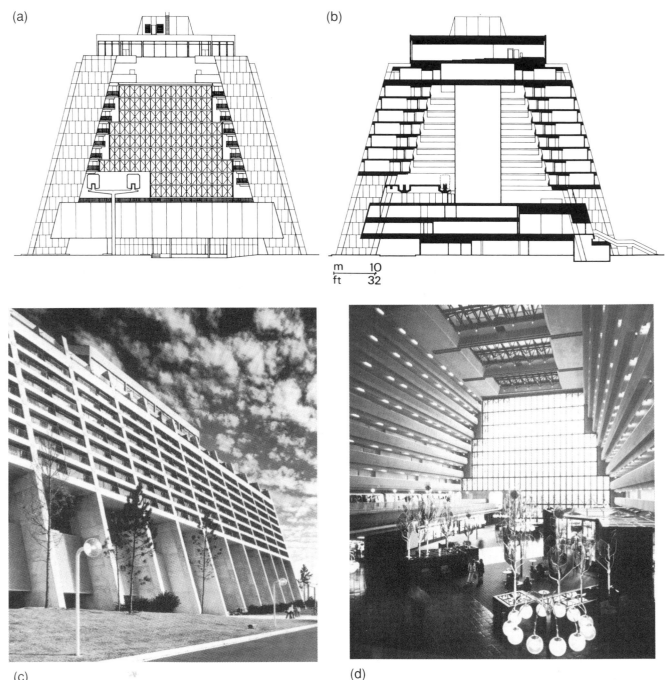

(a)

(b)

m ___ 10
ft ___ 32

(c)

(d)

Figure 5.28 *Contemporary Resort Hotel Walt Disney World, Orlando*
Fourteen-storey A-frame structure (a), (b), with rooms terraced up each side (c) to form a vast interior
lobby concourse through which a mono-rail passes (d). The end walls are glass sheeted. The 1050 room
units were pre-assembled steel construction (e), (f). Architects: Welton Becket and Associates

(e)

(f)

- Sensitive conservation areas in historical towns and traditional villages
- Restoration, conversion and/or extension of existing buildings
- Tourist destination in developing regions, using local materials and craft skills to express the vernacular character.

In addition to the envelope design and choice of cladding materials the scale of the building may need to be limited. In exotic surroundings, local design is best achieved in small units such as holiday villages or pavilion-style hotels.

Consideration must also be given to the fire hazard, maintenance and risk of damage from the use of local materials (e.g. timber) in framing or claddings. Some modification is usually required such as:

- preservation, fire retardation, insecticide, etc., treatment
- limitation of local materials to external claddings or representative areas, features and artifacts
- changes in construction method and substitutions to improve durability.

5.5 Noise control

5.5.1 Planning

Noise control is increasingly important in modern buildings because of:

- *external noise climates*: traffic, aircraft, car parking
- *internal activities*: discothèques, ballrooms, bars, leisure areas and pools
- *equipment*: mechanical plant, transmission noise, vibration
- *sound penetration*: reverberation in large interconnected areas resonance in lightweight structures, impact noise transmission.

Areas and rooms need to be rated in terms of the:

- amounts of noise generated (work areas, user activities)

- sensitivity to noise (bedrooms, meeting rooms).

By zoning, separation and screening, layouts can be planned to minimize the effects of one area on another. Examples include:

- separation of guestrooms from public areas
- screening of sensitive areas from external traffic noise (courtyard designs, sound 'shadowing' treatment of windows)
- grouping and screening of work areas.

Difficulties are most likely to arise in those rooms which have multiple uses or/and may be both noise producing (door banging, loud radio in bedrooms) and noise sensitive to others. Function rooms also need to be insulated from noise (speeches, seminars) and require acoustic design to avoid sound distortion due to prolonged reverberation and unequal absorption.

5.5.2 Standards: ambient noise levels

Acceptable background or ambient noise levels for particular rooms are expressed as noise criteria (NC) or noise rating (NR) values. These show the sound pressure levels over a range of frequencies which represent equal loudness – taking into account the sensitivity of human hearing to different frequencies of sound.

The numerical value of NC or NR curves corresponds to the decibel measurement at the centre frequency 1000 hz (Table 5.15).

5.5.3 Insulation

Standards of insulation are based on the difference in noise pressure levels inside and outside the room. This is usually expressed as the average reduction of noise decibels or measured over a range of frequencies such as the sound transmission Class (STC) rating (Table 5.16).

Table 5.15 NC/NR values

Room	NC or NR	Correction		
		Standard	*Location*	dB
Bedroom	25	High grade	Rural	–5
		Average	Resort	0
		Economy	City	+5
		Considerations		
Convention halls (over 50 seats)	25	Acoustic design for clarity of speech		
		Separation of service areas		
Meeting rooms (20 seat)	30	Sound insulation of partition		
Management office	40	Insulation from lobby		
Restaurant	45	Screening of kitchen		
Gymnasium	50	Separation from noise-sensitive areas		
General office	55	Reduction of internal noise		
Workshops	65			

Note: Lower NC ratings (–5) must be met for persistent pure tones (such as fan motors).

Table 5.16 Standards of insulation

Walls separating rooms		Average dB reduction or STC rating
Meeting rooms	– Adjoining areas, kitchens, toilets	45–50
	– Exterior	35–40
Convention halls	– Kitchen, toilets, plant	50–55
	– Entrance foyers, external corridors	45–50
Front office	– Lobby	35–40
Living rooms/suites and apartments	– Other rooms in same occupancy (except*)	40–45
Bedrooms	– Rooms of other occupancies, public corridors, lobbies	45–50
	– Mechanical plant rooms	50–55
	– Exterior	35–40
*Bedroom	– and exclusive bathroom	35–40

Construction of bedroom blocks is usually based on structural crosswalls which also provide a large mass and high density for good sound insulation and fire resistance. Attention must also be given to acoustic treatment of flanking paths (bathroom ducts, ceiling voids, interconnecting doors).

5.5.4 External noise

Entry of external noise may be:

* *direct*: through open or poor fitting windows, ventilators
* *indirect*: through resonance of the fabric (windows, walls, roof structure).

The noise climate of an area is generally determined by traffic but may also be generated by hotel operations and recreation activities (Table 5.17).

The main factor affecting noise entry into guestrooms is the window (Table 5.18).

5.5.5 Impact noise

This requires separate consideration. The transmission of impact vibration and noise by the structure (footsteps, door slamming) can be reduced by surface treatment (carpets, soft floor coverings, rubber buffers) and by isolation of the area (floating floors, lined walls).

Table 5.17 Noise climates

Approximate noise climates at night	dBa[a]
City centre, major traffic routes	70–50
Suburban and resort areas, secondary traffic	55–45
Rural areas, local traffic	50–43

Note: [a]Average decibel reduction. Varying with distance and time

The impact noise ratings (INR) necessary for concrete floor slabs in guestrooms and apartments are in the order of 18 to 22. This may be met by a carpet and floor pad or underlay (+20 to +30) but vinyl and composition flooring (+1 to +3) and even 3 mm (1/8") thick cork tiles (+10 to +15) are unlikely to be adequate.

Locks, fasteners, stays and closures for doors, coat hangers, etc. should have smooth quiet movement with nylon or similar bearings and rubber buffers or stops. Good fitting and correct hanging is essential. Wall recessed items should be staggered to reduce direct transmission.

Table 5.18 Typical values for noise entry through windows

Situation	Window	Average dB reduction or STC rating
Resort hotel, motels not directly facing highway	Single glazed 4 mm (1/8") glass, openable windows	18–20
Suburban hotels, tall blocks air-conditioned	Sealed, single glazed windows	23–25
Most hotels, windows insulated against heat loss	Double glazed 4 mm (1/8") glass with 20–50-(3/4–2") air gap	30–32
High-grade hotels facing busy streets, highway intersections or near airports	Double glazed with 200 mm (8") or wider space, acoustically lined	40–42

5.5.6 Noise for engineering services

The level of noise generated is often closely related to speed of movement of flow. As a rule, fans, motors and diffusers should function well below their maximum output ratings. Other steps to reduce noise disturbance include:

- location of plant rooms and roof mounted equipment away from noise sensitive areas
- isolation of machine-generated noise by confinement, separation and insulation. Reduction of noise transmission from vibration by the use of resilient mountings and connections
- correct size analysis, design, support and positioning of pipework, ducts and outlets
- attenuation of noise transferred through ductwork and sealing of voids.

5.6 Safety requirements

5.6.1 Legal framework

Requirements for safety are laid down in local ordinances, regulations and codes but the trend is towards broadly similar mandatory standards in all hotels catering for international tourism:

- *Building regulations and codes* governing constructional safety and function

- *Installation and performance standards* for electrical and mechanical services and equipment
- *Specific requirements* relating to fire protection and means of escape in event of fire; food hygiene; conditions for licences
- *Provisions for the health, safety and welfare* of employees in places of work
- *Conditions* for grading, classification, financial subsidy or mortgage
- *Insurance stipulations* to reduce the extent of risk or hazard
- *Obligations for maintenance* of premises in safe condition.

Safety features in all aspects of planning and design and requirements for fire egress have a major influence on the arrangement of rooms and circulations.

With increasing sophistication in technical equipment, the trend is also towards active protection with constant monitoring of conditions and automatic control of airflows and smoke penetration (see section 5.6.12).

5.6.2 Design features: checklist

General
Floors   Surface (non-slip). Demarcation of changes in level and steps

Steps	Location. Demarcation, visibility, edging
Stairs	Proportions. Width. Head clearance
	Flights (minimum 3: maximum 16 rises between landings)
	Handrails, balustrading. Landings
	Fire escape requirements (dimensions, protection materials, exits)
Ramps	Disabled guest circulation. Service circulations (carts, trucks)
	Inclines (10° maximum). Surfaces (non-slip). Handrails (both sides)
Doors	Dimensions. Door swings. Landing areas. Viewing panels. Panic bolts (fire escapes). Visibility of glass doors
Windows	Method of cleaning. Risk of accidental opening (locking). Risk of vertigo if sill height below 1120 mm (44″)
Balconies	Structural safety. Wind turbulence. Drainage. Sill height
Elevators	Requirements for access, support, control, maintenance and testing. Provisions for fire. Lighting. Landing areas. Alternative stairs
Corridors	Provisions against fire (fire resistance, combustible materials) and smoke penetration (closure of smoke doors). Signing. Lighting. Ventilation (smoke evacuation)

Guestrooms

Electrical	Wiring circuits. Protection (fuses, circuit breakers). Earthing or grounding. Locations of outlets and controls
Bathroom	Ergonomic design and layout (space, height, fittings). Positioning of controls. Showers (thermostat controls). Non-slip surfaces. Electrical safety (equipment). Emergency telephones
Kitchen	Space and layout (placing of equipment).
(self catering)	Lighting and ventilation. Electricity connections

Disabled	Access and circulation (spaces). Doors (operation). Appliances (design, fixing, stability)

Work areas

Planning	Space (work, circulation). Equipment (locations, space). Ergonomics (shelf heights, dimensions)
Equipment	Machinery (protection). Hot surfaces, flames. Electrical safety (separation, control)
Environment	Lighting. Ventilation (temperatures, humidity). Noise. Floors (cleansing, drainage, non-slip)

Management

Instruction	Information. Procedures (accidents, fires)
First aid	Training. Treatment facilities
Maintenance	Organization (planning, testing)

5.6.3 Fire safety

Requirements for fire protection and means of escape in the event of a fire have a major influence on the layout and construction of a hotel (see section 5.3.6). Fire safety is important in all hotels and resort complexes because of:

- large numbers of people sleeping on premises, in separate rooms, unfamiliar with the building and warning systems
- concentration of temporary visitors attending events: functions, conventions, restaurants, etc.
- staff on duty intermittently and in different departments
- fire loadings often high due to furnishings; many parts (kitchens, stores, workshops, garages) present a high fire risk.

Fire safety covers three main aspects:

- *Structural protection*: includes the *fire resistance* of the building elements and components and limitations on the use of *combustible materials* and finishes which have a high rate of *surface flame spread*.

- *Active protection*: covers the automatic detection of fire (heat, smoke, carbon dioxide), warnings and fire fighting equipment of various kinds.
- *Means of escape*: for the occupants in event of fire is concerned with travel distances to safe exits, identification and protection of escape routes and evacuations from the building.

5.6.4 Standards

Statutory requirements for fire protection and safety vary from one administrative authority to another and are mainly concerned with passive defence. Technical standards for safety, which are often deemed to satisfy local codes and regulations, are published by a number of institutions, for example:

USA: National Fire Protection Association (NFPA), National Bureau of Standards (NBS) and Underwriters Laboratories (UL).

Europe: International Standards Organization (ISO), European CEN and CENLEC Standards, British Standards Institution (BSI) and other national bodies.

5.6.5 Structural protection: fire resistance

Fire resistance is necessary to compartmentalize and delay the growth of fire whilst also protecting evacuation routes and the structure of the building.

The periods required for fire resistance depend on the class of use (hotel, assembly, parking areas, etc.), building height and floor or compartmented area (Table 5.19).

The figures indicated meet most code requirements but may be reduced for small buildings (Table 5.20).

5.6.6 Surface flame spread

To limit the rate of flames spreading across the surfaces of rooms (public areas, corridors), the class of finishes for ceilings and walls is usually specified. The requirements also consider the generation of inflammable and toxic gases and smoke, the risk of materials shattering, melting or distorting and the stability of fixings.

Categories
NFPA   5 classes from A (0) (non-propagating) to E (500) (very high rate)

BSI   0 (incombustible) to 4 (rapid).

Table 5.19 Fire resistance standards

Elements	Fire resistance period (minimum – hours)	
Structural frame Loadbearing and fire division walls	2–4	Depends on height and floor area[a]
Floors, roofs, Other external walls	2	Depends on distance to boundary and volume
Enclosures for stairs[b] elevator, etc., shafts	2	Doors usually 1 hr: self-closing
Guestroom walls to corridor.	1	Doors ½–¾ hr: self-closing
Interior partitions	1	Walls between guestrooms
Separation of ballrooms, enclosed restaurants, etc.	2	Nightclubs, discothèque, theatre may be 3 hr
Separation of enclosed parking, high-risk workshop and plant areas	2	Boiler house, generator, transformer, switchgear, laundry/dry cleaning, maintenance shops, furniture stores

Table 5.20 Fire resistance standards for small buildings

UK	Building height	Maximum area per storey[a]	Minimum fire resistance[b] Basement	Other
Structural elements	Up to 28 m	3000 m²	1½ hr	1 hr
	No limit	2000 m²	2 hr	1½ hr

Notes: [a]Floor or compartmented area.
[b]Periods may depend on use of automatic sprinkler systems.

Standards

Subject to local requirements, interior finishes are generally limited to:

Class B–C (26–75–200) or 1–2 for public areas
Class A–B (0–75) or 0–1 for lobbies, foyers and corridors.

The decorative treatment must also be taken into account. The use of automatic sprinkler systems may allow one class higher from that normally required.

Furnishings

Furniture and furnishings must also be considered:

- the use of flame-resistant materials and linings
- flame-retarding treatment of curtains and drapes
- prohibition of flammable and toxic materials (e.g. polyurethane foams).

5.6.7 Active protection (See Table 5.21 below)

Table 5.21 Provision in the event of fire

Examples	Typical provisions	(m)	(ft)	
Access for firefighting vehicles and appliances	Width	3.66	12	Wide hardstanding for hydraulic platform
	Clearance	3.66	12	
	Turning	18.0	62	
	Extended reach	20–30	65–100	
Fireman's lift	Required in buildings over six storeys with independent power, external access and protected enclosure			
Fixed equipment for manual operation	Wet and dry risers to hydrants and hoses located in main areas of circulation without 20 m (65 ft) of every part of the building. Mounted in recesses			
Automatic detection alarm and control systems	Temperature, carbon dioxide, smoke and fume activation of automatic alarm(s), indicator panels, electromagnetic release catches for smoke doors, exhaust and relief ventilation and dampers to isolate other ventilation ducts, water sprinkler and water curtain systems, elevator controls, etc.			
Portable appliances in areas of high risk (kitchen, boiler houses, workshops, electrical switchgear)	For control of small local fires, including fire blankets (fat fires), carbon dioxide (electrical), foam, dry power or vaporizing liquids. Appliances must be clearly marked with instructions, and regularly serviced			

5.6.8 Means of escape

Lifesaver codes lay down requirements to ensure a building can be fully evacuated within 2–3 minutes. The method of calculating the number and sizes of exits varies but usually covers the requirements given in Table 5.22 and 5.23.

5.6.9 Travel distances

The maximum distance to a protected exit is shown in Table 5.24.

Table 5.22 Room capacities: Maximum room occupancies based on areas

	m²/person	sqft/person
Restaurants and lounges	1.0–1.5	10–15
Bars, foyers (standing areas)	0.3–0.5	3–5
Guestrooms (two persons/room) over	10.0	(110 sqft)
Places of assembly	0.5–0.6	6–7

Table 5.23 Minimum number of exits from public rooms

Occupants	Exits
Up to 50[a]	1 (at ground floor level only)
Up to 500	2
Up to 750	3
Up to 1000	4

Note: [a]30 for small restaurants and bars above or below ground level.

Table 5.24 Maximum distance to a protected exit

	Conditions	Typical UK[a] (m)	USA[b] (m)	(ft)
Within rooms				
Ballrooms, conference halls, restaurants, lounges	2 or more exits	30[d]	45	130
Small restaurants and shops	1 exit	12[e]	60	200[c]
Apartments, suites	1 exit	9	15	50
Kitchens, boilerhouses	2 or more exits	12[d]		
Car parks (high-risk areas)	1 exit	6		
Through atrium space			30	100
Along corridors to protected stairs				
From any guestroom	2 directions	60[f]	30	100
			45	150[c]
	1 direction only	7.5	10.6	35[c]

Notes: [a]Based on requirements in London. Distances are direct to exit: actual travel distances may be 1½ times.
[b]Generally follow NFPA guidelines.
[c]With automatic sprinkler systems installed.
[d]Exits at angle of 45° from any position.
[e]Other than street level.
[f]Distance between exits. Self-closing smoke doors 30 m apart.

5.6.10 Widths of exits.

Corridors and stairs are based on a unit width of 560 mm (22in) (the average width of a person) with a minimum width of 2 units:1.1 m (44in) (Table 5.25).

Table 5.25 Exits by width

Persons per[a]	unit width
Ground floor exits:	
places of assembly	70–87.5[b]
Escape routes on	
guestroom floors	112[c]
Each staircase	112 + 50 per additional storey[d]

Notes: [a]Depending on local codes. Minimum 1.1 m (44in) wide.
[b]In steps of size: 87.5 maximum.
[c]Hazardous areas – may be reduced 50%.
[d]For each staircase. Assuming even distribution of persons.

Example

Conference hall areas	450 m^2
Maximum capacity (450 ÷ 0.6 m^2)	750
Aggregate exit width (750 ÷ 87.5×0.56)	4.8 m
Exits: minimum 3	each 1.6 m

(check: travel distance not more than 30 m)

5.6.11 Protected staircases: multistorey buildings

Typical requirements:

- At least 2 staircases normally required
- Sited on external wall with windows openable on each storey. Internal stairs must have automatic mechanical ventilation (section 5.6.12)
- Protected lobby or corridor to separate basement areas
- Minimum width 1.1 m (44 in): increased to 1.4 m (55 in) for buildings over 30 m (100 ft) height
- Stairs more than 1.8 m (72 in) wide must be in two halves (minimum 1.1 m width), separated by a central handrail.

Doors

Doors must open in the direction of escape without obstruction. Locked doors must have panic release mechanism. Revolving doors may not be acceptable unless there are side doors immediately adjacent and exit doors from places of assembly should normally have two equal leaves. Landings must be at least 900 mm(3'0") wide.

5.6.12 Smoke control

Provisions for control of smoke and hot gases include:

- ventilation of protected staircases and evacuation routes, with entry doors sealed against smoke penetration
- installation of exhaust fans at roof level in atriums, above lift shafts etc., with positive control of airflow movement away from corridors
- use of computer-controlled dampers and fans (with mechanical back-up system) to close air supply to areas affected by fire and maintain positive pressure in other corridors and stairwells.

All installation of fire and smoke control – including fireman's lifts, water pumps, computer-operated and manually controlled ventilation systems – must be connected to emergency power supplies.

5.6.13 Other provisions

Typical requirements:

Correct signposting	Size, colour and independent illumination detailed
Emergency lighting	Minimum 12 lux (1.2 lumens/sqft)
Smoke doors	Automatically self-closing with electromagnet catches
Warning systems	Automatic detection and alarm systems. Message relay to guestrooms. Manual break glass buttons. Indicator panels. Relay systems to fire authority

Table 5.26 Security

Application	Typical installations
Points of entry	
Windows and balconies	Low level and connected areas fitted with grilles and locks
Fire escape exits	Door release mechanism relayed to indicator panel in security office or reception desk
Employee's entrance	Visible to security office. CCTV cameras installed
Goods entrance	Loading dock fitted with metal shutter or grille. Goods receiving or storekeepers office adjacent. CCTV cameras may monitor loading dock areas
Public entrance	Visible from front desk and bell captain's station. CCTV system in entrance and lobby
Guest circulation	Elevator lobby visible from desk and/or CCTV system
Guestrooms	Master key locking or electronic card access systems installed. Internal dual lock facility
Belongings	
Safe deposit facilities	For guests (see section 6.3.8)
Strong room and safes	For cash and accounting adjacent to front desk and audit office
Baggage store	With street entrance (see section 6.2.5). Separate storage and baggage lift access may be provided near coach entrance
Hotel stores: high value goods	Entrance may be controlled by coded electronic card or security systems, windows etc. secured
Grounds and equipment	
Floodlighting	Used for dual recreation and security benefit
Lockable stores	For recreation and maintenance equipment
Fencing: if unavoidable	Unclimbable impenetrable ring fences separating vulnerable or hazardous areas
Closed-circuit TV systems	With directional lighting or infrared equipment to monitor grounds

Management obligation
Compliance with requirements (notices, signs, maximum capacities). Maintenance and regular testing or equipment and exits. Training and instruction of employees. Fire drills.

5.7 Security

5.7.1 Coverage

Security is an important consideration for guests in unfamiliar surroundings, for confidential meetings and for the control of loss and damage of property. In operational terms, security must be effective without becoming obtrusive or unduly restrictive (Table 5.26).

5.7.2 Systems

Security systems can be broadly grouped into four categories.

Automatic detection and warning apparatus
These cover various kinds of sensors which are connected to an amplified relay circuit which may activate an alarm and/or indictor panel. The sensors include:

- *magnetic pressure or vibration* contacts in entrances, doors, windows
- *infrared* beams across entrances and passages to operate doors
- *microwave or ultrasonic* waves for the volumetric protection of rooms.

Closed-circuit television systems

CCTV is widely used to monitor movements. Cameras must be carefully sited to avoid direct or reflected light glare, allow a traversing area of view and provide concealment. They are used for continual scanning, recording and closer observation with monitors mounted in the security office.

Locking systems

Door locks involve considerable cost in installation and replacement with the possibility of keys being lost or stolen. Mechanical locks may be based on replaceable lever or tumbler mechanisms and must include an internal night latch and/or bar facility. Master key systems provide for a hierarchy of keys allowing multiple access:

- *Master* – management (all guestrooms)
- *Sub-master* – housekeeper, security (complete floors)
- *Area-master* – housekeeping staff (floors, groups of rooms)
- *Individual* – guests (rooms)

Electronic systems

Keys may be substituted by cards printed with a code to operate a programmed sensor which controls the locking mechanism. Programmes can be varied for individual or multiple access and for specific periods of time. The card may also provide access to chargeable services and be used for automatic billing.

6

Hotel entrances, lobbies and circulations

6.1 Entrance

6.1.1 Signage

Signs and symbols are an important aspect of merchandising service to identify the hotel, provide information and direct visitors to the various facilities. At the same time, the graphic design must subtly suggest the status and character of the hotel in order to create and reinforce customer cognition, confidence and loyalty.

Signage and graphic design must be consistent throughout the hotel and coordinated with interior design.

Restrictions
- Size, design and illumination of signs are usually subject to planning controls.
- Siting outside the curtilage may be prohibited.
- The highway authority may install standard roadside signs.
- Licensing registration and grading symbols need to be displayed at the entrance.

Identification
- Graphic symbols may be incorporated in the building facade.
- The hotel name and insignia are usually located at side of door or *porte-cochère* and at the road entrance.
- Corporate styling is also represented in canopies, flags, exterior furniture and uniforms.

Directions
- Clear directions to the guest entrance, disabled access, function areas, recreation club and service areas.

Illumination
External lighting improves visibility and merchandising, security and safety. Systems include:

- floodlighting and feature lighting of buildings and gardens
- colonnade lighting of access roads, paths, parking
- direct or self-illumination of signs
- soft lighting of entrances, windows, interiors.

6.1.2 Landscaping

Landscaping softens the appearance of the building, provides screening and shelter for car parking and service areas, and an improved outlook for public areas and guestrooms. In larger sites the landscape plan encompasses recreational attractions (pools, tennis courts, golf courses, etc) as well as lawns and terraces for extension of hotel functions.

Generally, the landscape design provides a balance of natural and planted areas with hard pavings and features (water fountains, pools, sculptures) to provide focuses of interest. Mature trees are usually retained in site development.

The external landscaping is often complemented by indoor planted arrangements bringing a refreshing garden ambience into the building and serving to separate and screen particular areas. Interior landscaping may range from contemplative compositions (rock and sand gardens) to specific focuses (water features) and planted arrangements providing a neutral background or a conversation piece.

Key planning considerations for interior landscaping are the locations, degree of permanence, lighting and environmental conditions, accessibility, watering and drainage, stability, maintenance and replacement. Contract arrangements are usually employed.

6.1.3 Main entrance

The appearance presented by the main entrance and its approach is critical since this tends to typify the hotel. The entrance must be clearly defined and provide a good view of the interior.

The main features are:

Pedestrians (direct or from car park)	Distinctive paths (separated from traffic), signs and lighting (shadows avoided). Video cameras may be mounted for security
Taxis, cars	Traffic intensity and car parking (see section 5.2) Forecourt 5.5 m (22') or more wide. Circulation to car park. Provisions for taxi ranks, valet parking, waiting bays
Coaches	Minimum 1 parking bay:200 rooms. May lead to separate entrance for tour groups
Disabled	Signed routes with ramp inclines (maximum 1:10). Easily operated doors, wide corridors
Shelter	Canopy over entrance or *portes-cochère* (to extend cover) over main and banquet entrances. Clearance may be required

	for coaches (minimum 3.85 m) and emergency vehicles. Heating may be installed
Lighting	Soft lighting with recessed lamps in the underside of the canopy, screened wall lights and vestibule lighting illumination intensity increased from 200 lux (22 lumen/sqft) in the lobby entrance to 400 lux (45 lumen/sqft) at the reception desk
Security	Entrance visible from front desk. Video cameras, infra-red controls and automatic locking–releasing security systems may be installed
Luggage	A separate luggage entrance (at street level) may be provided with luggage storage, porterage desk and elevator(s) adjacent.

Separate entrances may be required for:

Banquets	For large numbers of conference and function users, with direct access to the foyer
Leisure club	Individual entrance for club reception, access to changing rooms also from hotel
Restaurants/shops	Additional street entrances for popular bars, cafés, restaurants (e.g. patisserie, brasseries, bistro style, English pubs)
Apartments	Serviced apartments, residential suites, offices, etc., with private foyer and elevators
Employees	Separated from guest areas, leading to control areas.

Space relationships

1. Resident guests

2. Front office

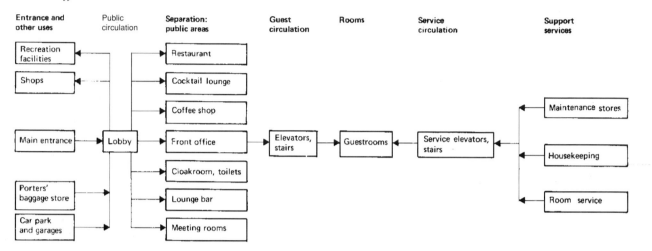

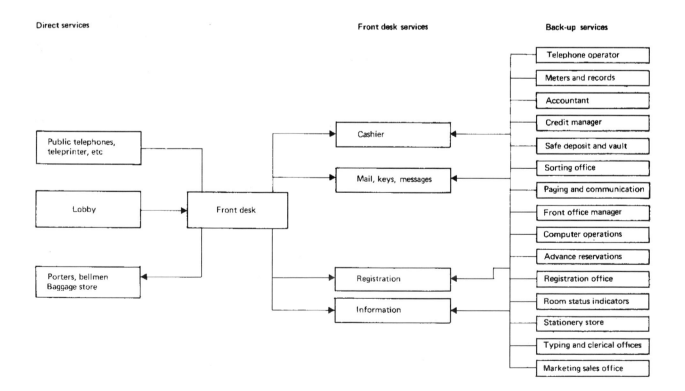

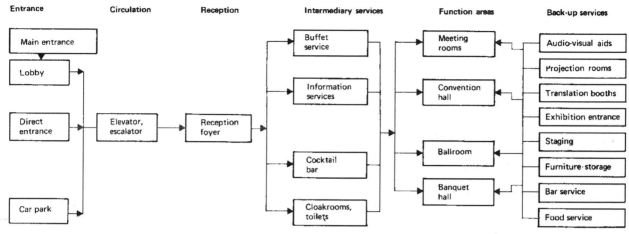

Figure 6.1 Functional relationships

6.1.4 Doors

Entrance doors must meet exacting functional requirements in addition to retaining a good appearance under conditions of repeated use. Alternatives are:

- Revolving – with double swing doors on one or both sides for luggage
- Double swing with single or double leaves, automatic or manual operation
- Sliding – automatically operated with swing doors for emergency use.

Non-revolving doors must be wide enough for a person carrying two bags or a trolley.

There should be a clear opening of:

Revolving doors 2.0 m (6.5 ft) internal diameter
Side doors 1.0 m (3.3 ft)–1.2 m (4.0 ft).

Doors must also meet safety and fire escape requirements which, in the case of revolving doors, include governors, sensitive edges and collapse or folding of leaves under pressure. Swing doors, as a rule, are not allowed to open out beyond the building line and must be recessed in the front wall.

Performance requirements for doors and frames include rain and wind exclusion, durability and retention of appearances, resistance to impact and scraping, ease of movement and closure, security against forced entry or breakage and safety in use – including the design of steps and thresholds.

Framing materials include bronze anodized aluminium, stainless steel and selected hardwoods. The choice of materials is usually coordinated with window design and shopfitting work in the lobby and retail areas.

Toughened glass doors are often used to reveal the interior but must be fitted with large distinctive handles or visible markings. The door furniture must coordinate with the design.

Entry of cold or hot air through open doors may be reduced by *vestibules*: normally 2.44 m (8 ft) minimum depth for swing door and baggage clearance with glass surround and transition lighting and heating/cooling. *Air curtains*: require careful temperature, height and velocity balance and are generally limited in use.

6.1.5 Changes in level

An elevated entrance is more impressive but steps are liable to cause accidents and difficulties in access for luggage, the disabled and elderly.

Location Steps set back at least 1.0 m and preferably 2.0 m from doorway and positioned in line with other obvious changes in space

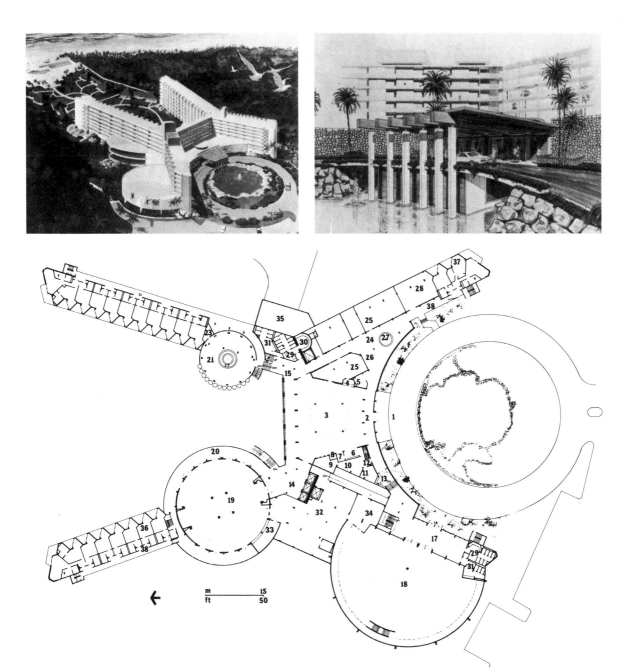

Key

1 Driveway
2 Main entrance
3 Lobby
4 Superintendent of service
5 Baggage
6 Registration
7 Cashier
8 Examination room
9 Accounting
10 Reception
11 Assistant manager
12 Stair down to executive offices
13 House phones
14 Elevator foyer
15 East foyer
16 Convention entrance
17 Convention foyer
18 Convention hall
19 Dining room
20 Terrace
21 Cocktail lounge
22 Bar
23 Bar storage
24 Shopping arcade
25 Shop
26 Activities desk
27 Car rental and travel information
28 Beauty shop
29 Women's toilet
30 Powder room
31 Men's toilet
32 Main kitchen
33 Display kitchen
34 Convention kitchen
35 Loading dock roof
36 Guestrooms
37 Executive suite
38 Open corridor

Figure 6.2 *Trelawny Beach Hotel: Jamaica*
Rendering of the *portes-cochère* and entrance to this luxury hotel. Architects: Morris Lapidus Associates

Lobby	Preferably on one level – unless deliberate to create separate areas. Stairs should have a minimum of three risers with central handrail if more than 2.2 m (7'2") wide
Visibility	Contrasting edges or nosings, preferably illuminated with recess lights
Damage	Edges of treads non-slip. Steps, corners and walls resistant to damage and marking.

6.2 Lobby or reception hall

6.2.1 Size

Usually the lobby acts as the hub of hotel activities, giving access to all or most of the public facilities as well as to the guestrooms. It includes circulation, assembly and waiting areas – with strategically located desks or stations for assistance – and leads directly to the front desk providing reception, information and cashier services.

The overall area depends on the size and grade of hotel, extent of activities using the lobby and the patterns of arrivals. Usually this is related to the number of rooms (Tables 6.1 and 6.2).

6.2.2 Design

As the main point of entry and initial contact the visual impression created by the design has a critical role in defining the style and character of the hotel:

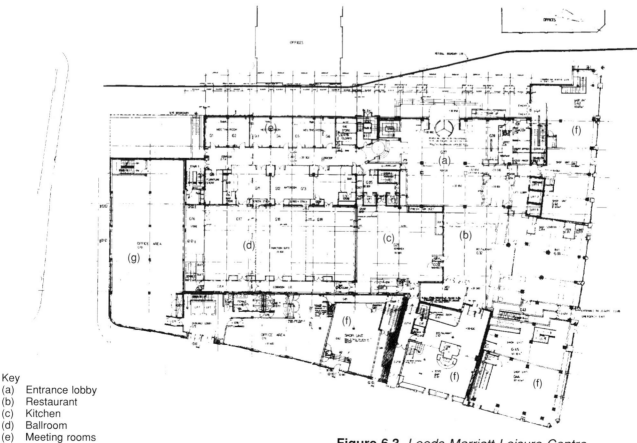

Key
(a) Entrance lobby
(b) Restaurant
(c) Kitchen
(d) Ballroom
(e) Meeting rooms
(f) Shops
(g) Office building

Figure 6.3 *Leeds Marriott Leisure Centre* Ground floor plan

(a)

(b)

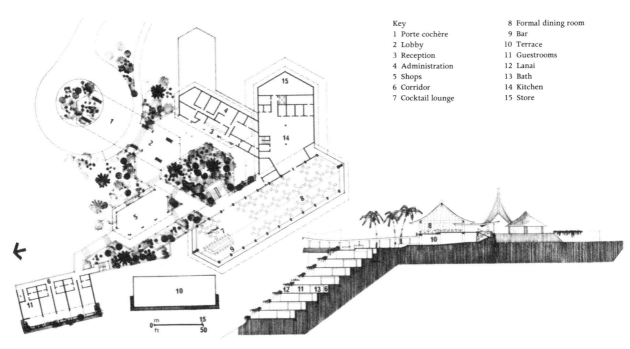

Key		
1 Porte cochère	8	Formal dining room
2 Lobby	9	Bar
3 Reception	10	Terrace
4 Administration	11	Guestrooms
5 Shops	12	Lanai
6 Corridor	13	Bath
7 Cocktail lounge	14	Kitchen
	15	Store

(c)

Figure 6.4 *Hotel Tahara'a Inter-Continental, Tahiti*
The site includes a plateau area 60 m (200 ft) above sea level (a) on which are located the public rooms
in the style of a Polynesian Longhouse (b). 200 guestrooms, accessible by elevator, are stepped 10 levels
down the slope towards the sea (c). Thousands of plants used for instant landscaping were grown during
the 1½ years of construction. Architects: Wimberley, Whisenand, Allison Tong and Goo. Walton
Photography

Table 6.1 Lobby area by type of hotel

Type of hotel	Lobby area/room (m²)	(sqft)
Budget hotels, motor and airport hotels	0.5	5
Resort hotels, city centre hotels	1.0	11
Hotels catering for large convention groups or having multiple activities (casinos, shops)	1.2	13

Table 6.2 Typical lobby space allocation: 200 guestroom city centre hotel

Area	m²	sqft	Notes
Front desk	15	160	7.5 m long
Circulation	100	1080	Entrance 12 m², elevator lobby 12 m²
Lounge seating	20	220	10 lounge seats
Retail space	10	110	Newsagent/gift desk
Cloakrooms, toilets	45	480	Including disabled
Bellman, concierge, telephones	10	100	
(Separate foyer for conference groups)			

- *Chain budget and mid-tariff hotels* tend to adopt a standardized layout and design features which are familiar and reassuring.
- *Large urban hotels*, which need to attract public interest, usually emphasize the expansive, even spectacular, extension of space as in atrium designs. In this case, the lobby usually includes restaurants, bars, kiosks, and lounges – on one floor or with mezzanine levels – sharing the same space.
- *Luxury hotels* generally adopt a more traditional arrangement of linked halls with emphasis on elegance and individual attention.
- *Resort hotels* often plan the lobby with visual links through to recreational areas and other attractions. Separate provision may need to be made for luggage handling.

The lobby also has a merchandising role:

- *hotel company* – through style, graphics, insignia
- *destination* – representative features, local artwork, displays
- *public facilities* – individual designs, themes, cross-advertising.

6.2.3 Planning

Circulation Planned circulation to front desk and guest elevators. Secondary routes to public rooms, shops, conference areas, etc. Circulation routes kept clear of obstruction and congestion. Minimum 2.125 m (7 ft) wide – two people with luggage side by side.

Direction Signs are required for directions and information including local regulations regarding safety, means of escape and registration. Graphic design must be coordinated with overall interior design and consistent throughout.

(a)

Figure 6.5 *Jerusalem Hilton*
Main lobby (a) of the 400 room hotel showing the arrangement of the front desk, offices and public areas. Plan of the lower ground floor (b). The hotel, which is adjacent to a large convention centre, occupies a site of 2.0 ha (5 acres) and includes three restaurants and a ballroom on the lower floor.
Architects: Y. Rechter, M Zarhy.
Structural Engineer: M. Peri.
Interior Design: Gad-Noy

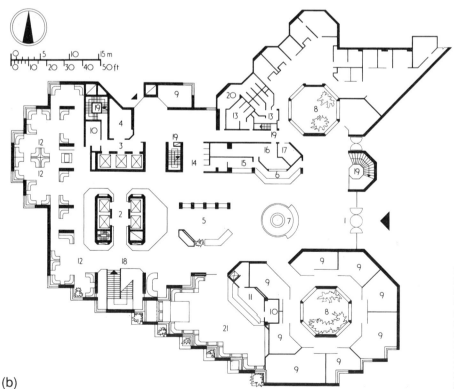

(b)

Key
1 Main entrance
2 Lift lobby
3 Service lifts
4 Luggage
5 Main lobby
6 Reception
7 Fountain
8 Patio
9 Shop
10 Pantry
11 Bar
12 Lounge
13 WCs
14 Telephones
15 Cashier
16 Front office
17 Manager's office
18 Stair to restaurant
19 Stairway
20 Powder room
21 Lounge bar

Assistance

Approved symbols may be used. Located within normal viewing pattern – not more than 30° above horizontal eye level. Local illumination may be used to draw attention.

In addition to the front desk separate stations or desks may be provided for:

- *Bell captain/porter* – permanent desk located near, and in view of the entrance, front desk and elevator lobby (see section 6.2.4)
- *Concierge* – for information, ticket sales, usually an extension of other desks
- *Conferences* – reception desk for groups and functions with meetings directory and portable host welcome signs
- *Front office manager* – portable table, with sign and two chairs.

Front desk

Main focus of activity and subject to intensive use. Set back at least 1.25 m (4 ft) from the circulation increasing to 6 m (20 ft) or more for large convention hotels. Positioned clear of columns with unobstructed view of entrance, guest elevator lobby and bell captain station for control and assistance. Direct access to front office (see section 6.3.1). In personalized high luxury hotels, tables and chairs may also be used for reception and host services

Lounge

Seating area separated from main circulations. Can be partially separate. Usually about 10% of lobby space but may extend to form a lobby bar for entertainment. High-quality furniture arranged in informal groupings with access for bar and/or refreshment service

Services

Cloakrooms and toilets, and provisions for disabled: see section 6.4.1

Public and house telephones

Located in quiet areas near front desk; should be acoustically treated, locally illuminated and fitted with shelving.

Promotions

Display cases and vitrines for commercial products. Design must be coordinated with shop-fitting work (usually in same framing materials) and hotel graphics. Cases are fitted with locks and interior lighting.

Miscellaneous – Brochure racks for hotel and local information, notice boards for travel agencies, etc. Similar control over location, design and use.

Retail space

The extent of retail space depends on the size and grade of hotel, location and commercial viability of shops. Several shops are usually provided in high-grade resort and city hotels, particularly in developing countries. A bakery–patisserie outlet may also serve as an extension for hotel sales. Alternative arrangements include:

- mixed-use shopping malls – occupying lower floors
- shops in extended arcade – with lobby and external access
- individual shops, stands or kiosks in lobby or atrium areas, external design, materials and signage being usually controlled to conform to the image and style of the hotel.

Retail concessions generally fall into four groups (Table 6.3).

Table 6.3

	m²	sqft
Desks, kiosks, stands (airline, tour agency, florist, autorental)	9	100
Small gift shops, jewellery, gifts	18–22	200–240
Mixed newsagent, tobacco, drugs	32–37	350–400
Specialist: book, shoes, dresses, bank/exchange	50–60	550–650

Beauty salons 50–60 m² (550–650 sqft) and barbers shops 32–37 m² (350–400 sqft) may be sited here or near the recreation areas.

Shops should have external access and parking space for deliveries. Kiosks and stands are usually movable but require electrical connections for lighting.

6.2.4 Luggage handling

In a large hotel, particularly for tour and convention groups, a separate entrance may be provided for luggage. This should have access to:

- *Bell captain or porterage station* equipped with house and external telephones, paging facilities and sorting shelves.
- *Luggage store* – area depends on tour or group departures: 0.05 m² per room; 250 room – 12.5 m² (135 sqft).
- *Luggage elevator*: with trolley access.

6.2.5 Materials

The lobby area is subject to intensive use and frequent refurbishment is generally difficult and disruptive. Durable materials are essential in areas subject to high traffic, impact or scraping. These are usually complemented by softer linings and furnishings which can be readily replaced and provide a balance for noise absorption, warmth and personalization of areas. The design and choice of materials will also be influenced by the style and sophistication of the hotel, its local environment and climatic conditions. Particular attention must be given to:

- durability, maintenance of appearance
- fire safety (see section 5.6)

Flooring materials include dense marble and terrazzo (with non-slip inserts in steps), decorative tiling, stone, vinyl and composition flooring – usually softened by carpet strips and squares. Carpeting may extend over the whole area with provision for replacement in areas of heavy traffic wear.

Walls are often dry lined to allow easy access to services and include laminated wood, plastic, metal and glass panelling for durability with decorative wall coverings for lounge and restaurant areas.

Ceiling construction may require large structural voids to house air-conditioning, lighting, sound, sprinkler and other engineering systems. Alternatively these may be largely confined to perimeter spaces allowing the central roofed area to be glazed for natural lighting.

Separation of functions within the lobby area may be indicated by changes in level (see section 6.1.5), flooring materials and ceiling heights, the arrangement of columns, furniture and balustrading and by the use of landscaping.

6.2.6 Engineering services

Engineering services and equipment must be carefully integrated into the design and this will influence positioning of equipment, the choice and architectural detailing of terminals and fittings and the void spaces required for concealment. Public areas of hotels generally require extensive services including the following.

Lighting

Lighting installations are planned to serve several purposes:

- *Decoration*: walls and window illumination, feature lighting
- *Identification*: signs, hazards, desks, stations, exits
- *Emergency*: independent of mains supply
- *Function*:

	Lux (lumen/m²)	Lumen/sqft
Generally	100	10
For daytime	200	20
Over reception desk	400	40

Supplementary lighting is required for desk recesses. Lamps must be shielded to avoid reflection on screens, direct glare and strong shadowing.

Heating, ventilation, air-conditioning

The sophistication of air-conditioning requirements depends on location and type of hotel:

High-grade hotels:	full air-conditioning generally installed with fan coil units supplied from central plant using a zoned system.
Smaller hotels:	modified heating– cooling systems more common.
Beach resort hotels:	lobby usually planned to utilize prevailing sea breezes for daytime cooling.

In mechanical systems, air movement results from infiltration and stack effects requiring draught lobbies. Air extraction is not normally required and primary air supply can be reduced to less than one change per hour. Temperature control is usually modulated to provide a transitional zone from outside conditions. Smoke extract system may be required (from atrium designs).

Public address systems

For background music and paging. Localized systems are usually provided with ceiling, cabinet or column-type speakers as required for the spatial area and height.

Fire protection

Smoke, gas and heat detection equipment with appropriate warning and indicating apparatus is essential. Automatic sprinkler systems are installed in lobbies and corridors used as fire evacuation routes.

Security

Cabling systems are required to camera mountings in strategic positions to monitor the entrance, desk area, elevator lobby and corridor to guest areas. Lighting must be coordinated.

Electrical

Extensive cabling systems are required with accessible ducts, trunking and cable trays providing physical separation, protection (grounding, earthing), electronic screening and means of isolation.

6.3 Front desk and front office

6.3.1 Reception services

The reception area provides for a number of activities:

- guest reception and registration
- cashier and accounting, money changing, deposit of valuables
- information, keys, mail, messages, brochures (concierge).

These services are provided over counters or desks which may be arranged as stations along a long counter (the front desk) or in separate areas. In either case, counter staff must have direct access to offices providing back-up information and supporting services (the front office) (Table 6.4).

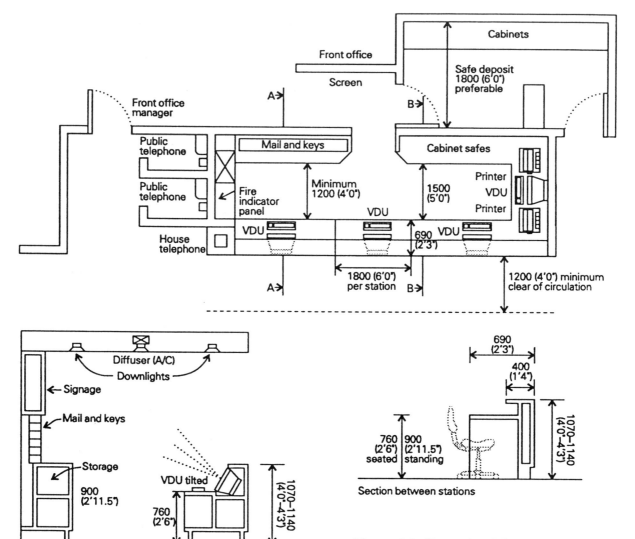

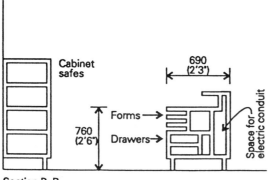

Section A–A

Section B–B

Section between stations

Figure 6.6 *Example of Front Desk for 250 room hotel*

Counter height 1070 mm (4'10") more personal but 1140 mm (4'3") provides better screening of work area.

Working height 760 mm (2'6") for seating, 900 mm (2'11"–3'0") for standing. Video display screens should be tilted to correct viewing angle and screened against light reflections. Keyboard heights adjustable. Safes are required for currency and cash etc. security. Guest safe deposit lockers may be provided in an adjacent room or in individual guestrooms.

Fire indicator panels are located in this area unless there is a specific security office to monitor conditions. The telephone operator's room is usually adjacent

Relationship

Table 6.4 Relationship between front desk services and back-up services

Front desk services	Back-up services
	Fire control room
	Meters and records
	Comptroller
	Accountant, cashier
Cashier	Safe deposit and vault
	Telephone operator
Mail, keys, messages	Paging and communication
	Front office manager
	Computer operations
	Reservations office
Registration	Mail sorting, copying
	Stationery store, records
Information	Typing and clerical office
	Marketing sales office
	Reception

6.3.2 Size and arrangement

Desk space requirements depend on the size of the hotel, grade or standards and patterns of arrivals and departures. Likely peak demands must be ascertained from the market analysis. Separate arrangements or supplementary registration desks may be needed to expedite the registration and checking out for large conventions, touring groups and flight departures.

Length
The desk is usually planned around 1.5–1.8 m (5–6 ft) equipped workstations, this length allowing for two accompanying guests, a degree of separation and privacy in transactions and space for equipment (Table 6.5).

6.3.3 Planning

Counters must be arranged as an integral part of the reception area and as a focus of interest. This area should be column-free to allow clear visibility and circulation. The lobby height may be reduced over the front counter for more concentrated local lighting intensities and acoustic treatment. Alternatively, an open desk arrangement may be used. Registration, cashier and information, keys and mail (concierge) sections should be in sequence with the adjacent registration–checkout stations being adaptable for either use. Signs must be simple and clearly visible from the lobby, positioned behind or over each area.

Easy access must be provided to the supporting front office areas through short passages or lobbies providing visual and noise screening (see section 6.3.7).

Table 6.5 Typical front desk provisions

Rooms	Desk length[a]		Stations[b]	Area[c]	
	(m)	(ft)		(m²)	(sqft)
50	3	10	1–2[d]	9.3	100
100–150	4.5	15	2–3	14.0	150
200–250	7.5	25	3–4	23.2	250
300–400	10.5	35	4–5	32.5	350

Notes: [a]Including concierge–information section. In larger hotels this may be a separate desk.
[b]For registration and cashier services. The central stations are made adaptable to serve both functions as required.
[c]Area of desk, work space and back fittings (excluding guest areas).
[d]Multipurpose use – including telephone exchange.

The desk may be a single straight counter or turned around a corner – in the latter case with the shorter turned section being used for concierge functions. All counters must be designed to screen the work areas from guest view – for confidentiality and security – both by positioning and angling equipment and by the arrangement of shelves and partitions.

Counters must be set back at least 1.25 m (4'0") from circulation routes increasing to 3.0 m (10'0") or more for a busy convention hotel – with separate group registration.

Working space behind the counter is a minimum 1.2–1.5 m wide (4'0"–5'0"). The back wall may be used for cupboards and racks or decorative features.

6.3.4 Counter design

Counters are provided with two overlapping worktops: typically 1050 mm (42") high, for convenient guest use and 760 mm (30") for a seated work area. The overall width should not exceed 690 mm (27").

The work counters need to provide space for equipment such as video display units (VDU) and panel boards. These are recessed and angled to allow clear visibility from a seated or standing position. Local lighting to workstations must be positioned to avoid glare, screen veiling or shadows.

Materials
Counter construction is usually of timber or metal framing with hardwood, laminated or moulded plastic surfaces or decorative durable panels such as marble and terrazzo.

6.3.5 Equipment

Technical advances with the use of computer-operated systems have revolutionized hotel operations, replacing mechanical card-indexing methods with electronic terminals and keyboards. Other major changes include the use of card access systems and credit/debit card transactions.

Front counters need to be designed to house terminals, printers and other equipment, to allow for servicing, replacement and extension without major reconstruction.

Front office equipment is generally specified or supplied by the hotel operating company and will depend on the type of hotel and sophistication of the systems used. Typical requirements include:

Reception (*each station*)	VDU and keyboard
	Room rack/room status panel
	Card key system/key drawer
	Stationery cupboards, racks
Concierge	Key slots, message indicator panel
	Wake-up system
	Brochure holders, stationery cupboard
	VDU and printers with information files
Cashier (*each station*)	VDU and keyboard
	Printer
	Cash register
	Credit card imprinter
	Stationery cupboard, files
Linked services	Safe deposit room
	Currency drawers, files
	VDU and printer for currency transactions
Associated areas	Telephone operator and facsimile/telex room
	Telephone meters
	Fire control system and indicator panel
	Paging and music system
	Security room and monitor screens.

Engineering services
Technical equipment is highly concentrated in this area and requires easy access for renewal or extension of cabling. Separated trunking or ducting must be provided for standard and low electrical voltages, telephones, screened cabling to video monitors, with colour-coded identification. Underfloor services are often used together with service voids in the deck and back counter.

6.3.6 Office requirement

Offices for hotel management and related needs can be grouped into three areas (Table 6.6):

- *Reservation and accounting offices*, closely associated with the front desk
- *Executive offices* which can be located elsewhere – with access to front office

Table 6.6 Office requirement

Area/room[a]	Offices	Location
Front office 0.65 m² (7 sqft)	Reception area Front office manager Reservations office Secretaries: reception, mail Credit manager Count room Cashier Safe deposit area Telephone operators Computer room Fire control room Accountant Controller Payroll manager[b] Accountancy workroom Secretaries	Adjacent to front desk Preferably associated with front desk services
Executive offices 0.25 m² (2.7 sqft)	Reception area Secretaries General manager Assistant general manager Food and beverage manager	Accessible to front office but may be sited on different floor
Sales and catering 0.35 m² (3.8 sqft)	Reception areas, secretaries Sales office Sales and marketing Manager Interview–meeting rooms	Preferably accessible to the banquet–conference area
Support 0.25 m² (2.7 sqft)	Circulation Storage, copying Toilets	
Specialist	Reception interview–training rooms Personnel office Housekeeper Engineer – Secretary, Assistant, plan rooms Chef Receiving office	Near employee facilities In housekeeping areas Near engineering workshops Adjacent to kitchen Adjacent to loading dock

Notes: [a]For high-grade (4 star) hotels of 250–500 rooms. Typical areas per room.
[b]Separate office for payroll manager located near accounting section.

- *Specialist offices* located in or near particular work areas.

The front office areas are detailed in section 6.3.7. These include offices dealing with mail, reservations, accountancy, control and front desk services. Meters, fire control panels, paging and communication, telephone operation and computer facilities are also usually located in this area.

In smaller hotels many of these functions are combined, the executive offices forming part of the front office area.

Space allocation

The front office, executive offices and sales and catering offices together represent the average areas per guestroom as shown in Table 6.7. These areas may be modified by hotel group centralization of some of the administrative functions.

6.3.7 Front office planning

Depending on the location, individual offices are usually clustered together around communal work areas (secretarial, accounting, sales, reservations). The front office and executive offices are either grouped together or planned to allow staff circulation separate from public areas. Staff toilets are also required in these areas.

Access to public areas is required at a number of places to facilitate operations.

Lobby	Front office manager – with reception area
	Banquet sales office – with reception area
Lobby or corridor	Executive offices – access for management.

In each case, views into the interior of the work areas must be screened.

In a small hotel, several of the functions can be combined and separate banquet and conference sales areas are not required. With increase in hotel size and sophistication more individual offices are required and the main offices are also larger (Table 6.8).

Table 6.7 Space allocation of office requirement (per guestroom)

Hotel grade	Area (m²)	(sqft)
High-grade hotels (4–5 star)	1.5	16
Mid-grade hotels (3 star)	0.9	10
Budget hotels (1–2 star)	0.3	3.5

6.3.8 Safe deposit areas

As a rule, hotels are responsible only for the loss of a limited value of guest belongings from rooms. Deposit facilities for valuables may take two forms:

- *Safe deposit area* adjacent to front desk
- *Individual safes* provided in guestrooms.

Safes must also be installed for cash received (deposits, payments), cash and currency changing transactions and payments (wages, petty cash).

In small hotels, safe deposit use may be over a section of the counter but a separate room is preferable to allow privacy. The safe deposit room must be accessible from both the lobby and front desk with a separate counter or integral sliding shelves. Banks of safe deposit boxes must be secured to the wall and an alarm fitted.

Safes in rooms are generally more convenient and preferable in high-class hotels. They may be securely mounted in a wall or closet and operated by separate lock or number code.

6.3.9 Telephone operation and other services

The telephone operator's room is often grouped with the front desk to facilitate duel use at night when minimal staff are on duty. Private automatic branch exchanges (PABX) are usually installed and the automatic switchgear and terminal equipment is housed separately (Table 6.9).

Table 6.8 Office sizes

Examples	200–250 rooms (m²)	(sqft)	400–450 rooms (m²)	(sqft)
Front office				
Reservations office	11	120	28	300
Front office manager	11	120	11	120
Rooms manager	(a)		14	130
Secretary	9	100	9	100
Credit manager	9	100	9	100
Cashier	(a)		11	120
Count room	11	120	14	150
Safe deposit area	4	40	5.5	60
Telephone operators	14	150	18	200
Fire control, security room	7.5	80	11	120
Computer room, etc.(b)	7.5	80	9	100
Accountant, auditor	(a)		9	100
Comptroller	11	120	9	100
Payroll manager	11	120	11	120
Accountancy work areas	14	150	28	300
Secretary	(a)		9	100
Storage copying	9	100	9	100
Executive offices				
Reception	14	150	18	200
Secretaries (1–2)	9	100	18	200
General manager	14	150	18	200
Assistant general manager	(a)		14	150
Food and beverage manager	11	120	14	150
Sales and catering				
Reception	14	150	18	200
Secretaries (0–2)	(a)		18	200
Sales office	14	150	28	300
Sales and marketing manager	(a)		14	150
Banquet manager	(a)		14	150
Conference services manager	(a)		14	150
Interview rooms	(a)		14	150
Copying, storage, etc.	7.5	80	14	150

Notes: (a)Combine with other functions.
(b)Depending on system and storage. Includes an area for public address system etc.
(c)Gross factor normally 0.25, including circulation space, toilets and stores.
(d)Room areas may vary with hotel company requirements.

The increased use of telephone, facsimile and associated services – particularly in city centre and convention hotels – result in this area being subject to intensive use. Access may be required to the Business Services Centre.

Other electronic services
Space provision to house technical equipment and ducting or trunking for cabling systems is required for:

Table 6.9 Telephone services for high-grade hotels (see section 10.5)

	Minimum area		Lines
	(m²)	(sqft)	
2 operator consoles	14	150	200–250
4 operator consoles	18	200	300–400

- background music, public announcement and paging systems
- television and radio systems (including in-house movies)
- clock systems
- closed circuit television monitoring and security systems
- metering of telephone and other guest services
- computer-operated systems (front office, accounting, energy, etc).

6.4 Cloakrooms and toilets

6.4.1 Planning

Toilet facilities (Table 6.10) are normally required near:

- *Main lobby*   } may be located
- *Restaurants and bars* } to allow dual use.
- *Banquet halls, conference rooms* – with nearby cloakrooms
- *Front office* – for staff.

Location

Public toilets should be sited discreetly adjacent to the corridors leading to restaurants and bars, but not directly accessible from street (security).

For separate banquet and conference users, toilets and cloakrooms are near the entrance foyer with generous circulation space and screening.

Space

Numbers of fitments and space requirements are dictated by the numbers of people accommodated.

Cloakrooms

Cloakroom facilities are essential for banquet, function and conference groups and some provision may be required for restaurant users. For security, attendant operated services are preferred. The counter should be set back at least 1.2 m from circulation area. Recommended area: 10.0 m² (108 sqft) per 100–150 seat covers. This allows for up to two-thirds of

Table 6.10 Toilet facilities

	Male public		Female public		Notes
	(m²)	(sqft)	(m²)	(sqft)	
Per guestroom	0.1	1.0	0.1	1.0	
Restaurant, function rooms					If greater than above
per 100 seat covers	13.0	140	13.0	140	
200–250	18.0	190	18.0	190	
300–400	23.0	250	23.0	250	
Disabled toilet	1.5×2.0 m		1.8×2.0 m		Recommended sizes:
	(5'0"×6'6")		(6'0"×6'6")		outward opening doors
			with vanitory shelf		

Notes: [a]Subject to legal standards. Based on 100% male or 100% female occupancy. Allows for screening or intervening ventilated space.

Table 6.11 Fitments for toilet facilities

Requirements	Examples
Floors, wall linings	Ceramic tiles, mosaics, terrazzo, marble, vinyl. Upper areas of walls may be plastered and decorated. Floors non-slip
Ceilings	Acoustic tiles (inert material)
Fitments	Corbel mounting (clear of floor) preferable with concealed cistern and pipework – with isolating valves and access for maintenance. Wash basins fitted with colour-coded tops, preferably spray type with lever operated wastes. Towel dispensers or air dryers installed. Tiled shelves for soap and cosmetics. Waste and disposal bins discreetly located
Lighting	Recess ceiling lamps. Screened (20–30 lumens/sqft)
Mirrors	Fitted over washbasins. Plain or tinted
Noise reduction Ventilation	Closures fitted on doors with rubber stops. Mechanical ventilation 8–10 changes/hour (legal minimum 3)
Automatic control	Where practicable automatic electronic control of lighting, flushing and hand-drying should be installed

visitor use, and includes counter and 1.2 m set back. Unattended area: similar space.

6.4.2 Design requirements

Toilet areas must include visual screening from public areas and a separately ventilated intervening space may be required for entry from a room. An ante-room or powder room should be provided where practicable. High-quality durable fitments and finishes are important to maintain standards (Table 6.11).

6.5 Circulation and transportation

6.5.1 Flow patterns

Hotel and resort activities involve extensive movements of guests, visitors, staff, goods and services. These need to be planned for convenience and operational efficiency while also meeting requirements for safety and security. The flow patterns of guests and visitors provide

the basis for planning most services including car parking (section 5.2), front desk registration and check-out (section 6.3.2), elevator requirements, demands on housekeeping and other departmental staff and engineering loading calculations.

In most cases it is necessary to provide services which will meet the peak demands, without excessive delay or waiting time and this usually involves some form of simulation modelling and computer analysis to predict results.

Simulation techniques are commonly used to determine the required capacities of elevators (numbers, sizes, speeds), numbers of registration clerks, restaurant seats, housekeeping staff, etc., in order to determine a satisfactory level of service.

Standards of provision vary depending on the sensitivity to cost (price) or the level of service. Thus, in budget hotels some degree of restriction and self-service is acceptable while in high-grade hotels services are highly personalized and planned to ensure rapid response and convenience.

6.5.2 Corridors and stairs

Public areas

In public areas, corridors represent a loss of space and adaptability. As far as possible, circulation should be through areas which have other uses (lounges, shopping malls, conference foyers) or which serve as focal points for multiple activities such as lobbies.

Other areas

The space taken up by corridors, stairs and elevators usually represents between 25% and 35% of the total built area of guestrooms and 15–20% of other areas.

6.5.3 Fire regulations

Travel distances

The number and positions of exit doors from rooms and the lengths of corridors between enclosed staircases are determined by the permitted travel distances (section 5.6).

Egress

Circulation through lobbies and foyers is usually acceptable for up to 50% of fire escape requirements if:

- protected (two hours fire resistance) from areas below
- constructed with linings which are non-propagating for fire or have a low rate of surface flame spread
- fitted with automatic sprinklers.

Construction

6.5.4 Corridor widths

Minimum widths for corridors and stairs are determined by the numbers of persons who might need to use these routes for fire escape. Widths also need to take account of wheelchair and trolley dimensions and the spaciousness expected in higher-grade hotels (Table 6.13).

6.5.5 Other requirements

Ceiling	Minimum 2.25 m (7.5 ft). Ceiling voids used to house engineering services including fire detection and sprinkler systems. Non-combustible or very low surface flame spread materials. Acoustic treatment.
Walls	Damage reduced by skirtings, fenders, panels. Exposed corners protected. Tough washable wall coverings. Access panels to room service ducts.
Floors	High-grade carpet preferable with close pattern and balanced colour to disguise shading and staining.
Safety	No projections into space. Floor coverings secured down. Changes in level by gradual ramp (1:20) or conspicuous steps (direct illumination, minimum three risers).
Noise	Sound insulation to guestroom minimum 40 dBa. Impact noise reduced by carpeting or resilient flooring. Absorption by acoustic ceiling tiles.

Table 6.12 Construction for fire resistance

	Minimum fire resistance periods	Notes
Doors to guestrooms	20–30 minutes	Self closing
Corridor walls	1 hour	
Protected staircases and exits	1 hour 2 hours	Up to three storeys four storeys or more

Table 6.13 Typical corridor widths

	m	ft
Minimum (restricted)	1.2	4'0"
Economy hotels	1.4	4'6"
Standard–high grade	1.5–1.9	5'0"–6'0"
With recessed doors (recessed width 2.0 m)	1.5	5'0"
Where service doors open out onto corridor	1.8–2.0	6'0"–6'6"
Secondary service routes allowing trolley access	1.2–1.4	4'0"–4'6"
Apartments (depending on number)	1.1–1.5	3'6"–5'0"

Engineering services   Vacuum cleaner connections and electronic socket outlets at 12.0 m (40 ft) maximum intervals. Each length of corridor should have fire detecting and warning systems with two manual operating points. Ventilation: independent from rooms with own exhaust and fresh air supply. Pressurized system may be used for fire escape staircases.

Lighting   Recessed wall or ceiling lights:

Illumination	Lux	Lumen/ sqft
Stairs, landings	100–150	10–15
Corridors (two circuits)	50 (night) –100 (day)	5–10
Emergency lighting (continuous use or automatic switch-over)	Minimum 20% of total	
Exit signs	Self-illuminated independent	

Visual impression   The apparent length of long corridors is reduced by increasing width and height at landings and intervals, variations in lighting and wall features.

6.5.6 Corridors for goods and services

Planned to provide efficient circulation between storage, working and service areas, with links to public areas at suitable points.

- Entry to public areas through vestibules (screening, noise reduction).
- Stairs avoided between related areas with frequent traffic.
- Floors non-slip. 1:12 reducing to 1:20 for long ramps or heavy trolleys. Walls durable allowing easy decoration and hygiene.
- Intermediary doors, dual, double swing with viewing panels and fenders.
- Good lighting and ventilation provided.
- Fire requirements apply (fire resistance, non-obstruction, exits).

6.5.7 Staircases

Staircase design is largely dictated by fire and safety requirements. The minimum flight for stairs is three rises and the maximum between landings sixteen risers. Codes stipulate the minimum clearances and widths, handrails and loading requirements.

Hotel staircases are often used as a design feature. The construction may be in decorative durable materials, such as marble, or other stonework with non-slip inserts to treads. To reduce noise, central strips of carpet or all-over carpeting on an incombustible base may also be used. The edges of steps must be distinguishable from the pattern.

Short-radius circular and monumental staircases may not be acceptable as fire escapes. As a rule, staircases and landings which lead from public areas should be protected by automatic sprinkler systems.

6.6 Internal transportation

6.6.1 Elevator services

Planning
The main guest elevators should be in sight of the front desk and preferably grouped together for economy and maintenance. Stairs should be adjacent to allow alternative and emergency use. Often the service elevators are grouped behind within the same structural enclosure, the service rooms and lobbies reducing noise transmission to guestrooms. In atrium designs, transparent elevators are often used as a feature but alternative enclosed elevators should also be provided for guests, and for baggage and service requirements.

Elevator lobby
Lobbies must be at least one third wider than the adjacent corridor. Ashtrays, mirrors, displays and seats may be provided but must not obstruct circulation. Lighting must be independent of corridor circuits. 150 lux (15lumen/sqft) is preferable.

Grouping
A bank of four elevators is usually the maximum. For larger numbers, elevators should be arranged in facing parallel rows of four, with lobby widths of about 3.5 m (11.5 ft) between banks of guestroom elevators and 4.2 m (14.0 ft) between those to public rooms. Advanced indicator lights and collective controls are normally required. Grouping is also used to distinguish elevators serving zones or groups of

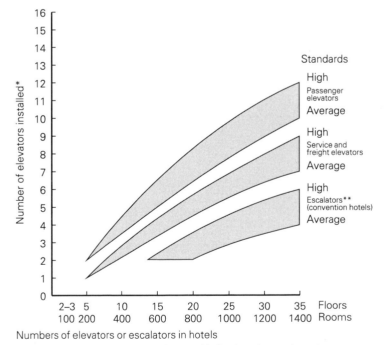

Numbers of elevators or escalators in hotels

* Depends on speed, acceleration, sophistication of controls and car size; approximate guide only. Does not include shuttle service to car park and express service to roof top restaurants.

** Escalator requirements are affected by the extent of public facilities, convention rooms, retail floors, etc.

Figure 6.7 *Numbers of elevators and escalators in hotels*

floors, and express elevators to penthouse or rooftop restaurants, etc.

Separation
Separate elevators are usually provided for:

Basement carpark — Terminates at lobby. Special safety provisions (isolating vestibule, fire protection, pressure ventilation).

Firemen's access — Required for high-rise buildings – to reach top of building within one minute. Within fire-protected enclose. Separate power supply and controls.

Leisure use — Leading directly to basement swimming pool, spa, leisure centre or outdoor recreational areas.

Machine room
Traction-driven equipment is normally located over the lift shaft in a rooftop or penthouse enclosure with clearance above the top landing, allowing for overrun. The machine room houses motors, pulleys, controls and a hoisting beam with space to enable cars to be removed for servicing. Provision must be made for easy access, for winter heating, filtered ventilation, noise and vibration control.

6.6.2 Types of elevators

Hydraulic — Operated by oil pressure, hydraulic elevators are relatively slow (about 0.5 m/s or 100 ft/min) but avoid the need for penthouse construction and strong supporting columns. May be installed in new or existing hotels for passengers or/and goods. Relatively quiet smooth movement over heights generally up to 9 m (30 ft) with a maximum of 18 m (60 ft). Drilling is required to accommodate the ram shaft and the power unit is usually sited adjacent.

Traction drive — Elevator suspended and moved by cables which pass over pulleys to counterbalance weights.

Table 6.14 Classification of passenger elevators

Light traffic	For small hotels and apartment buildings
up to four storeys	Single speed 0.5m/s (100 ft/min)
4–8 storeys	Two-speed 0.75–1.25m/s (150–250 ft/min) reducing to 1/3 speed on starting and stopping
Capacities	7–16 persons, 550–1100 kg (1200–1500 lb)
General purpose	For medium sized hotels up to sixteen storeys
4–8 storeys	Geared speeds 1.25 m/s (250 ft/min)
8–12 storeys	Geared speeds 1.75 m/s (350 ft/min)
12–16 storeys	Geared speeds 2.40 m/s (400 ft/min)
Capacities	16–22 persons, 1100–1600 kg (2500–3500 lb)
Intensive traffic	Large hotels, tower blocks, public rooms on upper floors. Express elevators. Zoning systems.
Over 12 storeys	Variable speeds 2.5–5.0 m/s (500–1000 ft/min) with controlled acceleration and levelling. Direct current motors installed.
Capacities	16–26 persons 1100–1800 kg (2500–4000 lb)

6.6.2 Technical features

Car design — Wider than deep. Door openings 1.0 m (3.5 ft) or more wide (double door preferable for easy entry). Interior linings designed to withstand intensive use. No projections. Smooth interior and edges. Mirrors. Good lighting and ventilation. Emergency stop, alarm and communication system. Automatic doors fitted with sensitive leading edges.

Safety — Structure stability and fire resistance (1 hour – shaft, ½ hour – doors). Smoke venting of shaft. Fire override controls with return to lobby or exit floor level. Emergency power, lighting and lifting gear. Safety of elevator machinery and cables, guide rails and counterweights. Provision of overload, overrun, terminal, speed limiting and levelling controls, landing and car door mechanisms.

Controls — Directional collective or dual (automatic/operative) controls. May be zoned for express service. Banks of elevators use interconnective collective controls and advanced signalling on landings.

Carrying capacity — Determined by maximum number of passengers to be carried over peak five-minute intervals. Usually based on guestrooms: 10% of maximum population, restaurants: 12%. Convention and banquet halls – higher coincidence of demand.

Waiting time — Depends on round trip time taken for car to return and numbers of cars installed. To provide good service at peak times: typical provisions:

Business and convention hotels 25–30 sec
Resort hotels 30–35 sec.

Numbers — Approximate guide: depends on speed, acceleration, sophistication of controls and car size.

6.6.4 Escalators

Escalators are used to transport large numbers of people over a limited number of floors, namely:

- multilevel shopping centres with hotel lobby on higher floor
- large convention, ballroom and exhibition rooms above or below ground level.

The floor area taken up by an escalator is extensive, but this may be justified by the high capacity and convenience (Table 6.15).

Angles of elevation are usually 30°, increasing to 35° in restricted space, with approach lengths of 1.8 m and 2.7 m (6 and 9 ft) at the top and bottom of the incline. Access to the machinery, which extends to about 1.2 m (4 ft) below landings, must be provided. Extensive safety devices are required including emergency braking, maximum load cut and automatic locking to prevent reverse movement. Fire safety provisions will usually require open

Table 6.15 Typical escalator provisions

Speed (m/s)	(ft/min)	Width (mm)	(in)	Capacity (persons/hour)
0.45–0.60	90–120	810	32	5000
		1000	40	7000

Figure 6.8 *Tower Hotel, London*
Relationship of the first floor service areas (a) and
guestroom floors (b) with central bank of
elevators. Architects: Renton Howard Wood
Associates

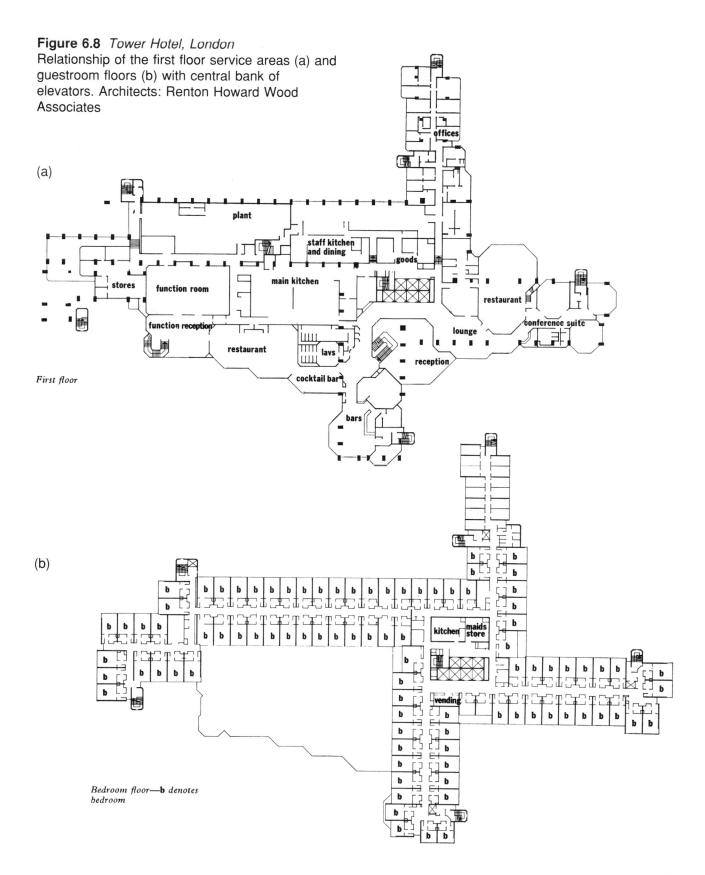

(a)

First floor

(b)

*Bedroom floor—**b** denotes
bedroom*

Table 6.16 Service elevator provisions

Requirements	Details
Dimensions	May need to accommodate furniture, trolleys, luggage, stretcher, food service equipment as well as staff transport. For furniture and trolleys: Car platform area 2.5×3.0 m (8×10 ft) Height – usually 2.6 m (8.5 ft) Capacity – freight 2800 kg (6000 lb) service only 1400 kg (3000 lb)
Design features	Robust with rustproof seamless linings for easy cleaning. Hinged foldable shelves may be fitted for trays. Good lighting and ventilation essential for hygiene. Telephone or intercom systems fitted.
Operational controls	For freight a single-speed 0.5 m/s (100 ft/min) is usually adequate for up to 8 floors. Faster service elevators have speeds similar to those for passengers and require automatic levelling. Control systems are generally simpler than passenger systems. Location indicator panels must be installed to reduce abuse. Safety and maintenance standards for elevators apply
Service rooms	Service elevator lobbies must be at least 2.1 m (7 ft) wide to allow temporary waiting of trolleys and carts without obstructing access. Typical requirements for service pantries, local service rooms and housekeeping rooms are illustrated in Figure 6.7

escalators to be automatically sealed in event of fire by a continuous curtain of water with directional exhaust ventilation to draw smoke away.

6.6.5 Service circulations

Efficient hotel operation depends on the correct planning of service circulation. Service elevators should open into a service lobby on each floor with housekeeping and room roof service areas adjacent. Separate elevator systems may be required for:

* heavy goods and freight – where storage is on a different level to delivery – and for exhibition and display equipment to convention halls
* food service only – for transfer of trays and trolleys from main to finishing banquet kitchens (dumb waiters) and for bar stocking.

Planning

The numbers of service elevators depend on number of guestroom floors, extent of food service to rooms and special requirements such as high-level restaurants and bars. Minimum ratios for guest:service lifts are 3:1 increasing to 3:2 for high-rise buildings with room service. Service of meals to rooms may be on an individual order basis or collective system in which one or more service elevators operate as mobile pantries travelling from floor to floor. Collective systems are efficient for standard limited needs (continental breakfast) and may be supplied direct or via supplementary pantries on more than one floor level (Table 6.16).

6.6.6 Engineering services

The need to incorporate engineering services and plant will influence and be affected by many aspects of hotel planning such as structural design, constructional grids and dimensions of components. Plant may be sited at rooftop level, in basements or/and adjacent to operational areas.

Enclosure of engineering services is necessary for protection, safety and appearance but must meet a number of requirements:

- *Protection* from mechanical damage, dampness, extremes of heat or cold.
- *Separation* to prevent contact between electrical wiring of different voltages and to reduce heat transfer between pipes, etc.
- *Access* with working spaces for servicing repair and replacement minimizing interruption of use and disturbances.
- *Identification* for easy location of faults.
- *Fire protection* to prevent penetration through floors or separating walls.

Vertical enclosure is provided by:
- Multiple service cores – with stairs, elevators, ducts, busbar systems, etc.
- Service ducts for pipework from bathrooms and electrical distribution.
- Chases recessed into walls for permanent pipes and cables.
- Cavity walls for front office and meeting rooms requiring extensive cabling.

Horizontal enclosures include:
- Engineering services floor separating guestroom storeys from public areas.
- Suspended ceiling voids with space for ventilation ducts and cable trays.
- Floor ducts and conduits formed during construction.
- Surface trunking and raceways in offices and work areas.
- Suspended access floors as an alternative in front office areas.

7

Guestrooms and suites

7.1 Planning and design

7.1.1 Marketing

Guestrooms represent between 65% (luxury) and 85% (budget) of the total built area of a hotel. The income from rooms is invariably the largest source of hotel revenue and makes the largest contribution to gross profit (see section 4.3.6).

The requirements for guestrooms are largely dictated by the market analysis (see section 3.3):

Main markets	Demand for single, double, twin and family rooms.
Fluctuation (seasonal, weekend)	Furniture and equipment needs. Adaptability.
Quality and grades	Standards of sophistication, room size and individuality, suites, room service.
Lengths of stay	Size of rooms, amount of furniture, wardrobe and drawer space, facilities in rooms, lounge–work areas.
Feasibility	Rationalization and space saving: construction method, equipment and furnishings budget, housekeeping needs.

7.1.2 Space saving

Room dimensions are critical. Reductions in the area of a room are multiplied by the number of rooms involved. A 12 per cent saving in room area represents more than the total space usually required for all public areas.

However, rooms which are too small are often visually restrictive or crowded, inflexible and difficult to service. Often this leads to increased wall and furniture damage.

Circulation

Usually between 25% and 35% of the total gross built area is taken up by corridors, stairs, lift shafts, associated service rooms and ducts. Typical plan configurations are illustrated in section 5.3.8 and circulation requirements are detailed in section 6.5.1.

7.1.3 Standardization

Rooms are mainly repetitive in size with various options of furniture arrangement. Standardization is important in:

- cost and time savings in construction and prefabrication
- uniform quality and pricing in chain operations
- efficiency in organization of room cleaning
- economy in bulk purchasing of equipment, furniture and furnishings
- rationalization of maintenance, work and replacements (see section 5.4.6).

In multistorey buildings, repetitive modules from floor to floor are essential for structural design and the location of service ducts.

Typical ratios

Table 7.1 Typical ratios of room types

	Single/double(a)	*Twin*	*Notes*
Resort hotels	15%	85%	Convertible family rooms
City/suburban hotels	50%	50%	With sofa bed
Budget hotels/ motels		100%	Standardized family rooms

Note: (a)Usually with double or queen-sized beds for flexibility.

7.1.4 Variations in room dimensions

In multistorey buildings:

- Column spacing to accommodate two room widths – usually within a practical limit of 7–8 m (23–26 ft). For maximum flexibility the inner rows of columns should coincide with the service ducts.

- Variations in lengths of rooms on each side of a double loaded corridor. Balconies may also be restricted to one side.
- Changes in room sizes in different wings of the building.
- Use of structural irregularity at corners and junctions to provide changes in room shape and suites.

7.1.5 Motels

Roadside inns and motels are generally 1–3 storey buildings allowing greater flexibility in layout. Repetitive units may be arranged:

- in pairs or clusters around service cores for the bathrooms
- in blocks with continuous or stepped facades, courtyards and other combinations to suit site contours, parking arrangements and boundaries.

Parking may be communal or immediately adjacent to the rooms.

Low rise construction allows wider scope for variations in shape while incorporating modular dimensions for economy in construction. Often, motel units provide convertible double/family rooms and sometimes include self-catering kitchenettes. Access to rooms may be direct (ground floor) via central or external corridors or by stairs to adjacent pairs of rooms.

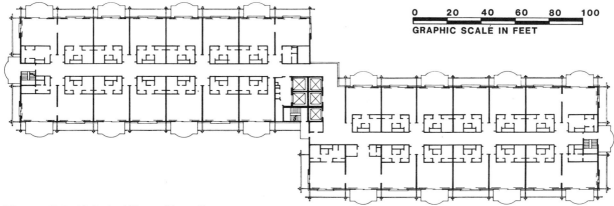

0 20 40 60 80 100
GRAPHIC SCALE IN FEET

Figure 7.1 *Kahala Hilton, Hawaii*
Typical guestroom floor

Figure 7.2 Motel Layouts. Basic arrangements for motel rooms. To allow comparison, the same guestroom unit has been used throughout.

(a)   In line, as in terraces or courts, with the bathrooms serving as noise screens. Each room enjoys an outlook which may extend as an individual terrace or lanai as an extension from the room.

(b)   Alternative stepped to give greater screening and privacy, or to suit the dimensions of the site.

(c)   In clusters, usually based on a module of four units, which may be linked to economize road and path construction. The example shows bathrooms grouped around a central service duct for easy maintenance access.

(d)   Interspaced with car parks, which may be covered car ports. Alternative (top) with front entrance, as with units which are arranged back to back or where the car park is separated.

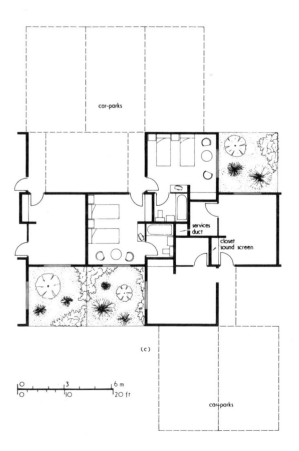

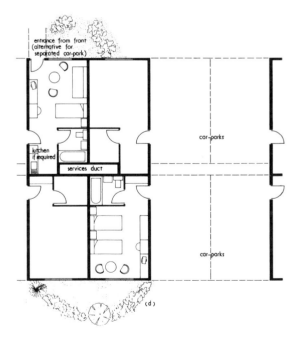

7.1.6 Village resort complexes

Room units in holiday villages and resort complexes are usually varied in style to create individuality and character. The density of building is disguised by landscaping and the retention or interplanting of trees to separate and screen groups of units. Layouts of village complexes are usually planned to provide:

- Separation of cars and service vehicles from the resort activities area.
- Transportation for luggage, maintenance and servicing of rooms.
- Rationalization of paths and engineering services (water, electricity, communications, drainage).
- Attractive relationships between the guest accommodation and public and recreational amenities of the resort.
- Efficient land utilization with space for future extension causing minimum disturbance.

Internal dimensions of units are usually standardized and may provide combinations of one, two or three rooms with convertible living/sleeping areas, uniform bathrooms and kitchenettes.

Construction often incorporates local building materials to reflect the character of the area but these may be limited to roof forms, walling and terraces.

7.2 Room dimensions

7.2.1 Functional zones

Rooms are planned to provide zoned areas for the various functions, each with sufficient activity space for convenient use and cleaning. For economy, zones should overlap to serve more than one purpose.

Minimum activity spaces

Lounge/work	Near window, daylight, views – movable furniture
Beds	Quiet area, away from window, screened from entrance
Dressing	Good lighting, mirror, chair/stool, multiple use
Luggage and storage	Near entrance, convenient access supplementary lighting
Bathroom	Internal, noise isolated, servicing access
Bedside	Controls, lights, telephone, access for making up
Circulation	Adequate width (luggage) other use of space.

7.2.2 Room widths

As a rule maximum benefit should be obtained from the outside walls (natural light, views) and the most critical dimension for hotel rooms is the width (Table 7.2). Increase of width reduces the numbers of rooms or increases length of corridors and the ratio of perimeter wall length:volume enclosed.

Table 7.2 Room widths

Width	m	ft	Comments
Minimum	3.0	10'0"	Suitable for single bed lengthwise. Otherwise inefficient, long narrow room
Standard	3.65	12'0"	Allows for crosswise beds with wall furniture and space between. Minimum 3.5 m (11'6") clear
Luxury	4.1	13'6"	Allows alternative lengthwise or cornerwise positioning of beds and generous spacing
Suite (minimum)	6.0	19'8"	Adjacent bedroom/ living room areas with minimum space

(a)

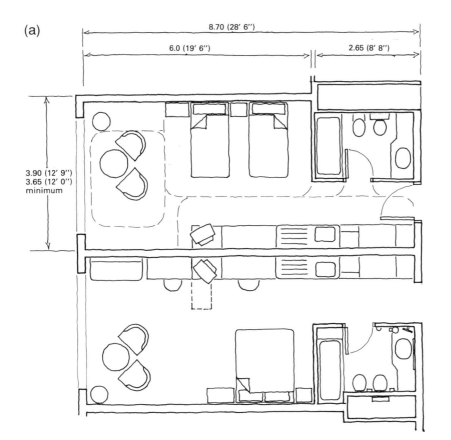

(b)

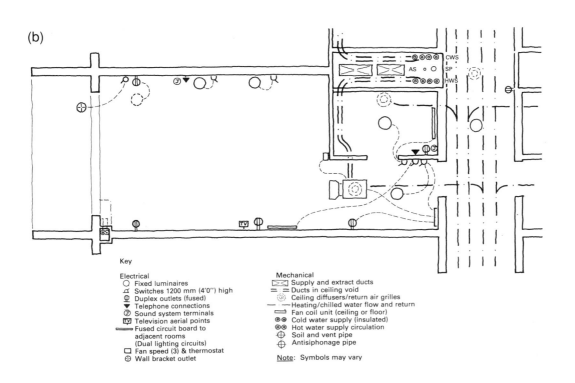

Key

Electrical
- ○ Fixed luminaires
- ⊿ Switches 1200 mm (4'0") high
- ⊕ Duplex outlets (fused)
- ▼ Telephone connections
- Ⓙ Sound system terminals
- TV Television aerial points
- ▬▬ Fused circuit board to adjacent rooms (Dual lighting circuits)
- ▢ Fan speed (3) & thermostat
- ⊕ Wall bracket outlet

Mechanical
- ⊠ Supply and extract ducts
- ═ ═ Ducts in ceiling void
- ⦂ Ceiling diffusers/return air grilles
- — ─ Heating/chilled water flow and return
- ⊏ Fan coil unit (ceiling or floor)
- ⊙⊙ Cold water supply (insulated)
- ⊙⊙ Hot water supply circulation
- ⊕ Soil and vent pipe
- ⊕ Antisiphonage pipe

Note: Symbols may vary

Figure 7.3 *Hotel guestrooms*

(a) High-grade hotel: standard twin bedroom showing usage spaces required around the furniture and fittings for planning room layouts.

(b) Alternative double or kingsized bedroom in high-grade hotel. This allows for a larger workstation and the option of a convertible sofa-bed.

(c) Electrical and mechanical outlets in high-grade bedrooms. Fan coil units are usually housed in the lowered lobby ceiling space, 460–600 mm (18–24"), with fresh-air ducts in the corridor ceiling. An alternative position for a floor mounted cabinet is also indicated. Emergency lighting and sprinkler systems (not shown) are installed in the corridor and may extend to the lobbies of rooms.

(d) Mid-grade hotel with twin beds and balcony. The bathroom is planned for a standard 1700×700 mm bath. An American 5 ft bath may be located in line with the duct.

(e) Alternative with 1.5 m, 60" or 72" bed and a fitted workstation. The bathroom layout allows for a bedroom door recess.

(f) Budget hotel with 1.5 m or 60" bed together with a single bed or convertible sofa. The washbasin may be located in the bedroom.

(g) Alternative for a budget hotel with a shower-room reducing the width to 3.15 m (10'4")

(h,i) Shadow Mountain Resort, W. Virginia. Proposed arrangement of rooms to provide separation of sleeping and living areas—extending on to a private balcony or terrace (lanai). Architects: Morris Lapidus Associates.

(j) Hotel Croatia de luxe, Cavtat. Compact room units, with balconies, angled to the corridor. Architects: S. Miličevič, Energoprojekt.

(k) Belo Horizonte Othon Palace Hotel. Based on a curved plan.

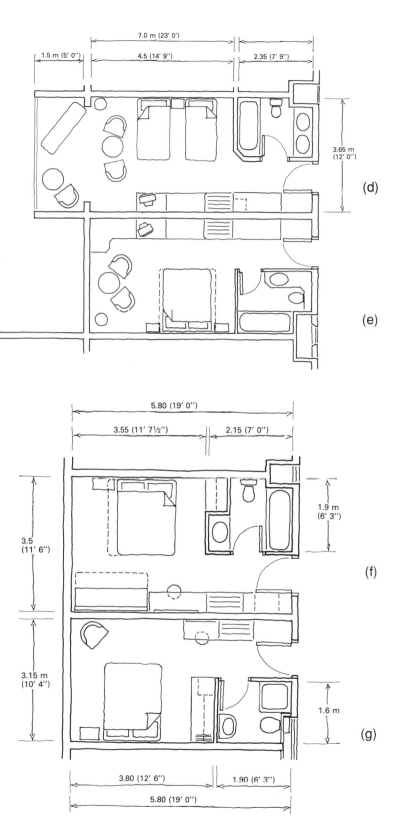

227

Figure 7.3 *Hotel guestrooms (continued)*

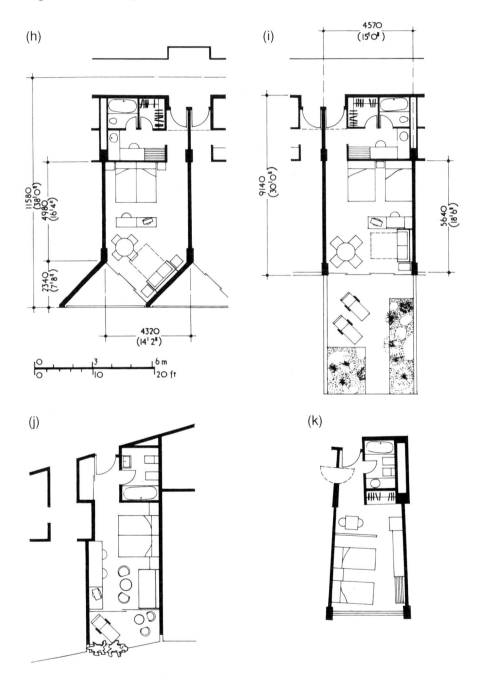

Standard rooms are normally based on a bed length of 2000 mm (79") with wall furniture widths of 600 mm (24") leaving a circulation and activity space of 1000 mm (40"). This room width can be reduced slightly for economy – minimum 3.5 m (11'6") – or increased to give a more spacious impression to 3.75 m (12'6") or 3.90 m (13'0"). Construction modules (to wall centres) add 0.2–0.23 m (8–9").

7.2.3 Room lengths and areas

Room lengths are generally more variable although they may be dictated by structural or site restrictions. The layout usually provides for bathroom/sleeping/working/day use areas to allow maximum benefit from natural light and views.

Bathroom dimensions are dictated by the number and spacing of fitments. A separate dressing area may be provided in luxury hotels.

The *sleeping area* extends about 2.40 m (8'0") for a metric double or queen-sized bed, 2.90 m (9'6") for metric twin beds and 3.70 m (12'2") for double–double beds allowing for side access.

The *day use area* is more flexible. Two easy chairs with coffee table takes up about 1.70 m (5'6"). This may be extended to 2.3 m (7'6") to accommodate a convertible sofa or settee. A similar space provides a good office/work area. The minimum is about 1.0 m (3'3") in economy units.

Internal areas

The dimensions summarized in Table 7.3 are representative although they will vary with location and constructional modules. American hotels are usually based on 5'0" bathtubs allowing more compact bathrooms. Budget hotel rooms often provide bedrooms for family use.

7.2.4 Extent of variation

In *budget hotels* the dimensions are more critical and shower rooms may be substituted for bathrooms. Some designs position the beds on different walls and others use bunkbed, folding or sofa beds to maximize the use of space and to accommodate market variations from singles to families.

Mid-grade hotels generally offer standard rooms. Typical ratios of twin beds:doubles (with or without convertible sofas) 3:1 for mixed markets and seasonal or weekend/weekday changes to 1:1 for business users requiring more lounge:working space. In most cases, rooms are to the same modular dimensions but corridors may also be offset to allow longer rooms on one side.

Luxury and high-grade hotels provide rooms with greater variety in size and arrangement. In cities with frontage space at a premium, emphasis may be given to length, with larger beds (72" king-size or 54" double–double) and furnished lounge areas. Bathrooms usually include four fitments and may extend to a dressing area with separate washbasin. Overall lengths are typically 8.4 m or 8.6 m. In other areas widths may be increased to 3.9 m or 4.1 m, the latter allowing beds to be repositioned.

Suites are provided as a proportion of the rooms (4 to 8%) in most high-grade hotels.

Table 7.3 Internal room areas

Hotel type	Room without bathroom or lobby (m)	(m²)	Bathroom only (internal)[a] (m)	(m²)	Overall including lobby area (m)	(m²)[c]
Budget	3.6×3.5 (11'9"×11'6")	14.70 136 sqft	2.15×1.9 (7'x 6'3")	4.09[b] 44 sqft	5.8×3.5 (19'×11'6")	20.3 66'6")
Mid-grade	4.9×3.6 (16'×12')	17.64 192 sqft	2.35×2.0 (7'9"×6'6")	4.70 50sqft	7.0×3.6 (23'×12')	25.2 276 sqft
High-grade	6.0×3.9 (19'6"×12'9")	24.20 249 sqft	2.65×2.2 (8'8"×7'3")	5.83 63 sqft	8.7×3.9 (28'6"×12'9")	33.9 363 sqft

Notes: [a]Metric dimensions include pipe ducts and are based on standard 1700 m (5'6") bathtub.
[b]May have compact shower room 2.8 m².
[c]Figures rounded.

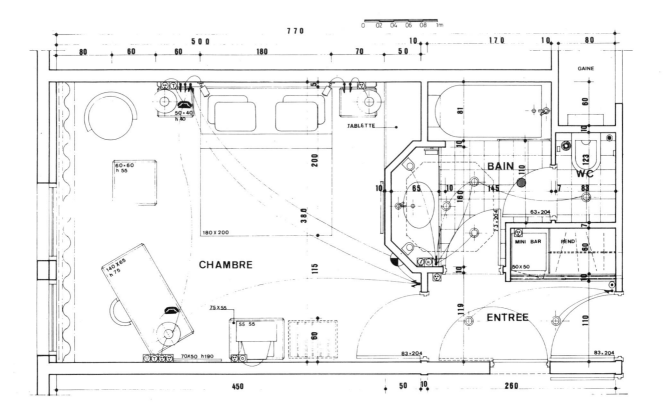

Key

⊛ Outlet: standard voltage
Ⓣ Telephone point
Ⓤ Outlet: universal voltage
Ⓡ Outlet: razor
⟼ Switch: simple
⤢ Switch: local
◉ Switch: general
Ⓩ Sound adjuster
◉ Television aerial
⊕ Loud speaker

1 Hanging closet
2 Mini bar
3 Luggage rack
4 Mirror
5 Shelf
6 Bedside cabinet
7 Chair and coffee table
8 Desk
9 Duct

Figure 7.4 *Hotel Sofitel*
Space requirements for guestroom furniture

These are economically located at the corners, ends or top floor of buildings – usually with other advantages of better outlook and privacy.

All-suite hotels offer suite combinations of rooms (see section 2.12) and high-ceilinged rooms may also be planned with sleeping and living areas at different levels.

7.2.5 Rooms for the disabled

With aging populations and increasing concern over equal opportunities, hotels must provide facilities for the handicapped and disabled. As a rule 1–2% of rooms must be equipped for disabled use.

Location

Rooms for the ambulant disabled are usually on the ground floor or easily accessible by elevator from an allocated carpark. Long ramp inclines should not exceed 1:20 and transitional strips are required over thresholds.

Corridors

Corridors must be at least 915 mm (3'0") wide and doors 815 mm (2'8") clear opening. Lobbies need to be 460 mm (1'6") wider than the latch side of the door. Doors to closets must be either narrow or sliding with hanging rails and shelves not higher than 1.37 m (4'6").

Bathrooms

A central turning space of 1.52 m (5'0") must be allowed, increasing the bathroom width to 2.75 m (9'0"). This may require the removal of one bed. The vanity tops should be 860 mm (2'0") high to allow 685 mm (2'3") knee space. Mirrors should extend down to 1.0 m (3'4"). Grab bars must be fitted on the headwall and sides of the bath and toilet. As a compromise the toilet seat height is usually 430 mm (17").

Bedrooms

Standard 3.65 m (12'0") wide bedrooms can be adapted with furniture rearrangement and modification. The eye level seated in a wheelchair is 1.07–1.37 m (3'6"–4'6") and switches should be 1.2 m (4'0") high. 910 mm (3'0") space should be allowed between beds and furniture. The optimum height for beds is 450–500 mm (1'6"–1'8") with toe space below. Dressing tables must allow 685 mm (2'3") knee space. A low window sill 610 mm (2'0") high is preferable for improved view.

7.2.6 Ceiling heights

Room ceiling heights are related to room areas – particularly lengths – and also tend to be higher in hot climates. The ceiling over the entrance lobby and bathroom may be lowered to house air-conditioning and extraction equipment (Table 7.4).

Table 7.4 Ceiling heights

	m	ft
Normal – over sleeping/living areas	2.5	8.2
Minimum	2.3	7.5
Preferable in hot climates	3.0	9.8
Bathroom and entrance lobby	2.2	7.2
Minimum	2.0	6.6

7.2.7 Balconies and terraces

Amenity space in the form of balconies and terraces can add significant costs (extension of building structure, loss of room space). There may be problems with security (access), wind funnelling and suction, waterproofing (at junctions), drainage, air-conditioning regulation in rooms and safety (raised thresholds, low wall or railing enclosure). Balconies and terraces are usually limited to resort hotel and apartment rooms which provide an attractive vista justifying the price differential.

A balcony may project outside the building facade or be focused into the area of the room. It can be angled or serrated to increase a side view, to catch the cooling sea breeze or to provide better screening from other rooms.

Balcony access allows easier window cleaning and may provide a secondary fire escape route. The projection also reduces the risk of vertical fire spread through windows and can give noise screening from car parks, roads and service areas.

Terraces may be formed by stepping back construction to utilize lower roof areas. This may be used on a steeply sloping site, or to reduce the abrupt outline of a large building by providing a relationship with the scale of the surroundings.

7.2.8 Noise reduction

Sensitivity to noise intrusion is high, particularly at night. Noise limitation involves both planning and specification requirements:

Insulation   Double glazing of windows and roof insulation (in susceptible areas). High mass party walls between rooms. Limited chasing. Dense floors with impact noise reduction (coverings, construction). Enclosure and acoustic insulation of pipework and ceilings.

Planning   Grouping together noise-generating areas (bathrooms, equipment). Back-to-back arrangement of room fittings.

Fittings   Adjustable closure of doors, closets, drawers. Design of coat hangers, locks, hinges.

Engineering   Pressure and velocity limitation in tunnels (pipes, ducts). Design of valves, faucets, cisterns, grilles, switches. Acoustic isolation of elevators and plant (see section 5.5).

7.3 Furniture and furnishings

7.3.1 Beds

The size and number of beds largely dictates the dimensions and layout of the room (see section 7.2.3)

Sizes

Heights (including mattress)
Typically 530–600 mm (20–24 in). Higher beds look more comfortable and are less tiring to make up. Lower divans (400–450 mm) make the room appear more spacious.

Glides or castors to allow easy movement. Usually at least 220 mm (8½ in) under clearance is provided for vacuuming and checking. *Headboards* are normally fixed to the wall to minimize damage. Typically 900–1000 mm (36–39 in) high, they may be framed and padded, straight or shaped to suit the room decor.

Essential features
- *Comfort*: upholstered quality of mattress and base.
- *Durability*: including edge reinforcement, retention of shape.
- *Quietness*: absence of creaking joints, springs, etc.
- *Standardization*: to allow interchangeability, replacement.
- *Safety*: inflammability, fire and smoke hazard.
- *Storage*: dismantling, mould resistance.

Supplements
Studio beds convertible into settees with easy movement of the base. *Foldup beds* top, side or centre hinged to reduce storage area: these may be stored in wall cupboards.

7.3.2 Furniture

Requirements for hanging and storage space and other furniture in guestrooms depend on

Table 7.5

| | American | | European | | | |
	Width (in)	Length (in)	Width (mm)	(in)	Length (mm)	(in)
Twin	39	80	1000	39½	2000	79
Oversized twin	45	80				
Double	54	80	1500	59	2000	79
Queen	60	80				
King	72/78	80				

Figure 7.5 *Space requirements for various items of guestroom furniture*

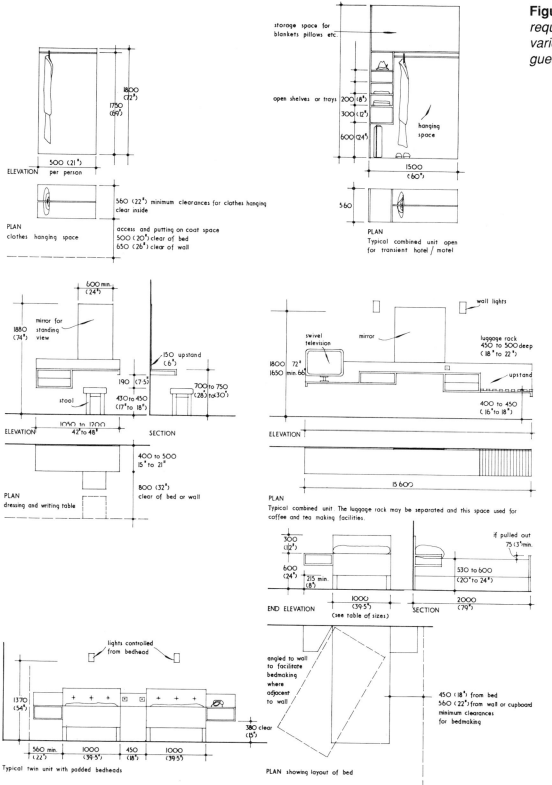

ELEVATION   per person

500 (21")

1800 (72")
1750 (69")

PLAN
clothes hanging space

560 (22") minimum clearances for clothes hanging clear inside

access and putting on coat space
500 (20") clear of bed
650 (26") clear of wall

storage space for blankets pillows etc.

open shelves or trays 200 (8")
300 (12")
600 (24")

hanging space

1500 (60")

560

PLAN
Typical combined unit open for transient hotel / motel

600 min. (24")

mirror for standing view
1880 (74")

150 upstand (6")

190 (7.5")

stool

430 to 450 (17" to 18")

700 to 750 (28") to 30")

1050 to 1200
42" to 48"

ELEVATION

SECTION

PLAN
dressing and writing table

400 to 500
15" to 21"

800 (32")
clear of bed or wall

wall lights

swivel television

mirror

luggage rack
450 to 500 deep
(18" to 22")

1800 72"
1650 min. 66"

upstand

400 to 450
(16" to 18")

ELEVATION

15 600

PLAN
Typical combined unit. The luggage rack may be separated and this space used for coffee and tea making facilities.

300 (12")

600 (24")

215 min. (8")

if pulled out
75 (3") min.

530 to 600
(20" to 24")

1000 (39.5")
(see table of sizes)

2000 (79")

END ELEVATION

SECTION

lights controlled from bedhead

1370 (54")

380 clear (15")

560 min. (22")   1000 (39.5")   450 (18")   1000 (39.5")

Typical twin unit with padded bedheads

angled to wall to facilitate bedmaking where adjacent to wall

450 (18") from bed
560 (22") from wall or cupboard
minimum clearances for bedmaking

PLAN showing layout of bed

233

Table 7.6 Hanging and storage space and other furniture

Hotel stay 1–3 nights: double/twin room[a]	High-grade (mm)	(ft)	Medium-grade[b] (mm)	(ft)	Optimum/minimum dimensions
Hanging space: wardrobe length	1200	48	900	36	Internal depth 560 mm (22 in) Rail height 160 mm (63 in) Overshelf 1750 mm (69 in)
	m²	sqft	m²	sqft	
Storage space: shelves, trays	1.50	16	1.10	12	Shelf height 200 mm (8 in) min increasing to 300–400 mm (12–16 in) at high and low levels. Tray depth 100 mm (4 in)
	Separate		*Combined*		
Writing and dressing tables (with drawers)	m² 1.00	sqft 12	m² 0.50	sqft 6	Depth minimum 400 mm (15 in) optimum 500–550 mm (20–21 in) Height 700–750 mm (28–30 in)
Luggage rack standard area[c]	0.45	48	0.45	48	Optimum height 450 mm (18 in) Depth 500 mm (20 in) Width 900 mm (35 in) Minimum 750 mm (30 in)
Bedside tables[d]	Each side		Outside/ between		Width minimum 375 mm (15 in) Up to 600 mm (24 in) Height 600–700 mm (24–27 in) Related to bed height
Loose chairs[e] and table	2–3 1		2 1		Chairs: lightweight, compact, upholstered. Tables: circular or rectangular

Notes: [a]For single rooms: standard furniture normal but may be reduced by 25% in economy grade.
[b]For resort hotels: increased hanging space 1200 mm (48 in); storage space 1.50 m² (16 sqft).
[c]For resort hotels: 2 luggage racks preferable. One may be portable or fitted with cushions and backrests as a seat.
[d]Housing lighting, telephone, sound system, etc. controls. Usually fixed.
[e]Low coffee tables with two comfortable chairs which may have rounded backs for easy repositioning. Luxury hotels may include settee. The tables must accommodate a tray, lamp and place settings or books. Dual purpose chair provided for dressing and writing table(s).

the grade of the hotel, number of people sharing the room and the length of stay (Table 7.6). Narrow tables increase room space but result in more damage/marking of wall.

7.3.3 Quality and specifications

Furniture and furnishings in hotels are subject to more intensive use, strain and damage than domestic units and call for more exacting specifications. Particular points for attention are:

- *Surfaces* – resistant to burns, varnish, solvents, ink, etc. stains and scratching. Vulnerable areas protected (toughened glass, mats)
- *Support* – anchorage in walls for cantilevered furniture and fittings
- *Framework* – stays, hinges, locks must be simple, strong and quiet in operation
- *Maintenance* – provisions for checking, replacement of components and renovation
- *Coat hangers* – nylon glides with detachable hanger for easy movement, reduced noise.

Extent of loose furniture

To save space and assist room cleaning, most large items of furniture are fitted into the construction but beds, chairs and coffee tables are invariably loose to allow for making up and rearrangement. In luxury hotels, the dressing, writing and side tables are usually individual items of furniture.

7.3.4 Other fittings

Mirrors	Fitted mirrors with screened lighting above or adjacent. *Bathroom*: may be extra wide for illusion of space. *Full length*: at least 1.37 m (4'6") long. Fitted in lobby. *Dressing table*: top 1.9 m (6'3") for standing view.
Lamps	At bedside, over dressing table, in living area in addition to lighting in lobby and closet.
Features	Planters, decorative artwork.
Drinks refrigerator	Fitted in cabinet to suit room decor.
Television console	On wall bracket or turntable allowing adjustment.
Room safe	In cupboard or wall recess. Programmed.
Telephone	Usually located on bedside table. Extension to lounge (suite).
Facsimile	Terminal fitted near worktable.
Computer	Power point installed above or under worktable.
Wastebins	Compatible with design.

7.3.5 Decor and furnishings

Decoration and furnishings need to satisfy several requirements:

Appearance: light, visually extending colours, co-ordinated designs.

Durability: adequate life expectancy. Resistant to damage discolouring.
Cleaning: easy cleaning, removal, laundering/dry cleaning.

Walls are usually painted or covered in vinyl paper with redecoration every 1–3 years. Framing or protection is required to edges and external corners.

Finishes: guestroom

Floor	Usually carpeting (see below). Tiles may be suitable for resorts in hot climates.
Walls	Painted or vinyl paper. Framing or protection is needed to edges and external corners.
Woodwork	Painted or pre-finish doors and cabinets. Frames may be painted in matching or contrasting colours.
Ceilings	Usually soffit of floor slab. Acoustic treatment. Painted.

Finishes: bathroom

Floor	Ceramic with falls to drain outlet.
Walls	Ceramic or marble tiles to 1.4 m (4'6"). Painted above.
Ceiling	Usually accessible tiles or slats. Painted.

Finishes: furnishings

Carpeting	Medium-grade (high-grade in corridors) with mark and shade camouflaging with muted colours and patterns.
Curtaining	Coordinated mesh and lined drape curtains usually provided in half sections. Resistant to sunlight, fading, creasing.
Bed overlay cushions	Coordinated design, neat fitted finish, resistant to soiling and wear with intensive use.
Linen	Four to five sets per bed (for laundering etc.). High-quality linen required with alternative blankets or duvet covers.

Towelling Bath, hand and face towels for each occupant and floor covers. May be woven with hotel motif. Bathrobes may be disposable.

Linen and towelling are included in operators' supplies: provision made for storage.

7.3.6 Electrical outlets

Receptacle outlets (socket) Minimum three. Positioned no more than 3 m (10 ft) apart on ring main with isolating switches and correctly rated fuses.

Shaver outlet Supplied through transformer. With 200/250–100/150 V selector switch and isolator.

Lighting circuits Three to five independently controlled circuits. *Entrance foyer* (closet interior operated by door opening). *Main*, central and side lights (with local switches). *Bedside*, each side with local switches. *Bathroom*, above mirror and centrally recessed. Dressing area.

Multiple connection With control panel for radio, telephone, automatic relay systems (morning calls, messages, fire alarm, etc.), facsimile terminal.

Telephone Bedside location with extensions to lounge/work area and bathroom (emergency).

Television Power and aerial system connections (with metered in-house film system). Preferably on swivel base or arm for easy movement.

Dispense cabinet Terminal power with isolating switches.

Room status Terminal point to room status system.

Energy control Automatic systems operated by door key and/or window opening.

Door lock Electronic door-locking system.

Air conditioning and heater controls Relay to fan motor and thermostat regulator.

Fire detection Sensor and alarm with automatic sprinkler in lobby if installed.

Electrical distribution to guestrooms is normally through panel boards on each floor. 25% spaceways should be allowed. Circuit wiring must be to approved engineering standards with overload protection and grounding. Specific precautions are required for electrical outlets in bathrooms. At least three circuits should be installed for each pair of rooms with separate circuits for the foyer, bathroom and main room. Voltages of supplies in different countries range from 115 to 240 (single phase). The wiring load is usually estimated on 20 amps per guestroom (see section 10.3).

7.3.7 Environmental control

Mechanical services to rooms range from natural ventilation with space heating to centralized air-conditioning allowing individual adjustment. Natural ventilation is common in temperate climates, particularly for resort and budget accommodation. For extremes of high or low temperature it is necessary to provide space cooling or heating and this may involve part or full conditioning of the air circulation. Similar requirements apply where windows must be closed because of noise etc. Details of design standards and air-conditioning systems are summarized in Chapter 10. Key considerations include:

System: Unitary or centralized circulations

Appearance: Building design, location of plant and equipment, integration

External: Noise, heat/steam emission, condensation, access

Locations: Under window. In lowered ceiling over lobby and bathroom

Controls: Fan speeds (3). Temperature (range), cutout (window opening)

Noise limits: Night-time levels NC 30 – standard NC 25 – high grade

Operation: Versatility, efficiency, maintenance, relative costs.

7.3.8 Bathroom planning

Apart from some budget hotel and hostel designs, *en suite* shower or bathrooms are provided for each guestroom. Bathrooms are invariably arranged back to back sharing common vertical service ducts and pipework and confining noise.

Options

- *Internal to guestrooms*: with service access from corridor. Using mechanical ventilation and installed lighting.
- *Between guestrooms*: reducing width of building by some 4.5 m (14.8 ft) for restricted site or courtyard designs.
- *On external walls*: allowing natural lighting and ventilation but with reduction of windows to guestrooms.

Internal bathrooms are most common giving a more efficient plan area and better utilization of the outside walls. Lighting and air extraction equipment are usually installed in a lowered ceiling with plenum air supply units fitted above the ceiling of the entrance foyer to the room.

Layout

Bathroom dimensions are mainly dictated by the number of fixtures and the size of the bath.

7.3.9 Bathroom design

Fixtures

Bathtub

- Standard 1700×750 mm (5'6"×2'6"). Minimum 1525 mm (5'0") long.

- May be lowered by recessing floor to accommodate waste outlet and trap (accessible).
- Fitted with adjustable shower extension and containing curtain or screen.
- Taps colour coded with supply thermostatically controlled.
- Lever-operated waste outlet. Recessed soap holder and grabrail fitted.
- Retractable drying line installed above bath.

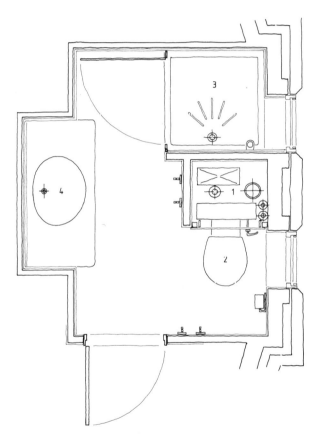

Figure 7.6 *Shower room suite: Arcade Hotel*
Detail of the shower room suites for the Arcade Hotel, Birmingham, using prefabricated units. The internal area is 2000×2360 mm (78.7×92.9"). Designer: Fowlers Design and Build. Clients: Arcade (UK) Properties Ltd

1 590×563 mm enclosure for WC cistern, hot & cold water pipes, soil and vent pipes and airduct.
2 WC pan
3 815×815 mm shower cubicle
4 1200 mm vanity unit

237

- Whirlpool tubs, 1700×915 mm (5'6"×3'0") may be installed (in spa hotels) and separate shower cubicles.

Water closet
- May be partially screened or separated from bathroom.
- Siphonic closets are more efficient. The fitment may be corbelled from the wall leaving floor clear for easy cleaning. Flushing cisterns may be enclosed in adjacent duct.

Bidets
- Standard requirement in luxury hotels forming part of the suite. Corbelled fixtures preferable. Anti-siphonage connections to hot and cold supplies with thermostatically controlled mixing valve and waste outlet.

Washbasins
- May be pedestal-mounted basin 630×485 mm (25×19 in) but usually fitted as vanity unit in an extended shelftop.
- Dual vanity basins or a second unit in the dressing area may be provided for twin rooms.
- Taps must be colour coded (red, blue) with mixer valve and green for drinking supply (refrigerated).
- Simple lever-operated wastes fitted.

Bathroom items: checklist
- Toilet roll holders or dispensers (duplicated)
- Towel rail and overhead rack
- Clothes hook. Dressing robe
- Shaving mirrors on extended swivel bracket
- Emergency telephone
- Music relay speaker with volume control
- Retractable washline (over bath)
- Hairdryer (fitted)
- Soap trays (recessed)
- Glass holders
- Wastebin
- Weighing scales
- Lighting: general, concealed above mirror
- Floor drainage and outlet drains (with seal).

7.4 Servicing of rooms

7.4.1 Requirements

Efficient room cleaning and servicing with minimum disturbance to guests requires provision for:

- *Separation*: service elevators, lobbies, housekeeping rooms and pantries, separate from guest circulations.
- *Transport*: carts and trolleys for housekeeping supplies, food service etc., linen chutes.
- *Equipment*: socket outlets, vacuum points, access to service ducts and fire-fighting equipment, equipped service rooms.
- *Control*: room indicators and status systems, housekeeping offices and stores.

7.4.2 Service areas

Service elevator	Requirements detailed in section 6.6.5.
Service lobby	Width 2.1 m (7 ft) to 3.0 m (9 ft) with space for parked and waiting carts, trolleys and equipment provided on each landing, separate from guest circulation.
Construction	Walls usually smooth concrete, blockwork or plaster, painted with edges protected from damage. Floors vinyl, composition or epoxy resin, level, smooth and noise reducing. Corridors screened from noise and bright lights.
Housekeeping	Usually one per floor serving each guestroom wing.
Linen rooms	Located adjacent to service elevator (entered through lobby) and/or at end of corridor adjacent to service stairs (emergency exit).
Area	Typically 3.0×4.2 m (9×14 ft) for 30 rooms depending on construction module. Separate areas provided for

Linen chutes

clean linen racks and storage supplies, trolley cart parking (1 cart per 15 to 18 rooms), soiled linen containers, trash bags, cleaners, sink and shelving.

In larger hotels, chutes may be installed to convey used linen to the laundry receiving/sorting area on a lower floor. Chutes are usually smooth galvanized steel sheeting fitted with angled openings on each floor, having self-closing fire-resisting doors. Minimum opening 450×450 mm (18×18in). Shafts must be ventilated and fitted with sprinklers.

Trash

Removed in disposable bags by cart or separate chute to collection container. Similar requirements.

Food pantries

Where room service of food is provided, separate pantries or kitchens are required. A pantry may serve one or several floors depending on access to service elevator. Typical area 3.0×4.3 m (10×14 ft).

Construction

Designed as food room with non-absorbent, cleansable walls, floors, work surfaces. Walls usually tiled up to 1.8 m (6 ft).

Equipment

Depends on extent of centralization. Usually includes equipment for beverages, icemaking and light meals (refrigerator, toaster, boiling top, microwave oven, grill, convection oven), benching, sink, storage cupboards (china, silverware, trays) and trolley park.

Services

Service rooms require adequate benchtop power points, good lighting – 400 lux (40 lumen/sqft). Ventilation – three air changes/hr plus extraction over equipment. Cold – preferably chilled – drinking water in addition to hot and cold supplies and drainage.

Employee WC

May be required in large hotel for housekeeping staff. WC and washbasin installed in separately ventilated cubicle (six air changes per hour) with intervening lobby.

Entrance to corridor

Service doors must be at least 1050 mm (42 in) wide, preferably double-leaf 1375 mm (54 in), self-closing and recessed back from the corridor. Doors should be fire resisting (½ hour), sound insulated, resistant to damage and designed to match the decor.

8

Public facilities

8.1 Extent of provisions

8.1.1 Variations

The range and scale of public facilities in a hotel are determined by three main factors:

- Type of hotel and market emphasis
- Size (number of rooms), location, extent of competition
- Non-residential use of hotel facilities.

Hotel grading or company requirements usually specify minimum standards for particular categories of hotels. In some situations, such as isolated tourist resorts, the markets for inclusive packaged holidays will require extensive food, beverage, entertainment and leisure facilities. Specific provisions will apply in accommodating conventions and business meetings and hotels may market their facilities for local banquets and other functions.

Many small *staging inns and budget hotels* economize in capital cost and operation by providing only the minimum public space. In roadside locations, café-restaurant services may be operated fully independently.

Hotel-garni and *bed and breakfast establishments* minimize food service to reduce staffing costs and in guesthouses communal facilities are shared with the host family.

In *leisure tourism accommodation* generally the trend is towards independent choice including self-catering. Most resort developments provide the option of rented units (rooms, suites, apartments, villas) which have individual kitchen facilities. In condominium-style resorts

– individually owned and time-shared – emphasis is given to real estate development with units clustered around private recreational focuses. Restaurants, cafés and bars tend to be small-scale, franchised or independently operated and widely varied in theme and style of service.

8.1.2 Areas per room

See Table 8.1 opposite.
See also section 4.2.3.

8.2 Food service outlets

8.2.1 Marketing

Food and beverage play an important role in distinguishing hotel standards, attracting outside interest and promoting repeat custom. However, the operating expenses and allocated overheads (initial cost, replacements, energy, management) are generally high and the utilization of hotel restaurants tends to fluctuate widely (see section 4.3.6).

Planning and development of food and beverage outlets requires detailed analysis of trends in consumer preferences (in food choice, surrounding and style of service), rationalization and more efficient use of space and facilities and location and design to attract wider custom.

Residential take-up of restaurant places varies widely during the day. In a representative city hotel the demand may range from 80–90% at breakfast, 15–20% at midday to 30–40% in the

Table 8.1 Public areas per room, by hotel type

Hotel type	Seats and net areas per room[a]								
	Restaurants, cafés			Bars, lounges			Function, meeting rooms[b]		
	Seats	m²	sqft	Seats	m²	sqft	Seats	m²	sqft
Deluxe hotel[c]	1.0	2.0	22	0.8	1.6	17	1.5	2.4	26
City centre hotel[d]	0.8	1.5	16	0.8	1.4	15	3.0	4.5	48
High-grade resort hotel[c]	1.5	2.8	30	0.8	1.6	17	2.0	3.0	32
Resort village	0.6	1.1	12	0.8	1.4	15	1.0	1.4	15
Suburban hotel[e]	0.9	1.6	17	0.6	1.0	11	2.0	2.8	30
Motor hotel[f]	0.8	1.4	15	0.4	0.6	6	1.9	1.4	15
Airport hotel[d]	0.8	1.4	15	0.6	1.0	11	2.5	3.5	38
Budget hotel[g]	0.6	1.0	11	0.3	0.4	4	–	–	–
All-suite hotel[c]	0.6	1.2	13	0.3	0.6	6	1.5	2.4	26

Notes: [a]Depends on particular location and marketing. For gross areas (access, cloaks) add 20–25%. With kitchens and stores (gross) add 40–50%
[b]Including foyer/reception area.
[c]Several lounges and meeting/function rooms.
[d]Attracting conferences and banquets.
[e]Also provincial towns.
[f]Limited conference/function demand.
[g]May be reduced or omitted.

evenings. This variation is even more pronounced in transient accommodation. One solution may be to group accommodation with restaurants and cafés which are operated independently (roadside inns, budget hotels, resorts).

Food and beverage space may also be rationalized by providing in-room facilities or collective room service for 'continental' breakfast. Where restaurant choice is limited, the design may allow for easy changes in style, lighting and ambience, including the introduction of alternative buffet service.

Non-residential use of restaurants is often promoted by the introduction of more popular food concepts, variety of choice, daytime informality and convenient entrance. Areas may be separated to cater for business lunches or group functions. Cross-advertising, special promotions and created events are commonly used to attract wider attention.

8.2.2 Range of choice

The style of restaurant and range of choice depends largely on the size of hotel and requirements set by grading or company policy. Although a large dining room or coffee shop is needed for the concentrated breakfast demands and for tour and conference groups, smaller, more intimate areas offer extended variety of choice without greatly increasing the space. Most medium-sized hotels provide two restaurants and larger hotels three or four (Table 8.2).

8.2.3 Relationship to kitchens

In planning restaurant requirements, the need for adjacent kitchens or service pantries must be considered:

Adjacent to main kitchen: Savings in kitchen space, equipment and staff. Higher operational efficiency with detailed planning.

Table 8.2 Style of restaurant and range of choice

Hotel size (rooms)	Coffee shop, café[a], brasserie (seats)	Main or speciality restaurant (seats)	Ethnic or gourmet restaurant (seats)
50	50–75	–	–
150	80	60	–
250	100	60	50
Space provision/seat[b]	1.6 m²	2.0 m²	2.0 m²

Note: [a]Excluding poolside, café-bar and other club facilities. This area is also used for breakfast meals with buffet or table service.

[b]The area required per seat is dictated mainly by the size and spacing of the furniture, proportion of tables seating two persons and arrangements for food service (buffet, table service, etc.).

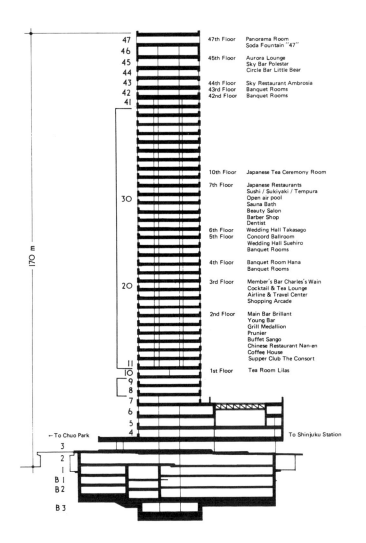

Figure 8.1 *Keio Plaza, Inter-Continental Hotel, Tokyo*
The Keio Plaza hotel is part of a vast skyscraper redevelopment of Westside Tokyo. Occupying a land area of 14 500 m² (158 000 sqft) with a plot ratio of 8:1 the hotel accommodates 200 guests with multiple dining and convention facilities. Architects: Nikon Architects

(b)

Figure 8.2 *Furama hotel, Singapore*
The furama shows a typical Japanese restaurant arrangement (a). Constructional finishes and decorative features provide a quiet, unobtrusive background complementing the warm natural wood of the furniture (b). Architects and designers: Kano Kikaku Sekkeisha, Y. Shibata and Associates

(a)

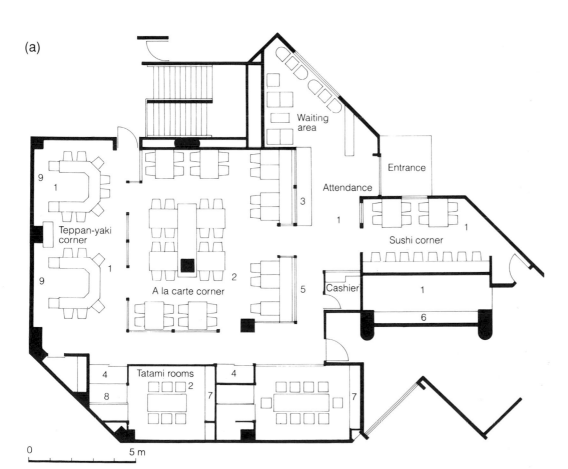

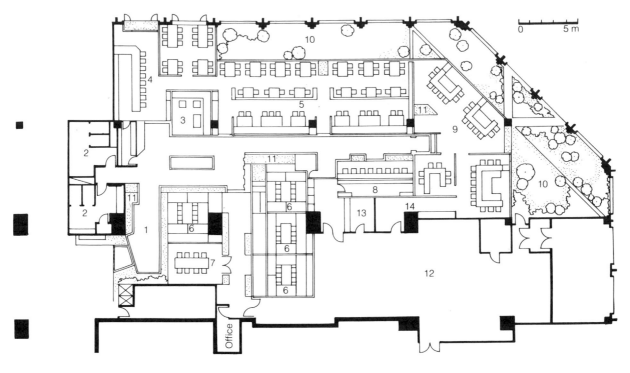

(a)

(b)

(c)

Figure 8.3 *Shangri-La Hotel, Kuala Lumpur*
Designed by Kanko Kikaku Sekkeisha, the Shangri-La restaurants (a) include an *à la carte* restaurant (b), waiting area and bar, sushi bar, tempura counter, teppanyaki restaurant and tatami rooms. Traditional landscaping features provide an interesting backcloth (c).

(a) Ground floor

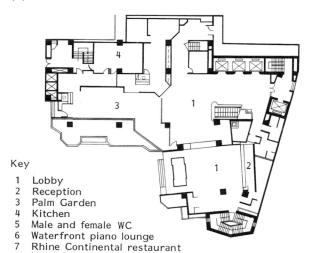

Key

1 Lobby
2 Reception
3 Palm Garden
4 Kitchen
5 Male and female WC
6 Waterfront piano lounge
7 Rhine Continental restaurant

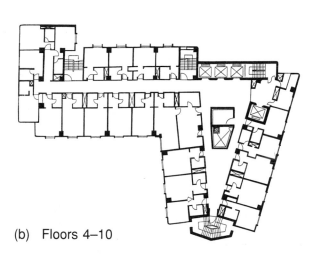

(b) Floors 4–10

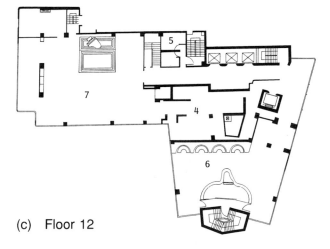

(c) Floor 12

Figure 8.4 *Hotel Riverview, Taipei*
The Hotel Riverview is centrally located between business/commercial and cultural/temple areas of Taipei. Each of the 220 rooms has a scenic view of the river and city.

Faced in red brick, the mid-rise building of twelve storeys has restaurants and banquet rooms on four floors including a continental restaurant and piano lounge occupying the top floor

Remote or on another floor: Requiring separate satellite or service kitchen with 25–35% duplication of space, equipment and work.

Kitchen details are given in section 9.3.

8.2.4 Design development

The design of a food service facility generally follows an evolving sequence of steps:

• Marketing, location, operation and finance considerations

• Development of the food concept and service style
• Planning circulations, layouts and seating arrangements
• Technical requirements and service integrated into the design
• Interior design details, including furniture, furnishings and equipment
• Complementary requirements, tableware, uniforms, graphics.

In hotel development this procedure tends to divide into two separated stages with marketing and space allocation being decided as part of the initial planning and interior design when the building shell is completed. The same procedure applies to individual cafés, restaurants and bars in resorts.

Markets	Characteristics, level of demand, average spend, preferences, trends.
Location	Advantages, space, access, relationship to entrance, kitchens etc.
Operation	Operating hours, number of covers, turnover, staffing, food preparation.
Concept	Menu style of preparation and service theme for design, key functions.
Ambience	Emphasis on sophistication, intimacy, sociability, entertainment.
Service style	Exhibition cooking, buffet style, counter seats, table waited, table-side carts.
Circulations	Public entrance, reception, cloaks, cashier, aisles, service routes.
Service	Access, screening, service stations, table clearance, counter service.
Seating plans	Space per seat, groupings, perimeter and interior views, personalization.
Technical	Engineering services, equipment, locations, access, integration, protection.
Equipment	Service counter design, station equipment, terminals, special effects.
Features	Focuses for interest, theme features, artwork, plants, screens.
Furniture	Table sizes, shapes, adaptability, styles of chairs, seats, carts, stations.
Decor	Treatment of walls, ceilings, floors, windows, doors. Colour and lighting schemes.
Fittings	Luminaries, sound system, air diffusers, grilles, fire safety, controls.
Furnishings	Carpets, curtaining, linen, uniforms, changes from daytime to evening.
Tableware	Menu and service style: china, silver, glassware, table appointments.
Graphics	Signage, menu, presentation, information display, printing needs.
Special	Access and seating for disabled, reduction–extension of areas.

8.2.5 Main characteristics

See Table 8.3 opposite.

8.2.6 Adaptability

Restaurant design may allow for some adaptability to suit varying requirements:

Spatial	With soundproofed partitioning to create separate area for private dining or functions. Spill-over into adjacent atrium or external terraced areas to provide lively café-style atmosphere.
Lighting	High spatial illumination in daytime. Low background with table lighting at night. Changes in tone and direction of lighting (dual circuits, dimmer switches, adjustable fittings).
Service	Changes in mode of service and uniforms from exposed table tops, place settings, simplified menu, buffet-style service to table linen, sophisticated tableware, à la carte menu.
Decor	Use of screens, reversible panels, relocatable curtains and pictures.
Furniture	Stackable chairs, adaptable table tops (square, round) linked for extension. Wheeled serving counters and stations.

Major changes incur considerable costs in storage and duplication of equipment as well as extra labour and disruption.

Table 8.3 Characteristics of food and beverage outlets

Type	Operation	Characteristics
Coffee shop Café Brasserie	Open 18+ hours/day. Limited menu of broad appeal. Informal atmosphere. Quick service	Individual stylized design. Bright and lively ambience. Fitted bar for counter or buffet-style services may include counter seating. Combination of booth, banquet and loose furniture. Usually closely grouped, with seat areas screened by planters, etc. May spill out into atrium or terrace
Main restaurant	Main meal periods. Cyclical table d'hôte menu with à la carte 'option'. Formal atmosphere. Waited/buffet service	Traditional design reflecting character and sophistication of hotel. Entered through foyer space with host station. Seating plans arranged around external views or internal focuses of interest. Tables and chairs, mainly for two, in small groups with some separation and privacy. High quality linen and tableware
Speciality restaurant	May be limited to midday and evening. Specific à la carte menu and style of service	Theme-based design with emphasis on food speciality, ethnic or local character, display and presentation. Furniture, tableware, furnishings and equipment specifically designed. Authentic features incorporated. Styled uniforms and graphic design
Entertainment restaurant Night club	May be separate, purposely designed room or provided by rearrangement of furniture in restaurant and/or lounge	Loose furniture – although raised balcony or alcove seating may be provided round perimeter. Equipped with dance square, special lighting and sound systems. Service entry from performers changing rooms and equipment store. Acoustic separation from other areas

8.2.7 Other outlets

Increased sales of food and beverages may be created through a number of other outlets:

Lobby, atrium	Refreshment service, display carts and decorative stands.
Recreation	Food and beverage counters, open-air restaurants, pool bars, club members' lounges.
Serviced apartments	Direct or pantry preparation service with corridor linkage or vehicle distribution.
Bakery/patisserie	Shop sales of confectionery etc. products.
Resorts	Franchised outlets for centrally produced food.

8.3 Lounges and bars

8.3.1 Location

Lounges and associated bars or refreshment service are often provided:

* in or near the lobby for waiting and meetings between guests and visitors

(a)   Exterior

(b)   Restaurant

Figure 8.5 *Kuusamon Hotel, Kuulama, Lapland*
Located on the edge of the Artic Circle, the Kuusamon Hotel occupies a site of 5 hectares (12.5 acres),
providing 44 guestrooms with restaurants, a dance hall, small casino and swimming pool. The design
reflects the character of the area and features an octagonal tent-like roof as well as exposed hewn
stonework in the facades. Architects: SOK Building department. Chief Architect: Pauli Lehtinen

- for entertainment, social relaxation, including piano or cocktail bars
- in association with high class restaurants and other services
- for conference groups and functions as informal breakout areas.

The emphasis placed on beverage services depends greatly on the location of the hotel and its market orientation. In city centres the lobby tends to be a popular meeting place for visitors and guests. In resorts and convention hotels evening entertainment is important. Traditional pub-type bars are often used in inns and hotels in Europe.

In smaller and mid-grade hotels beverage services are usually rationalized into a common lounge-bar located near the entrance.

8.3.2 Features

Lobby lounge and bar
Lounge seating is required in or adjacent to the lobby usually taking up some 10% of this space. The lounge must be clearly visible but separated from desk areas and circulation. Service of beverages and light refreshments is provided through a small dispense bar with access to the kitchen or local pantry. A piano may be provided for quiet entertainment.

Entertainment lounge
An entertainment lounge may be located on higher or lower floors having easy access, fire egress and acoustic separation from other areas of the hotel.

Design emphasis is focused on the cocktail bar, stage and dance areas and external views are not necessary. Themed designs are often adopted to create a dynamic image. The lounge usually includes a piano or small stage with a dance area and may allow extension into other public space. Extensive technical systems must be installed to provide for varying requirements and control (lighting, sound, acoustics, fire safety, air-conditioning, bar and other equipment). Bar services are also required for nightclub, discothèque and other entertainment facilities.

Other lounges
Separate lounge areas may be required for exclusive use by guests (including library and writing rooms) and by conference groups. These

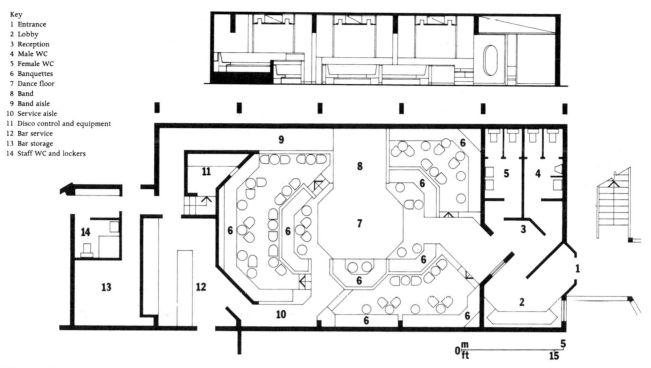

Key
1 Entrance
2 Lobby
3 Reception
4 Male WC
5 Female WC
6 Banquettes
7 Dance floor
8 Band
9 Band aisle
10 Service aisle
11 Disco control and equipment
12 Bar service
13 Bar storage
14 Staff WC and lockers

Figure 8.6 *Othon Palace Hotel, Bahia, Brazil*
Plan and section of basement nightclub showing ceiling service ducts and raised outer banquette seating. Architects: Paulo Casé, Luiz Acioli, LA Rengel. Interior Design: de Polo Associates. Operators: Othon Palace Hotels

---

are designed for quiet, comfortable relaxation with lounge chairs arranged in small groups.

8.3.3 Design

In restaurant design emphasis is usually given to the views out of windows (of scenery or recreational activities). Lounges are normally orientated around the bar and entertainment areas. Factors to consider are:

Markets	Residential and local markets. Characteristics, spending power.
Competition	Local facilities available. Popularity.
Alternatives	Options. Suitability for hotel standards and clientele.
Operation	Access to stores, cellars, operating hours, staffing, controls.
Emphasis	Lounge relaxation, bar focus, entertainment activity.
Location	Need for visibility, external access, noise confinement, fire exits.
Areas	Seating capacity, space allocation, bar area.
Support	Cloakrooms, toilets, performers' rooms, stage areas.
Technical	Mechanical and electrical services, locations for equipment.
Theme	Character, atmosphere, style of fittings and furniture.
Bar	Siting, access to stores, space, design, pumplines, equipment.
Furniture	Bar seating, table groupings, seat variations.
Fittings	Lighting, sound systems, microphones, controls.
Design	Features, decorative treatment, colour scheme, graphics.

249

1 Front desk
2 Elevator hall
3 Lounge
4 Seating
5 Display
6 Night club entrance
7 Bathers' entrance
8 Service Lobby
9 Safe deposit
10 Beauty salon
11 Barber's shop
12 Control
13 Male WC
14 Female WC
15 Footbath
16 Vestibule
17 Bar
18 Stage/dance floor
19 Duct spaces
20 Staff WC and lockers

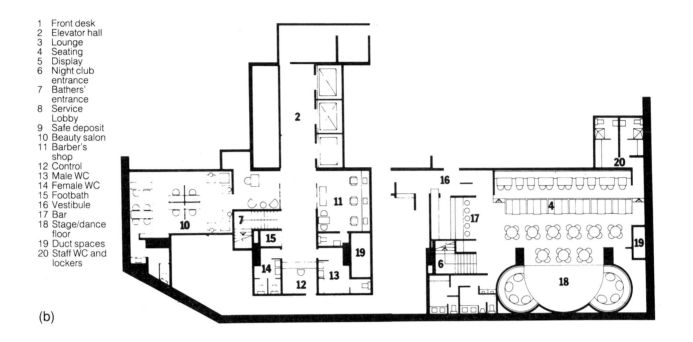

(b)

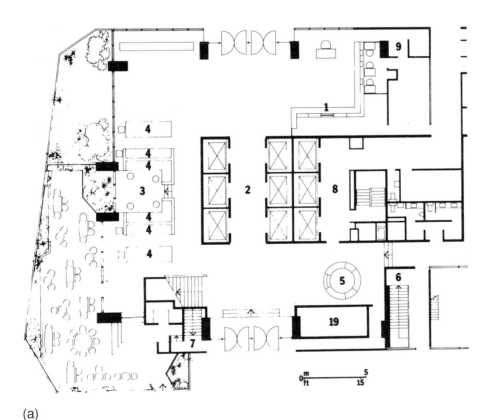

(a)

Figure 8.7 *Othon Palace Hotel, Rio de Janeiro, Brazil*

The entrance lobby, reception and lounge are at street level (a). Guestrooms occupy the 5th and 28th floor of a tower block, typically 27 rooms on each floor around a central circulation/services core. The hotel includes a rooftop swimming pool on the 29th floor.

Plans of the nightclub and bar at first basement level are also shown (b). On the same floor are a barbers shop and beauty parlour with a separate entrance for bathers. Architects: Pontual Associates. Consulting Architect: W. B. Tabler. Interior Design: de Polo Associates. Othon Palace Hotels

8.4 Conference, banqueting and function rooms

8.4.1 Marketing benefits

The provision of facilities for group functions offers a number of advantages:

- Association conventions, large conferences and exhibitions mainly occur outside peak tourist seasons. Convention expenditure is typically 2 to 2.5 times that of transient users.
- Facilities for meetings – often with food service – are regularly used by business visitors and local companies.
- Social functions and banquets generate demands at weekends, and high food and beverage revenues.
- The rooms can be hired for exhibitions, product launches, receptions, parties and other events.

Function and meeting space in hotels is generally multi-functional to allow higher utilization although purpose-designed lecture theatres may be provided in executive conference centres and specialized business suites. Hotels may also be part of large congress and exhibition complexes.

8.4.2 Areas

In most city centre hotels of high grade, the function areas account for 2.0–3.0 m² per guestroom: in resort and suburban hotels this reduces to 1.0–2.0 m² per guestroom, depending on market emphasis (Table 8.4). Luxury hotels and other hotels of mid-grade generally omit large ballrooms but usually include a suite of rooms for business meetings and social functions.

8.4.3 Planning

Function areas require careful evaluation and planning to allow efficient use and flexibility to meet widely varying demands:

- *Space requirements*: based on estimated numbers (see section 8.4.2), hotel occupancies, optimum size of convention groups, competition.
- *Structural requirements*: location for large column-free spaces: separation of structures,

(Continued on page 260)

Table 8.4 Typical ratios of space:250 room hotel[a] Total area 550–750 m² (6000–8000 sqft)

	Theatre style	Banquet layout	Classroom style[b]	
Ballroom or main hall	240 to 400[a]	200 to 320	125 to 200	Divisible into three. Foodservice
Banquet room or subsidiary hall	100	80	50	May be divisible to two. Foodservice
Meeting rooms	50×2		25×2	
Board rooms	25×2		12×2	
Foyer	60–100 m²			One-third of main hall. Shared for other circulation, toilets, etc
Gross factor	0.20			

Notes: [a]With high provision for conventions and functions.
[b]Theatre style 0.8 m²/seat. Banquet 1.0m²/seat. Classroom 1.6 m²/seat maximum capacity.
[c]Depending on competition and demand for larger conferences and banquets.

HOTELS

(a)   Third floor plan

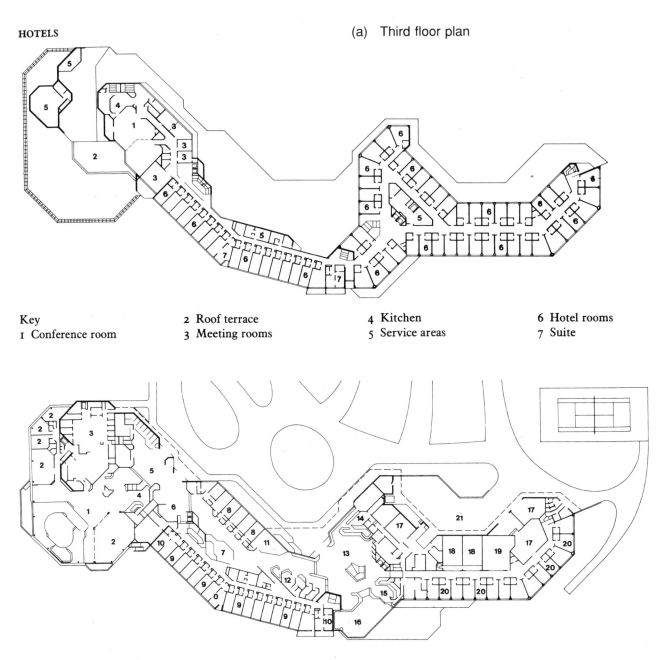

Key			
1 Conference room	2 Roof terrace	4 Kitchen	6 Hotel rooms
	3 Meeting rooms	5 Service areas	7 Suite

(b)   Second floor plan

Key	
1 Restaurant	12 Hairdresser
2 Meeting room	13 Lobby
3 Kitchen	14 Reception
4 Bar	15 Bar
5 Lobby	16 Lounge
6 Roulette	17 Admin and service
7 Winter garden	18 Upper part of squash
8 Offices	courts
9 Hotel rooms	19 Table tennis
10 Suite	20 Invalid rooms
11 Children's playroom	21 Service yard

(c) First floor plan

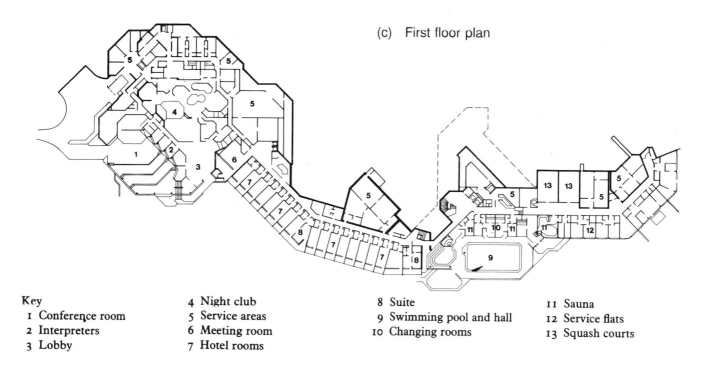

Key

1 Conference room	4 Night club
2 Interpreters	5 Service areas
3 Lobby	6 Meeting room
	7 Hotel rooms

8 Suite	11 Sauna
9 Swimming pool and hall	12 Service flats
10 Changing rooms	13 Squash courts

Figure 8.8 *Rantasipi Hotel, Laajavuori, Jyväskylä, Finland* Following enlargement this hotel has fully equipped meeting facilities for up to 400 participants and 176 hotel rooms (337 beds) on four floors. The buildings' contoured cast concrete facings and extensive glass panels blend into the rocks and trees of its lakeland setting. The hotel offers a wide package of facilities for recreation and physical fitness as well as for working sessions. There are a night club, swimming pool, sauna, two squash courts, solarium, casino, games room, children's playroom, restaurants and bars. Nearby is the Laajavuori winter and lakeland sports centre. Architects: Finnish Architects Company. 2nd Stage: Holma, Lerber, Roinnen, SAFA

(d) The windows of the hotel reflect its wooded setting

(a) South elevation

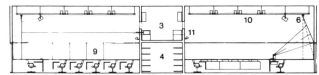

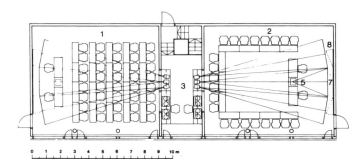

(b) Plan of conference room

(c) Auditorium

(d) Team working room

Key

1 Maximum fitting, 2 + 40 seats
2 Square fitting, 2 + 22 seats
3 Operating room with projectors and CCTV-centre with monitors and tape recorders
4 Storage
5 Overhead projector
6 Screens
7 White-board
8 Flaps
9 Magnetic tracks for fixing flaps
10 Grid for audiovisual installations
11 Servo-controlled TV-camera

Figure 8.9 *Sandpiper Hotel, Hyvinkää, Finland*
The Sandpiper Hotel was built to provide high standard conference and recreational facilities and then extended to provide a training centre – operated with the hotel – for an insurance company. In the vacations, weekends and evenings, the hotel is able to meet requirements for tourism and leisure. The hotel has 383 beds, two swimming pools, indoor games, squash courts, a gymnasium and 1100 seats in the restaurants and nightclub. In addition to an auditorium of 220 seats and conference room for 100, there are 9 conference rooms for 42 and 27 syndicate rooms. The main market is for groups of 30–40. Adjacent conference rooms are served from a common projection room. Photos: Martti I. Jaatinen. Owner: Sandpiper Hotel Chain/Rantaloma OY. Architect: Anna-Maija & Martti I. Jaatinen

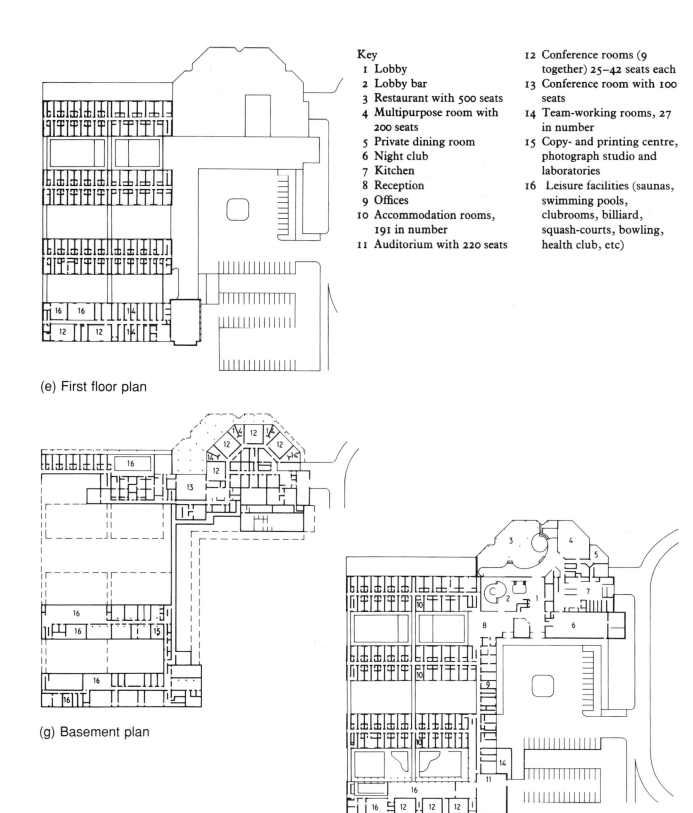

Key
1 Lobby
2 Lobby bar
3 Restaurant with 500 seats
4 Multipurpose room with 200 seats
5 Private dining room
6 Night club
7 Kitchen
8 Reception
9 Offices
10 Accommodation rooms, 191 in number
11 Auditorium with 220 seats
12 Conference rooms (9 together) 25–42 seats each
13 Conference room with 100 seats
14 Team-working rooms, 27 in number
15 Copy- and printing centre, photograph studio and laboratories
16 Leisure facilities (saunas, swimming pools, clubrooms, billiard, squash-courts, bowling, health club, etc)

(e) First floor plan

(g) Basement plan

(f) Ground floor plan

(a) Architects concept.

Figure 8.10 *Miyako Hotel, Tokyo*
The Miyako hotel is located in 2.3 ha (5.5 acres) of landscaped gardens. There are 500 guestrooms and suites, a variety of restaurants, a shopping arcade and extensive facilities for health and fitness. In addition to the function rooms, there is a ceremonial hall for weddings with dressing rooms and photographic studios. The ballroom can accommodate up to 1000 delegates and the banquet hall seats 350.
Architects: Minoru Yamasaki

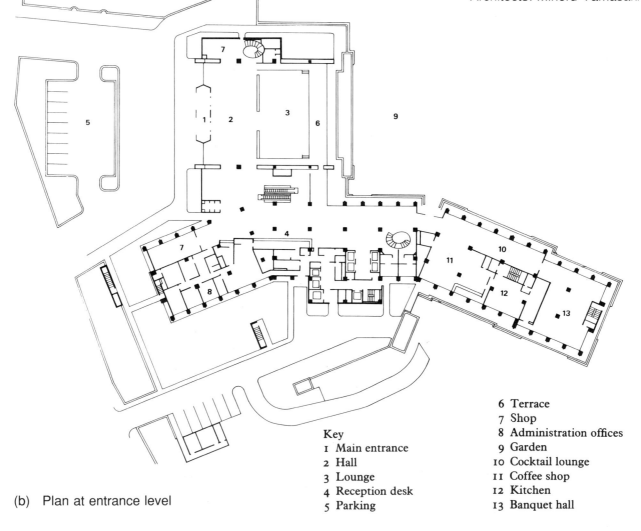

(b) Plan at entrance level

Key
1 Main entrance
2 Hall
3 Lounge
4 Reception desk
5 Parking
6 Terrace
7 Shop
8 Administration offices
9 Garden
10 Cocktail lounge
11 Coffee shop
12 Kitchen
13 Banquet hall

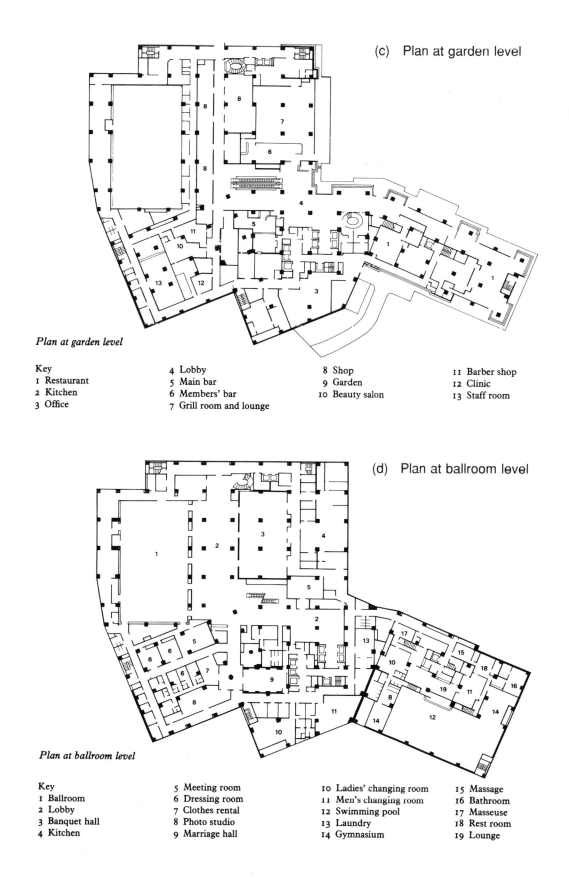

(c) Plan at garden level

Plan at garden level

Key
1 Restaurant
2 Kitchen
3 Office
4 Lobby
5 Main bar
6 Members' bar
7 Grill room and lounge
8 Shop
9 Garden
10 Beauty salon
11 Barber shop
12 Clinic
13 Staff room

(d) Plan at ballroom level

Plan at ballroom level

Key
1 Ballroom
2 Lobby
3 Banquet hall
4 Kitchen
5 Meeting room
6 Dressing room
7 Clothes rental
8 Photo studio
9 Marriage hall
10 Ladies' changing room
11 Men's changing room
12 Swimming pool
13 Laundry
14 Gymnasium
15 Massage
16 Bathroom
17 Masseuse
18 Rest room
19 Lounge

257

(a) Al Bustan Palace Hotel

(c) Al Maha lounge

(b) Al Bustan café

(d) Al Sindbad club

Figure 8.11 *Al Bustan Palace Hotel, Oman*

Described as the most spectacular hotel in the Middle East, the Al Bustan Palace Hotel (a) was built at a cost of $200 million to accommodate the Gulf Cooperation Council Summit in 1985 and other Heads of State meetings. Located in a beautiful sandy cove the development required construction of new roads through the mountains and a separate village for employees.

The Al Bustan Palace consists of an octagonal main building and two wings providing a total of 210 double rooms and 48 suites. There are eight floor levels in the main building with the main entrance at level 4 leading to a vast atrium topped by a golden dome. The suites occupy the top three floors and level 8 houses eight palace suites.

Levels 1, 2 and 3 contain a complete Congress Centre with separate entrances to a large auditorium and ballroom supported by reception areas, meeting rooms, a fully equipped theatre, health club and medical clinic. A total of 17 banquet and reception rooms can cater for a thousand people; in addition there is a choice of four restaurants. Back-of-house and plant rooms are mainly concentrated on level 3 near the service and staff entrance.

There are a total of thirteen guest elevators, four of which serve the VIP suites, and eight service elevators. Although highly functional with modern facilities this outstanding hotel reflects the architecture of the region. Exquisite filigree and arabesque details, moorish tiles and damask drapes, adopted throughout, express the Islamic inspired design policy fostered by His Majesty Sultan Qaboos. Architect: David Blatchford/ Philippou (Cyprus). Builders: J. & P. (Oman). Project Managers: Valtos, Oman. Hotel Operators: Inter-Continental Hotels

(e)   Banqueting room

Figure 8.11 *Al Bustan Palace Hotel, Oman (continued)*

Key
a   Main entrance
b   Al Bustan café
c   Al Maha lounge
d   Al Sindbad club
e   Banqueting and
     reception area
f   Al Marjan restaurant
g   Hotel reception
     (level 4)
h   Swimming pool
i   Health club
j   Open air theatre

k   Oman auditorium
     (level 3)
l   Majan ballroom
     (level 3)
m   Staff entrance
     (level 3)
n   Staff facilities
o   Loading bay
p   Storage
q   Main kitchen
r   Laundry
s   Engineering

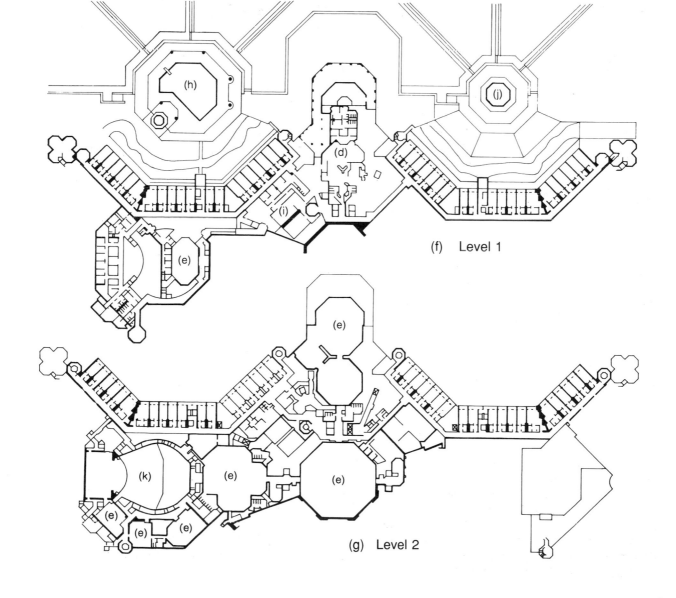

(f)   Level 1

(g)   Level 2

(Continued from page 251)

fire-resisting construction, external and internal noise insulation.

- *Access* from hotel lobby. Separate entrance for non-residents. Additional car parking. Reception/registration facilities. Access for exhibits and handling requirements.
- *Grouping*: of meeting/function rooms and arrangement to utilize common areas (entrance, foyer, cloakrooms, toilets).
- *Number and capacities* of separate rooms and divisible areas to meet varying requirements. (Plenary sessions, seminars, syndicates, meals). Means of separating foyer areas for privacy. Fire escape requirements, travel distances, protection of egress routes.
- *Circulations* for food and beverage service to each function and banquet area with access to storage (furniture, equipment).
- *Planning of service and storage areas* for efficient operation. Banquet kitchen/pantry, supplied from main kitchen (0.2–0.3 m²/seat). Furniture and equipment stores are usually 5–10% of the hall areas.
- *Specific requirements*. AVA systems and equipment. Simultaneous interpretation, projection, televising and press facility requirements. Access and restrooms for VIPs and speakers.
- *Engineering services*. Zoning and balancing requirements, location of plant, systems, installation and access needs, control points.
- *Dual use* of selected guestrooms and suites as syndicate rooms, etc. Located on same or adjacent floor with additional storage for furniture.

8.4.4 Foyers

Serving as an assembly, reception and breakout space the foyer is usually one-third the area (0.3 m²/seat) of the ballroom or main halls. This area may be divisible or separated into ballroom and conference suite areas to allow independent use. Access is required from the lobby and any secondary entrance area, with portable desks for reception/registration information. Service access for the kitchen or pantry must be provided for refreshments.

Cloakrooms and toilets must be based on the maximum occupancy and planned to meet intensive use without congestion. Areas of 0.10 m²/seat for males and 0.12 m²/seat for females are representative up to 400 with lower ratios above.

Foyers are usually designed with a durable neutral decor, complementary to the main hall, and provide for a number of requirements:

Noise screening From external or noise-generating areas within the hotel with acoustic linings and carpeting (section 5.5).

Fire safety Serving as egress route with fire-resistant separator and surfaces with low flame spread and low smoke generating ratings. Incorporating automatic detection, alarm and sprinkler systems, emergency lighting and exit signs.

Sound system Paging, music and directions.

Air-conditioning Zone controlled and balanced with the halls. Regulated fresh air supply. Exhaust ventilation for smoke removal.

Signage Clear directions, room identifications, noticeboards, etc. in consistent style.

Stations Portable counters and trolleys with service connections located to avoid route obstruction and congestion.

8.4.5 Ballroom and convention halls

Ballrooms provide a large flexible space which can be used for conventions, exhibitions, social activities, banquets or dances. These areas are usually divisible by movable partitions to create a range of smaller rooms (Table 8.5).

Division into three provides full, two-thirds and one-third size options and allows the middle space to serve for furniture storage and sound isolation when the outer rooms are used for different activities.

Table 8.5 Ballroom divisibility

Halls area	Length:width	Length division
250 m² and over	2:1	into 3
Less than 250 m²	3:2	into 2

Heights

Table 8.6 Ceiling heights are related to the size of the hall (Table 8.6).

	m	ft	*Notes*
Large ballrooms	3.6–4.2	12	4.6 m (15') for exhibitions
Medium capacity/conference halls	3.0–3.1	10	
Minimum for function rooms	2.7	9	

In addition to creating a good visual impression of grandeur and dynamism the height is important in assisting uniform ventilation, clearance for slide projection, chandeliers, etc., and for exhibition displays. However, excessive height can give rise to sound reverberation, temperature gradients and lamination of air as well as difficulties in dividing halls and the resultant disproportionate heights in the smaller areas. One solution is to limit the full height to central light wells with lower perimeter and separating surrounds as a decorative feature.

8.4.6 Ceiling construction

The perspective of the ceiling is a major consideration in the design of the ballroom and its dividing rooms. In addition the construction must incorporate many functional requirements including access to technical equipment:

- *Air-conditioning* ducting, terminals and diffusers, including the loading and insulation of roof-mounted plant and balanced zone control equipment.
- *Lighting systems* with a combination of decorative lamps, general lighting, track lighting arrays, exhibition and special lighting requirements, emergency lighting, dimmer switches and controls for separate circuits.
- *Fire detection and alarm systems* automatic sprinkler installations. Ceiling materials to satisfy low surface flame spread (section 5.6.6), low smoke generation and secure fixing requirements.

- *Acoustic treatment* over the whole or part to reduce reverberation time to 0.8 seconds or less in use.
- *Ceiling voids* will require separation above the lines of partitions to meet fire-resistance periods – usually ½ hour – and sealed sound flanking paths.
- *Thermal and sound insulation* (particularly near airports, railways, major roads) under roof construction and plant (section 5.5.4).
- *Mechanical equipment* for moving partitions, projection screens and other retractable equipment.

8.4.7 Walls and partitions

Damage is likely to arise from furniture rearrangement, exhibitions, spillages and handling. The lower part of walls may be panelled or protected by skirtings and dado rails. Upper areas are usually decorative with acoustic absorption but must meet fire and surface flame spread requirements. Walls must accommodate extensive technical services with outlets and terminals at some 3 m (10 ft) intervals (low and standard voltage outlets, telephone jackpoints, CCTV circuits, communication systems and computer network links).

Partitions
Movable partitions are invariably required for all large halls to increase flexibility of use. Some of the methods used are given in Table 8.7.

Panels may be moved by hand or be electrically operated. To achieve high standards of sound insulation, double partitions may need to

Table 8.7 Methods for partitioning large halls

Type	Component	Noise insulation techniques
Sliding	Tracks	Sealed by expanding strips etc. along edges
Perpendicular folding	Sections	Insert and overlap joints tightened together
Horizontal folding	Continuous	Flexible sheets or joined panels, hollow filled
Housed against wall or in recesses	Rigid panels	Resilient linings and heavy cores, edge sealing
Housed in ceiling or floor	Panels or continuous	Flexible or rigid as above, wall edges sealed
Relocated or demountable[a]	Panels	Pressed against or fixed to sealing strips or stiffened frame

Note: [a]Removed to store or reposition.

be used. Masking sound may be introduced into the intervening space (see section 5.5.2).

8.4.8 Doors and windows

As a rule, doors should open outwards and be recessed to avoid obstruction.

Main entrance doors should be central, in proportion with the room, at least 2.4 m (8 ft) and usually 3.0 m (10 ft) high. Requirements include attractive durable facings and furnishings, silent easy opening and closure, fire resistance and sound insulation. A vestibule may be provided. Viewing lenses and indicator panels should be fitted.

Exit doors must open outwards, with panic bolts and locking release mechanism, approved signs and emergency illumination. Exit and egress routes must comply with local fire code and security requirements (section 5.6).

Windows may not be necessary in larger ballrooms but natural light is beneficial in smaller function and meeting rooms. Mechanized blackout blinds with automatic lighting should be provided.

8.4.9 Floors

Spring floors are preferable for frequent ballroom use with means of locking and carpet

Table 8.8 Floor loadings

	kN/m²	lb/sqft
Large ballrooms, dance halls[a]	5.0	104
Stages	5.0	104
Meeting rooms, function rooms[b]	3.0	63

Notes: [a]May be increased to allow concentrated wheel loads for exhibits.
[b]Seated areas.

covering for functions. This is usually limited to the central area. More commonly, removable dance squares are used over fitted carpeting.

Grids of ducts may be provided for technical services in line with partitions and other identified positions for stations or stage requirements.

Design floor loadings depend on the intended use (Table 8.8).

8.4.10 Furniture and special equipment

Essentially furniture should be:

- lightweight but strong: stackable into mobile carriers
- linkable to form rows: interchangeable (e.g. tops and frames)

- styled to suit character of room and hotel
- durable, resistant to staining, scraping and marking
- protected to prevent damage to floor or walls.

Typical seat plans for conference and banquet organizers must be prepared. These must provide for views – of the stage, top table, screens, etc., seat spacing and circulation needs. Special requirements include a stage dais or bandstand and audio-visual aid equipment.

Stage dais or bandstand
A raised platform (permanent or portable) will usually be required to improve view and direct sound for lectures and entertainment. Steps, curtain rails and back screens should be provided in addition to a speaker's dais or desks.

Audio-visual aid equipment
This may be provided, hired or supplied by the organizers, but provisions must be made for installed cabling, controls and ancillary equipment. Separate booths may be warranted for slide and cine projection sound and lighting controls and simultaneous language interpretation:

Cine/slide projection	Stands. Electrical and control connections.
Screens	Portable, permanent or retractable. Size and viewing pattern.
Sound amplification	Microphone points, sound controls, positions and types of speakers. Recording facilities.
Interpretation	Requirements, extent of relays, positions and facilities for interpreters.
Music	Background sound systems, control and synchronization.
Lighting	Types of luminaries, locations, dimming and sequence controls.
Television	CCTV systems. Positions and mountings for cameras and monitors. External relays.
Telephone	Jackpoints in key areas including booths.

8.4.11 Services

Technical services
High-standard engineering services with sophisticated controls are required to ensure environmental quality, flexibility to meet varying requirements and energy management. To allow division of space, the engineering systems and equipment need to be designed for each area as well as for the whole (see chapter 10). Water supplies and drainage are required near the area.

Food and beverage services
Ballrooms and banquet areas (including divided spaces) need to have individual service access from the kitchens or pantries supplying food and beverages. Close proximity is essential to ensure rapid service and the banquet kitchen is equipped with large capacity refrigerators and ovens (often combined) based on the maximum numbers and menu choices to be provided.

Basic preparation of food may be carried out in the main kitchen requiring some system of food transportation between the kitchen areas. Service access is also required to the beverage stores and wine cellars and for furniture, equipment and exhibits (see section 9.3.1).

Service entrances
The planning of furniture layout must be related to service entrances which must be positioned and designed to minimize:

- crossing of room, distraction of activities, speeches, etc.
- risk of accidents, spillages
- disturbance from penetration of noise or brighter light
- view of work areas.

The last two usually require screening and the interspacing of a service vestibule.

8.4.12 Other facilities

Meeting rooms

Smaller meeting and function rooms often have a high utilization. They are usually grouped together and are of various sizes, designed and fitted out for alternative seating plans. Partitioning may be used to increase flexibility. If no other banquet rooms are provided, some of the rooms may have service access.

Scaled-down technical requirements for ballrooms apply.

Lecture theatres, cinemas

Executive conference centres and hotels with a specialized requirement for executive training and conferences may also include purpose-designed lecture theatres and/or cinemas. These areas have raked floors with permanent stepped seating and fixed equipment ensuring better viewing and communication.

Specialized facilities are used in association with general meeting rooms and banquet areas.

8.5 Leisure and recreation facilities

8.5.1 Range of provision

The extent and types of facilities provided in hotels varies widely, depending on:

- location and marketing emphasis, including local club membership
- number of rooms, grading and level of charges
- availability and cost of land.

Budget hotels	Games room, outdoor pool, children's play area
Small family hotels	
Mid-grade urban hotel	*Health club*: gymnasium/exercise room, aerobics room, squash courts. Swimming pool, spray/whirl pools, sauna, solarium[c], rest area, beautician/hairdressing salon. Massage rooms[a]. Changing facilities, club bar and lounge. Billiard room[a].
High-grade resort	*Health club*: indoor facilities.
hotels and resort complexes	Outdoor: swimming pool, tennis courts, handball/volleyball, putting green, boules[a], children's play area, changing rooms.
	Country Golf course (miniature, 9 or 18 hole, driving range)[a] Jogging/parcours. Outbound trails, riding school,[a] archery,[a] clay pigeon shooting,[a] fishing,[a] river canoeing/boating.[a]
	Sea or lakeside Beach bathing – with shelters, snorkelling, scuba diving, wind surfing, dinghy sailing, boating, fishing, yacht and motor boat moorings, marina,[b] game fishing.[b]
	Mountain Access to ski-lifts and pistes, ice skating rinks,[b] ski room, ski lounge, games room.

Notes: [a]Depending on space and market advantages.
[b]Usually provided on a resort basis.
[c]May be omitted because of health risk.

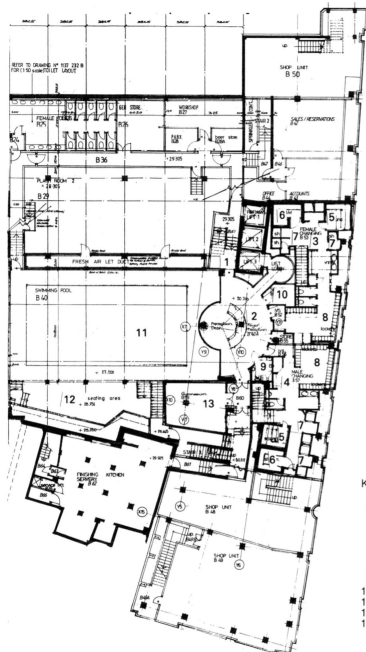

Figure 8.12 *The Leeds Marriott*
Opened in 1993 the Leeds
Marriott is owned and operated by
Scotts Hotels and includes a
separate office area to the side
and rear. On the ground floor are
street frontage shop units, around
the foyer and restaurant, with a
large function meeting room suite
extending to a mezzanine floor.

The basement houses a large
health club with a 15 m pool and
back-of-house areas. There are a
total of 246 rooms and 12 corner
suites. Standard rooms are 3.6 m
wide (3825 mm centres) with
corridors off centre giving 7.4 m
and 6.2 m internal lengths
(including bathroom) for twin and
single rooms respectively
(11'10"× 24'3" and 20'4").
Developers: Scotts Hotels.
Architects: Cobban & Lironi

Key
1   Entrance
2   Reception
3   Female changing
4   Male changing
5   Sauna
6   Showers
7   Cubicle access
8   Lockers
9   Disabled wc
10 Solarium
11 Swimming pool
12 Seating area
13 Gymnasium

(a)   Plan of health club leisure centre

(a) Front elevation and porte cochere

Figure 8.13 *Leisure Club, Stoke on Trent Moathouse*
Standing on the site of a redundant industrial complex which was landscaped as the setting for Stoke's Garden Festival the new Moat House is linked to the historic home of the Wedgwood family which has been converted to form meeting rooms. Designed to blend in with the hall, the hotel has 147 guestrooms, a function suite for 400, bars, a restaurant and basement leisure club.

Extending over 500 m² this basement leisure club serves resident and club members. It includes an 11 m swimming pool, spa bath, steam room and sauna, a fully equipped gymnasium and large studio with a sprung floor for aerobics, dance and exercise programmes accommodating up to 20. Developers: Queens Moat Houses plc. Architects: Nellist Blundell Flint Partnership. Structural Engineers: Kenchington Ford plc, Alfred McAlpine. Interior Design: Trevillion Interiors; Taylor Swimming pools

Figure 8.13 *Leisure Club, Stoke on Trent Moathouse (continued)*

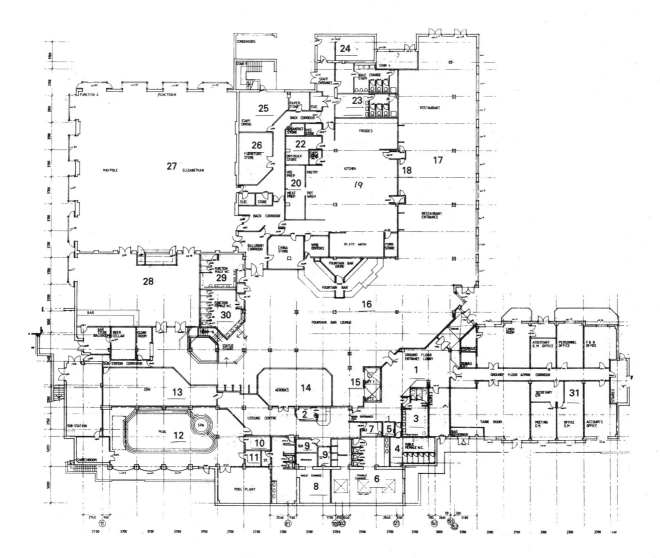

Key

Ground Floor
 1 Entrance lobby
 2 Reception: Leisure centre
 3 Public: Male wc
 4 Public: Female wc
 5 Disabled wc
 6 Female changing
 7 Beautician
 8 Male changing
 9 Sun rooms
 10 Sauna
 11 Steam room
 12 Pool and spa
 13 Gymnasium
 14 Aerobics
 15 Elevators
 16 Fountain bar lounge
 17 Restaurant
 18 Carvery
 19 Kitchens
 20 Preparation areas
 21 Chef's office
 22 Food storage
 23 Staff changing
 24 Wine store
 25 Staff dining
 26 Furniture store
 27 Ballroom (divisible)
 28 Ballroom bar
 29 Functions: male wc
 30 Functions: female wc
 31 Executive offices

(c) Ground floor plan of leisure club

8.5.2 Consideration

Table 8.9 Considerations involved in leisure and recreation facilities

Benefits	
Marketing attraction	For both business and leisure users
Promotional use	To increase room sales at weekends, in low season, etc.
Club membership	Generating fees, charges and other sales.
Difficulties	
Large capital cost	On built areas, fitting out and equipment
Extensive land areas	Pools, tennis courts, play areas, golf courses.
Drainage/irrigation and constructional works	Pools, golf courses, tennis courts, marinas
Need for constant qualified supervision	For safety, health checks, cleaning, engineering services (treatment plant, ventilation)
High operating costs	Expenses of energy, water purification, laundry, cleaning
High maintenance	Repairs/replacements of materials, equipment, upkeep of grounds, greens, beaches, lighting etc. systems
Short periods of use	Seasonal use of many outdoor areas. Short life-cycles for specialized equipment

Health and safety considerations increase with spa facilities – particularly with concentrated occupancies of heated spa pools and changing areas.

8.5.3 Planning requirements: indoor areas

Facilities specified Grouped into areas of dual/alternative use, associated activities, 'wet' and 'dry' areas. Specific areas for children. Spectator provisions.

Changing areas Separate changing areas usually required for sexes. Located at entrance to recreational area with separate in–out circulation. Cubicles and lockers based on guest and club members. Usually two cubicles (minimum) plus two per 100 for each separate area (Table 8.10).

Location Relatively low value areas may be used – basement, interior. Natural lighting not essential. In resort hotels, may be adjacent to outdoor recreation (alternative choice, shared changing areas, linked pools)

Access Direct access from guestrooms (without crossing lobby) by

Table 8.10 Changing areas[a]

Hotel	m²	ft²
150 rooms	50–60	540–650
250 rooms	65–75	700–800

Notes: [a]Includes towel issue, separated areas each with lockers, cubicles, watercloseIs, showers, wash basins, dryers.
[b]Additional facilities may be required for club members based on 0.9 m² (10 ft²) per person.

Space

Table 8.11 Area and height of dry areas

	m²	sqft	Notes
Fitness room	25–50	270–540	5 to 10 stations
Gymnasium/ aerobics studio	50–80	540–860	12 to 28 persons

Height: 3.5 m (11'6") small fitness rooms
4.0 m (13'0") larger gymnasia, dance studios

Relationship elevator(s) and stairs. Separate entrance for club members and public with reception/control area.
Internal and external pools may be used as focus for revenue-generating areas (cafés, pool bars, party rooms).

Noise Effect of noise on guestrooms and sensitive areas. Direct absorption and insulation requirements.

Engineering services Control of humidity, odour, balanced ventilation. Energy management and reclaim systems. Water recycling and treatment (ozone, chlorine). Location of plant: access for servicing.

8.5.4 Dry areas

Separation
Gymnasium, fitness rooms, dance/aerobic studios and similar areas must have 'dry' access to changing rooms (to avoid floor wetting, damage, slipperiness).

Finishes
Walls must be designed for easy maintenance. One wall should be fitted with mirrors (toughened glass). Wall bars may be fitted. Floors must be durable, warm, partly resilient, splinter-free and resistant to impact damage. For gymnasia, hardwood strips are common while synthetic carpeting or vinyl covering is used for equipment rooms. Acoustic ceilings may be used to reduce noise levels.

Technical services
Temperatures are usually maintained at 12–16°C in high-activity areas with 3–5 changes/hour. Uniform lighting giving 200 lux (20 lumen/sqft) is required. Fittings must be recessed and shatterproof (safety glass).

8.5.5 Equipment

Exercise equipment falls broadly into three groups:

- Cardio-vascular exercise, body toning, stretching, improvement of fitness and health.
- Weight training, body building and improvement of stamina.
- Gymnastic activities, wall bars, trampoline.

New equipment is constantly being developed and the layout should allow for flexibility, the

Table 8.12 Space required for exercise equipment

Room area[a] (m²)	Examples of equipment	Unit space[b] m²	sqft	Number
25	Exercise cycles	3.5	38	2
	Pacer machine	6.0	65	1
	Rowing machine	5.0	54	1
	Free weights	6.0	65	1
	Reception/supervision	1.0	11	
50	Exercise cycles	3.5	38	4
	Pacer machine	6.0	65	1
	Stairmaster	6.0	65	1
	Rowing machine	5.0	54	1
	Skiing exerciser	5.0	54	1
	Pneumatic weights	5.0	54	2
	Free weights	6.0	65	1
	Reception/supervision/rest	3.0	32	
40	Nautilus circuit			
50	Aerobic, dance studio[c]	3.0	32	12–16

Notes: [a]Net area. Gross factor 1.25 including storage.
[b]Unit space for planning: area occupied by machine plus 0.5 m.
[c]Per person, in class.

equipment is usually arranged in rows on two or three sides of the room. At least one wall should be mirrored. Free space should be allowed in front of wall bars and at least 1.0 m clear between equipment (Table 8.12).

8.5.6 Changing and 'wet' areas

Supervision
In most hotels the supervision area is located to serve a dual role of reception (entrance, towel issue) and supervision of the pool area. First aid and safety equipment must be provided.

Changing
Cubicles are usually 920 × 1070 mm (36" × 42") fitted with mirrors, seats, clothes hooks and door locks. A disabled cubicle 2000 × 2000 mm (6'6" × 6'6") may be provided with ramped or level access through the area. The changing area should provide full-size lockers, hairdriers, mirrors and seats. Toilets (separate for sexes), shower and foot sprays/baths are sited between the changing and pool areas.

Massage
Separate massage/treatment cubicles 2.8 × 2.2 m (9'0" × 7'3") may be provided with direct access from the changing area. Solariums are not now recommended.

Swimming pool
Indoor pools are usually rectangular and relatively small: 4.6 × 9.1 m (15 × 30 ft) to 7.6 × 15.2 m (25 × 30 ft). Most of the area may be a uniform depth of 1.2 m (4 ft) reducing to 0.9 m (3 ft) at the shallow end. Deeper pools – usually 1.8 m deep (6 ft) – should have a resting ledge at a depth of 1.2 m (4 ft). The deck area is mainly 2.0 m (6'6") wide increasing to 2.8 m (9'0") for a rest area with loungers. The deck area may also extend to include circular jet and surge pools.

Table 8.13 Planning standards for wet areas

	Unit space[a] m²	sqft	Notes
Swimming pool	8.0	86	Water area only[b]
Whirlpool, jacuzzi	2.0	22	Total including 0.5 m surround
Sauna, steam bath	2.0	22	Cabinet space only[b]
Shower and foot baths	1.0	11	

Notes: [a]Unit space per person based on average high occupancy.
[b]Not including surround or access.

Saunas usually form part of this area and are provided with associated showers or plunge pools (Table 8.13).

8.5.7 Equipment and environment

Water treatment
Water circulation and treatment plant is usually located in the vicinity of the pool. Treatment includes filtration, sterilization (with chlorine or ozone), pH adjustment and heating. Plant areas must allow for access for equipment and servicing drainage and ventilation to remove fumes. Inflow is usually at the shallow end with outflow over edge channels and at the deep end.

Pool equipment
- Underwater lighting with access covers and protected fittings
- Jet surges, with pump circulation and time control
- Markings and depth indicators. Temperature indicator
- Safety and first aid equipment, lifebelts, instructions
- Cleaning equipment.

Finishes
Throughout the wet areas, non-slip ceramic or vitrified floor tiles must be used laid with a 1:24 slope to drains. The lower 2.0 m (6'0") walls must be tiled extending to full height in showers, etc.

Environment

Table 8.14 Environment of changing and wet areas

	Typical temperatures (°C)	Air changes/hour
Activity areas	12–16	3–5
Changing areas	26–28	8–10
Pool area	27–28	4–8
Other areas	24–26	3–5
Water – swimming	24–26	
– leisure pool	28–30	

Energy recovery
High energy consumption is required for space heating/ventilation, pool water heating and domestic hot water. Energy savings of 45–65% are achievable using heat pump and water heat exchange equipment.

8.5.8 Associated facilities

The facilities of larger hotels normally include hairdressing/beauty salons and may extend to massage treatment, rest areas and medical examination rooms (Table 8.15).

Table 8.15 Planning standards for associated facilities

| | Unit space | | Notes |
	m²	sqft	
Massage and treatment rooms	8.0	86	Plus 2.0 m² equipment
Hairdressing and beauty rooms	7.0	75	Average high occupancy
Rest areas	6.0	65	Loungers
Café-bar	2.0	22	Spacious

8.6 External recreation areas

8.6.1 Planning

Leisure activities near the hotel tend to be grouped into two areas: focused on the swimming pool or associated with tennis courts and other games areas. Planning requirements regarding facilities, changing areas, access, relationships, noise and engineering services apply (section 8.5.3). External leisure areas are carefully integrated into the landscape and may be sited within a natural background setting (polluted lake, inaccessible or rocky beach, mountain vistas).

8.6.2 Swimming pools

Swimming pools are a key attraction in resort hotels, not only for recreation but as a focus for sunbathing and spectator interest. The pools are often free-form and combined with landscaping, planted areas, linking channels, fountains and other features. In larger resorts, individual pools or linked sections may be provided for swimmers and non-swimmers with a separated paddling pool/play area for children within view.

Location	Direct elevator access without passing through the lobby. Sited with sea, beach or garden background. Used as a focus of interest for guestrooms, cafés, bars. Screened from external view. In urban areas rooftop pools may be used.
Orientation	Exposed to maximum sunlight: mid-morning–late afternoon. Sheltered from strong prevailing winds.
Size	25.0 × 12.5 m (82 × 41 ft) – larger hotels and resorts 15.0 × 8.0 m (50 × 25 ft) – large hotels 9.0 × 4.5 m (30 × 15 ft) – small hotels (usually with free-form outline).
Deck	Minimum 1.2 m clear for access to pool. 3.2 m width including sunbathing increasing to 6.2 m for larger pools. Smooth, non-slip, resistance materials with drainage away from pool.
Depth	Indicated by markings. May be gradual slope 0.9–1.8 m (3–6 ft) deepening to 2.4 m (8ft) or uniform level 1.2 m (4 ft). (The depth must be increased for diving.)
Drainage	Overflow from the pool may be drained in recessed perimeter channels or through surface gratings – increasing the water levels.
Features	Underwater lighting, illumination of cascades and sprays. Shadow-free safety lighting. All lighting and circuits protected. Diving boards not recommended. Safety notices posted. Whirlpools, jacuzzis, showers in extension of

surround. Pool bar may form an extension to the pool or an adjacent area.

Support Lockers, changing rooms, towel issue, storage area. Plant and equipment rooms with service access. Safety equipment, telephone and first aid room.

8.6.3 Other recreational facilities

Tennis courts and associated areas are usually sited in a less prominent area: often landscaped to create a garden view for guestrooms. Generally a minimum of two courts are provided. Golf and other activities require more extensive grounds and may be shared with other resort hotels or club facilities.

Golf

Regulation	18 hole	6000 m course	40–60 ha (100–150 acres)
	9 hole	3000 m course	20–30 ha (50–75 acres)
Practice	3 hole course		8 ha (20 acres)
Pitch & putt green	18 holes		3 ha (7.5 acres)

Bowling green

6 lane	50 m × 50 m	0.25 ha (0.6 acres)

Tennis courts

Four court tennis centre, including surround	0.15 ha (0.4 acres)

9

Back-of-house operational areas

9.1 Goods entrance

9.1.1 Goods receiving area

- The unloading area must be covered and enclosed (with shutters) for weather protection, exclusion of vermin, containment of noise, litter etc., and security. Extended screening may be required from hotel areas.
- A minimum platform of 2.0 m (6'0") width is required for offloading at vehicle tailboard height : 1.2 m (4'0")
- A receiving office for control checking and weighing deliveries should be immediately adjacent. The purchasing office should also be directly accessible.
- Temporary holding storage must be provided – but most deliveries are immediately transferred to main stores.
- Preferably stores should be located adjacent with direct corridor access: minimum width 2.0 m (6'0"), maximum ramp 10%. Double swing doors with viewing panels are required.
- If transfer to another level is necessary, one goods elevator for each loading bay should be installed. These should be independent of room service circulation requirements.
- In hotels with large convention and exhibition areas provision must be made for receiving and transferring exhibits and stand displays direct to the halls.

9.1.2 Refuse and garbage

- Transfers and storage of refuse and garbage must be kept separate from goods received.

- The shape and size of containers, bins and skips is dependent on the system of vehicle collection and handling.
- A refrigerated storage room is usually provided for food garbage.
- A compactor is required with screening to confine noise and debris.
- Separate storage for bottles is necessary and a glass crushing machine may be warranted.
- Where refuse chutes are used, level access is required to the collection point. Isolating and fire control equipment must be installed.
- A suitably equipped washing area for containers is required.
- All surfaces must be smooth and impervious with high fire resistance. Water hoses, non-slip floors with drainage must be provided.

9.1.3 Relationship

See Figures 9.2 and 9.3 on pp. 276 and 277.

9.2 Employee facilities

9.2.1 Number of employees

Staffing requirements depend on the grade, degree of personal service, occupancy rates, the range of food and beverage facilities and extent to which laundry maintenance and other functions are contracted out. Variations in the relative costs of employment and the level of education and training also result in differences from one country to the next.

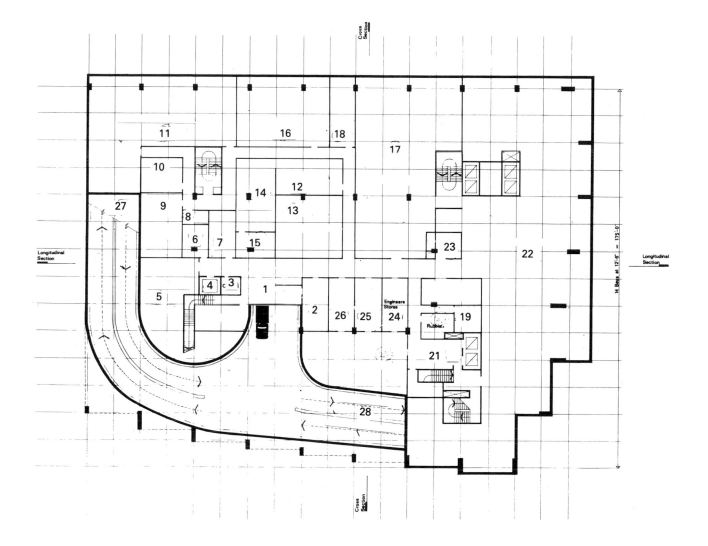

Key

Receiving area
1 Receiving platform
2 Garbage sorting
3 Control
4 Freight elevator
5 General storage
6 Trash
7 Empties

Employees area
8 Timekeeper
9 Telephone and switchroom
10 Personnel office
11 Employee lockers and wc
12 Staff dining room
13 Employee dining room
14 Kitchen
15 Dishwashing

Housekeeping
16 Housekeeping
17 Valet and laundry
18 Print shop
19 Soiled linen
20 Rubbish
21 Service elevator
22 Boiler and machine room
23 Engineer's office
24 Engineer's stores
25 Upholstery shop
26 Paint shop

Circulation
27 Ramps to Ground level
28 Ramps to car-park basement

Figure 9.1 *Inter-Continental Hotel, Piccadilly, London*
Basement floor on a restricted hotel site with service access shared with car park.
Architects: Frederick Gibberd & Partners

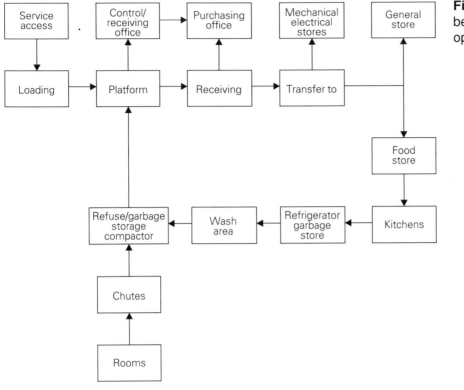

Figure 9.2 Relationship between the back-of-house operational areas

Numbers

Table 9.1 Typical ratios of staff per room

Typical ratios(a)	Staff per room(b)
Luxury resort hotels	1.4:1
High-grade convention hotels	0.9:1
High-grade city centre hotels	0.7:1
Mid-grade resort hotels	0.6:1
Mid-grade urban hotels	0.5:1
Minimum service hotels and motels	0.25:1 to 0:10:1
Apartments, condominiums (depending on services)	0.10:1 to 0.05:1

Notes: (a)Based on Europe, N. America, Australasia. Increased by 50% in developing countries.
(b)Equivalent full-time employees.

Distribution

Table 9.2 Staff ratios by department

Department	Employees per 100 rooms(a)
Front desk, lobby	8.3
Housekeeping	11.3
Food and beverage	29.6
Telephone, minor operations	4.1
Administration – general	6.3
Marketing – sales	2.8
Property operations	3.0
Other	3.6
	69.0

Notes: (a)Typical of good grade city centre hotels in Europe. Increased by 50 to 100% in developing countries.
Source: Based on *Worldwide Hotel Industry* 1993, Horwath International.

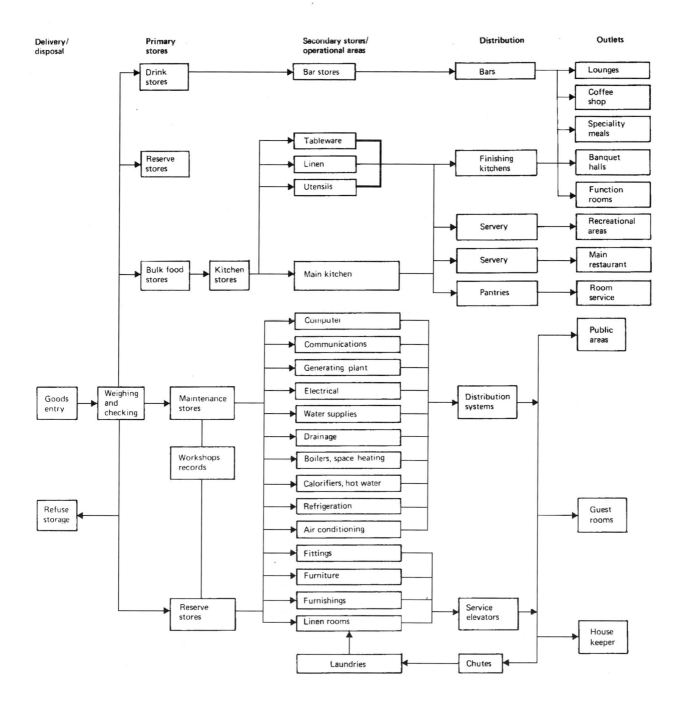

Relationship to sales

Ratio of employee costs per department may be expressed as:

- Sales per employee

- Productivity index: $\dfrac{\text{sales}}{\text{employee costs}}$

Payroll costs generally represent 25–30 per cent of total hotel expenses.

9.2.2 Employee facilities

In view of the large numbers of people employed (both full-time and part-time), high

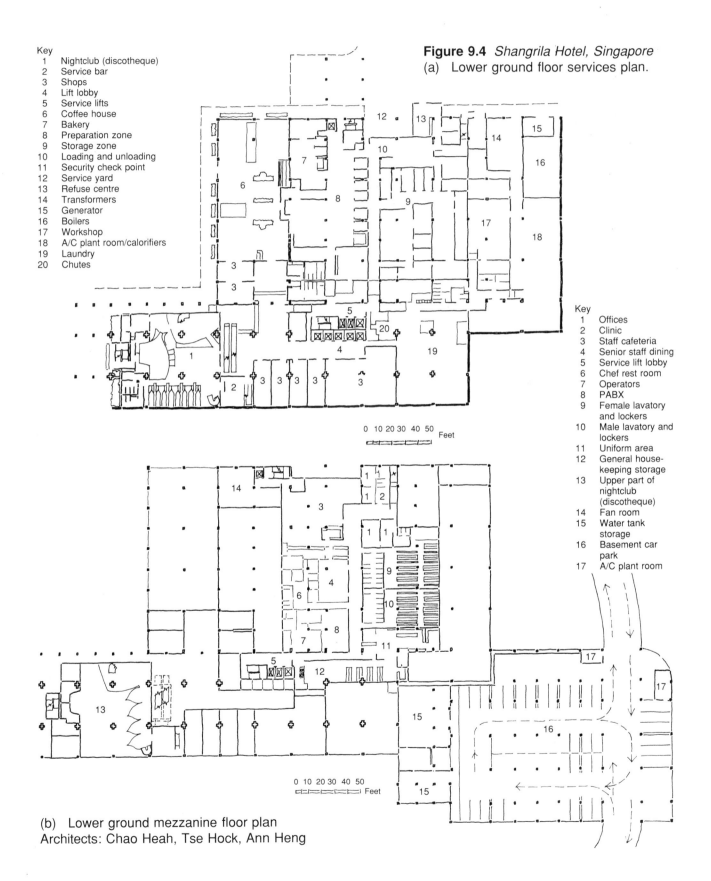

Key
1   Nightclub (discotheque)
2   Service bar
3   Shops
4   Lift lobby
5   Service lifts
6   Coffee house
7   Bakery
8   Preparation zone
9   Storage zone
10 Loading and unloading
11 Security check point
12 Service yard
13 Refuse centre
14 Transformers
15 Generator
16 Boilers
17 Workshop
18 A/C plant room/calorifiers
19 Laundry
20 Chutes

Figure 9.4 *Shangrila Hotel, Singapore*
(a) Lower ground floor services plan.

Key
1   Offices
2   Clinic
3   Staff cafeteria
4   Senior staff dining
5   Service lift lobby
6   Chef rest room
7   Operators
8   PABX
9   Female lavatory
    and lockers
10 Male lavatory and
    lockers
11 Uniform area
12 General house-
    keeping storage
13 Upper part of
    nightclub
    (discotheque)
14 Fan room
15 Water tank
    storage
16 Basement car
    park
17 A/C plant room

0 10 20 30 40 50 Feet

0 10 20 30 40 50 Feet

(b) Lower ground mezzanine floor plan
Architects: Chao Heah, Tse Hock, Ann Heng

seasonal and labour turnover rates and the use of shift systems, there is a need for careful planning and control of employee areas. Generally, hotels offer meals and other services to employees as part of their remuneration and provide uniforms, changing facilities and training opportunities. Facilities must comply with employment legislation covering matters such as health and safety in places of work, conditions for employment and training and food hygiene, as well as ensuring security.

9.2.3 Planning

A separate entrance should be provided for employees, leading via timekeeping and security offices to personnel areas and changing facilities. Corridors giving access to back-of-house work areas should be separated from those used by the public or guests (Figure 9.4).

9.2.4 Residential accommodation

Hotels normally provide an apartment within the building for the general manager and may include other on-site accommodation for key staff.

Other residential requirements depend on:

- remoteness, local population base, competition
- seasonality and use of supplementary foreign or student labour.

Staff rooms may be provided in part of the hotel, an annexe, converted houses or separate hostel-type buildings. In developing countries, large-scale tourism projects usually include the planned provision of a township for hotel employees, ancillary workers and their families complete with its local infrastructure.

The costs of large-scale employee accommodation may represent 10 per cent of the development cost. However, employee benefits are normally taken into account in setting wage rates and can contribute to a reduction in labour turnover and absenteeism costs as well as improvements in standards and productivity.

9.2.5 Security and personnel

The security office must have a clear view of the employee entrance and may be supplemented by video monitoring of movements. Timekeeping

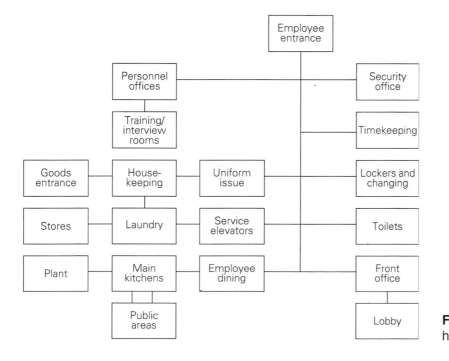

Figure 9.5 Arrangement of back-of-house work areas

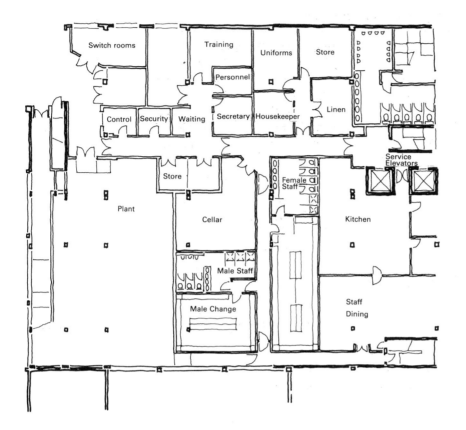

Figure 9.6 *The Leeds Marriott* Employee changing facilities in the basement

equipment is located in an adjacent area for control. Associated offices, depending on size of hotel, are provided for personnel offices, interview and training rooms, the paymaster and purchasing agent. A first aid room should be available (Table 9.3).

9.2.6 Changing and toilet facilities

Typical standards for sanitary provision are given in Table 9.4.

A separate locker must be provided for each employee for uniforms and outdoor clothing. Separate changing rooms with showers, washbasins and WC facilities adjoining must be available for each sex (Table 9.5).

Changing and toilet facilities must be well ventilated (10 airchanges/hour) and heated or air-conditioned as required to reduce condensation. Strict security must be provided with individual lockers for all employees – part-time employees may be allocated a specific area.

Table 9.3 Size of security and personnel areas

Typical areas	150 rooms (m²)	sqft	250 rooms (m²)	sqft
Security, timekeeping	8.0	90	10.0	110
Personnel Interview, training[a]	} 25.0	270	39.0	420
Purchasing	–	–	11.0	120
Total	33.0	360	60.0	650
Area per room 0.20–0.25 m² (2.2–2.7 sqft)				

Note: [a]Dual purpose. Including first aid facilities in area.

9.2.7 Restrooms: staff feeding

Usually restrooms are combined with canteens for employee food service (Table 9.6). A separate area may be provided for supervisory and administrative staff.

Table 9.4 Typical standards for employee sanitary provision

Fittings	Residential hostels	Non-residential staff [b] Male	Female
Waterclosets	(shared) 1 for 9 persons	1 for 1–15 2 for 16–35 3 for 36–65 4 for 66–100	1 for 1–12 2 for 13–25 3 for 26–40 4 for 41–57 5 for 58–77 6 for 78–100
Urinals		1 for 7–20 2 for 21–45 3 for 46–70 4 for 71–100	
Washbasins[a]	1 per bedroom and 1 per bathroom		
Bathrooms	As for WCs		
Cleaners' sinks	Minimum 1 per floor		

Notes: [a]Washbasins must also be provided in food handling areas.
[b]Separate facilities are usually provided for front office use.

Table 9.5 Employee changing room and associated facilities

Typical areas[a]	Per employee [b] (m²)	(sqft)	Per guestroom (m²)	(sqft)
WCs and washing room	0.4	4		
Locker and changing room[c]	0.6	6	0.6	6

Notes: [a]Based on 100–200 room hotel of good grade.
[b]Ratio of space for male:female facilities depends on local pattern of employment. Normally 1:1.
[c]Includes changing cubicles and showers.

Table 9.6 Provision for staff feeding

Typical areas	Per seat[a] (m²)	(sqft)	Per guestroom[b] (m²)	(sqft)
Staff feeding	0.9	10	0.2	2

Notes: [a]With compact seating plan.
[b]Allowing for staggered use: 20% at one time.

9.3 Food preparation and storage

9.3.1 Range of facilities

Hotel food preparation and beverage services fall broadly into three groups (Table 9.7).

Table 9.7 Hotel food preparation and beverage services

Food service outlets	Preparation areas
Multiple choice of restaurants and bars including extensive banquet areas. Individual room service	Main kitchen near stores with satellite kitchens adjacent to each restaurant and banquet room. Service pantries on guestroom floors
One or two restaurants and function rooms on same floor	Main kitchen serving restaurants and function rooms direct
Minimal food service in hotel. Separate restaurant(s) available. (Budget hotels. Holiday villages)	Vending machine and/or facilities may be provided in individual rooms

First floor main kitchen
1 Preparation areas for meat, fish, vegetables, fruit and cold foods
2 Cold rooms and chilled stores
3 Dry store
4 Trolley bay
5 Offices
6 Western kitchen with back bar fryer, charcoal range, fry top range, charcoal broiler and sink
7 Oriental kitchen with back bar open top range, kwali range, rice steamer
8 Serving counters
9 Beverage service counter
10 Dressing table
11 Bread and dessert service
12 Delicatessen shop
13 Dishwashing area
14 Banquet production: steaming and boiling pans
15 Oriental kitchen
16 Western kitchen
17 Pick-up table
18 Meeting room
19 Toilets

Figure 9.7 *Hyatt Aryaduta, Jakarta*
The main food production area of the Hyatt Aryaduta is located on the first floor adjacent to the restaurants and banquet rooms. The facilities include extensive cold storage, separate preparation areas, cooking sections for Western and Oriental food with their own serving counters and a central dishwash area. The banquet kitchen is adjacent and there is also a delicatessen shop. Foodservice Consultants: Christian K. Potzold, Singapore. Hotel operators: Hyatt Hotels

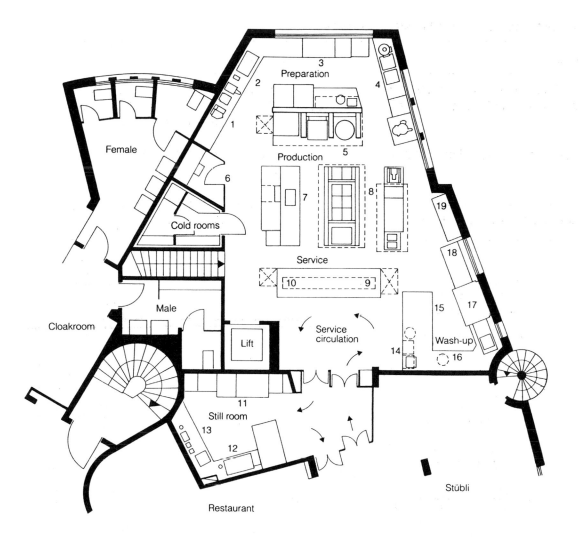

Figure 9.8 *Kongress Hotel Davos, Switzerland*
This 160 bed hotel has a ground floor kitchen
based on the traditional French-style layout.
Storage rooms and staff feeding areas are located
in the basement. Foodservice Consultants:
Therma Grosskuchen AG. Clients: Kongress
Hotel, Davos

Preparation area
Service circulation
1 Cold meat preparation
2 Cold dishes, coupes, glaces
3 Pastry preparation
4 Vegetable preparation

Main production area
5 Boiling pan and bratt pan on trunions, with floor drainage channel
6 Garde manger
7 Rotisseur
8 Entremetier

Service counter
9 Hot service
10 Cold service

Still room
11 Wine, mineral and milk storage
12 Beverage counter with boiler and coffee machines
13 Fruit juice and milk dispensers, mixer, toasters

Dishwashing area
14 Soiled dish counter with overshelf and under-counter waste bins
15 Under-counter glass-washing machine
16 Rack slide with inset sink and drainer
17 Dishwashing machine
18 Pot sink
19 Pot rack

9.3.2 Planning

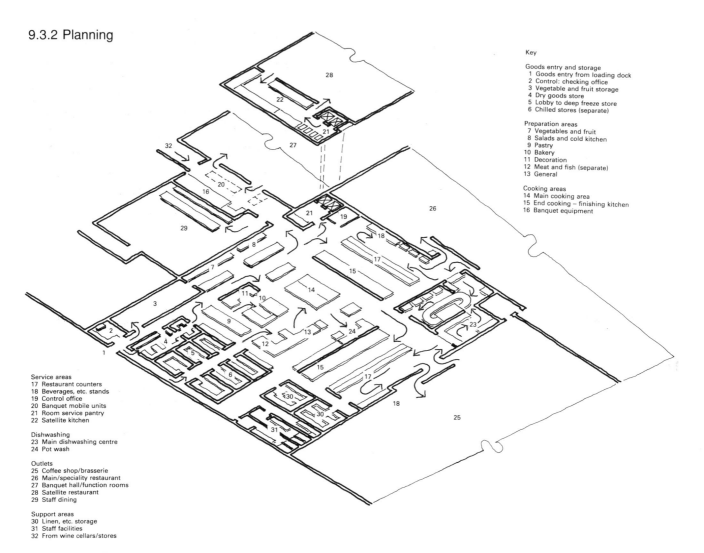

Figure 9.9 *Foodservice circulations in a large hotel*

9.3.3 Catering systems

Food production is invariably organized into one or more systems which enable the operations to be rationalized. Catering systems allow labour and equipment to be more effectively used and provide control over food and energy costs, hygiene and quality. Most systems are based on that described in Table 9.8.

Other arrangements include centralization of bakery, butchery and vegetable preparation for one or several hotels and associated restaurants.

9.3.4 Areas

Net areas are usually based on the number of seats or covers in the restaurants or banquet halls served (Table 9.9).

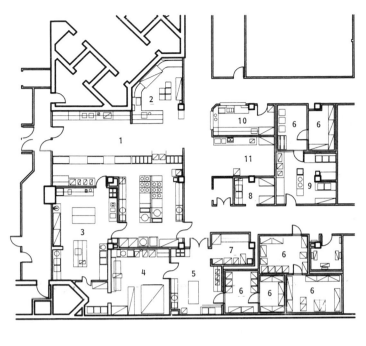

(b) View of main servery

Key

1	Main kitchen servery	7	Chocolate and decoration
2	Dishwashing	8	Pot wash
3	Vegetable kitchen	9	Meat preparation
4	Bakery	10	Service bar
5	Pastry preparation	11	Room service
6	Cold rooms		

0 2 4
  1 3

(a) Plan of kitchen

Figure 9.10 *Foodservice kitchens*
The kitchens of the Holiday Inn Crowne Plaza are designed to serve two restaurants and a patisserie with a total of 416 seats, function rooms seating 400 and room service for the 298 guest rooms and suites. Architect: Dr Hyati Tabanlioğlu

Table 9.8 System for organization of food production

Operation	Benefits	Location
Central production ↓	Economies of scale	Main kitchen in hotel or off-site
(a)Chilling +1 to 3°C or freezing −20°C ↓	1–3 days in advance 1–3 months storage	Part of main kitchen
Transportation ↓	Insulated or refrigerated	Integrated with equipment
Storage until required ↓	Individual variety	In or near finishing kitchen
End cooking/finishing	Freshly cooked	Finishing kitchen adjacent to restaurant or banquet hall

Notes: (a)*Cook and chill system* – for banqueting and internal use.
   Cook-freeze system – for remote off-site production.

Table 9.9 Kitchen areas

Area per seat	High-grade hotels		Mid-grade hotels		Economy hotels	
	(m²)	(sqft)	(m²)	(sqft)	(m²)	(sqft)
Main kitchen and stores[a]	1.2	13	1.0	11	0.7[d]	7.5
Satellite kitchen[b]	0.3	3				
Banquet kitchens[c]	0.2	2				

Notes: [a]Storage requirements depend on frequencies of deliveries.
[b]Including local dishwashing.
[c]0.15 m² increase in main kitchen; 0.05 m² banquet pantry
[d]Using part convenience food.

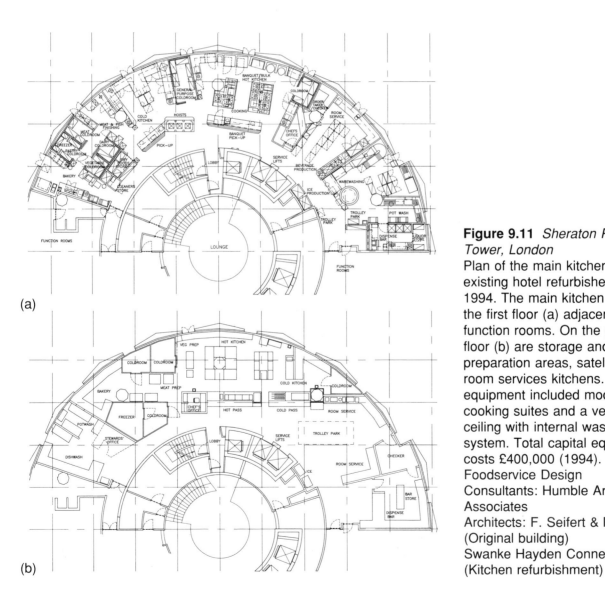

(a)

(b)

Figure 9.11 *Sheraton Park Tower, London*
Plan of the main kitchens of existing hotel refurbished in 1994. The main kitchen is on the first floor (a) adjacent to function rooms. On the ground floor (b) are storage and preparation areas, satellite and room services kitchens. New equipment included modular cooking suites and a ventilated ceiling with internal wash system. Total capital equipment costs £400,000 (1994).
Foodservice Design Consultants: Humble Arnold Associates
Architects: F. Seifert & Partners (Original building)
Swanke Hayden Connell (Kitchen refurbishment)

9.4 Laundry and housekeeping

9.4.1 Laundries

Laundry services may be provided by:

- linen rental or contracts with outside commercial laundries
- centralized services for the area operated by the hotel group
- hotel-operated laundry within premises.

The policy will depend largely on the size and standards of the hotel, costs and difficulties of providing space and operating a laundry. Advantages of self-operation arise from better control, including fast return of linen to use, increased life of articles and lower charges. Even in hotels using contracted-out arrangements, it is common to provide one or more automatic washing machines for staff use and guest valet–laundry services.

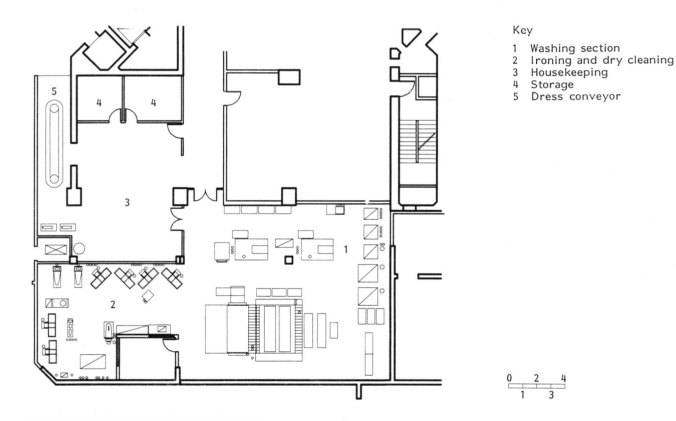

Key

1 Washing section
2 Ironing and dry cleaning
3 Housekeeping
4 Storage
5 Dress conveyor

Figure 9.12 *Holiday Inn Crowne Plaza, Istanbul*
Laundry layout for this 298 room hotel

Table 9.10 Typical quantities of linen per occupied room

	kg	lb
High-grade hotels	5.9	13
Average hotels	4.5	10
Low-tariff hotels	2.7	6

Typical quantities of linen per room are given in Table 9.10. These include restaurant staff uniforms and limited laundry services for guests. Laundry requirements are usually based on:

70% flatwork (sheets, table cloths, napkins)
25% tumble dried (towels)
5% uniforms and miscellaneous (including guest items).

9.4.2 Areas

Space requirements depend on the number of guestrooms and extent of restaurant and banquet services.

Table 9.11 Typical laundry and housekeeping space requirements per guestroom

	m²	sqft
Laundry	0.65–0.79	7.0–8.5
Housekeeping	0.33–0.46	3.5–5.0

9.4.3 Planning

Laundry areas generate steam, high humidity, noise and vibration and are best located at ground or basement level with housekeeping areas adjacent. The layout must be planned around the movement of linen to ensure correct sequencing and control.

9.4.4 Equipment

Laundry equipment typically includes programmed washing machines, hydro extractor, tumble drier, flatwork ironer (with spreading and folding), garment press and manual ironing boards. Tabling must be provided for initial sorting, shaking out after washing and assembly following ironing.

The flatwork ironer is the largest item and generally determines the layout of the area. A dry cleaning machine is often provided in an adjoining area for uniforms and guest valet services.

9.4.5 Construction and services

Laundry and housekeeping areas present a high fire risk from lint dust and surfaces must be smooth and impervious. Steam is commonly used for heating and processing. Ventilation rates normally provide 15–20 airchanges/hour with separate extraction over steam equipment and dry cleaners. Large quantities of water are required (Table 9.12) and efficient floor drainage must be provided as well as supply and waste connections to individual equipment.

Table 9.12 Typical water requirements for laundry areas

	litres/kg	gal/lb of linen
Cold water	15	1.5
Hot water	31 (at 82°C)	3.0 (at 180°F)

Good illumination must be provided with moisture-proof fittings, over all work areas (Table 9.13).

Table 9.13 Required illumination in laundry and housekeeping areas

	Lux	lumen/sqft
Laundry	160	15
Stores	160	15
Drycleaning, pressing	260	20
Repair and sewing work	320	30

9.4.6 Housekeeping

Quantity of linen required per room, assuming efficient turnaround of laundry service, is given in Table 9.14. These figures include one set in reserve.

Table 9.14 Quantity of linen required per room

	Sets per room
High-grade hotels	4–5
Mid-grade tourist hotel	3–4

Space for linen sorting, storage, reserves, repair work, stocktaking, supervision and issue must be located near the laundry. The housekeeping area generally takes up about 0.4 m² (4 sqft) per guestroom. Requirements for the housekeeping areas are:

Heating and ventilation	Airflow exhausted towards laundry
Shelving on adjustable racks	600 mm (24 in) wide or more up to 1.5 m (5 ft) high
Access for circulation	1070 mm (42 in) aisles
Repair/sewing room	Located nearby with seats and worktables.

Supervision
One or more offices must be provided for housekeeping administration located to allow control of linen and uniform issue and storage areas.

9.4.7 Other storage areas

Reserve stores
In addition to reserves of linen and uniforms, secure storage is required for replacement silver, glass and china with one or more separate areas for general storage (Table 9.15). Total area = 0.2 m² (2 sqft) per room.

Table 9.15 Reserve stores

Additional furniture storage	Location near
For changes in layout and function	Banquet and conference rooms
For guest requirements (beds, cots, cribs, TV sets)	Guestrooms
Public areas (baby chairs, extra chairs)	Restaurants

9.5 Engineering

9.5.1 Areas

Provisions for hotel maintenance vary widely. The trend is towards rationalization with greater use of contract or group services.

Extensive workshops are provided to maintain high standards in large hotels and in situations such as isolated resorts where external services are inadequate (Table 9.16).

Table 9.16 Workshop requirements per guestroom

	m²	sqft
Engineering workshops, office and stores	0.3–0.5	3–5[a]
Plant rooms	0.9–1.4	10–15[b]

Notes: [a] Increased to 0.9 m² (10 sqft) in developing countries.
[b] Reduced in budget hotels.

9.5.2 Relationships

Plant is also located at or near roof level (air-conditioning, water supplies) and on intermediate service floors (Figure 9.14).

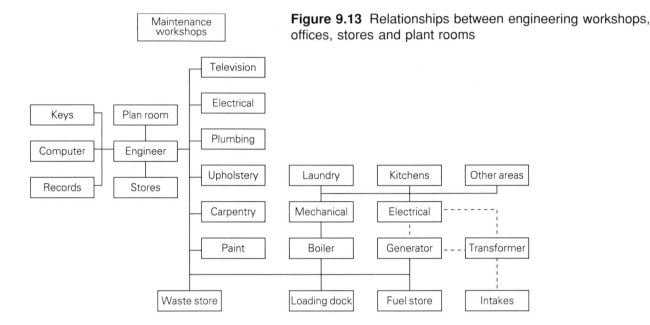

Figure 9.13 Relationships between engineering workshops, offices, stores and plant rooms

9.5.3 Requirements

Loading dock	Height of platform and clearance. Ramps. Handling facilities (cranes, pulleys, trucks). Goods lift: capacity, size.
Plant	Location – effect of noise and vibration. Access for servicing and removal of plant. Space requirements for large equipment.
Engineer's office	Location, relative to workshops. Communication and recording systems. Information and record files. Workstations.
Computer room	Energy management system. Maintenance programmes. Data sources. Equipment monitors.
Plan room	Plan filing cabinets, table and wall charts. Drawing equipment.
Maintenance workshops generally	Wide double doors: 1800 mm (72 in) fully opened. Fitted with workbenches, racks, trays. Electrical trunking with socket/receptacle outlets. Durable smooth surfaces. Good uniform lighting 300 lux (30 lumen/sqft). Ventilation rates. 2–3 airchanges/hour increased where exhaust ventilation required.
Carpentry	Long racks for timber and sheeting. Workbenches with power equipment and exhaust ventilation. Fire precautions (automatic detectors, alarms and sprinklers).
Paint shop	Adjacent. Fire resistant separation of areas and fire precautions. Compressors and spray equipment in separate booth with exhaust ventilation and fume separation.

Upholstery   Adjacent to carpentry. Fitted with sewing and work benches. Floor work areas. Fire precautions and fireproof storage of materials.

Electrical   Adjacent to plumbing with extensive shelf, rack and tray storage and workbenches. Circuit and lamp testing equipment.

Television shop   Repair benches with racks and trays. TV antenna system.

Key cutting   Separate secure area for key cutting and lock repair.

10

Environmental standards: technical installations

10.1 Coverage

10.1.1 Importance

Table 10.1 Considerations relating to technical installations

Considerations		Typical values
Capital costs	Engineering services and equipment	30–32% of building costs
Annual costs	Property operations and maintenance, energy, etc.	8–12% of revenues
Life-cycle	Depreciation of equipment: – computers, operating systems – catering and laundry equipment – mechanical plant	 2–5 years 5–10 years 10–15 years
Legal responsibilities	Safety, security, hygiene, conditions in workplaces	
Standards of hotel	Range of guest services, level of sophistication, comfort	
Maintenance	Standards, quality control, programming of work	
Variations	Climatic and diurnal ranges, changes in function and seasonal use	

Engineering services and equipment are becoming increasingly sophisticated to meet the higher standards demanded by discerning guests but also to provide for higher utilization of internal space and allow better control of performance and operating costs.

10.1.2 Economies

The costs of equipping and servicing public areas are relatively high and low-tariff hotels and inns may achieve savings by omitting or rationalizing restaurant facilities. With low-rise construction, up to three storeys, elevators may be omitted and – depending on location – air-conditioning may not be necessary in the rooms.

10.1.3 Public utilities

Engineering services include water supplies, sanitation and drainage, disposal of garbage; heating, ventilation, air cooling and conditioning, refrigeration; electrical distribution and equipment, communication and transmission facilities, elevators and transportation systems, catering, laundry and other operational equipment; and installations for control, security and efficient management.

In most situations hotels can use supplies provided by public utility services but in isolated resorts and developing areas the lack or unreliability of public supplies may require private installation of water supplies, treatment and storage; electricity generation; sewage treatment; and other infrastructure works.

Hotel development may also include:

Generation of electricity — For combined heat and power systems to achieve energy savings and revenue (from sale of electricity).

Sewage treatment — To prevent local pollution of beaches, etc., and enable recycling of effluent for land irrigation.

10.2 Water supplies and drainage

10.2.1 Quantities and extent of treatment

Large quantities of water are required in hotels for personal use, food preparation, cleaning and other domestic purposes, and possibly for firefighting, cooling, boilers, laundries, swimming pools and recreational use, irrigation of grounds and pavement cleansing (Table 10.2).

Domestic supplies — Must be pure, sterilized and protected from contamination, heat and frost. Drinking supplies separated. Outlet valves and taps must not become submerged.

Dishwashing and laundry — Treatment to reduce hardness and staining may be required.

Firefighting — High-pressure supplies to hydrants and sprinkler systems from two sources (storage and mains). Mains supply protected from contamination.

Boilers, heating and cooling plant — Treated water stored and recycled separate from other supplies.

Swimming pools — Cooling water circulation sanitized. Water continuously recycled, filtered, heated or cooled, and sterilized with residual trace of chlorine or ozone.

Irrigation — Clean water and/or treated sterilized effluent, free from silt and undecomposed material.

Table 10.2 Average water requirements

Average quantities	Per head per day	
	(litres)	(US gallons)
Hotel guests	135	35
Resident employees	90	24
Non-resident employees	45	12
Hostels	90	24
Restaurants	7.5	2 per meal

Notes: Average consumption within premises only.
Total usage in resorts may rise to 300 litres (80 gals)/guest.
Maximum rate of use rises to above three times the average flow.

10.2.2 Sources

In remote areas private supplies may be obtained from:

- *Underground aquifers* extracted from wells and boreholes.
- *Catchment surfaces* draining to storage tanks and cisterns.
- *Seawater desalination* using evaporation, freezing or osmotic processes.

Potential sources must be tested for reliability in drought conditions and extent of storage required.

10.2.3 Distribution within the premises

Storage capacity	1–2 days supply minimum. In high-level cisterns or pressurized tanks (at least two to allow maintenance).
Pressure	Boosting of supply pressure may be required for high-level buildings. Distribution zones limited to about ten storeys. All pumping equipment duplicated with means of isolation and drainage.
Drinking supplies	Taken separately from mains supply. May be chilled. Colour coded.
Domestic hot water	Indirectly heated in calorifiers near areas of use with secondary circulations to floors of rooms, kitchens, laundries, etc.

Supply temperatures			
	Domestic hot water	50°C	120°F
	Dishwashing: sinks	60°C	140°F
	Rinsing/sterilizing	82°C	180°F
	Laundry	72–82°C	160–180°F
	Chilled water	10°C	50°F

Hot water storage		Litre/ head	Gal /head
	High-grade hotels	45	10
	Budget hotels	32	7

10.2.4 Firefighting

Water pressure in tall buildings is regulated by zoning between 83 kN/m² (12 psi) and 552 kN/m² (80 psi).

Hose reels and hydrants are placed adjacent to escape routes (adjacent to staircase enclosures) 20 m (70 ft) apart to give a discharge rate of at least 0.4 litre/s (5 gal/min)

Sprinklers with automatic opening at a set temperature 57–71°C (135–160°F) are installed 2.6 to 4.3 m (12–14 ft) apart in corridors, public rooms and lobbies. Most systems are dual activated by smoke or fumes.

10.2.5 Waste and soil installations

Guestrooms
Vertical soil and waste pipes are normally installed in ducts between pairs of bathrooms allowing short branches from the fittings on each side to be connected at each floor. Provision must be made for access (sealed), anti-siphonage and ventilation of each of the stacks.

Much of the plumbing work can be prefabricated prior to installation and complete assembled bathroom units may be supplied with fittings in place ready for connection.

Kitchens and laundries
Drainage to kitchens includes waste connections for sinks, waste disposal units and water-filled equipment as well as for floor washing. Similar provisions apply to laundries. To reduce drain blockage it may be necessary to install grease traps and/or silt chambers.

10.2.6 Drainage and sewage disposal

In most situations, drainage systems provide for separation of foul water from surface water to facilitate sewage treatment.

Surface or storm water
This can be discharged direct to streams and lakes (natural or artificial) and used for landscaping cooling systems, emergency

firefighting and other practical uses. The risk of flooding must be assessed from peak intensities of rainfall, based on probability factors, areas drained and permeability of surfaces. Large areas of car parking and buildings may substantially alter the rate of run-off.

Foul water
Foul water collecting as sewage is conveyed in drainage systems laid at gradients to give a self-cleansing velocity of about 0.76 m/s (2.5 ft/sec). It may be necessary to collect and pump the sewage to higher ground for treatment to avoid beach pollution:

- Pipe sizes – 100 and 150 mm (4 and 6 in) common
- Gradients – minimum 1 in 80 to 120
- Access – at major junctions and changes in direction of gradient
- Ventilation – at head of each major branch and at lowest point.

Treatment
Sewage treatment may take several forms but provides for settlement and removal (or decomposition) of sludge and oxidation of suspended organic matter. Tertiary treatment may include chlorination of the effluent:

Settlement: Septic tank, sedimentation, activated sludge
Oxidation: Biological filter or land irrigation, air diffusion in tanks.

Sewage works tend to produce odour and attract flies and need to be carefully sited away from the buildings, beach and leisure areas (Table 10.3).

Table 10.3 Sewage treatment standards

Typical standard for effluents	Maximum parts per million
Biochemical oxygen demand (5 day)	20
Suspended solids	30

10.3 Electrical services

10.3.1 Lighting

Lighting installations are designed to serve a variety of functions – merchandising, security, directions, decoration and ambience – as well as to provide adequate illumination.

Luminaires
Generally a range of luminaires is installed with emphasis on:

- *Incandescent lamps* for warmth and sociability in near positions in lounges, restaurants or bedrooms.
- *Tubular fluorescent lighting* for general diffused lighting and work areas. With colour blending. Including permanent supplementary day lighting and concealed background illumination.
- *Discharge lamps* for high-intensity lighting of large halls and outdoor areas.

Fittings
Fittings may be:

- *Direct or semidirect* type for suspending low over tables, counters, desks, equipment or bedside reading.
- *General diffusing* for background illumination and in work areas.
- *Indirect* around perimeters, along corridors and to supplement general lighting.

10.3.2 Standards

Standards are recommended by the Illumination Engineering Society and Institution of Building Services Engineers (UK).
    Levels of illumination (Table 10.4) are dictated by:

- the need for accuracy, alertness and speed of working
- avoidance of excessive contrasts and glare (expressed as the limiting glare index).

Table 10.4 Levels of illumination

Situation	Scalar lumination (lux)	(lumens/sqft)	Limited glare index	Notes
Outdoor car parks	10	1		Increased to 20 lux over goods yards
Entrance lobby day(night)	200(100)	20(10)		Higher intensity at entrance during daytime (transitional zone)
Reception area	400	40		Increased locally to 600 lux over workstations. Light screened
Toilets, cloakrooms	200	20		
Public rooms (background)	100	10		
Corridors day(night)	100(50)	10(5)	22	Higher levels for cleaning in daytime. 200 lux in elevator lobbies
Guestrooms (general)	100	10		
Bedhead, writing desk	200	20		
Kitchen (general)	200	20	22	
Preparation, cooking, service	400	40	25	600 lux over serving counters. Infrared lamps for food lighting
Laundry, housekeeping	200	20	25	400 lux for hand-ironing, spotting, checking; 600 lux for needlework repairs
Stores, workshops	200	20	25	400 lux over workbenches, machinery; 600 lux in drawing offices
Offices	400	40	19	Balanced, screened, lighting in computer rooms, telephone operators (glare index 16)
Staff areas	100	10		Increased to 200 lux in staff canteen

10.3.3 Trends

Energy saving Increase of lumens emitted for a given voltage (installed flux) by substitution of lamps of higher efficacy, eg, tubular fluorescent lamps 45–55 lumens/watt, incandescent lamps 8–12 lumens/watt.

Brighter decoration Improving the utilization factor of artificial and natural light. Brighter decor also tends to make rooms appear more spacious and to improve sociability.

Life cycle Replacement of lamps to maintain efficiency and performance.

Use of external lighting systems To extend recreation activities.

10.3.4 Electrical services: standards

As with other services and equipment, electrical installations are subject to national codes and regulations stipulating standards of quality, performance and protection in the interests of safety. Reference should be made to the National Electrical Code (NEC), National Fire

Protection Association (NFPA) and Underwriters Laboratories (UL) in the USA and relevant IEC and CENLEC European standards.

10.3.5 Primary and emergency supplies

Supplies

Electricity mains supplies to hotels are generally three-phase AC with a cycle frequency of 50 or 60 kHz. Supply voltages vary from one country or undertaking to another, the most common being 120/208 V and 277/480 V in the USA and 240/415 V in the UK.

Individual hotels and resorts may generate their own electricity:

- in isolated areas or where the mains supplies are inadequate or unreliable
- in combined heat and power systems to achieve energy savings and (where appropriate) supply electricity to other consumers
- for emergency needs (see below).

Transformers

Mains supplies are generally conditional on the installation of a transformer which may be located externally (fenced off) or in a transformer room or vault within the building, near the main switchgear room. The transformer room must have good access, fire protection, air cooling and drainage.

Minimum capacity 150% of peak local requirements.

Emergency generators

Equipment is duplicated where possible to limit the extent of any failure. In the event of mains failure an automatic transfer switch enables supplies from battery and generator to be brought into use.

The location of the emergency generating plant is important in view of the noise, fuel space, ventilation and maintenance requirements.

Emergency supplies

Usually based on 30% of normal maximum demand:

- Lighting all exit signs, 50% of stairways and 20% of corridors, 10–20% of lighting in public areas
- Telephones, fire alarms and warning devices
- Firefighting apparatus (pumps, compressors, etc.)
- All sewage pumps and water pumps needed to maintain hot and cold supplies and partial heating or cooling
- Passenger elevators (with selector switch)
- Partial services to kitchens
- All food refrigerators and cold rooms.

10.3.6 Demand loads

Demand loads of equipment determine the current-carrying capacities and ratings of conductors and phase distribution both for individual branch circuits and the feeder and distribution submains (Table 10.5).

Branch current loadings may be estimated on the basis of:

- general lighting loads, including socket or receptacle outlets of 15 amp or less rating
- individual load ratings of connected equipment (cooking, heating, laundry, air-conditioning and mechanical plant).

Table 10.5 General lighting loads (based on NEC minima)

	Watts/m²	Watts/sqft
Hotel rooms	27	2.5
Motel and budget hotel rooms	22	2
Apartments, family rooms	32	3
Hotel lobby and reception	65	6
Restaurants	32	3
Offices and administration	55	5
Shops, coffee shops	32–55	3–5
Function rooms	32–55	3–5
Convention rooms	46–66	4–6
Major exhibit halls	220–270	20–25

Feeder and distribution submains serving large areas of a hotel may assume demand factors of less than 100% of the maximum calculated loading on branch circuits served depending on the probability of some diversity in demand.

The maximum calculated loading must include capacity for future increases, power factors of equipment and other peak conditions affecting simultaneous use.

10.3.7 Future developments and extensions

Growth of electrical consumption in hotels has been in the order of 25–30% in ten years with developments in operating equipment (accounting, computing and control equipment, electric cooking, coldrooms, elevators) and in more demanding standards of accommodation (television, self-catering, air-conditioning in rooms). Provision for future needs should allow 10–25% spare ways in conduits, raceways, switchboards and panel boards (including protection devices).

10.3.8 Distribution

Mains distribution may be based on:

Radial distribution	Feeders from main switchboards direct to principal areas of consumption (kitchens, laundry, lobby, function rooms, guestrooms, etc.) and other buildings on site (holiday villages).
Ring main distribution	Feeder cable extending round site or premises serving subsidiary distribution panels in each area. Allows easier isolation and future connections with economy through greater diversity factors in demand.
Rising main distribution	Suitable for tall hotel and apartment buildings. Rising mains – in the form of insulated cables or enclosed busbars – supply distribution panel boards for each floor.

10.3.9 Installations

Standards of practice are specified in local codes and regulations. The following is intended only as a guide:

Physical separation	High voltage, standard voltage, emergency and low voltage conductors in separate compartments.
Protection	Correct rating of conductors. Effective electrical insulation and mechanical protection. Overload devices (fuses, circuit breakers) against excessive current. Grounding or earth leakage circuit provision.
Environment	Protection of conductors and equipment from excessive heat, cold, condensation and moisture. Specific requirements apply to use of electrical apparatus in bathrooms, laundries and kitchens (water, steam corrosion). Shaver points (multivoltage). Boiler houses, garages, fuel stores (fire hazard). Computer and telephone equipment (moisture, screening).
Support	Cables and wires supported in vertical and horizontal runs, particularly in common ducts and service ways.
Access	At connections, junctions, switches, pull points. At intervals not exceeding 60 m and two bends.
Fire risk	Ducts and risers fire-stopped between compartments. No combustible material in enclosures.

Enclosure of cabling

Rigid metal conduit	Cast-in floor concrete (e.g. in rooms). Built or chased into walls (e.g. in restaurants, lobbies). Suspended in ceiling

	space on hangers (in corridors).
Flexible conduit	Connections to machines (metal). In protective covers to switch wiring in plaster walls. Underground.
Exposed metal raceways	Cable trays or troughs in service areas, machine rooms, ceiling voids.
Rectangular ducts in hollow walls, floors	Areas of concentrated services (offices, reception, kitchens, rooms).
Vertical ducts	For risers and panel board equipment in service cores.
Surface trunking with removable covers	For computer rooms, offices, workshops to allow relocation of equipment.
Accessible floor service voids	Computer rooms, telephone operators, conference and exhibition rooms

10.4 Heating, ventilation and air-conditioning

10.4.1 Codes and standards

Reference should be made to guides and technical memoranda by professional bodies etc., the American Society of Heating, Refrigeration and Airconditioning Engineers (ASHRAE), the Chartered Institution of Building Services Engineers (CIBSE) and relevant ISO and European CENS standards.

10.4.2 Outdoor design criteria

Outdoor design temperatures are usually based on the probability of occurrence of extreme conditions (Table 10.6 and 10.7).

Special consideration must be given to:

- *diurnal variations* in temperature due to high radiation loss at night which may require daytime cooling to alternate with heating at night
- *prevailing sea breezes* which may be utilized to reduce air-conditioning loads in resort hotels
- *degree of exposure to wind* affecting surface heat loss
- *solar heat absorption and penetration* – orientation and times of exposure to solar radiation. Effects of thermal storage.

10.4.3 Internal design standards

These depend to some extent on comparison with outside conditions and on the nature of use of each room.

Table 10.6 Probability of extreme conditions

	Probability factors	
	Summer	Winter
For high-grade hotels in USA	1½ or 2½%	Median of extremes
For hotels in temperate climates (United Kingdom)	2½ or 5%	99% or 97½%

Table 10.7 Example of outdoor design conditions

	Cooling	Heating
UK outdoors Temperatures	28°C dry bulb 20°C wet bulb	−4°C Saturated

Guestrooms

Table 10.8 Design standards for guestrooms (based on CIBSE recommendations)

Environmental conditions		Air-conditioning		Notes
		Day	Night	
Winter	°C	24[a]	24[a]	} Lower temperature adjustment
	°F	75	75	
Summer	°C	22	20	} Higher temperature adjustment
	°F	72	68	
Relative humidity		40–60%	40–60%	Double glazing may be required to reduce condensation
Fresh air supply	g/sec	25	25	Subject to local codes
	lb/hr	200	200	
Air filter efficiency	%	95	95	
Noise level	NC			Maximum
Standard		35	30	
High-grade		30	25	
Maximum air movement	m/s	0.15	0.15	Overfloor areas up to 2 m (6.5 ft) height.
	ft/min	30	30	

Notes: [a]22°C for space heating only.

Public rooms

The temperature of heated public space and offices may be limited to 20°C (68°F) by statutory regulations to conserve energy (Table 10.9).

Comfort

The above temperatures are dry resultant temperatures which are a product of air and radiant temperatures and air velocity. This is a better indication of conditions for comfort and applies generally in all areas apart from kitchens and plant rooms.

10.4.3 Fresh air allowances

The quantity of fresh air introduced into air-conditioned spaces should not normally be less than 8 litre/sec (17 cfm) per person. Where the ceiling height (as in large ballrooms) makes volumetric standards inappropriate an alternative rate of 15.5 litre/sec per m² (3 cfm/sqft) may be used (Table 10.10).

10.4.5 Natural ventilation of rooms

Natural ventilation is commonly used in budget and mid-grade hotels in resorts, holiday villages and condominium developments. It is also more practical in many back-of-house areas.

Natural ventilation allows the use of openable windows and is simple and economical. It is normally combined with space heating and may be supplemented by fan aircooling or unit conditioners.

Rates of airchange for natural ventilation are listed in Table 10.11.

Table 10.9 Typical design standards for public rooms

Area	Cooling[a]			Heating[b]		
	°C	°F	%RH (max)	°C	°F	%RH (min)
Restaurants, bars, lounges	22		60	21		40
Conference rooms	22		60	20–21[b]		40
Lobby, foyer	27			18–20[c]		
Corridors, stairs	23		60	20		25
Computer etc., equipment and stores	27			18–20	64–68	[d]
Kitchens	23			15–18[e]	60–64	[f]
Mechanical and electrical equipment	30			18		
Internal swimming pools				30		
Changing rooms				25		

Notes: [a]Temperature may fluctuate ±1°C.

[b]Adjustable in each conference room.

[c]Depending on outside conditions. Air curtains may be used.

[d]Condensation avoided.

[e]Minimum 15.6°C (60°F) in work areas.

[f]Larger plant requires only frost protection and ventilation.

Table 10.10 Fresh air supply per room

Room	Recommended		Minimum	
	(litre/s)[a]	(cfm)[b]	(litre/s)[a]	(cfm)[b]
Guestrooms	12	30	8	25
Apartments	12	20	8	15
Restaurants	18	15	12	12
Cafeterias	12	15	8	10
Cocktail bars	18	30	12	25
Meeting etc. rooms	25	40	18	30
Dance halls	12		8	
Offices	12	15	8	10
Small shops, stores	12	20	8	15

Notes: [a]Europe

[b]United States of America

Table 10.11 Rates of airchange for natural ventilation

Rooms	Airchanges per hour
Guestrooms, bedrooms	1
Living rooms, foyers, circulation areas	1.5
Public rooms, dining rooms, work areas[a]	2.0
Entrance lobbies, sanitary facilities, changing and drying rooms	3.0

Note: [a]Low occupancies.

10.4.6 Mechanical air circulation

Mechanical circulation is required to provide the higher rates of air changes necessary to maintain suitable conditions and remove pollutants, heat and high humidities. Fan-operated equipment may be direct or extended by air ducting to remote areas and includes the following.

Systems
Exhaust systems in kitchens, internal bathrooms, toilets, garages and for smoke control. *Plenum systems* for controlled distribution of supply air to specific areas. *Air conditioning systems* providing treatment, regulation and circulation of fresh and recycled air.

Balancing

Exhaust and plenum systems must be balanced to ensure even distribution of fresh or conditioned air and positive removal of pollutants. Balancing of high rates of extraction (kitchens, laundries, toilets) usually involves part controlled distribution of make-up air, part inflow from adjacent areas.

Smoke control

Provisions must include automatic switchover to fire mode in areas of risk (garages, circulation areas, atriums) to enable controlled extraction of smoke and direction of airflows. Fire mode systems include dampers, release vents and emergency fans for smoke exhaustion and air pressurization.

Automatic fire dampers are also required in exhaust ducting from cooking and laundry equipment and garages.

10.4.7 Rates of air change: operational areas

Air flow rates in operational areas are generally governed by exhaust requirements. Specific conditions apply in the following areas.

Boiler house

Direct entry must be provided for combustion air based on 150% theoretical requirements. Cooling air is also needed to provide suitable ambient conditions.

Generating plant

Adequate fresh air for internal combustion (with efficient exhaust) and cooling.

Plant rooms

(Transformer, switchgear, telephone equipment, refrigeration plant mechanical plant, elevator machinery, etc.). Well ventilated with filters if necessary to maintain ambient temperatures to standards specified by manufacturers, maximum 32°C (90°F). Exhaust fans may be required.

Kitchens

Ventilation is dictated by high rates of extraction above equipment (Table 10.12).

Easily removable grease filters and automatic fire dampers are required over cooking equipment. Ductwork must have sealed access points for internal cleaning.

A large proportion of air exhausted (60–80%) is made up of air supplied (heated or cooled) to preparation areas. The balance is usually by air flow from the restaurant extracted over the serving counters.

Laundries

15–20 airchanges/hour. Large items of equipment (tumble driers, rotary irons) and dry cleaning machines require individual exhausts.

Public toilets

10 airchanges/hour based on an extract rate of 6.4 litre/m^2 (1.25 cfm/sqft). Supply air usually 50% with balance from corridor. Fans must be duplicated with automatic switchover and the exhaust systems must be separate from other ventilation.

Enclosed car parks and loading docks

Six air changes/hour extraction rate with one-third at low level, two-thirds at high level to

Table 10.12 Ventilation in kitchens

Zone	Air changes/hour	Based on area
Over kitchen area	20–30[a]	20 litre/s/m^2
Over cooking area	40[b]	

Notes: [a]Depending on concentration of equipment and canopies.
[b]Determined by face velocity over extraction loads.

ensure cross-ventilation. Precautions must be taken to reduce risk of fire and smoke entering other areas (separation, fire dampers, discharge outlets, sparkproof machinery, pressure ventilation of lobbies, etc.).

Food stores

Local air refrigeration is essential for chilled (+1 to +3°C) and frozen (–20°C) temperatures. Garbage stores may also be chilled. Refrigeration plant may be largely centralized or individually self-contained. Centralized systems allow heat recovery for domestic hot water supplies.

10.4.8 Air-conditioning

Air-conditioning is generally a necessary requirement in lobbies, restaurants, bars, meeting rooms and ballrooms. In higher grade hotels (4–5 star) guestrooms should also be air-conditioned and have individual controls. Air-conditioning equipment may range from individual self-contained units to centralized systems.

10.4.9 Unitary equipment and multi-unit decentralized systems

Based on packaged systems, self-contained units have lower initial costs and allow individual operation but tend to be noisy and obtrusive.

Guestrooms	
Through-the-wall and split packaged units	Units contain circulating fans, air filters, direct expansion refrigerator coil, compressor and air-cooled condenser. Typical ratings 2.5–3.5 kW (¾–1 ton R). May include heating element or reverse cycle heat pump.
Multi-unit decentralized systems	Including variable refrigerant volume direct expansion (VRV) systems combined with localized ventilation plant and heat exchanger. Up to eight indoor units connected to one external condenser.

Public spaces	
Self-contained package units	Larger floor standing, cabinet conditioners with ratings up to 17 kW (5 tons R) which may be directly aircooled or water-cooled with a remote cooling tower.
Split package systems	Multiple air handling units served by aircooled compressor–condensing equipment which may be remotely located (on roof etc.) and noise insulated. Includes VRV systems.

10.4.10 Central systems for guestrooms

These provide for central treatment and distribution of primary (fresh) air through ducts to terminals in which the balance of air is recycled from the room.

Fan coil units	Incorporate fans for discharge of primary and secondary air (filtered) over heating or cooling coils.
	Fan coil units may be sited under the window, on adjacent party walls or in lowered ceiling space above the entrance vestibule or bathroom (mounted horizontally).
	Heating water is usually supplied at 49–60°C (120–140°F) and chilled water no less than 7°C (45°F) with four- or two-pipe circulations. Fans have two or three speed motors with selector switch and thermostat regulator. Noise levels measured 1 m from the grille should not exceed NC 30.
	Variations: *Versatemp reverse cycle heat pump* systems.
High velocity induction units	Use centrally supplied fresh air to induce air recirculation within room. Primary air must be related to the bathroom extract. Mounted in similar locations.

High velocity dual duct systems

Separate hot and cold air from central plant supplied through terminal air mixing unit in each room. Allows good control but requires relatively large ducting.

Exhaust systems

Removal of air from a guestroom is usually through exhaust systems in the bathroom and supply grilles must be positioned to avoid short cycling of air flows.

Exhaust registers should be located near the water closet and provide 6 airchanges/hour (minimum 3) 19–30 litre/s (40–60 cfm). Noise levels measured at the bathroom door should not exceed NC 30.

10.4.11 Central systems for public spaces

To provide independent control, isolation and flexibility to meet varying conditions each public space requires a separate air supply. This may be provided from an independent unit or multizoned system and include return air ducts for reconditioning or discharge of exhausted air to balance the fresh air requirements.

Individual

Air-conditioning unit located near to the area served (plant rooms or roof mounted) with precautions against noise and vibration. Supply air is usually ducted direct to ceiling diffusers or wall registers.

Multizone

Distribution of conditioned air may be through:
- *Variable air volume (VAV) systems* with dual hot and cold ducts to attenuation and mixing boxes serving each zone.
- *Single duct to fan coil units* for terminal cooling or heating.

10.4.12 Distribution

Ductwork supplying primary air may be designed for high-velocity distribution with air speeds of 15–25 m/s (3000–5000 fpm) or local velocities of 3.7.5 m/s (600–1200 fpm). Ducts may be formed from galvanized sheet steel or spirally wound, circular or oval section tubing. The ductwork may be exposed or housed in ceiling voids and vertical service cores. Precautions against noise include correct sizing, streamlining, supporting and attenuation treatment.

10.4.13 Specific areas

Entrance lobbies and foyers

High rates of natural ventilation are likely due to infiltration and stack effects. Equipment with high heating or cooling capacity installed (fan coil or induction units). Temperatures can be modulated to allow transitional zone. Specific provision must be made for automatic switchover to fire mode for smoke evacuation and directional control of airflows (see section 10.4.6).

Restaurants, cocktail lounges, coffee shops

Supply air may be provided from individual air-conditioning units or dual duct zoned system. Ceiling diffusers usually installed and air flow may be concentrated over or under windows (to balance heat loss/gain) and around the bar or servery (areas of activity). A flow of 290–380 litre/s (600–800 cfm) per diffuser and a temperature differential of 9–10°C (16–18°F) is suitable for normal ceiling heights.

Extraction is provided over servery areas and balanced with the kitchen requirements.

Private dining rooms, meeting rooms

The air-conditioning system must have a wide range of adjustment using terminal heating/cooling equipment. Air is exhausted in crossflow towards the bar and servery. Noise levels should not exceed NC 35.

Ballrooms, conventional halls

In divisible rooms each separated area must have individual controls requiring either self-contained air circulation or primary plant supplying terminals with temperature and air flow adjustment. Air inflows and exhausts must be balanced to give even distribution with changing conditions of space and function.

10.4.14 Central heating systems

Air-conditioning	Using tempered air. Usually supplemented by perimeter space heating, local heating in bathrooms, etc.
Direct electric heating	With local air convector or panel heating appliances (portable or fixed) in which the heating elements are protected against fire risk and hazard.
Low pressure hot water	Most common being relatively safe and simple in operation. Suitable for compact buildings.

Operating temperatures	°C	°F
Convector heaters, radiators	80	175
Fan coils (2 pipe systems)	60	140

Medium and high pressure hot water (MPHW, HPHW)	*Operating temperatures*	°O	°F
	MPMW typically up to	120	250
	HPHW	150–	300–
	(less common)	180	350

Subject to rigorous legal and insurance requirements. Used in very large hotels and for district heating of resorts – with calorifiers in individual properties.

Steam heating   Alternative to MPHW in larger hotels and multiple developments. Specific applications (after conversion) in laundries, kitchens, dishwashing and cleaning.

10.4.14 Domestic hot water

Hot water for washing and cleaning may be provided by directly heated boilers, immersion/electrode boilers or calorifiers (steam or hot-water heated). Calorifiers must be located near areas of use, with secondary circulation of the hot water to minimize delay and waste. Structural support, access for servicing, control and drainage, insulation of hot and cold supplies and noise must be considered in the planning stages.

10.4.16 Heat sources

Boilers

Sectional boilers are most common for LPHW installations: horizontal fire tube boilers (usually package type) are generally suitable for larger premises. Two boilers are usually installed, each capable of operating independently and sized to meet 75% (or 80 and 60%) of peak load to allow for seasonal fluctuations. In larger premises and resort systems, three boilers, each 50% peak load, may be installed.

Combined heat and power generation (chp)

Combined installations enable individual hotels and resorts to generate all or part of the electrical load in addition to recycling the waste heat for space and/or domestic hot water heating. Surplus electricity may be sold to public undertakings or used for storage heating or cooling. A number of generating units are used to allow flexibility and higher overall efficiency.

Solar energy

Utilization of solar energy is generally cost-effective in summer resort hotels for domestic hot water, swimming pool and specialized communication equipment applications. Passive equipment is normally installed and the siting of solar collecting panels, header tanks and pipework is critical in relation to exposure (incident angles), screening (unsightly appearance) and maintenance (cleaning, etc.).

Heat energy

Most new equipment is designed for increased energy efficiency and may include options for heat recycling from cooling condensers, hot wastes (laundry, dishwashing) and hot gases (regenerative or recuperative systems).

10.4.17 Fuels

The choice of fuel depends on availability and cost.

Small to medium-sized hotels generally use gas or light viscosity oil with electricity for supplementary heating. In larger hotels and resorts, medium viscosity oil may provide an alternative.

Oil storage (2.2 m³/tonne) and pumping have to be determined and burners are usually of the pressure jet automatic type supplied individually or on a ring main system. *Safety controls* are legally required to ensure warning and isolation of pressure variation, fire water or flame failure, smoke emission and other hazards.

10.4.18 Gas installation

Supplies

Gas may be supplied in the form of natural gas (methane) or oil gas supplied from mains or liquefied gas (propane, butane) from local storage in pressurized containers.

Uses

As a fuel for combustion in boilers, heat exchangers, storage or instantaneous water heating systems, combined heat and power generators, cooking equipment and incinerators.

Mains gas supplies are extensively used in city and urban hotels allowing more flexibility than liquid or solid fuels. Gas-fired boilers may be installed near roof level to free space at ground level for other uses. *Portable liquefied gas* can provide an alternative fuel for cooking and for specialized grilling equipment.

10.4.19 Requirements

Gas installations must meet local code and regulation requirements for metering, control, safety, protection, air supply, damper and flue arrangements.

As a rule, gas burning equipment is not interchangeable and burners, air regulators, governors, safety devices and controls are specific to the properties of the gas. Special structural and ventilation precautions apply to storage areas for portable gas.

10.4.20 Location of plant

Large-scale plant requirements include water treatment and storage, air handling, heating, refrigeration, electricity generation, elevator machinery and fuel storage. The location for such equipment may be specific (e.g. elevators) or allow a degree of centralization with other associated plant. Locational considerations must take account of noise, vibration and heat or fume emission, floor loadings, access for servicing and replacement and ventilation requirements:

- *roof mounted* designed to profile, with roof access and screening
- *ground level* for accessibility and near storage
- *basement* with air intake and ventilation shafts
- *intermediary service floor* for high-rise buildings, above public rooms
- *separate energy supply centre* for resort services and district distribution.

Chilling and cooling equipment

Central plant supplying chilled water to air-conditioning units requires the installation of at least two refrigeration–chilling units each capable of supplying 60–70% of the total load. Cooling towers for dissipation of heat must also

(a) Plan of basement technical centre

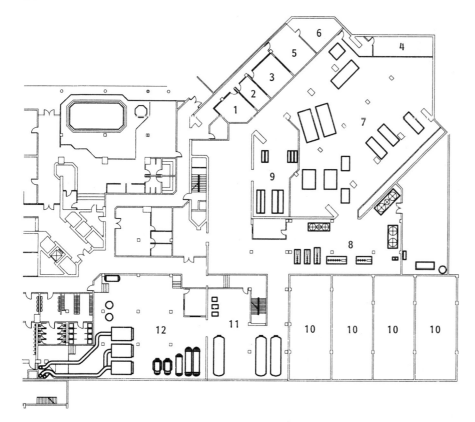

(a)

```
0 2 4    10        20
 1 3 5         15
```

Key

1	Security room	7	Air-conditioning equipment
2	Technical room	8	Water supply pumping equipment
3	Chief engineer	9	Chilling equipment
4	Automatic control centre	10	Water storage
5	Equipment	11	Hot water storage
6	Electrical distribution	12	Boiler room

Figure 10.1 *Basement technical centre*
Plans of the technical plant area in the 298 room
Holiday Inn Crowne Plaza Hotel, Istanbul.
Architect: Dr Hyati Tabanlioğlu. Mechanical
engineer: Ersin Gudol. Electrical engineer: Bulent
Cedetas

(b) View of mechanical centre

be duplicated and must be sited to avoid nuisance (noise, humidity, maintenance, frost damage) usually at or near roof level.

Boiler plant

May be at ground/basement level for access and near storage or grouped with air-conditioning equipment at rooftop level. Chimney heights are subject to local control depending on the type and output of the plant and the dispersion of effluent gases (CO_2, smoke, condensation).

10.4.21 Control and administration

Engineering control panels are required for central systems to indicate operating conditions of all remote components and plant performance. The trend is towards computerized sensing control and automatic regulation of systems in the interests of energy management. Installation may provide for:

- fully automated control (intelligent buildings)
- remote station recording and adjustment (regional energy management of group hotels)
- integrated computer programming (engineering services, security, maintenance).

Engineering offices, control rooms, plan and record rooms and associated workshops are generally grouped close together in order to give convenient access to the equipment areas. (see section 9.5.2).

10.4.23 Energy conservation

Energy costs in a high-grade hotel typically account for 4–5% of all revenues. Reductions in energy use may be required for commercial savings, load reductions (in plant capacity, peak tariff charges) and to comply with legal standards (insulation, temperature, limitations, etc.). In most countries, substantial incentives are provided for energy-saving improvements to existing buildings and other innovative developments.

Energy savings may be achieved in several ways but need to be considered in relation to their cost-effectiveness (payback period) and other benefits.

Solar heat gain (cooling load)

Position, screening and insetting of windows. Use of venetian blinds, (external, double or between windows) vertical blinds, canopies and deflecting screens and reflective glass (specific locations). Solar heating systems.

Fabric heat loss or gain

Maximum thermal transmittance (U). Values and heat flow rates in winter and summer conditions are stipulated in building regulations and codes. Use of heavy window drapes and privacy mesh curtains.

Ventilation loss

Reduction of infiltration and air leakages by fitting and edge sealing of windows and doors. Control of extraction and air-conditioning loss through opened doors and windows.

Lighting

Substitution of tungsten filament lamps with luminaries of higher efficacy and exhaustion of air over light fittings to reduce cooling load.

Domestic hot water

Improved secondary circulation and insulation of hot and cold pipes. Reduction of temperature to 50°C (122°F). Use of spray taps and showers.

Air-conditioning and space heating/cooling

Zone control and monitoring of temperature inside and out. Use of reverse cycle and thermal storage systems.

Heat recovery

Recuperation or regenerative use of exhaust heat from dishwashers, cooling water, etc. Combined heat and power systems (see section 10.4.16).

Monitoring and regulation

Energy management systems enabling rapid response, correction and optimization of energy use (see section 10.4.21).

Control

Central reduction of heating temperature (to 18°C) from 0100 to 0500 hours. Zone control to isolate unused areas. Use of door card or key to activate or isolate room heating/air-conditioning.

10.5 Telecommunications and sound systems

10.5.1 Telephone systems

Equipment for external telecommunications is regulated by the public operating company. Systems vary in complexity with a trend towards increasing sophistication in guest and operating facilities.

Private automatic branch exchange PABX/PBX	Direct dialling and metering. Automatic connection of outgoing and extension calls. Used in hotels with more than 50 extensions.
Private manual branch exchange PMBX	All incoming and outgoing calls routed through the operator. Limited to ten outside lines (two operators). For small hotels located adjacent to reception desks.
Private manual exchange	Independent internal system for communications between extensions (guests, administration, security). May be used in parallel with public telephones.
Intercom system	Direct wired and radio controlled for administration, maintenance or security contact.

10.5.2 Private automatic branch exchanges

Equipment specifications are usually based on:

- capacity of the exchange: numbers of lines and extensions
- system of connection: switchgear equipment
- facilities provided.

Space requirements

Table 10.13 PABX space requirements for a 250 room hotel

	m²	sqft
Telephone exchange	3–4 consoles[a]	300–320 lines
Telephone operator's room	18.6	200
Autoswitch equipment and terminal equipment	37.2[b]	400
Telephone operator's restroom, lockers and toilets	18.6	200

Notes: [a]Including facsimile transmission and separate access.
[b]12 m² per 100 extensions.

10.5.3 Facilities

Guest lines

Numbering	Matching telephone extension and room numbers.
Operator's desk	Indicator panel for identification of calls.
Connection to service lines (message/mail, reception, room service, laundry/valet, concierge)	Single-digit numbers used. Automatic routing to operator if occupied. Wake-up systems – personal or taped for multiple calls.
Connection to other guest lines	Operator barring on request or generally (at night).
Outgoing local and national calls	Automatic. Metered. Long distance calls itemised.
Outgoing international calls	Direct dialling or via operator. Metered. Itemized. Cheapest line route selected.
Incoming calls	Via operator, direct or transferred to message board. Messages may be voice recorded.

Administration

Operational staff	Departmental lines, service lines (all other calls via operator).
Departmental offices	As above plus administration and local calls.
Executive offices	As above plus two service lines.
Senior management	As above plus two service lines and one private line.

10.5.4 Developments

The network for communication with individual rooms provided by telephone lines can also be used for other control and information systems.

Local control panel	For room facilities, television, music, curtains.
Loud-speaker	Fire alarm, specific evacuation instructions.
Detection signalling	Smoke sensors. Entry to unoccupied rooms.
Room status	Indication of room cleaning, availability.
Room allocation	Automatic metering on registration.
In-room checkout	To control TV display of guest folio of charges.
Business services	Connections for facsimile and computer data transmissions.
Network conferencing	Multiple line connections for group discussions.

10.5.5 Other telephone requirements

Emergency and maintenance locations:

- guest and service elevators and motor houses; engineering plant rooms
- kitchen, servery, restaurant, bar, pantry, stores
- every third/fourth landing of emergency fire stairways

- in guest bathrooms.

Public telephone locations:

- main lobby
- ballroom or function room foyer
- recreational club
- employee restrooms.

Group reservation telephones are sited on the reception desk convenient for public use. Other public telephones should have shelves, be individually screened by booth enclosures or acoustic hoods, grouped together and located in a relatively quiet area to one side of circulation routes.

10.5.6 Telephone operator's room

Freestanding cabinets for desk or counter mounting	Up to 200 extensions, 44 exchange lines, 12–24 connecting links.
Cord-type consoles with 2 or more panels, grouped as suites	Unlimited extensions.

Cordless consoles may be separated

10.5.7 Switching equipment

Switchgear is mounted in a separate room located adjacent or near to the operator's rooms. The equipment consists of multiswitches and relays in modular frames which may be mounted in dustproof cabinets (in small installations) or rows of switchracks. The development of electronic equipment has allowed large savings in space.

Telephone apparatus is usually powered by a 50±4 volt relay supply provided through a battery and autocharger or direct mains transformer unit. Indictor and alarm signals automatically show various faults.

Large equipment rooms must be designed to suit equipment mountings: with ceilings 2.8 m (9'3") or higher; smooth, dust-free flooring and painted walls; and good access (with doors opening outwards). Internal temperatures may need to be maintained between 15.5 and 18.5°C (60–65°F) with good ventilation, fitted with filters. Larger installations require a separate battery or transformer room.

10.5.8 Distribution

Distribution is through pairs of cables collected into bunches which must be protected from damage, moisture or electrical contact. These must be separated from higher voltage supplies (see section 10.3.9).

Horizontal distribution	• ceiling void or raised service floor (offices) • surface trunking or raceways • hollow skirting
Vertical distribution	by risers in ducts and shafts
Branches	from junction boxes.

Terminals in guest rooms are usually on each side of the party walls adjacent to bedside cabinets. Extensions may be installed to lounges (suites), work areas (executive rooms) and bathrooms (emergency). Developments include the use of glass optical fibre for cabling systems.

10.5.9 Background music and paging

Sound systems include facilities for selecting, amplifying and distributing music from radio or music centre (CD player, tape deck) to multiple speakers located in various parts of the hotel or resort. Microphone circuits are connected for messages (paging) and public announcements, with transmission to selected areas.

Systems broadly fall into two groups:

• *general* – extending over both guest and staff working areas, or
• *local* – for specific rooms and their associated foyers for seminars, functions, exhibitions, etc.

Local and general systems should allow for interconnection.

Speakers may be of the cabinet, column or ceiling type to harmonize with the decor. Column or reflex horn speakers may be used externally, e.g. around swimming pools.

To ensure clarity there should be:

• relative large numbers of speakers
• multiple channels – to different areas
• variable volume settings – in public areas
• individual selection and control in guest areas.

10.5.10 Television and radio systems

Requirements for television reception and distribution depend on local conditions and the arrangements which may be made for leasing and installing equipment.

A master antenna television system is usually installed with specific channel antennae, signal amplification in stages and coaxial cable distribution to outlets in guestrooms, lounges, bars and staff restrooms.

Receiving dish aerials for satellite stations and cable television services should also be incorporated into new designs.

Developments
The television cable and screen may be used for a range of other services, for example:

Closed circuit TV in-house entertainment	Internal distribution using unallocated VHF channels.
Local information	Using interactive enquiry systems.
Computer connections	For portable equipment including games.
Self check-out	Extension of in-house system. Folio of charges displayed by dialling code number.

Television sets must be mounted or secured on tables, shelves or brackets which allow a wide angle of view and swivelling without damage or hazard from trailing cables. Remote control is preferable.

Radio broadcasting is normally through a central sound transmission system but AM/FM antennae installations may be used for individual reception – such as in separate apartments.

10.5.11 Audio-visual aid equipment for conventions and exhibitions

The range of equipment may provide:

- *Closed circuit television* cameras, screen displays and recording equipment with line transmission to other areas (seminars, conference relays).
- *Television projection systems* for large audience viewing.
- *Teleconferencing networks* through business satellite communication systems using dish aerials for transmission and reception.
- *Slide projection* with remote control and linked sound transmission. Including projection booth and equipment store for large halls.
- *Overhead screen projection* with angle adjustment screens.
- *Tape recording* and editing facilities.
- *Music and microphone facilities* through local sound systems.
- *Telephone connections.*
- *Simultaneous interpretation* with wired services to purpose-designed booths or portable interpretation stations.
- *Speaker's lectern* with auto-cue facilities.

10.6 Computerized operating systems

10.6.1 Applications

The rapid development of computerized equipment and customized software for information processing has led to many applications in hotel operations. These may stand alone or be fully integrated systems and broadly cover the following main areas of management:

Front office   Including reservations and accounting systems

Property   Energy management, life safety, security monitoring, and property maintenance systems.

Departments   Food and beverage control, inventory control and ordering, housekeeping, work scheduling and payroll systems.

Individual   Desktop and personal computers for general or specialized work: financial analyses (spreadsheets), word processing, electronic filing (database) systems, graphics packages, etc.

10.6.2 Arrangement

Systems can be interlinked to form an *integrated computerized system* in which entries made at any system terminal automatically update the files in parallel systems.

Standalone systems handle a more limited range of jobs and are usually designed for a specific aspect of hotel operations such as reservations or accounting. With the increasing capacity and versatility offered by microcomputers the trend is towards the installation of multisystems interfaced where required to provide integration.

10.6.3 Typical installations

- *Large hotels – 300 rooms plus.* Dual minicomputers used to back up each other and support a large number of terminals. Direct links to other systems and devices.
- *Medium hotels – 100–300 rooms.* Two or more microcomputers each supporting a small number of terminals with some interfacing for transfer of data.
- *Small hotels – 25–50 rooms.* One or more standalone computers supporting up to four terminals.

In each case, individual computers will also be used for office and department functions.

10.6.4 Range of facilities

Reservations   Automated reservation, room allocation and direct billing systems. Marketing reports. Analysis of sales. Room availability for individuals and groups. Guest profiles and history. Room assignment. Payment method. Deposit crediting.

Front desk   Registration: telephone and room notification. Credit card verification. Issue of card/keys. Guest accounts: continuously updated. Point of sale charging (see section 6.3.5).

Accounts   Guest accounts. Night audit. General ledger. Accounts payable. Discounting. Travel agent accounts. Referral credits. Financial reports. Performance analysis. Payroll accounts. Inventory files, continuous updating.

Telephone   Automatic metering. Itemized charging. Route selection. Message notification. Warning and wake-up services. Room status system (see section 10.5.4.)

Television   In-room entertainment, information and account portfolios (see section 10.5.10.)

Security   Room access control, sensory monitoring of space. Fume and smoke detection. Alarm activation, zoning, checking. Automatic switchover to fire mode control. Smoke evacuation, pressure ventilation (see section 10.4.6.)

Energy management, engineering controls   Monitoring of environmental conditions. Optimization and adjustment of flows. Zone regulation. Out-station data transmission to central computer. Maximum demand control, load shedding. Fault location, automatic switchover facilities. Maintenance records. Programming and costing (see section 10.4.21.)

Food and beverage operations   Menu costing. Recipe formulation. Stock control. Production programming. Staff scheduling.

10.6.5 Construction of computer rooms

For large offices and computer rooms, floors should be in removable panels suspended over a void accommodating ventilation ducting, communication and power supply cabling. Distributed floor loadings are in the order of 3.5 kN/m^2 (70 lb/sqft). The minimum ceiling height is 2.4 m (8 ft), with 3.0 m (10 ft) preferable in larger rooms.

Table 10.14 Optimum conditions: sophisticated equipment

Environment	Optimum range	Notes
Temperature	21±3°C	Minimum 10°C
Relative humidity	50±10%	Heating required to prevent temperature falling below dew point
Air filtration	95% efficiency at 5 microns	
Illumination	500 lux (50 lumens/sqft)	Uniform fluorescent lighting of balanced daylight colour

Surfaces must be non-dusting, noise-absorbent and fire resistant with low rate of surface flame spread. Fire-sensing equipment with CO_2 extinguishers and alarms must be installed. Sensitivity to environmental conditions will depend on the sophistication of the equipment. As a rule, air filtration, temperature and humidity control are required (Table 10.14).

For screen viewing work critical requirements are:

- room illumination relative to brightness of screen (eye strain)
- directional angle of light (viewing, glare)
- height and inclined angle of screen (back strain, view distortion)
- position and height of keyboard relative to user: seated or standing (ergonomic efficiency, repetitive use injuries).

11

Maintenance and refurbishment

11.1 Financial aspects

11.1.1 Quality control

Maintenance cannot be isolated from the initial planning of hotels; decisions on architecture, interior design, plant and equipment will have a major influence on subsequent costs of energy, upkeep and replacement. Maintenance and life-cycle refurbishment is also market-driven by the need to compete, to maintain market shares and retain grading and tariff levels.

Account must also be taken of indirect costs, loss of performance and quality control:

- *difficulties and delays*, particularly in cleaning and housekeeping adding to labour costs
- *loss of revenue*, due to failure, breakdown and closure of areas for repair
- *loss of quality and goodwill*, due to interruptions, inefficiency and declining standards
- *risks to safety, security* and infringement of legal and insurance requirements.

11.1.2 Costs

As a proportion of total revenues, typical annual allowances are:

Property operations and maintenance 4–6%
Energy and utilities 4–5%

The real costs of maintenance are difficult to assess since much of this work often overlaps with other budgets:

- Leasing of equipment and furniture

- Depreciation allowances for replacement of furniture, fittings and equipment (including life-cycle refurbishments) 4–6% per year
- Building rents, including maintenance of the building shell, where the hotel occupies leased premises
- Common charges for estate management and maintenance of condominium and timeshared properties.

11.1.3 Life-cycle replacement

Provision for replacement and renewal of equipment, fittings, furnishings and decoration is made by estimating a reasonable life expectancy for each type of item. Life-cycles depend on obsolescence, wear and tear; the relative costs of maintenance, cleaning and replacement; the inconvenience, loss or damage which could result from neglect or breakdown, and the standards of the hotel in terms of image, grade and price.

In preliminary estimates, depreciation allowances are usually based on 20–25% replacement of FFE over each five-year period. Maintenance schedules take into account appropriate life-cycles for major renewals or refurbishment (Table 11.1).

11.1.4 Replacement schedules

Replacement and refurbishment programmes are subject to changes in requirements and circumstances as well as cost considerations. In general, the frequency and timing of work will depend on:

Table 11.1 Life-cycles for major renewals or refurbishment

Renewal/Replacement	Period (years)
Public rooms	
Refurbishment: renewal of carpets, fittings and furniture	5–8[a]
Guestrooms	
Decor, furnishing fabrics	2–4[b]
Carpets, electrical fittings	5–8
Furniture	7–10[c]
Bathroom fittings	10–15[c]
Capitalized leased equipment	5–8[d]
Electronic, communication and computer equipment	5–8[d]
Food service, kitchen and laundry equipment	7–10[e]
Major engineering plant	10–15[f]
Hotel buildings	20–25[g]

Notes: [a]Major refurbishments planned to fit in with the concept life-cycle of the restaurant, bar, etc.

[b]Two-year decoration usually combined with fabric and carpet cleaning.

[c]May require renovation instead of replacement.

[d]Affected by obsolence, introduction of new systems.

[e]Ten years for heavy-duty equipment.

[f]Major overhauls and replacements. Servicing and maintenance carried out regularly.

[g]For amortization of loans. Building renovation likely.

- *Changes in market conditions* need for upgrading or modifications to the facilities
- *Phasing of work* in line with the seasonal reductions in occupancies and other refurbishment needs
- *Hotel performance*: putting back or advancing non-essential work to balance accounts or gain tax benefits
- *Legal and insurance standards*: obligations to meet new requirements
- *Difficulties* of replacement in terms of access, damage, other disturbance, cost and loss of revenue.

11.2 Maintenance work

11.2.1 Terminology

Maintenance is defined as work undertaken to keep or restore every facility to an acceptable standard. This work may be organized and carried out with forethought, control and records (planned maintenance) or carried out on an emergency basis when the need arises (Figure 11.1).

Planned maintenance may be:

- *Preventive* to reduce the likelihood of failure or breakdown of plant and equipment by providing regular attention and servicing (e.g. elevators, mechanical and electrical plant, kitchen and laundry equipment).
- *Corrective* to restore the area or facility to an acceptable standard (e.g. redecoration, refurbishment of rooms).
- *Running maintenance* facilitated by the installation of duplicate equipment (pumps, fans, plant) and independent access.
- *Shutdown maintenance* requiring the closure of rooms or equipment, best planned to enable other work in the area to be carried out at the same time.

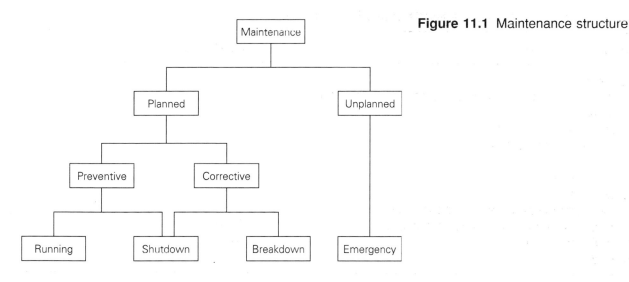

Figure 11.1 Maintenance structure

- *Breakdown maintenance* applying to the numerous small items of equipment which require replacement at irregular times for which advance provision can be made by way of spares, materials, labour and equipment.

Effective breakdown maintenance relies on an efficient system of reporting and recording defects through the operating departments (housekeeping, front office, food and beverage services, etc.). Good storage facilities and efficient organization of work are also critical.

Breakdown maintenance can only be used in areas which affect few people, where the equipment is fail-safe and where no other serious danger (e.g. from fire, injury or collapse) may arise.

11.2.2 Designing out faults

Many inherent defects in buildings and equipment only become apparent after a period of use. Spaces, materials, equipment and fittings or their fixings may be found to be unsuitable for the conditions experienced in hotels and resorts. The reasons may be general (lack of durability, susceptibility to damage, blockage or failure; poor retention of appearance) or more specific such as inadequate clearances for cleaning or servicing.

In each case, recording, analysing and reporting back this experience of maintenance and performance is a valuable aid to future design, modifications of equipment and specifications.

11.3 Planned maintenance

11.3.1 Introducing a system

As a preliminary to any planned scheme it is necessary to prepare a detailed inventory of all the items within each area of the premises. Such scheduling is laborious and advantage may be taken of the initial specifications used for the building and engineering contracts. The main headings should include: area, sub-area, item, component and reference.

11.3.2 Nature and frequency of maintenance

In each case it is necessary to 'determine' the type of maintenance work required. This tends to fall in four main areas of work:

- Routine inspection either by maintenance staff or through procedures for noting and reporting defects, by other employees and occupants.
- Cleaning, lubricating, servicing, adjustment and other regular preventive maintenance for plant and equipment.

- Redecoration and renovation work, periodic dry cleaning and laundering of furnishings, resurfacing and recovering of furniture and other forms of corrective maintenance.
- On the spot repairs and replacements, emergency work requiring immediate attention.

The frequency and extent of work involved depends on the:

- risk of damage or hazard which might result from neglect and failure
- legal and insurance standards
- importance in terms of annoyance and loss of customer goodwill
- effect on efficiency of operation and staff morale
- standards and image projected by the hotel.

Routine inspection procedures for plant and machinery must be arranged either with maintenance personnel employed directly or under maintenance contracts arranged with suppliers. The latter arrangement is usually necessary for specialist equipment, such as elevators, internal communication equipment, television receivers.

Routine inspection of guestrooms, staff rooms and public areas is most economically combined with other work. Efficient and simple systems for recording defects (checklists) and reporting and recording complaints by other employees must be established. Detailed inspection of all areas by maintenance personnel is necessary before, during and following major renovation work carried out under contract.

Preventive maintenance details are normally based on plant manuals and instructions provided by equipment manufacturers. Insurance and other requirements will lay down procedures and intervals for tests on safety.

Corrective maintenance is very dependent on management policies, budgets and standards. Guidance on cleaning and other treatment and life-cycles for replacement is usually provided by the suppliers. The responsibility for maintenance may be passed back to the suppliers by

the use of hire, leasing or supply and maintenance contracts.

Breakdown maintenance requires careful assessment of stores and workshop facilities. This is greatly aided by rationalization of equipment and furniture. Questions of interruption, disturbance, night work and the types of work to be done by direct employees and by contractors must be determined.

11.3.3 Scheduling of work

Planned maintenance facilitates the:

- scheduling of work at times when it causes least inconvenience or loss of income, such as in the low season, and in a way which enables all the related work to be done at the same time
- contracting out of work

Schedules are of many kinds. For easy identification, simple colour-coded wall charts may be used to show when rooms will be out of use and the nature of work to be carried out. More detailed specifications will be drawn up to enable the work, replacements and contracts to be organized in advance. Estimates can be obtained and cost limits laid down for different areas. The maintenance can be scheduled over several years to avoid wide fluctuations in costs during any financial period and budgets can be determined.

11.3.4 Contract work

Most hotels employ some direct staff for emergency and routine preventive work. The trend is, however, towards more contracting out of maintenance. Contract work has many advantages: it is usually simpler to administer once the procedures and contracts have been established, it is often more expedient to use the resources of a specialist company (skills, plant, purchasing) and the period of employment is entirely productive.

Contracts do involve much greater preparation. The quality of the work and effectiveness depend on the specifications and conditions of contract; there are also potential security risks unless the work area is confined. Contract work is also used in most motels and apartment buildings, which have the minimum permanent staff.

11.3.5 Staffing

The numbers and trades of maintenance personnel employed in a hotel or motel will depend on the availability of contractors in the area. Other considerations which will affect staffing are the age, grading and size of the hotel, use of shift duties, responsibility for improvement, conversion and refurbishing work, extent of restaurant and banqueting provision, and external maintenance of grounds. In modern practice, the range is usually 5–10 maintenance staff per 100 rooms. The higher ratio is typical of a high-grade hotel with some engineers employed on three eight-hour shifts.

For residential accommodation, as in tourist resorts, maintenance supervision and security needs are often interdependent. Routine cleaning, servicing and ground maintenance work for areas used in common is usually carried out by direct employees, but external painting and building work is invariably let under contract. One of the problems arising from the variable nature of hotel and property maintenance is the under-utilization of trade skills. Greater efficiency can be obtained with organization of maintenance on a group basis, but this is then very dependent on good communication facilities and management. Typical staff structures include engineers (about half the total), electricians, plumbers, carpenters, painters, cleaners, storemen and groundsmen. Specialist telephone, television and electronic engineers may also be employed.

11.3.6 Stores

Planned maintenance relies on the ready availability of suitable materials and spares. At the same time, because of economic and space limitations, stocks must be kept to a reasonable minimum. An efficient system of stock monitoring and control is essential. This must ensure that spares are replaced as they are used and that demand for additional items (such as in corrective maintenance) is anticipated. The latter may be part of the planning procedure; for example complete replacement of specified fittings or components may be scheduled at fixed intervals of time. Records of defects also indicate replacement needs.

Stores must be properly costed and accounted for in the work carried out.

11.4 Administration

11.4.1 Components

Each aspect of maintenance requires individual consideration.

1. *Reporting*. Method of obtaining information about faults or deficiencies. This will include:

   - *Liaison* with other departments
   - *Inspection check-lists* and instructions to non-specialist staff
   - *Work requests*, with copies for the department concerned and reference file. Work requests may be written or transmitted electronically (e.g. telautograph).

2. *Instructing* personnel by means of:
   - *Day schedules* of work for each employee
   - *Equipment cards* giving details of each item of equipment, spares and components for reference and correspondence
   - *Job procedures* listing the routine work involved in cleaning, servicing, lubricating
   - *History cards* providing summary record of previous work, entered each time maintenance is carried out
   - *Schedules* of furnishings and furniture providing details of materials, finishes, etc., and instructions for cleaning, laundering, resurfacing and other maintenance.

3. *Recording* details of new items supplied, specifications, warranties, instructions and

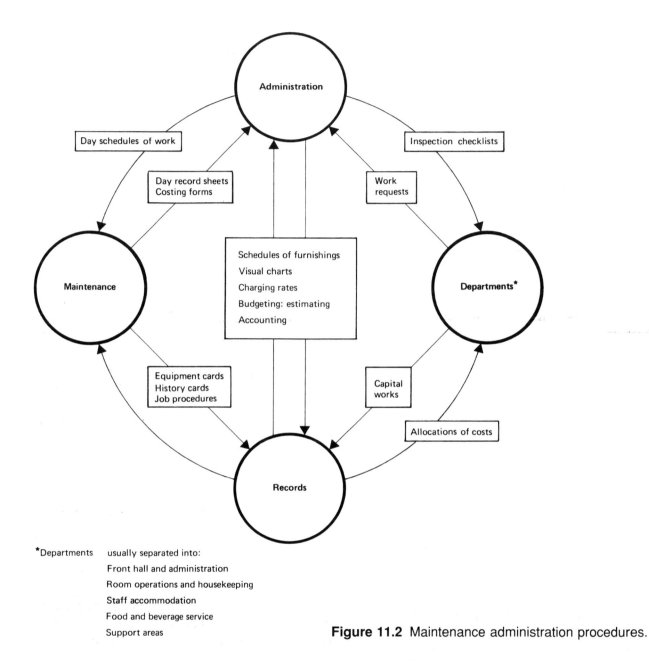

*Departments usually separated into:
Front hall and administration
Room operations and housekeeping
Staff accommodation
Food and beverage service
Support areas

Figure 11.2 Maintenance administration procedures.

costs, which should be entered on equipment cards, schedules and accounts. All of this information is useful for re-ordering and obtaining spares and replacements. It is also valuable when comparing performances and costs of alternatives and in designing out faults. History cards also contribute to this 'feedback' of information.

Records also include reference summaries such as:

- *Visual charts* showing programmes of planned maintenance for different areas of the hotel
- *Rooms* required for corrective maintenance work at particular times.

Table 11.2 Guestroom maintenance schedules

	Redecoration etc.	Replacement
2nd year	Room painted, curtains cleaned, carpet cleaned, furniture polished, fittings inspected	
4th year	Room painted as 2nd year except for replacements, i.e. carpet cleaned, furniture polished, fittings inspected	Curtains, chairs covered
6th year	Room painted as 2nd year except for replacements, i.e. curtains cleaned, carpet cleaned, chairs cleaned, furniture polished, fittings inspected	Waste paper bins, door stops
8th year	Room painted as 2nd year but colour change, i.e. furniture polished, fittings inspected	Curtains, carpets, curtain cords, chairs covered, electric fires, towel rails, bedspreads, quilts
12th year	Room painted as 2nd year	Curtains, chairs covered, luggage stool, waste paper bins, door stops, shaving plugs, centre light fittings, wall light fittings, TV points

4. *Specifying* work to be carried out under contract and drawing up conditions for contract work. In carrying out work (e.g. to guestrooms) the time allowed while the room is out of use is often limited and attention must be given to the scheduling of different jobs. In other cases (e.g. in public areas) the work may be restricted to certain areas or times.

5. *Accounting* includes day-to-day costing of jobs and long-term budgeting:

   - *Costing forms* with details of charging rates for labour and material calculated
   - *Schedules* of monthly and annual costs of maintenance attributed to different departments
   - *Estimates* of future expenditure or maintenance based on projected costs for work scheduled ahead.

11.4.2 Maintenance administration procedures

The schedule for maintenance of guestrooms is given in Table 11.2.

The tenth year is as year 2. Furniture replacement in theory is based on a ten-year cycle in bedrooms. In practice, it is changed about every twelve years depending on condition. Restaurant furniture is usually based on an eight-year cycle.

Example: 3-day room redecoration programme:

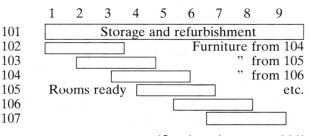

Room | Dates

(Continued on page 326)

321

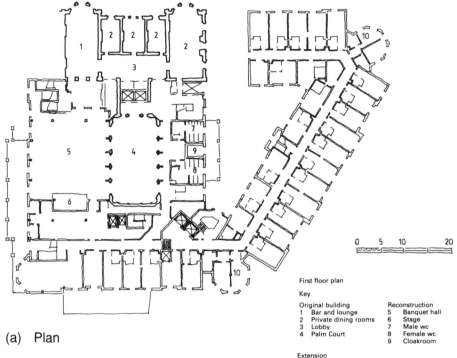

(a) Plan

First floor plan

Key

Original building		Reconstruction	
1	Bar and lounge	5	Banquet hall
2	Private dining rooms	6	Stage
3	Lobby	7	Male wc
4	Palm Court	8	Female wc
		9	Cloakroom

Extension
10 Guestrooms and corner suites

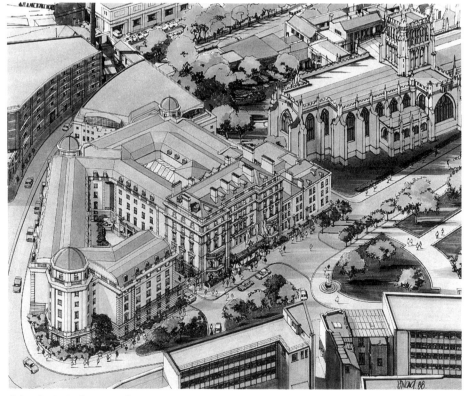

(b) Artist's impression

(c) Palm court

Figure 11.3 *Royal Swallow Hotel, Bristol*

The Swallow Hotel group's redevelopment of the crumbling old Royal Hotel, one of the landmarks in Bristol since 1863, provided a catalyst for regeneration of a large run-down part of the city centre adjacent to the Cathedral.

All of the 242 bedrooms, including 15 octagonal corner suites, are incorporated in a new seven-storey building which wraps round the side and rear of the restored Royal Hotel. The latter was completely stripped and refurbished to provide opulent public rooms including a large leisure club, Palm Court restaurant and four floors of conference and banquet rooms incorporating the latest audio-visual technology including teleconferencing links. Servicing is via a tunnel running under the site.

Development costs of the hotel were over £40 million ($60 million) and included funding of part of the new roadworks. The work extended over three years leading to the opening in September 1991. Developer: Swallow Hotel. Architect: Caldwell Denny & Bryan. Structural Engineer: McDowell. Interior Design: Peter Inston Design Co.

(d) Terrace restaurant

11.5 Major refurbishments

11.5.1 Investment

Reinvestment in major updating or renovating work usually arises when:

- a hotel has become uncompetitive due to outdated standards and lack of life-cycle refurbishment

- the benefits of the site, building character and known markets offer the prospect of increased business.

This usually occurs when hotels are acquired by companies seeking expansion and/or representation in locations where prime sites are limited.

Sale values of existing hotels closely follow cycles of economic activity, reflecting changes in market demand and yields. This is illustrated by

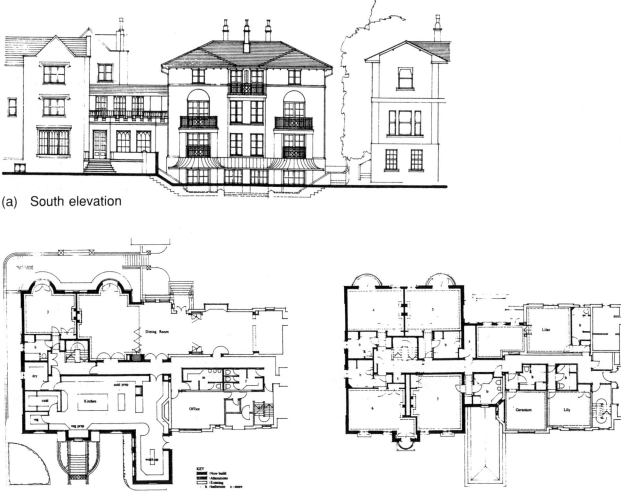

(a) South elevation

(b) Ground floor plan

(c) First floor

Figure 11.4 *Priory Hotel, Bath*
Extension of this listed Georgian building in the city of Bath called for extensive research and care in design. Faced in Bath stone, the new four-storey wing incorporates a larger dining room and new kitchen with ten *en suite* bedrooms for this award-winning small hotel. Architects: David Brain Partnership

(a)   Sketch design for reconstruction of the Palm court

(c)   Entrance

(b)   View of Palm Court

(d)   Restaurant design

Figure 11.5 *The Langham Hilton*
The Langham was London's first grand hotel and, when opened in 1865 by the Prince of Wales, it was the capital's largest and most sophisticated building and quickly became the fashionable gathering place of London. Bomb-damaged during the Second World War the building had been converted for use as BBC offices.

Over a five-year programme 1987–1991, the old Grade II listed building has been sensitively extended, modernized and restored, to recreate its original opulent style. Interior design: Richmond International. Architects: Ralph Halpern

(Continued from page 321)

the escalation in UK hotel prices in the boom years 1983–89, followed by an average 40% drop in valuation per room in the 1990–93 recession. Similar increases, fuelled, in part, by investment tax credits, were experienced in the USA in 1981–86, with oversupply and decline in occupancies causing a 17% decrease in weighted average selling prices in 1990–91 alone (see section 1.4).

Costs of renovation vary widely and retrofitting of building components requires individual design and detailings. In older buildings the work usually involves remodelling and extension to increase the number of rooms.

Costs of acquisition and renovation are normally less than new build and renovation works may attract grant aid in addition to tax credits. The costs of added blocks of rooms is often 25% less than an equivalent new hotel and give higher returns. Refurbishment work may be carried out in stages to fit in with seasonal occupancies and warrant a higher grading.

11.5.2 Nature of work

The extent of works may range from replanning for major reconstruction, new extensions and engineering systems to simple redecoration and refurbishment of specific rooms. However the closure of parts or the whole of the hotel provides an opportunity to install other systems at the same time.

Table 11.3 indicates the main works which are usually involved.

(a) Bedroom

(b) Suite

(c) Bar

Figure 11.6 *The Dorchester Hotel, London*
To allow refurbishment and restoration to the highest standards it was decided to temporarily close one of the world's premier hotels. Bedrooms have been totally replanned, with new fully marbled bathrooms, within the confines of the external walls and corridors. Distinctive features of the many Grade II listed interiors of this palatial building have been meticulously retained and restored while also carefully housing new air-conditioning and other technical equipment. To complete the renaissance of the Dorchester three new public areas plus a ballroom suite have been formed within the original building envelope. Interior design: Richmond International. Architects: John R Harris

Figure 11.7 *Le Meridien Hotel, Piccadilly, London* Occupying a prime site overlooking Piccadilly, the conversion of the Meridien Hotel included the addition of a conservatory-style coffee shop on the first floor integrated with the existing facade. Interior Design: Richmond International

11.6 Conversions

Conversion of other types of buildings to hotel use may arise from:

- lack of suitable sites and hotels in an area
- availability of buildings of history and character which do not have other viable uses.

The properties may range from stately houses and chateaux to redundant dockland buildings, halls and palaces – even rows of houses.

Conversion costs are generally higher than in new buildings because of the need for sensitive adaptation and conservation of the fabric. Difficulties may arise from the high proportion of public rooms, tall ceilings, lack of *en suite*

(Continued on page 333)

327

Table 11.3 Major refurbishment

Area	Constructional changes	Engineering systems	Furnishings, etc.
Rooms	Replanning divisions. Extensions. Conversions – suites. Bath/shower rooms. Fitting new windows, doors, locks, safes	AC/vent/heating. Lighting, power. Telephone, TV, video. Plumbing. Room management systems[a]	Bathroom fittings. Furniture, mirrors. Carpets, furnishings. Lamps, equipment. Decoration, signage. Terminal equipment
Circulation	Replanning of corridors, stairs, lobbies, elevators, service rooms, chutes, protection of evacuation routes	Elevators (guest service, goods), AC, lighting, power, vacuum systems, emergency telephones. Fire safety[b], sprinkler and security systems[c]	Linings, decoration, carpeting, light fittings, signage. Fire resistant enclosures
Lobby and front office	Changes in layout. Redesign of lobby, toilets, rental spaces, front desk, safe deposit, offices and business centre	As above. House telephones. Telephone exchange. Public address and hotel management systems[d]	As above. Lounge furniture, furnishings, piano bar, uniforms, graphics
Public rooms	Changes in food concept, replanning interior design, bars, counters, kitchen planning	AC, lighting, power. Energy management. Background music. Restaurant/bar. Management systems.[e] Fire safety[b]	Furniture, carpets, furnishings, lamps, decoration features. Food service equipment, tableware, menus, graphics uniforms
Meeting rooms	Division of areas. Movable partitions. Foyers, cloakrooms. Direct access. Service circulation storage	As above. Computerized control. AVA projection systems. Interpretation systems	Furniture – meetings, banquets, seminars. Stage PA and AVA equipment. Food/bar service
Recreation areas	Extension, conversion or renovation to form swimming pool, surge pools, sauna, changing rooms, gymnasium, bar	AC/vent/heating, lighting, power, PA, TV monitoring, energy management, safety systems	Changing room furniture, fitness equipment, signage. Lighting, TV cameras
Back-of-house	Replanning of loading docks, kitchens, laundries, stores. Staff facilities. Plant rooms	AC/vent/heating, lighting, power. Refrigeration. Energy management.[f] Security, safety and maintenance systems[g]	Wall and floor linings, ceilings. Laundry and kitchen equipment. Stores, carts. Waste compactors. Employee toilets, showers and lockers. Dining room furniture

Notes: Computerized systems and associated work.

(a)*Room management* Room status, energy adjustment, security monitoring, telephone metering, guest services, facsimile, in-room accounting. Video folio display, in-room movies, interactive information. (Section 10.5.)

(b)*Fire safety* Detection, sprinkler systems, portable extinguishers, smoke door closure, alarm and indicator panels, emergency generator, pressurization of stairs, smoke exhaust systems. (Section 5.6.)

(c)*Security* Electronic card access, internal fasteners, opening sensors for emergency doors; television monitoring of entrances, goods yards, lobbies, alarms in cashiers and safe deposit areas, room safes. (Section 5.7.)

(d)*Hotel management* Reservation, guest history room allocation, accounting, invoicing, employee records. (Section 10.6.)

(e)*Restaurant–bar management* Computerized ordering, recording, point of sale accounting, stock take and re-ordering menu and recipe costing. (Section 10.6.)

(f)*Energy management* Monitoring of internal and external conditions, optimization of energy flows, zone controls, peak load shedding, energy cut-out for unoccupied rooms, improved insulation, energy reclaim systems from equipment.

(g)*Maintenance* Work scheduling, costing, programming inventory listing, stock taking and re-ordering. (Section 10.6.)

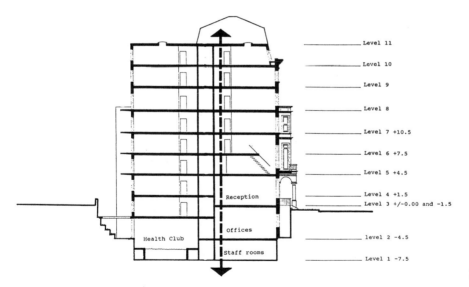

Figure 11.8 *Proposal for conversion of terrace London*
Conversion work involves careful planning to fit appropriate room dimensions within existing facades. This proposal illustrates the insertion of an intermediary floor at level 6 forming a mezzanine bedroom area in the front rooms.

Rear rooms are increased by new extensions and the basement is utilized for a health club and support areas. Complementary mansard roof extensions at the centre and ends of the terrace are added to house elevator machinery and plant. Architects: DSMP Architectural Services Ltd

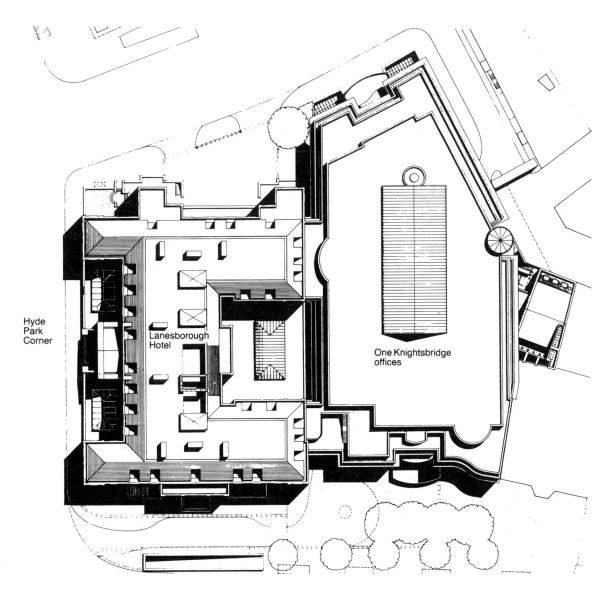

(a) Plan of hotel and adjacent office building

Figure 11.9 *The Lanesborough Hotel, London*
Overlooking Hyde Park Corner, the dilapidated St Georges Hospital of 1829 has been transformed into one of the most imposing neo-classical hotels in London. With renovation costs (at $120 million), partly offset by the adjacent development of an office building, the Lanesborough provides 95 guestrooms and luxury suites at a cost of £1.0 million per room ($ 1.49 m).

On the ground floor a series of arched spaces form the entrance hall and traverse axis linking drawing rooms, library bar, lounge on one side and the dining room and conservatory restaurant on the other. Period authenticity has been maintained throughout the grand public areas. Although the bedrooms are small for a luxury hotel they are cosily furnished in Victorian style incorporating hidden services and the latest technology. Developers: St George's Investment (UK), The Grosvenor Estate. Architect: Fitzroy Robinson Partnership. Services Engineers: Oscar Faber Partnership. Interior Design Consultant: Ezra Attia Associates. Hotel Operators: Rosewood Hotel Group

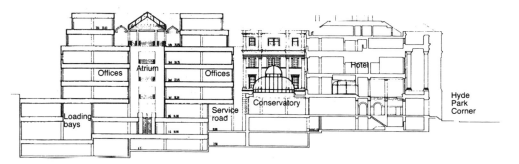

(b) Section

(c) Typical floor plan showing (in part):
   – general arrangement of the rooms
   – secant pile wall and new steel
     framework to secure the original
     brick walls

(*Steel Construction Today*,
November 1992, courtesy
of Fitzroy Robinson)

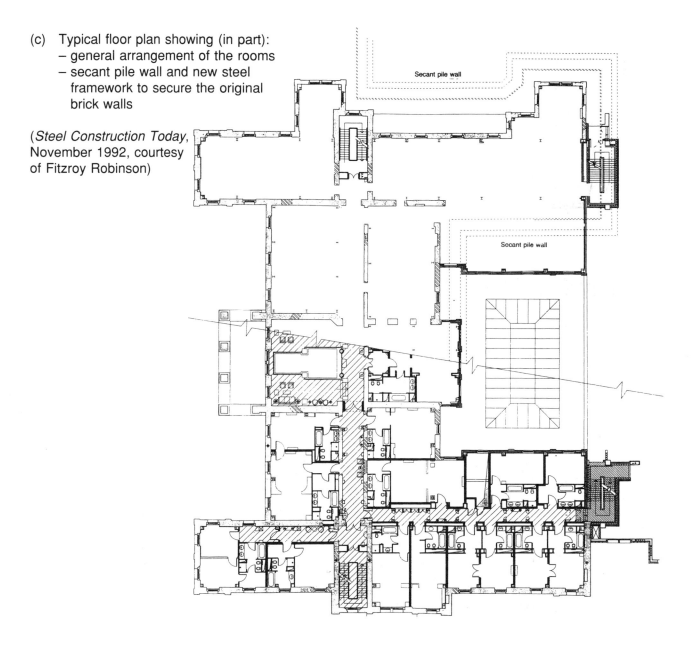

(a)

(c)

Figure 11.10 *Four Seasons Hotel, Milan*
Retaining the ambience of the 15th century
refurbished monastery, this deluxe hotel, opened
in 1992, has only 98 rooms and is the smallest of
the Four Seasons hotels. There are light and airy
doubles around the cloistered garden (a) and two-
storey suites with vaulted ceilings along glassed-in
promenades (b). View of the lobby (c). Design:
Paolo Peroni

(b)

(Continued from page 327)

bathrooms and the need to install extensive air-conditioning and other engineering systems. When converted such buildings offer unique character, often in prime locations. Projects may be government sponsored (Paradors in Spain, Pousadas in Portugal), independent or commercially grouped and assisted by heritage grants and other incentives. Conversion works are also widely used for self-catering and condominium developments.

Redevelopment is thus able to make a positive contribution to both conservation and tourism.

Selected bibliography

Planning, design and maintenance

Borsenik F.D. and Stutts A.T., (1992) *Management of Maintenance and Engineering Systems in the Hospitality Industry*, John Wiley, New York, 3rd edn

Davies T.D. and Beasley K.A., (1988) *Design for Hospitality: Planning Accessible Hotels and Motels*, Nichols, New York

International Hotels Environment Initiative (IHEI), (1993) *Environmental Management for Hotels*, Butterworth-Heinemann, Oxford

Kazarian E.A., (1983) *Foodservice Facilities Planning*, AVI Publications, Westport, 2nd edn

Larrose G. and Poulain J.P., (1986) *D'Ingenierie Hoteliere*, LT Editions Jaques Lanore

Lawson F. R., (1973) *Restaurant Planning and Design*, Architectural Press, London

Lawson F.R., (1973) *Design of Commercial Foodservice Facilities*, Watson-Guptill, New York

Lawson F.R., (1976) *Hotels, Motels and Condominiums*, Butterworth Architecture, Oxford

Lawson F.R and Baud-Bovy M., (1977) *Tourism and Recreation Development: A Handbook of Physical Planning*, Architectural Press

Lawson F.R., (1981) *Principles of Catering Design*, Architectural Press, London, 2nd edn

Lawson F. R., (1981) *Conference, Convention and Exhibition Facilities*, Butterworth Architecture, Oxford

Lawson F.R., (1995) *Restaurants, Clubs and Bars: Planning, Design and Investment*, Butterworth-Heinemann, Oxford, 2nd edn

Rutes W. and Penner R., (1985) *Hotel Planning and Design*, Watson-Guptill, New York

Hotel and foodservices marketing and management

Buttle F., (1986) *Hotel and Foodservice Marketing*, Cassell, London

Coltman M.M., (1994) *Hospitality Management Accounting*, Van Nostrand Reinhold, New York, 5th edn

Davies B. and Stone. S., (1991) *Food and Beverage Management*, Butterworth-Heinemann, Oxford, 2nd edn

Horwath and Horwath, (1992) *Hotels of the Future: Strategies and Action Plans*, Horwath Consulting, London

International Hotel Association, (1987) *Hotel 2000 Study*, IHA, Paris

Jones P. and Lockwood A., (1989) *Management of Hotel Operations*, Cassell, London

Jones P. and Merricks P., (1994) *Management of Foodservice Operations*, Cassell, London

Jones P. and Pizam A., (1993) *The International Hospitality Industry: Organisational and Operational Issues*, Pitman/John Wiley, London

Knowles T., (1994) *Hospitality Management*, Pitmans, London

Lockwood A., and Davis B., (1994) *Food and Beverage Management: A Selection of Readings*, Butterworth-Heinemann, Oxford

Lundberg D.E., (1990) *The Hotel and Restaurant Business*, Van Nostrand Reinhold, New York, 5th edn

Medlik S., (1993) *Dictionary of Travel, Tourism and Hospitality*, Butterworth-Heinemann, Oxford

Medlik S., (1995) *The Business of Hotels*, Butterworth-Heinemann, Oxford, 2nd edn

Messenger S. and Shaw H., (1993) *Financial Management for Hospitality, Tourism and Leisure Industries*, Macmillan

Morrison A.M., (1989) *Hospitality and Travel Marketing*, Delmar, New York

Mullins L.J., (1990) *Hospitality Management: A Human Resources Approach*, Pitman, London

Murdick R.G., Render B. and Russell R.S., (1990) *Service Operations Management*, Allyn and Bacon, Boston, Mass

Riley M., (1991) *Human Resource Management*, Butterworth-Heinemann, Oxford

Teare R. and Boer A., (1991) *Strategic Hospitality Management*, Cassell, London

Teare R. and Olsen M., (1992) *International Hospitality Management: Corporate Strategy in Practice*, Pitman, London

Teare R. (ed), (1992) *Managing Projects in Hospitality Organisations*, Cassell, London

Teare R. and Ingram H., (1993) *Strategic Management*, Cassell, London

Teare R. (ed), (1994) *Marketing in Hospitality and Tourism: A Consumer Focus*, Cassell, London

Tourism policy, marketing and development

Baum T. (ed), (1993) *Human Resource Issues in International Tourism*, Butterworth-Heinemann, Oxford

Boniface B. and Cooper C.P., (1994) *The Geography of Travel and Tourism*, Butterworth-Heinemann, 2nd edn

British Tourist Authority, (1993) *Guidelines for Tourism to Britain, 1993–1997*, BTA, London

Bull A., (1991) *The Economics of Travel and Tourism*, Pitman, London

Burton R., (1991) *Travel Geography*, Pitman, London

Cooper C.P. et al, (1993) *Tourism Principles and Practice*, Pitman, London

Edgell D.L. (Sr), (1990) *International Tourism Policy*, Van Nostrand Reinhold, New York

Frechtling D.C., (1994) *Practical Tourism Forecasting*, Butterworth-Heinemann, Oxford

Getz D., (1991) *Festivals, Special Events and Tourism*, Van Nostrand Reinhold, New York

Gunn C.A., (1994) *Tourism Planning: Basic Concepts and Cases*, Taylor and Francis, 2nd edn

Hall D.R. (1991) *Tourism and Economic Development in Eastern Europe and the Soviet Union*, Belhaven Press, London

Harrison D., (1992) *Tourism and the Less Developed Countries*, Belhaven Press, London

Holloway J.C., (1989) *The Business of Tourism*, Pitman, London, 3rd edn

Inskeep E., (1991) *Tourism Planning: An Integrated and Sustainable Development Approach*, Van Nostrand Reinhold, New York

Jefferson A. and Lickorish L., (1991) *Marketing Tourism: A Practical Guide*, Longman, Harlow, 2nd edn

Johnson P. and Thomas B. (eds), (1992) *Perspectives on Tourism Policy*, Mansell, London

Law C.M., (1993) *Urban Tourism*, Cassell, London

Lickorish L.J., (1991) *Developing Tourism Destination Policies and Perspectives*, Longman, Harlow

Lundberg D.E., (1990) *The Tourism Business*, Van Nostrand Reinhold, New York, 6th edn

McIntosh R.W. and Goeldner, C.R., (1990) *Tourism Principles, Practices, Philosophies*, Wiley, New York, 6th edn

Medlik S. (ed), (1991) *Managing Tourism*, Butterworth-Heinemann, Oxford

Mill R.C., (1990) *Tourism: The International Business*, Prentice Hall, London

Pearce D., (1989) *Tourism Development*, Longman, Harlow, 2nd edn

Pearce D., (1992) *Tourism Organisations*, Longman, Harlow

Smith S.L.J., (1989) *Tourism Analysis: A Handbook*, Longman, Harlow

Swarbrook J., (1995) *The Development and Management of Visitor Attractions*, Butterworth-Heinemann, Oxford

Theobald W., (1994) *Global Tourism: The Next Decade*, Butterworth-Heinemann, Oxford

Torkildsen G., (1992) *Leisure and Recreation Management*, E. & F.N. Spon

Williams A.M. and Shaw G. (eds), (1991) *Tourism and Economic Development*, Belhaven Press, London, 2nd edn

Witt S.F., Brooke M.Z. and Buckley P.J., (1991) *The Management of International Tourism*, Unwin Hyman, London

Journals and periodicals

Architects Journal

Caterer and Hotelkeeper

Cornell Hotel and Restaurant Administration Quarterly

Hotels

International Journal of Tourism Managemant

Leisure Management,

World Tourism Organization News and Information Bulletins

Series

Bridges T. (ed), *Integrated Approach to Resort Development, World Tourism Forecasts to 2000, Compendium of Tourism Statistics*, WTO, Madrid

Cooper C.P. (ed), *Progress in Tourism, Recreation and Hospitality*, Belhaven Press, London

Horwath and Horwath, *Worldwide Hotel Industry* and *European Hotel Industry*, Horwath Consulting, London

Johnston R. (ed), *International Journal of Service Industry Management*, MCB University Press, Bradford

Pannell Kerr Forster Associates, *Trends in the Hotel Industry (International)* and *Eurotrends*, PKF, London

Peters J. (ed), *Facilities*, MCB University Press, Bradford

Plimmer F.A.S. (ed), *Property Management*, MCB University Press, Bradford

Teare R. (ed), *International Journal of Service Industry Management*, MCB University Press, Bradford

Venmore Rowland P. (ed), *Journal of Property Finance*, MCB University Press, Bradford

Waters S.R. (ed), *Travel Industry World Yearbook*, Child and Waters, New York,

Index

WITHDRAWN